AF698531

NEW ESSAYS ON THE NATURE OF LEGAL REASONING

This is the first book to bring together distinguished jurisprudential theorists, as well as up-and-coming scholars, to critically assess the nature of legal reasoning. The volume is divided into three parts.

The first part, 'General Jurisprudence and Legal Reasoning', addresses issues at the intersection of general jurisprudence – those pertaining to the nature of law itself – and legal reasoning.

The second part, 'Rules and Reasons', addresses two concepts central to two prominent types of theory of legal reasoning.

The essays in the third and final part, 'Doctrine and Practice', delve into the mechanics of legal doctrine and practice, from a legal reasoning perspective.

Volume 14 in the series Law and Practical Reason

Law and Practical Reason

The intention of this series is that it should encompass monographs and collections of essays that address the fundamental issues in legal philosophy. The foci are conceptual and normative in character, not empirical. Studies addressing the idea of law as a species of practical reason are especially welcome. Recognising that there is no occasion sharply to distinguish analytic and systematic work in the field from historico-critical research, the editors also welcome studies in the history of legal philosophy. Contributions to the series, inevitably crossing disciplinary lines, will be of interest to students and professionals in moral, political, and legal philosophy.

General Editor

Prof George Pavlakos (Glasgow)

Advisory Board

Prof Robert Alexy (Kiel)
Prof Samantha Besson (Collége de France and Fribourg, CH)
Prof Emilios Christodoulidis (Glasgow)
Prof Sean Coyle (Birmingham)
Prof Mattias Kumm (New York and Berlin)
Prof Stanley Paulson (St Louis and Kiel)
Prof Joseph Raz (Columbia Law School and King's College London)
Prof Arthur Ripstein (Toronto)
Prof Scott Shapiro (Yale Law School)
Prof Victor Tadros (Warwick)

Recent titles in the series

Volume 8: Private Law and the Value of Choice
Emmanuel Voyiakis

Volume 9: Freedom and Force: Essays on Kant's Legal Philosophy
Edited by *Sari Kisilevsky and Martin J Stone*

Volume 10: The Nature and Value of Vagueness in the Law
Hrafn Asgeirsson

Volume 11: Law's Humility: Enlarging the Scope of Jurisprudential Disagreement
Triantafyllos Gkouvas

Volume 12: Rightful Relations with Distant Strangers: Kant, the EU, and the Wider World
Aravind Ganesh

Volume 13: The Making of Constitutional Democracy: From Creation to Application of Law
Paolo Sandro

Volume 14: New Essays on the Nature of Legal Reasoning
Edited by Mark McBride and James Penner

New Essays on the Nature of Legal Reasoning

Edited by
Mark McBride
and
James Penner

• HART •
OXFORD • LONDON • NEW YORK • NEW DELHI • SYDNEY

HART PUBLISHING
Bloomsbury Publishing Plc
Kemp House, Chawley Park, Cumnor Hill, Oxford, OX2 9PH, UK
1385 Broadway, New York, NY 10018, USA
29 Earlsfort Terrace, Dublin 2, Ireland

HART PUBLISHING, the Hart/Stag logo, BLOOMSBURY and the Diana logo are trademarks of Bloomsbury Publishing Plc

First published in Great Britain 2022

Copyright © The editors and contributors severally 2022

The editors and contributors have asserted their right under the Copyright, Designs and Patents Act 1988 to be identified as Authors of this work.

All rights reserved. No part of this publication may be reproduced or transmitted in any form or by any means, electronic or mechanical, including photocopying, recording, or any information storage or retrieval system, without prior permission in writing from the publishers.

While every care has been taken to ensure the accuracy of this work, no responsibility for loss or damage occasioned to any person acting or refraining from action as a result of any statement in it can be accepted by the authors, editors or publishers.

All UK Government legislation and other public sector information used in the work is Crown Copyright ©. All House of Lords and House of Commons information used in the work is Parliamentary Copyright ©. This information is reused under the terms of the Open Government Licence v3.0 (http://www.nationalarchives.gov.uk/doc/open-government-licence/version/3) except where otherwise stated.

All Eur-lex material used in the work is © European Union, http://eur-lex.europa.eu/, 1998–2022.

A catalogue record for this book is available from the British Library.

Library of Congress Cataloging-in-Publication data

Names: McBride, Mark, 1978- editor. | Penner, J. E. (James E.), editor.

Title: New essays on the nature of legal reasoning / edited by Mark McBride and James Penner.

Description: Oxford, UK ; New York, NY : Hart Publishing, an imprint of Bloomsbury Publishing, 2022. | Series: Law and practice reason; volume 14 | "In July 2020, the plan was to host a workshop on legal reasoning in Singapore, with the aim being to collect and integrate the papers into a volume … The physical workshop was a casualty of Covid-19, but around that time we did our best to thrash out some ideas via Zoom."—ECIP introduction. | Includes bibliographical references and index.

Identifiers: LCCN 2021062199 (print) | LCCN 2021062200 (ebook) | ISBN 9781509937653 (hardback) | ISBN 9781509958801 (paperback) | ISBN 9781509937677 (pdf) | ISBN 9781509937660 (Epub)

Subjects: LCSH: Law—Methodology—Congresses.

Classification: LCC K212 .N49 2022 (print) | LCC K212 (ebook) | DDC 340.1—dc23/eng/20220202

LC record available at https://lccn.loc.gov/2021062199

LC ebook record available at https://lccn.loc.gov/2021062200

ISBN: HB: 978-1-50993-765-3
ePDF: 978-1-50993-767-7
ePub: 978-1-50993-766-0

Typeset by Compuscript Ltd, Shannon
Printed and bound in Great Britain

To find out more about our authors and books visit www.hartpublishing.co.uk. Here you will find extracts, author information, details of forthcoming events and the option to sign up for our newsletters.

Contents

PART III
DOCTRINE AND PRACTICE

List of Contributors

Larry Alexander is Warren Distinguished Professor of Law and Co-Executive Director of the Institute for Law and Religion at the University of San Diego, USA.

Scott Brewer is Professor of Law at Harvard Law School, USA.

John Horty is Professor in the Department of Philosophy and Affiliate Professor in the Department of Computer Science at the University of Maryland, USA.

Grant Lamond is University Lecturer in Legal Philosophy at the University of Oxford, UK.

Barbara Baum Levenbook is Professor Emerita at the Department of Philosophy and Religious Studies, North Carolina State University, USA.

Nicole Lokstadt is a doctoral student based at McMaster University, Canada.

Mark McBride is Assistant Professor at the National University of Singapore.

Rob Mullins is Senior Lecturer at the TC Beirne School of Law, University of Queensland, Australia.

James Penner is Kwa Geok Choo Professor of Property Law at the National University of Singapore.

Adam Rigoni is Senior Lecturer at Arizona State University, USA.

Fred Schauer is David and Mary Harrison Distinguished Professor of Law at the University of Virginia, USA.

Fábio Shecaira is Adjunct Professor at the Faculty of Law, Federal University of Rio de Janeiro, Brazil.

Emily Sherwin is Frank B Ingersoll Professor of Law at Cornell Law School, USA.

Sundram Peter Soosay is an independent scholar.

Katharina Stevens is Assistant Professor at the University of Lethbridge, Canada.

Introduction

MARK McBRIDE AND JAMES PENNER

WHILE THERE HAS been a recent burst of interest in the nature of legal reasoning – which at its core may be taken to involve investigation of precedent, distinguishing, overruling and reasoning by analogy, but whose parameters extend far beyond that core – no single volume has brought together a group of distinguished jurisprudential theorists of legal reasoning.

In July 2020, the plan was to host a workshop on legal reasoning in Singapore, with the aim being to collect and integrate the papers into a volume (alongside a small number of other additional contributions from those unable to attend). The physical workshop was a casualty of Covid-19, but around that time we did our best to thrash out some ideas via Zoom.

This collection of essays brings together esteemed philosophers, as well as more junior scholars, to assess critically the nature of legal reasoning. All of the 13 essays are cutting-edge, and none has been published previously.

The volume is divided into three parts. Part I, 'General Jurisprudence and Legal Reasoning', contains four essays, by Fred Schauer, Barbara Levenbook, Fábio Shecaira and Adam Rigoni. The essays address issues at the intersection of legal reasoning and general jurisprudence – that branch of the philosophy of law pertaining to the nature of law itself. While it would be a surprise if these two topics did not have a rich intersection, it is notable that they are often pursued independently of one another. More specifically, Schauer explores the intersection between law as a normative order (Kelsen's terminology) and the activities and decision-making behaviour of lawyers and judges. Levenbook develops a methodology of creating and testing proposed theories of legal content, and considers its compatibility with certain positions in general jurisprudence. Shecaira, meanwhile, interrogates the idea that it is necessarily the case that legal reasons are general, and also (relatedly) whether judges have an obligation to ground legal decisions on general reasons. Finally, Rigoni, in an essay that nicely segues into the second part of the collection, discusses the compatibility of the so-called reasons model of precedential constraint with various movements in general jurisprudence.

Part II, 'Rules and Reasons', contains five essays, by Mark McBride, Grant Lamond, John Horty, Larry Alexander and Emily Sherwin, and James Penner. The essays address issues in some sense descending in a level of abstraction from the first part, and delving into two concepts central to two prominent types of theory of legal reasoning, namely, rules and reasons. The first three essays in this part form a triptych. McBride offers a cautious defence of a rule model of legal reasoning vis-à-vis rival reasons models, with much of his energies devoted to critiquing Lamond. Lamond, in turn, takes the opportunity to revisit and rearticulate his prominent reasons model of precedential constraint. In the last essay of this trio, Horty takes the opportunity to pick up on several aspects of Lamond's rearticulation. The last two essays in this part switch from models of legal reasoning based on these concepts to interrogation of one of these concepts itself, namely, rules. Alexander and Sherwin review some of their seminal work on rule following, and go on to explore and consider, by way of contrast, the nature and functions of legal standards. Penner, meanwhile, considers whether or not Wittgenstein's insights into the nature of rule following have any practical or theoretical significance for understanding the rules of law, and the way they are understood to be followed.

Part III, 'Doctrine and Practice', contains four essays, by Sundram Peter Soosay, Katharina Stevens and Nicole Lokstadt, Rob Mullins and Scott Brewer. The essays address issues in some sense descending in a level of abstraction from the second part, and delve into the mechanics of legal doctrine and practice, from a legal reasoning perspective. Soosay, drawing upon a number of long-standing doctrinal controversies drawn from English contract, tort and criminal law, argues that to 'think like a lawyer' is inherently practical in nature, a form of concrete professional activity not so unlike the methods or practices employed by doctors and engineers. Stevens and Lokstadt examine some of the (neglected) presuppositions of the adversarial model of civil trials. Mullins considers how we should best conceive of justification defences, for instance the criminal law's permitting us to use force in self-defence. Brewer, meanwhile, drawing upon detailed analysis of a few well-known US contract law cases, drills into a central aspect of his logocratic method, namely, abduction in legal argument.

While we cannot – and did not – aspire to exhaustively cover the vast landscape of legal reasoning, our more modest hope is that these essays can move some central debates forward in some significant ways.

Part I

General Jurisprudence and Legal Reasoning

1

On the Relationship between Law and Legal Reasoning

FREDERICK SCHAUER*

FOR LITERALLY MILLENNIA, theorists of various stripes have sought to provide an understanding and sometimes a definition of the social phenomenon commonly called 'law'. And for a time measured more in centuries than in millennia, theorists – usually not the same ones – have sought to explain the processes by which lawyers argue and reason and by which judges reach their decisions, all commonly subsumed under the heading of 'legal reasoning.' But are law and legal reasoning the same thing? And if not, what are the differences, and why should we care about them?

It turns out that the relationship between law and legal reasoning can explain many – albeit not nearly all – of the differences among some of the major strands of twentieth- and twenty-first-century legal philosophy. Exploring those differences may consequently tell us at least something about law, something about legal reasoning and perhaps something about the enterprise of legal philosophy itself.

I. THREE THEORISTS

A. Ronald Dworkin and the Tradition of Unity

From his earliest to his last writings, Ronald Dworkin focused his attention on courts and the process of judging.[1] And he also, in a marked departure from

* This essay was prepared for the Legal Reasoning Workshop at the National University of Singapore. I am grateful to Mark McBride and James Penner, both as the organisers and for their helpful comments, and to Michael Green for valuable insight about Kelsen.

[1] Thus, in Ronald Dworkin (1986) *Law's Empire*, Cambridge, MA: Harvard University Press, arguably his most important work, and the place where he develops his own perspective most extensively, the opening line of the book is 'It matters how judges decide cases.' And when Dworkin goes on to say that '[j]urisprudence is the general part of adjudication, silent prologue to any decision at law' (ibid, 90), he punctuates his willingness – indeed, eagerness – to view the enterprise of legal philosophy as emerging from and dependent on the process of adjudication.

much of the contemporary jurisprudential community and from the bulk of post-Hartian legal philosophy, steadfastly refused to offer anything resembling a crisp account of the necessary (or essential) properties of law, or of the concept of it.[2] In his later writings Dworkin did distinguish among sociological, doctrinal and taxonomic concepts of law,[3] but it is not clear what phenomenon or phenomena Dworkin was explicating the concept of. At times he seemed to be seeking to describe, explain and justify an attitude,[4] at other times he appeared to be focusing on the behaviour of judges, lawyers and other actors within a particular cluster of modern legal systems in developed democracies,[5] and at still other times he trained his attention on identifying that which entitled a society to use its power of coercion.[6]

Whether any of these characterisations of Dworkin's enterprise is correct I will leave to those more interested in Dworkinian exegesis than I am. Nevertheless, Dworkin is usefully taken as representing the position that identifying law involves identifying the sources – or inputs, to use a less pleasing but also less theory-laden term[7] – that legal actors use in making decisions, or that non-legal actors use in making decisions in alleged reliance on, or guidance by, law. In deploying *Riggs v Palmer*[8] as a datum in support of his account of law, Dworkin relies heavily on what Judge Earl for the majority in the New York

[2] See William Ewald (1998) 'Posner's Economic Approach to Comparative Law' *Texas International Law Journal* 33: 381–86, 386, n 26; Philip Soper (1987) 'Dworkin's Domain' *Harvard Law Review* 100: 1166–86. Examples of Dworkin's resistance to offering a definition of 'law', or to specifying the essential properties of the concept of law, include Ronald Dworkin (1987) 'Legal Theory and the Problem of Sense' in *Issues in Contemporary Legal Philosophy: The Influence of HLA Hart*, ed Ruth Gavison, Oxford: Clarendon Press, 9–21, 15–16; Ronald Dworkin (1983) 'A Reply by Ronald Dworkin' in *Ronald Dworkin and Contemporary Jurisprudence*, ed Marshall Cohen, Totowa, NJ: Rowman & Allanheld, 247–300, 250–52. I emphasise 'post-Hartian' because the bulk of *The Concept of Law* is situated well within the anti-essentialist philosophical milieu within which Hart operated. See Frederick Schauer (2013) 'Hart's Anti-Essentialism' in *Reading HLA Hart's* The Concept of Law, eds Luis Duarte d'Almeida, James Edwards and Andrew Dolcetti, Oxford: Hart Publishing, 237–46.

[3] See especially Ronald Dworkin (2006a) 'The Concepts of Law' in *Justice in Robes* (Cambridge, MA: Harvard University Press, 223–40; and Ronald Dworkin (2006b) 'Hart and the Concepts of Law' *Harvard Law Review Forum* 119: 95–104.

[4] Dworkin (n 1) 45–86, 410, and especially in the book's concluding paragraph (at 413).

[5] Dworkin (1983) (n 2) 260–62. And, more generally, Ronald Dworkin (1977) *Taking Rights Seriously*, London: Duckworth, 14–130.

[6] Dworkin (n 4) 190–92.

[7] Talk of 'legal sources' will, for the jurisprudential cognoscenti these days, elicit connections with the 'sources thesis' developed by Joseph Raz, and which is an essential component of his 'exclusive positivism' account of the concept of law. See Joseph Raz (1979) *The Authority of Law: Essays on Law and Morality*, Oxford: Clarendon Press, 45–52; Andrei Marmor (2002) 'Exclusive Legal Positivism' in *Oxford Handbook of Jurisprudence and Philosophy of Law*, eds Jules Coleman and Scott Shapiro, Oxford: Oxford University Press, 104–24. Raz may or may not be correct, but I want to think of 'sources', at least preliminarily, as simply the things that lawyers rely on in argument and that judges use in making decisions. And that is why it might be better to think of them as 'inputs', with the question of which inputs are law and which are not being exactly the point at issue.

[8] *Riggs v Palmer*, 22 NE 188 (NY 1889).

Court of Appeals actually used to support his decision. If Judge Earl and others actually do use principles to support an outcome, then, for Dworkin, these (and other) principles have become part of the law. And if, as in *Henningsen v Bloomfield Motors*,[9] the principles that judges use are moral principles that have not (unlike the principles in *Riggs*) previously been used or recognised as valid in the legal system, then such moral principles are also part of the law. Importantly, as we shall see, at no point does Dworkin say that the use of moral principles is a common feature of adjudication and of legal reasoning but that such principles are nevertheless not part of the law. For Dworkin, therefore, the best account of what judges and other legal actors actually do, described at the appropriate level of generality, is also an account of law. Or, to put it differently, for Dworkin what judges use in making decisions is law, and if we want to find out what the law is in a jurisdiction, we will want to identify and examine the materials that judges use in reaching and justifying their decisions – and that lawyers use in arguing to those judges.

When understood in this way, there is little to distinguish Dworkin from some of his seeming adversaries, at least with respect to the relationship between law and legal reasoning. Hart, most prominently, offered a conception of what he labelled the 'ultimate rule of recognition' – the criterion determining what counted as valid law – that imposed no constraints on the types of norms or sources or inputs that could qualify as sources of law in some jurisdiction.[10] Whatever inputs officials actually used in making their decisions in the name of the law – internalised, in Hartian terminology – would thus count as law in that jurisdiction.[11] Most obviously, this included moral inputs,[12] and the position

[9] *Henningsen v Bloomfield Motors*, 161 A2d 69 (NJ 1960). *Henningsen* is actually a better case than *Riggs* for Dworkin's challenges to legal positivism and to the idea of a rule of recognition. The principle at work in *Riggs* – 'no man shall profit from his wrong', as it was put in the 19th century – was well recognised, and explicitly so, within the legal canon at the time, as the *Riggs* majority made clear. Not so, however, with *Henningsen*'s unconscionability principle, and thus *Henningsen* provides somewhat better support for the view that legal decision making sometimes draws on moral principles not previously explicitly recognised by the applicable rule of recognition. I put aside whether this is or is not a successful challenge to legal positivism, but Dworkin thinks it is, and from that perspective *Henningsen* works much better than *Riggs*.

[10] HLA Hart (1961) *The Concept of Law*, 3rd edn, eds Penelope A Bulloch, Joseph Raz and Leslie Green, Oxford: Oxford University Press, 2012, 100–10. Legal systems contain myriad rules of recognition, as with the constitutions that 'recognise' statutes as law, and the statutes that 'recognise' administrative regulations as law. But at the top (or the base, to use a different spatial metaphor for the same idea) of this hierarchy is the ultimate rule of recognition, whose authority is a matter of acceptance and existence and not a matter of legal validity, and which is the ultimate determinant of the kinds of things that count as law in a jurisdiction and the kinds of things that do not.

[11] See Matthew Kramer (1999) *In Defense of Legal Positivism*, Oxford: Oxford University Press; WJ Waluchow (1994) *Inclusive Legal Positivism*, Oxford: Oxford University Press; Julie Dickson (2012) 'Legal Positivism: Contemporary Debates' in *Routledge Companion to Philosophy of Law*, ed Andrei Marmor, New York: Routledge, 48–64.

[12] See Andrei Marmor (2011) *Philosophy of Law*, Princeton, NJ: Princeton University Press, 92–97.

commonly known as inclusive legal positivism,[13] and which Hart labelled 'soft positivism' when he announced his conditional agreement with it in the 'Postscript' to *The Concept of Law*,[14] is nowadays associated with the view that moral principles can count as valid legal inputs if, contingently, they are accepted by officials as authoritatively relevant to their decisions in the name of the law. And as Dworkin pointed out, with no little sense of self-satisfaction, the space between his picture of law and that offered by inclusive legal positivism is quite small.[15] Accordingly, legal positivism as understood by (the later) Hart and by the inclusivists uses what legal officials – judges, most prominently – actually do and actually rely on as the way of identifying what counts as law.[16] And if for Dworkin and the inclusive positivists what judges (and lawyers) actually and explicitly do and actually and explicitly use is plausibly understood as legal reasoning then there is little, if any, space between the concept of law and those actual practices of legal argument and legal decision making that are commonly described as legal reasoning.

Much the same can be said, although perhaps more tendentiously, about another family of views that appears again intriguingly similar to Dworkin in this dimension, although plainly not in many others. And here I am talking about American Legal Realism. Holmes plainly overstated things when he defined law in terms of '[t]he prophecies of what the courts will do in fact',[17] but his claim nevertheless, as with Dworkin's, treated the behaviour of the courts, and by implication their modes of reasoning and decision making, as largely congruent

[13] See Kenneth Einar Himma (2002) 'Inclusive Legal Positivism' in *Oxford Handbook*, eds Coleman and Shapiro (n 7) 125–65. An earlier label was 'incorporationism', as used in, most prominently, Jules Coleman (1982) 'Negative and Positive Positivism' *Journal of Legal Studies* 11: 139–64, and Jules L Coleman (1998) 'Incorporationism, Conventionality, and the Practical Difference Thesis' *Legal Theory* 4: 381–425. Even earlier, see David Lyons (1977) 'Principles, Positivism, and Legal Theory' *Yale Law Journal* 87: 415–35; E Philip Soper (1977) 'Legal Theory and the Obligation of the Judge: The Hart/Dworkin Dispute' *Michigan Law Review* 75: 473–519.

[14] Hart (n 10) 238–76. I say 'conditional agreement' because Hart accepted soft positivism only insofar as the moral norms that a rule of recognition might recognise were in some sense objective: ibid, 254. And James Penner suggests to me, plausibly, that even Hart's 'agreement' was cautious, even avoiding direct criticism (ibid) of Raz's contrary position.

[15] Ronald Dworkin (2006a) 'Thirty Years On' in *Justice in Robes* (n 3) 187–222, esp at 188, where Dworkin describes Coleman's inclusive positivism as 'so stunningly like my own'. Obviously, there is a difference between the natural law position that morality is necessarily a criterion of legality and the soft positivist position that morality may, contingently, be a criterion of legality. But because Dworkin never maintained that his account of law was a necessary account of the role of morality in determining legal validity in all possible legal systems in all possible worlds, the differences between Dworkin and the soft positivists, at least at the conceptual level, are smaller than is commonly supposed. Dworkin's account of the role of morality in actual legal decision making (that is, at the sub-conceptual level), however, was substantially exaggerated. See Frederick Schauer (2004) 'The Limited Domain of the Law' *Virginia Law Review* 90: 1909–56; Frederick Schauer (1997) 'Constitutional Invocations' *Fordham Law Review* 47: 1295–1312.

[16] See Frederick Schauer (2017) 'What Counts as Law,' *Valparaiso University Law Review* 52: 1–17.

[17] Oliver Wendell Holmes (1897) 'The Path of the Law' *Harvard Law Review* 10: 457, 461.

with how he understood the very idea of law.[18] Much the same can also be said about the work of the other Legal Realists. Although Karl Llewellyn's observation that 'what these officials do about disputes is, to my mind, law itself'[19] is commonly caricatured, distorted and taken out of context,[20] it does represent the focus of Llewellyn and of most of the other Realists[21] on the actual behaviour of judges in developing their accounts, even if not their definitions, of law. Llewellyn may be unfairly saddled with the literal reading of the foregoing quote, as Twining makes clear,[22] but there is little doubt that he and most of his intellectual fellow-travellers would have been impatient, at best, with trying to separate the idea of law from the reasoning and decision-making processes of those who operated within the legal system.

B. Hans Kelsen and the Universal Incompleteness of Law

The receptiveness of theorists and theories as otherwise diverse as Ronald Dworkin, the inclusive legal positivists and the American Legal Realists to the substantial overlap between conceptions of law and accounts of what judges and other legal actors do becomes particularly interesting once we appreciate the extent to which there is a decidedly different view and consequently a different tradition. And here the major figure, and the starting point for this different tradition and different account of law, is Hans Kelsen. Using the illuminating metaphor of a frame without a picture, Kelsen notably insisted that no legal act – no judicial decision, for example – could be completely determined by the law.[23]

It is not immediately clear what Kelsen meant by this, especially because he also insisted that law was a gapless enterprise.[24] On the face of it, it appears

[18] I say 'very idea' to emphasise that Holmes, as with most of the other Legal Realists, would have had little patience with conceptual analysis of the concept of law, however much he may well have presupposed a particular concept of law. See Brian Leiter (1998) 'Realism, Hard Positivism, and Conceptual Analysis' *Legal Theory* 4: 533–47.

[19] KN Llewellyn (1930) *The Bramble Bush: On Our Law and Its Study*, New York: Columbia Law School, 12.

[20] See William Twining (2012) *Karl Llewellyn and the Realist Movement*, 2nd edn, Cambridge: Cambridge University Press, 147–52.

[21] See Frederick Schauer (2013) 'Legal Realism Untamed' *Texas Law Review* 91: 749–80. Although Llewellyn avoided opining on the 'nature' of law, and although he felt it important to distinguish law from the entire social order, he nevertheless insisted that law's 'technical measures and [] personnel' need to be understood as necessarily conjoined. See Karl N Llewellyn (1938) *The Theory of Rules*, ed Frederick Schauer, Chicago, IL: University of Chicago Press, 2011, 91–94.

[22] And see also Frederick Schauer (2011) 'Editor's Introduction' in Llewellyn (n 21) 1–3.

[23] Hans Kelsen (1967) *Pure Theory of Law*, tr Max Knight, Berkeley, CA: University of California Press, 245, 348–56; Hans Kelsen (1934) *Introduction to the Problems of Legal Theory*, tr Bonnie L Paulson and Stanley L Paulson, Oxford: Clarendon Press, 1992, 80. And see, for particularly important explication, Pierluigi Chiassoni (2019) *Interpretation without Truth: A Realistic Enquiry*, Cham, Switzerland: Springer, 103–24.

[24] See Eugenio Bulygin (2013) 'Kelsen on the Completeness and Consistency of Law' in *Kelsen Revisited: New Essays on the Pure Theory of Law*, eds Luís Duarte d'Almeida, John Gardner

that viewing law as gapless and viewing law as necessarily incomplete are directly opposed positions. But a closer look reveals that the two positions are not opposed, at least from a Kelsenian perspective. To Kelsen and his followers, law consisted of a hierarchy of authorisations (*Stufenbau*, in German), with the highest norm authorising the creation of lower-order norms, and those lower-order norms authorising the creation of even lower-order norms, and the lowest-order norm authorising its application – interpretation – to particular facts and particular events.[25] But each of those authorisations was, to Kelsen, necessarily incomplete, remaining to be filled out by the authorised law-making or law-applying official from among a menu of authorised possibilities. When seen in this way, the alleged inconsistency disappears. Each of these authorisations is indeed a frame without a picture, but the authorisations themselves, at whatever level, are comprehensive, leaving nothing that is neither authorised nor unauthorised.[26]

There is obviously a great deal more to the Kelsenian picture than this snapshot of just one aspect reveals, but the key point, at least for my purposes here, is that for Kelsen the choice among legally-authorised options is a choice that the authorised official necessarily makes on the basis of political, moral and sociological factors. And these factors are not, according to Kelsen, themselves law, or part of the law.[27] For Kelsen, no legal act, including the acts of interpretation and applying the law to particular facts or particular decisional opportunities, is completely determined by the law.

The relevance of this to my inquiry here should now be clear. For Kelsen, what officials *do* in creating lower-order norms is not itself based on law, no more than what legislators do in engaging in the legally authorised act of legislating is based on law. Legislators derive their power from the law, and exercise it, hopefully, within legal limits, but what they do in pursuance of that power and within those limits is not itself derived from law, based on law or, simply, law, even if the product or output of those efforts is law. For Kelsen, the frame of law is a necessary input into a judicial (or other official legal) act, but it never, by itself, determines the output. And so too, from a Kelsenian perspective, is the act of applying the law to particular facts, as with the typical (in a juryless system) judicial decision. Again, those decisions are for Kelsen authorised by law, and bounded by legal limits, but not themselves law, and not themselves based on law.

and Leslie Green, Oxford: Hart Publishing, 225–43; Inés Weyland (1986) 'Idealism and Realism in Kelsen's Treatment of Norm Conflicts' in *Essays on Kelsen*, eds Richard Tur and William Twining, Oxford: Clarendon Press, 249–72.

[25] See Stanley L Paulson (2019) 'Hans Kelsen on Legal Interpretation, Legal Cognition, and Legal Science,' *Jurisprudence* 10: 188–221.

[26] Stanley L Paulson (1980) 'Material and Formal Authorisation in Kelsen's Pure Theory' *Cambridge Law Journal* 39: 172–93.

[27] See, for a view about Kelsen that concludes much the same thing about legal *powers*, Christoph Kletzer (2019) 'Book Review' [of Maris Köpcke, *Legal Validity: The Fabric of Justice*] *American Journal of Jurisprudence*, 64: 275–80, 277–78.

What emerges from this picture, therefore, is the conclusion that, for Kelsen, what judges do in reaching a decision is not itself law, even if it is bounded and constrained by law, and even if judges necessarily must determine the contours of those boundaries and constraints. But the actual substantive decision is, for Kelsen, not itself uniquely determined by the law.[28] And thus, unlike Dworkin, unlike (my reading of) inclusive legal positivism, and unlike the American Legal Realists most obviously, Kelsen sees law and the decision-making activities of judges as conceptually distinct acts.

C. Joseph Raz and the Distinction Between Law and Legal Reasoning

Although interpreting Kelsen on the relationship between law and the reasoning of judges and other law appliers is, like much of the Kelsen *oeuvre*, sometimes obscure and often contested, a much clearer example of the same conclusion can be found in the work of Joseph Raz. As the leading and possibly founding figure in what is now known as *exclusive legal positivism*,[29] Raz maintains that the use by legal actors of what appear to be non-legal sources – morality, most obviously – does not *ipso facto* convert those non-legal sources into law, or into sources of law. A particularly effective example, for Raz, comes from the use by one jurisdiction of the law of another jurisdiction. If the law of France provides that a provision of a contract should be interpreted according to the law of the place where the contract was made, and if the contract was made in Italy, then a French court interpreting that provision of that contract will apply Italian law.[30] In doing so, however, it is not making the law of Italy the law of France. It is applying Italian law only by virtue of a direction in French law telling the court to apply Italian law.[31]

Raz uses the example to illustrate that the law, as understood by Raz, can point to all sorts of things that should be used in making legal decisions, but that does not make those things law.[32] And this leads Raz to the further conclusion

[28] If we accept the distinction between hard and easy cases, as developed by Hart and implicitly accepted by the early Dworkin, see Lawrence Solum (2010) 'The Unity of Interpretation' *Boston University Law Review* 90: 551–78, we might conclude that Kelsen believes that there are no easy (legal) cases.

[29] See n 7.

[30] Here I help myself to an assumption about French conflict of laws law, a topic about which I know nothing. But the point is not undercut by my ignorance.

[31] Raz (n 7) 46. And see, to the same effect and in expanding in various ways on Raz, Matthew Kramer (2000) 'How Moral Principles Enter into Law' *Legal Theory* 6: 83–108; Adam Perry (2020) 'Law's Boundaries' *Legal Theory* 26: 103–23; Scott J Shapiro (2009) 'What is the Rule of Recognition (and Does It Exist)?' in *The Rule of Recognition and the US Constitution*, eds Matthew Adler and Kenneth Einar Himma, New York: Oxford University Press, 235–68.

[32] Thus, a 'judge's legal obligation can – and often does extend beyond applying legally valid norms. In particular, it can extend – via directed powers – to applying *morally* legally binding norms.' Mark McBride (2017) 'The Inner Logic of Exclusivism (and Inclusivism): Raz's Foreshadowing' *Australian Journal of Legal Philosophy* 42: 81–120, 117.

that although there may be many things that are part of legal reasoning – defined as the reasoning and argumentative practices of lawyers and judges – those are not part of the law. And thus law is, for Raz, one thing, and legal reasoning and its sources are something else.

Although Raz's distinction between law and legal reasoning is implicit in much of his writing, it is most explicit in a 1998 article responding to a claim about law's autonomy made by Gerald Postema.[33] Here Raz offers a distinction between what a legal actor might use to identify the law and what that actor – prototypically a judge – would use or do to reach a conclusion. There is a difference, for Raz, between reasoning to the law (locating the law) and reasoning from the law (going from the law to a conclusion).[34] The latter, Raz insists, includes many things that are not law in a way that the former, by Raz's definition and understanding, does not. Raz offers as an example the practice of interpretation, which is different from the law. And he could have added, from his perspective, the use of logic, language, grammar, arithmetic and many other things that are used by a judge or other legal actor in reaching a conclusion or making a decision,[35] but which are not themselves law.[36]

Thus, Raz talks of 'the role of law in legal reasoning',[37] a phrase that would make no sense for Dworkin and any others who would equate the two. But for Raz, 'In legal reasoning, legal rules and standards appear among the reasons inclining the argument toward one conclusion or another. But they compete with other reasons.'[38] Accordingly, Raz appears to accept, here and elsewhere, that the task of identifying the law is in some way autonomous, in that it does

[33] Joseph Raz (1998) 'Postema on Law's Autonomy and Public Practical Reasons: A Critical Comment' *Legal Theory* 4: 1–20, esp at 4–9, responding to Gerald J Postema (1996) 'Law's Autonomy and Public Practical Reason' in *The Autonomy of Law: Essays on Legal Positivism*, ed Robert P George, Oxford: Clarendon Press, 79–118. And see also Joseph Raz (1995) 'The Autonomy of Legal Reasoning' in *Ethics in the Public Domain: Essays in the Morality of Law and Politics*, Oxford: Clarendon Press, 326–40.

[34] On this distinction, see the useful elaboration in Fábio Shecaira (2014) 'Gardner on Legal Reasoning' *Law and Philosophy* 33: 747–72, esp at 749–50.

[35] See Leslie Green (2018) 'Legal Positivism' in *Stanford Encyclopedia of Philosophy* at https://plato.stanford.edu.

[36] In making a claim that is interesting, albeit peripheral to my arguments here, Raz says that one of the non-legal aspects of any judicial decision in a common law country is the determination that 'there is nothing in the situation that would justify modifying the law, or its application to the case, by this court on this occasion': Raz (1995) (n 33) 4. Implicit in Raz's claim, and in restricting it to common law countries, is what seems to be the premise that defeasibility is not a necessary feature of law and not a necessary feature of a code-based legal system, although it may be a defining feature of common law adjudication. This claim seems correct to me, apart from whether it is Raz's claim or not. See Frederick Schauer (2012) 'Is Defeasibility an Essential Property of Law?' in *The Logic of Legal Requirements: Essays on Defeasibility*, eds Jordi Ferrer Beltran and Giovanni Battista Ratti, Oxford: Oxford University Press, 77–88; Frederick Schauer (1998) 'On the Supposed Defeasibility of Legal Rules' *Current Legal Problems 1998*, ed MDA Freeman, Oxford: Oxford University Press, 223–40.

[37] Raz (1998) (n 33) 5.

[38] ibid, 6.

not require use of moral (or, it is worthwhile to note, non-legal in any other way) criteria. This is what Raz thinks of as reasoning *to* the law. But once the law is so identified, then reasoning *from* the law to a judgment, an application or an interpretation is a largely different and not strictly legal enterprise.

II. DOES IT MATTER?

It might be tempting to suppose that the distinction between the more capacious views about law, or about the definition of the concept of law, associated with Dworkin, the inclusive legal positivists and the American Legal Realists, on the one hand, and the less capacious views of Kelsen and Raz, on the other, is a mere terminological dispute. But that would be a mistake. Showing why that is so, however, takes us into a serious methodological dispute about the nature of legal theory, and only after that issue has been addressed can we truly answer why the dispute actually matters.

A. Is Legal Theory Descriptive?

What are theorists doing when they offer theories (or accounts, or whatever) of the nature of the concept of law? Under one view, and here Raz is again the most explicit, a theory of law is a description. It is neither normative nor prescriptive but simply aims to provide an account of just what the concept of law *is* in some culture.[39] But we need to be careful here. For Raz and those who agree with him, the claim is not that the concept of law is the same in, for example, the contemporary United Kingdom as it is in Somalia or as it was in fourteenth-century France. And the claim is certainly not that the basic legal institutions and the understandings of law are uniform across time and space. Although so-called legal pluralists properly stress that both legal institutions and understandings of the nature of law vary dramatically, culturally and temporally and geographically,[40] Raz is emphatic in accepting that a theorist offering a theory of law is offering 'our' theory of law, where 'our' refers to the culture in which and from

[39] See especially Joseph Raz (2005) 'Can There Be a Theory of Law?' in *Blackwell Guide to the Philosophy of Law and Legal Theory*, eds Martin P Golding and William A Edmundson, Oxford: Blackwell, 324–42. See also Joseph Raz (1998) 'Two Views of the Nature of the Theory of Law: A Partial Comparison' *Legal Theory* 4: 249–82.

[40] See, among the more prominent contemporary legal pluralists, Brian Z Tamanaha (2017) *A Realistic Theory of Law*, Cambridge: Cambridge University Press; William Twining (2019) *Jurist in Context: A Memoir*, Cambridge: Cambridge University Press; William Twining (2009) *General Jurisprudence: Understanding Law from a Global Perspective*, Cambridge: Cambridge University Press. Also relevant is Susan Haack (2018) 'The Pragmatist Tradition: Lessons for Legal Theorists' *Washington University Law Review* 95: 1049–82; and the various essays in Tomasz Gizbert-Studnicki and Jerzy Stelmach (2007) *Law and Legal Cultures in the 21st Century: Diversity and Unity*, Warsaw: Wolters Kluwer Polska.

whose standpoint the theorist is theorising. It is our theory of law that enables us to tell whether Somalia, say, has law from *our* perspective, and doing so is not inconsistent with Somalians' having a very different concept of their law or our law from the one that we happen to have.

This digression into pluralism aside, the basic claim of Raz, of Hart in the 'Postscript' to the *Concept of Law*,[41] of Julie Dickson[42] and of Matthew Kramer,[43] among others,[44] is that we can describe and/or explain the concept of law without in any way prescribing what the concept of law ought to be.[45] There are of course significant issues regarding the methodologies of description and explanation, many of which involve question about the 'data' of jurisprudence.[46] Nevertheless, all practitioners of descriptive conceptual analysis of the concept of law in the modern analytic positivist tradition insist that they are not telling any society what its concept of law ought to be, and not, at least in the guise of describing and explaining the concept of law, prescribing what any lawyer, judge or legal actor what to do,[47] or prescribing what any society ought to permit or require its lawyers, judges and other legal actors to do, or prohibit them from doing.

Even assuming that non-prescriptive and non-morally-evaluative description of the concept of law is possible,[48] however, it hardly follows that prescription is impossible. Law is not, of course, a natural kind. It is created by human beings

[41] Hart (n 10) 238–76.

[42] Julie Dickson (2001) *Evaluation and Legal Theory*, Oxford: Hart Publishing, esp at 30–37.

[43] See, among many works, Matthew H Kramer (2012) 'What is Legal Philosophy?' *Metaphilosophy* 43: 125–34.

[44] Perhaps, with qualifications, Michael Giudice (2015) *Understanding the Nature of Law: A Case for Constructive Conceptual Explanation*, Cheltenham: Edward Elgar; Brian Leiter (2007) *Naturalizing Jurisprudence: Essays on American Legal Realism and Naturalism in Legal Philosophy*, Oxford: Oxford University Press, 164–81; Scott J Shapiro (2011) *Legality*, Cambridge, MA: Harvard University Press. And perhaps, with even more qualifications, Jules Coleman (2001) *The Practice of Principle: In Defence of a Pragmatist Approach to Legal Theory*, Oxford: Oxford University Press, 175–79; Leslie Green (2008) 'Positivism and the Inseparability of Law and Morals' *New York University Law Review* 83: 1035–58. And see the useful discussion in Brian H Bix (2019) *Jurisprudence: Theory and Context*, 8th edn, Durham, NC: Carolina Academic Press, 3–30.

[45] An insightful analysis of the nature of description in legal theory is Brian Bix (1999) 'On Description and Legal Reasoning' in *Rules and Reasoning: Essays in Honour of Fred Schauer*, ed Linda Meyer, Oxford: Hart Publishing, 7–28. See also Brian Bix (1995) 'Conceptual Questions and Jurisprudence' *Legal Theory* 1: 465–80.

[46] See Gerald J Postema (2018) 'The Data of Jurisprudence' *Washington University Law Review* 95: 1083–96.

[47] It was not always so. Jeremy Bentham, more or less the founder of modern analytic legal positivism, conceived his enterprise in a very different way. See Frederick Schauer (2015) 'The Path Dependence of Legal Positivism' *Virginia Law Review* 101: 957–76. But compare Jules Coleman (2001) 'Incorporationism, Conventionality, and the Practical Difference Thesis' in *Hart's Postscript: Essays on the Postscript to the Concept of Law*, ed Jules Coleman, Oxford: Oxford University Press, 99–148; Jules Coleman (1982) 'Negative and Positive Positivism' *Journal of Legal Studies* 11: 139–62, 145–47.

[48] Among the best and most careful defences of such conceptual analysis is Veronica Rodriguez-Blanco (2003) 'A Defense of Hart's Semantics as Nonambitious Conceptual Analysis' *Legal Theory* 9: 99–124.

in human societies. It is, in precise terminology, an *artifact*, and thus similar in its non-natural character to important artifacts such as countries, corporations and money, and to less important ones like football, opera and stamp collecting.[49] But once we recognise the artifactual nature of law, and thus the artifactual nature of the concept of law, we must recognise as well that just as artifacts can be created, so too can they be re-created.[50] In other words, the existence at some point in time (or span of time) of a particular concept of law in a particular culture, and the existence of the ability to describe and to explain that culture's concept of law, is not inconsistent with the enterprise of conceptual revision. If some culture has some concept of something, it would be open to that culture to have, looking forward, a different concept – or a different understanding, to put it more simply – of much the same thing.

If a culture can have one concept of *X* – or, simply, concept *X* – at time one, and if that culture can have a different (or at least improved, even if not dramatically different) concept of *X* at time two,[51] then it follows that someone at time two could believe that the concept at time two was better in some way or for some purposes than the concept at time one, or that the concept at time one was better in those ways or for those purposes than the concept at time two. And it follows from *this* that, although value-free description of a concept at a particular time is arguably possible,[52] so too is the enterprise of conceptual revision. And such conceptual revision might include not only, less controversially, simply sharpening the existing concept, but also, more controversially, shifting it in some way. If one concept is better (for some purpose, or to achieve some goal) than another, then urging that an improved one replace an unimproved one is an entirely sensible project, and one not inconsistent with the quite different project of conceptual description and explanation.[53]

[49] See Luke Burazin, Kenneth Einar Himma and Corrado Roversi (eds) (2018) *Law as an Artifact*, Oxford: Oxford University Press.

[50] Frederick Schauer (2005) 'The Social Construction of the Concept of Law: A Reply to Julie Dickson' *Oxford Journal of Legal Studies* 25: 493–501.

[51] Putting aside the question whether *X* is the same at time one and time two, and putting aside the question of what we perceive as *X* at time two is the same thing that we perceived as *X* at time one.

[52] Whether description that is free from the injection or influence of moral and political values is controversial throughout the social sciences. For scepticism about the purity (or even the possibility) of the descriptive/explanatory project in the philosophy of law, see Ronald Dworkin, (2006c) 'Hart's Postscript and the Point of Political Philosophy' in *Justice in Robes* (n 3) 140–86; Stephen R Perry (2001) 'Hart's Methodological Positivism' in *Hart's Postscript*, ed Coleman (n 47) 311–54. But note that Dworkin does not claim that all description is value-laden, nor that value-free conceptual analysis is universally impossible. He maintains only that values are an essential part of interpreting *evaluative* concepts, of which law is one. See Stephen Guest (2013) *Ronald Dworkin*, 3rd edn, Stanford, CA: Stanford University Press, 66–67.

[53] On the projects of conceptual choice and conceptual revision, often these days described as conceptual engineering, see especially Matti Eklund (2017) *Choosing Normative Concepts*, Oxford: Oxford University Press, 192–203. And see also, on choosing and revising, rather than merely describing, our concepts, Sally Haslanger (2012) *Resisting Reality*, Oxford: Oxford University Press; Alexis Burgess and David Plunkett (2013) 'Conceptual Ethics I' in *Philosophy Compass* 8: 1091–1101; Alexis Burgess and David Plunkett (2013) 'Conceptual Ethics II' in *Philosophy Compass* 8: 1102–10. Note that this kind of conceptual revision is decidedly not about, *pace* comments to me by

The question of what some culture's concept of law *ought* to be was the starting point for both HLA Hart and Lon Fuller in their memorable 1958 debate in the pages of the *Harvard Law Review*.[54] Although Hart and Fuller disagreed about almost everything, they did appear to agree that disobedience of profoundly immoral official directives was desirable, and that a society could and should *choose* the concept of law that would best facilitate this desirable practice. For Fuller, this meant denying to such evil directives the status and label of law, while for Hart it meant being explicit about the fact that recognising and designating as law some directive from someone with a gun and a uniform (or a robe) said nothing about the very different question whether it should be obeyed.[55] But both appeared to agree that a legal positivist conception of law or a natural law conception (including Fuller's procedural variety of it) were stances and concepts that could be selected, rather than (or in addition to) being stances that could at a particular moment in time be identified, described and explained.

Hart's commitment to the possibility of choosing, evaluating and revising a concept of law to serve moral goals was reiterated in *The Concept of Law*, where he explicitly describes making a 'reasoned choice'[56] between competing concepts of law, a choice to be made on the basis of deciding which one is superior to another because of its ability to 'assist our theoretical inquiries, or advance and clarify our moral deliberations, or both'.[57] This commitment to a concept of law as something chosen is, of course, in tension with Hart's claim in the 'Postscript' to be engaging solely in description, and that is why Julie Dickson identifies Hart's position(s) on the matter as 'awkward'.[58] But Hartian exegesis

James Penner, urging the replacement of some institutions or phenomena with other ones. It is about how we should understand, or frame or group the institutions and phenomena we have. One need not recommend change either in the institutions we think of as legal institutions, or in the first-order understandings we have of morality to recommend that the two be considered, for example, necessarily conjoined or necessarily separate. The question is how we should categorise and comprehend the phenomena of the world, and not what those phenomena should be.

[54] HLA Hart (1958) 'Positivism and the Separation of Law and Morals' *Harvard Law Review* 71: 593–629; Lon L Fuller (1958) 'Positivism and Fidelity to Law – A Reply to Professor Hart' *Harvard Law Review* 71: 630–72.

[55] See Frederick Schauer (1996) 'Positivism as Pariah' in *The Autonomy of Law: Essays on Legal Positivism*, ed Robert George, Oxford: Clarendon Press, 31–56.

[56] Hart (n 10) 208.

[57] ibid, 209.

[58] Julie Dickson (2009) 'Is Bad Law Still Law? Is Bad Law Really Law?' in *Law as Institutional Normative Order*, eds Maksymilian Del Mar and Zenon Bankowski, Aldershot: Ashgate, 161–83, 164. And here I take issue with Leslie Green, who argues that although Fuller was engaged in prescription, Hart was simply trying to understand and not to 'advise' anyone or anything. Leslie Green (2008) 'Positivism and the Inseparability of Law and Morals' *New York University Law Review* 83: 1035–58, 1036. But although that is a plausible (although in my view an attenuated) interpretation of the 1958 Hart in the *Harvard Law Review*, it is in direct conflict with Hart's language three years later in *The Concept of Law* – 'reasoned choice', '[I]f we adopt', '[I]f we adopt' (again), '[I]f we adopt' (still again), 'an effort to train and educate men', 'preferring the wider concept of law' and so on throughout pp 209–12. Perhaps the 'Postscript' suggests that Hart came to regret this language, but to interpret this earlier and canonical language as denying prescription is to read into what Hart said more than Hart's language can bear.

aside, I want to accept that a concept (or understanding) of law is something that a culture or society can choose, even if it does so slowly, incrementally and at best only semi-intentionally. And I want to accept as well that one implication of the ability of a society to choose or adopt (or adapt) its concept of law is the ability of a particular theorist or commentators to urge the choosing of one concept rather than another. Of course such an urging by a legal philosopher is unlikely to have, at most, any but the smallest real-world effect, and even then only over time and only in implicit coordination or conjunction with the urgings of many others. But the same could be said about Aristotle on virtue, Kant on lying and Rawls on justice. The point is only that normative legal theory, even normative legal theory about the concept of law, is not only possible but also has a long and distinguished history.[59]

B. The Explanatory Failures of the Capacious and the Narrow Conceptions

The foregoing methodological digression behind us, we can then turn to the normative question whether it would be better to understand law and legal reasoning as largely similar, even if not exactly congruent, as Dworkin, perhaps the inclusive positivists and perhaps the American Realists would have it, or instead as two obviously connected but plainly distinct ideas, as Kelsen, Raz and various Razian exclusive positivists see the matter. And if we understand this, now, as a choice, then one way of making the choice, following the Hart quotation above from *The Concept of Law*, is on the basis of attempting to achieve explanatory clarity, which is hardly an unimportant aspiration. But as the foregoing discussion has emphasised, it is hardly the only possible aspiration, and conceptual revision or conception choice to achieve substantive moral, political or other goals is, at the very least, possible.

Now, however, things get messy, because it turns out that neither the option of treating law and legal reasoning as largely congruent, nor the option of treating law and legal reasoning as largely distinct, is particularly satisfactory. If we understand law as incorporating all of the things that lawyers do and all of the things that judges (and other legal actors) use in making their decisions – in adjudication, especially – we wind up failing to capture the distinctiveness of the domain of the law. Raz observes, correctly and as noted already, that interpretation requires more than just the law in his strict and narrow sense. But if we unpack 'interpretation', we can see that making a judicial decision, or arguing before a judge, requires use of the semantics and pragmatics of language, of logic

[59] The issue is only preliminary for purposes of this chapter. For my more extensive thoughts along these lines, see Frederick Schauer (2018) 'Law as a Malleable Artifact' in Burazin et al (n 49) 29–43; Frederick Schauer (2021) 'Normative Legal Positivism' in *Cambridge Companion to Legal Positivism*, eds Patricia Mindus and Torben Spaak, Cambridge: Cambridge University Press, 61–78.

in the informal sense, of basic arithmetic and sometimes more sophisticated mathematics and statistics, and of all of the tools of rigorous and non-rigorous empirical inquiry.[60] To give just two examples, similar to each other and well-known throughout the common law world, the Law Lords in *Donoghue v Stevenson*[61] made their decision not only on the basis of their knowledge of the Scots law of delict and of the traditional doctrine of privity of contract, but also on the basis of what they knew about snails (live and dead), ginger beer bottles (opaque and non-opaque), the nature of ginger-beer bottling, the nature of the café business and much more.[62] And in the American predecessor and counterpart of *Donoghue v Stevenson*, Judge Benjamin Cardozo in *MacPherson v Buick Motor Company*[63] relied on his knowledge – some of his own and some supplied by counsel – of automobiles, automobile wheels, the automobile manufacturing industry, the automobile selling business, dangerous (and safe) products generally, the knowledge of consumers about automobiles and so on.

The question is whether all of this should be understood as law. Once we understand the pervasiveness of policy, political and moral considerations in judicial decision making, understanding all of these domains and sources of judicial enlightenment as law risks losing what seems to be distinctive about the domain of the law and about the idea of legal sources. Indeed, even if we take *Riggs v Palmer* as representative, which it was not,[64] it is still noteworthy that the majority opinion there of the New York Court of Appeals, even as it relied on various sources from antiquity and other jurisdictions past and present, and even as it relied somewhat on common sense and common knowledge, restricted its explicit and cited reliance mostly to things that resembled law in the most traditional sense. Indeed, once we recognise that Dworkin's distinction between principle and policy,[65] whatever its normative merits, is wildly inaccurate descriptively,[66] we are led to the conclusion that too capacious an understanding of law, one that would include the full universe of inputs into judicial decisions and the entire array of argumentative practices of lawyers, winds up seeking to explain so much that it actually explains very little.

At the core of the inclusive positivist idea is the insight, derived from Hart, that a society could in theory decide that pretty much anything could count

[60] See Matthew Kramer (2007) 'Why the Axioms and Theorems of Arithmetic Are Not Legal Norms' *Oxford Journal of Legal Studies* 27: 555–62. See also Perry (n 31).

[61] *Donoghue v Stevenson* [1932] AC 562 (HL).

[62] A great deal more. See Matthew Chapman (2010) *The Snail and the Ginger Beer: The Singular Case of Donoghue v Stevenson*, London: Wildy, Simmonds & Hill.

[63] *MacPherson v Buick Motor Company*, 111 NE 1050 (NY 1916).

[64] See Frederick Schauer (2004) (n 15), 1937–39.

[65] Dworkin (n 1) 221–24, 243–44, 310–12, 338–39.

[66] See especially Melvin Aron Eisenberg (1988) *The Nature of the Common Law*, Cambridge, MA: Harvard University Press; Melvin Aron Eisenberg (2007) 'The Principles of Legal Reasoning in the Common Law' in *Common Law Theory*, ed Douglas E Edlin, Cambridge: Cambridge University Press, 81–101. See also Robert J Sharpe (2018) *Good Judgment: Making Judicial Decisions*, Toronto, CA: University of Toronto Press, 105–24.

as a 'recognised' (in the rule of recognition sense) source of law, and therefore as law.[67] But however profound this idea is, and profound indeed it is, by itself it cannot explain the reality of the fact that the domain of legally recognised sources in all developed democracies is not even close to coextensive with the domain of all of the sources that would be considered legitimate in social, political and even moral debate.[68] The inclusive positivists are right to stress that all of this is contingent and not necessary, but the contingency of the real does not make the real any less real.[69] And whether it be inclusive legal positivism, or the Dworkinian conflation of moral, political and legal sources, or the American Legal Realist tendency to do much the same thing from a different starting point, all of these perspectives run the risk, one that is often realised, of offering a description that so flattens our decisional experiences, or so flattens the decisional practices of people calling themselves lawyers and judges, that we wind up with an impoverished understanding of how law as we know it actually works. And we wind up as well with little understanding of the important social and institutional phenomenon that we can call the 'differentiation of law'.[70] In a world in which courts appear different from legislatures and administrative agencies, in which judges appear different from presidents, prime ministers and parliamentarians, and in which the books published by the West Publishing Company, Butterworth's and their equivalents appear different from those published by most publishers of fiction and non-fiction, law has a salient institutional presence. Perhaps that institutional presence is merely superficial or sociological. But perhaps it is not, and an account of law that cannot explain what appears to be so visible a differentiation may suffer from a failure of explanatory ambition. Indeed, even as normative matter it may be valuable to

[67] Hart was right to mock John Chipman Gray for distinguishing law from sources of law: Hart (n 10) 1–2, 141. If the sources of law are not law then the only thing that is law is the decision of the judge based on those sources, an account that fails to explain how law, as law, can guide, constrain or do pretty much anything else.

[68] See Schauer (2004) (n 15).

[69] And thus I suspect, albeit with no hard evidence for my suspicion other than what I know about Hart's life story (see Nicola Lacey (2004) *A Life of HLA Hart: The Nightmare and the Noble Dream*, Oxford: Oxford University Press; Neil MacCormick (2008) *HLA Hart*, 2nd edn, Stanford, CA: Stanford University Press, 1–16), that Hart's initial perception of the idea of a rule of recognition was inspired by his almost nine years of practice as an equity barrister, practice that focused quite narrowly on a relatively small array of recognised legal materials. And if I am correct about this then it may be that the very idea of a rule of recognition comes closer, empirically and sociologically, to the exclusive positivist idea than it does to inclusive positivism, even as it remains theoretically compatible more with the latter than with the former.

[70] See Frederick Schauer (2015) *The Force of Law*, Cambridge, MA: Harvard University Press, 154–68. Even if it is impossible to 'demarcate' the realm of the legal from the realm of the moral, or from other non-legal realms, see Brian Leiter (2011) 'The Demarcation Problem in Jurisprudence: A New Case for Skepticism' *Oxford Journal of Legal Studies* 31: 663–77, and thus even if the realm of the legal overlaps with various other realms, the centre of gravity of the legal may be different from the centre of gravity of the realms of morality, politics, policy and science, among others. And if that is so, then looking for the indicia of differentiation may be sensible even if looking for demarcation is a fruitless enterprise.

think about which questions are best addressed by institutions with particular legal competence and which questions are best left to others. Dworkin appears to recognise this issue when in *Law's Empire* he stresses the difference between principle and policy, but, given his views about the permeability of the boundaries between the legal, the moral and the political, he turns out to have little to say about institutional design once we recognise that courts, especially in the common law world, have long been in the policy business.

Yet if the flaw in a too-easy assimilation of laws and legal reasoning is that it misleadingly ignores the extant distinctiveness of the category of methods and sources conventionally referred to as 'law', the flaw in the exclusivist explanations of Kelsen, Raz and others is just the opposite. The flaw of the exclusivist perspective, at least in the hands of some of its prominent proponents, is that of dumping the entire universe of the non-legal into the same undifferentiated basket, a basket that Kelsen and Raz appear to believe is of little concern to legal theorists.[71] If this is so, however, we may then wind up with an impoverished view of what legal theory might wish to do.

To be more specific, if it is the case that much of what lawyers and judges do, especially in their use of policy and morality, is not something that is law and not something that is of concern to legal theorists,[72] then it turns out the exclusivist or Kelsenian approach to the enterprise of legal theory will leave too much of what lawyers and judges do out of that enterprise, which in a different way may also be a form of narrowness of theoretical scope and theoretical ambition.

III. TAKING STOCK

So we have come a long way from the initial question – whether law and legal reasoning are the same thing, and, if not, how they differ. But it turns out that answers to that question map onto the more familiar divide between the capacious conceptions of law represented by Dworkin, inclusive legal positivism and American Legal Realism, on the one hand, and the exclusivist conceptions of Kelsen and Raz, on the other. And the answers also map onto more familiar questions about the relationship between law and adjudication.

These mappings, however, are hardly the end of the story. For it then turns out that both of these conceptions – law and legal reasoning as coextensive,

[71] Raz is explicit on the point. 'The sociology of law provides a wealth of detailed information and analysis of the functions of law in some particular societies. Legal philosophy has to be content with those few features which all legal systems necessarily possess.' Raz (n 7) 104–05.

[72] It is not necessarily the case that a lack of interest in the non-law dimensions of legal reasoning, legal obligation and legal practice follows from characterising those dimensions as something other than law. Legal theorists or legal philosophers might still be interested in theorising about things that are not law in a strict sense. But it is unlikely as an empirical matter that labelling those things as 'non-law' will facilitate that interest.

and law and legal reasoning as distinct – have, as explanatory approaches, their virtues and also their vices. And then we might want to ask just what it is that we want to know – just what questions are we interested in asking and answering, and just which account of the relationship between law and legal reasoning will assist in addressing those questions. If we are interested in determining the effect, if any and how much, and on what, of the kinds of materials that are published by West Publishing and Butterworth's and Sweet & Maxwell, then only a narrower and exclusivist conception of law will facilitate this empirical inquiry.[73] And if we are interested in explaining why we expect lawyers and judges to have legal training, why morality and politics and policy do not appear on bar examinations, and why law libraries typically contain the books they do, once again only the more narrowly targeted inquiry that is associated with the exclusivist programme can serve this function.

If, by contrast, we are seeking to explain what lawyers and judges actually do, then the more capacious understandings of law, understandings that do not distinguish law from the reasonings of lawyers and judges, may provide the key to this understanding. If actual legal decision making is pervaded by morality, politics and policy, the blanket dismissal with 'that's not law' is singularly unsatisfying. And so also with too insistent a preoccupation on the distinction between a theory of law and an account – or theory, if you will – of adjudication.[74]

The even larger lesson of this may be that it is a mistake to think of the debates and differences I have tried to explain here as competing and mutually exclusive explanations of the same phenomenon. Each of the positions explored here tells us something, and if at the end of the day we are unable to declare a winner and a loser, that consequence may be a virtue and not a vice, or, in the contemporary vernacular, a feature and not a bug.

[73] See Brian Leiter (2007) *Naturalizing Jurisprudence: Essays on American Legal Realism and Naturalism in Legal Philosophy*, Oxford: Oxford University Press, 56–57, 134–35; and, earlier, Leiter (n 18) 547.

[74] See Leslie Green (2005) 'General Jurisprudence: A 25th Anniversary Essay' *Oxford Journal of Legal Studies* 25: 565–80. See also Juan Vega Gómez (2011) 'The Hart Fuller Debate Re-Revisited' *Jurisprudence* 2: 261–71, 269–70.

2

The Law of the Street

BARBARA BAUM LEVENBOOK*

IT IS RELATIVELY uncontroversial that some degree of efficacy in guiding and governing the conduct of lay law subjects is a necessary condition for the existence of a legal system. Many theories of legal content are compatible with the following picture of efficacy: most law subjects do what the law directs them to do and refrain from doing what the law prohibits.[1] On this picture, efficacy might result from happy accident. Law subjects need not believe that they are conforming to law, neither do they need to have justified beliefs about legal content. What is important is that they behave in a certain way. They might believe it is a required way but be mistaken about what requires it (eg thinking they are following norms of courtesy or morality).[2]

However, I join others who contend that this picture is too limited. It makes legal rule following by lay law subjects peripheral (if not incidental) to the idea of an existing legal system. To alter, slightly, the fanciful situation described by St Exupéry in chapter X of the children's book *The Little Prince*, suppose a king were to live on one asteroid and to observe his subjects (through a telescope, for instance) on a nearby asteroid.[3] Suppose, further, the king were then to command of his subjects what he has observed they were going to do anyway,

* I am grateful to Connie Rosati for suggesting the title of this chapter. The penultimate version of this chapter was presented as the inaugural guest lecture for the University of Durham Centre for Law and Philosophy in December 2020. I wish to express my appreciation to the organiser, Kara Woodbury-Smith, and all of the participants on that Zoom event. I am indebted to Michael Pendlebury, Kenneth Ehrenberg, Adam Rigoni, Mark McBride, James E Penner and Maggie O'Brien for comments on earlier drafts from which I have greatly benefitted, and to Hrafn Asgeirsson for many fine discussions and for ideas that I have adapted.

[1] Some legal philosophers would add that in cases of deviance, the requirement or prohibition must be applied or would be applied by courts and other law-applying and law-enforcing organs. See Burazin's excellent discussion of the various conceptions of efficacy, Luka Burazin (2017) 'The Concept of Law and Efficacy' in *Encyclopedia of the Philosophy of Law and Social Philosophy*, eds Mortimer Sellers and Stephan Kirste, Dordrecht: Springer, https://doi.org/10.1007/978-94-007-6730-0_231-1.

[2] Indeed, on some particularly thin conception of efficacy, the behaviour need not be causally traceable to the existence of any of the local laws.

[3] In the book, a king lives on an asteroid and the little prince gets to visit various asteroids.

but in such a way that the subjects do not and cannot learn of the command. On the picture I reject, we now have a significant necessary condition for the existence of a legal system; and this conclusion is absurd. We have a necessary condition for an odd, perhaps self-delusional, game played by the king. However, this game, except for the normative structure that creates the role of the monarch (if, indeed, there can be one in the circumstances[4]), bears no important resemblance to an existing legal system.

Instead, I suggest that (at a minimum) in existing legal systems it must also be possible for lay law subjects to have epistemic access to the legal content that purports to guide their behaviour.[5] This epistemic access conclusion falls out of three assumptions. The first is that legal systems, to be legal systems, must aim at guiding the behaviour of their law subjects, and the second is that this is a sensible goal. The third is that guidance by legal content paradigmatically requires that legal content (under some description mentioning its status as law) enter into the practical reasoning of the guided.[6] Those guided by legal content must know it. Since it is not sensible to aim at what is impossible to achieve, epistemic access by lay law subjects must be possible in a legal system (to a sufficient degree).

These reflections yield a tool for assessing theories of legal content: scrutinise the account that the theory can offer of how, if at all, a legal system can attain the goal – guide behaviour of lay law subjects – under real-world conditions (to a sufficient or significant degree). Can lay law subjects have (enough) epistemic access to legal content pertaining to them under real-world conditions, given the practicalities of typical existing legal systems, and if so, how?

The latter is not (entirely) an empirical question. It is asking for implications of a theory of legal content, the conditions under which (according to the theory) lay law subjects can have epistemic access to this legal content. It is then asking how these conditions match real-world conditions, which is an empirical question of course.

The importance of the answer to my dual question for theories of legal content has long been under-appreciated. If the conditions do not match, we are given a theory of something that cannot do one of the things it aims at under the conditions in which it allegedly exists. Then the fact that legal systems do

[4] It may be that the description of this example is incoherent; on some philosophical accounts of law, conditions creating a monarch would also be missing. In that case, imagine a self-styled king instead.

[5] There is general agreement among prominent legal positivists that a necessary condition for a legal system to exist is widespread obedience to the legal norms or standards that direct behaviour. See, eg, HLA Hart (1994) *The Concept of Law*, 2nd edn, Oxford: Oxford University Press, 113–14; Joseph Raz (1980) *The Concept of a Legal System*, 2nd edn, Oxford: Oxford University Press, ch 9. I defer to experts on Kelsen to determine if he can be included in this group, since the answer is not clear to me. In addition, see Robert Alexy (2002) *A Theory of Constitutional Rights*, 2nd edn, tr Julian Rivers, Oxford: Oxford University Press, 31–34. A standard view is that obedience has an epistemic component.

[6] See n 54 for an explanation of the insertion of 'paradigmatically'.

exist requires a rejection of one or more of the assumptions laid out in the foregoing introductory paragraphs. These assumptions have enough traction and plausibility that only compelling arguments for rejecting them (that is, for the incompatible theory of legal content) would justify their rejection. I am not aware of any such compelling arguments.

Instead, such an incompatibility gives us reason to prefer alternative theories of legal content according to which law can (or perhaps does to a reasonable extent) achieve the goal under real-world conditions. Of more importance for present purposes, in evaluating these preferable theories of legal content, consideration of theoretical virtues, such as elegance, simplicity and explanatory significance give us reason to prefer some candidates to others. This criterion of adequacy for theories of legal content will be primarily used in what follows.

In this chapter, I will present a partial theory of legal content that answers the question, 'Can lay law subjects have sufficient epistemic access to legal content pertaining to them under real-world conditions, given the practicalities of typical existing legal systems, and if so, how?' The theory presented here answers affirmatively with economy and explanatory significance.[7] As I shall argue, holistic theories of legal content, such as Greenberg's and Dworkin's, and two mainstream non-holistic theories of legal content – the view that legal content is set entirely by official intentions and the view that legal content is set entirely by official interpretive conventions – answer the question affirmatively only at prices my account avoids. For this reason, I will argue, my theory is superior to these four theories in accounting for the possibility (indeed, in many instances the actuality) of lay epistemic access in existing legal systems.

A word of caution is appropriate at this point. Theories of legal content are metaphysical theories, not epistemic theories[8] (although it is arguable Dworkin's is both). As Sellars, citing Aristotle, once warned, we should not confuse the order of being (a metaphysical claim) with the order of knowing (an epistemic claim).[9] For example, based on behaviour, we may know that a person is in a particular psychological state. Further, we may normally use that behaviour to justify the assertion that the psychological state obtains. Yet it does not follow that the metaphysical determinant of that psychological state is the behaviour (rather than, eg, a particular physical state of the brain).[10] Conversely, if the metaphysical determinant of a psychological state is a particular physical state of the brain, it does not follow that one must know this physical state of the brain obtains in order to know that someone is in the psychological state.

[7] This is not wholly new work on my part, but it is a development and connection of strands of a theory that has been emerging in my work over several years.

[8] That is to say, they are accounts of what constitutes legal content, rather than about how to recognise or know the content of law in legal systems.

[9] Wilfrid Sellars (1991) 'Reply to Aune' in *Wilfrid F Sellars Papers*, Archives of Scientific Philosophy, Archives & Special Collections, University of Pittsburgh Library System, 1–19, 14, fn 4.

[10] I am indebted to Michael Pendlebury for the example.

However, if there is a correlation between the determinant (the physical state) and something else (particular behaviour), the behaviour can be a justification for a belief about the psychological state.

I will show that, on the four rival theories of legal content, either it is not plausible to hold that lay law subjects can use the determinants that the theories identify to justify their beliefs about legal content in existing legal systems, or that the account of their doing so is *ad hoc*. I will then consider whether lay law subjects can have epistemic access to legal content through their awareness of the second correlate of a correlation with the determinants alleged by the theory. If so, and if the theory of legal content in question is true, then lay law subjects may have justified true beliefs about legal content and be well on their way to having epistemic access to legal content. They would have epistemic access under real-world conditions in existing legal systems.[11]

On my approach, in contrast, there is no conceptual room for a correlation between the determinants of legal content and the basis on which lay law subjects naturally rely when their beliefs about legal content pertaining to themselves are both true and justified. To a significant extent, the determinants and this basis are the same. Law is, at its core, centred upon the shared understandings or dispositions to understand of law subjects. More precisely, the legal content of statutes and judicial decisions is built around, and preserves, a core of understandings, dispositions and meaning assignments that is the province of anyone with sufficient linguistic ability, relevant socialisation, access to statutory texts (or texts of other written regulatory instruments) and accurate knowledge of certain facts about judicial decisions.

In other words, and in somewhat dramatic terms, I will advance the view that there is at the centre of law a 'law of the street'.

I. SOME PRELIMINARIES

I am offering only a partial theory of legal content. It is not a theory about the content of constitutive rules, rules of recognition or legal principles as understood by Dworkin – if there are any – in a legal system. For present purposes, I am assuming that statutes, judicial decisions, constitutional provisions, administrative rules, other regulatory instruments such as by-laws and common law doctrines are all inputs whose output, according to the type of theory I advance, is the content of local (jurisdiction-specific) law. I am not offering a theory about why these things are inputs, nor about what grounds them. I am offering a theory about what determines their legal content individually

[11] Lay law subjects may in addition believe that the requirements and prohibitions in question are legal ones. Yet these law subjects might not know, according to these theories, the real (ie metaphysical) reasons the legal content is law.

(if they have such a thing), and what determines the legal content they jointly create.[12]

Even this last characterisation is too broad. I omit all claims concerning constitutional legal content, for I suspect one must say special things on that topic.[13] If it turns out that I am mistaken, so much the better for the view I advocate.

I am interested solely in legal content that may provide epistemic guidance to lay law subjects. There can be epistemic guidance by legal permissions and the granting of powers – for example through a wills statute – but for simplicity's sake, I will omit discussion of such guidance and concentrate on directives.[14]

One of the ideas that I will be relying on is that the notion of law – in the central case, the case Hart described as 'municipal law' and the case most legal philosophers discuss – is inseparable from the notion of an existing legal system. What I mean by this is that thinking about fictional legal systems, hypothetical legal systems and archaic legal systems all entail thinking about legal systems that could have existed or might have existed or did exist. That makes the existence conditions for legal systems relevant to accounts of this sort of law.

I should also make it clear that I am interested in the implications of existence conditions for legal systems guiding human beings as humans are actually constituted, as opposed to drawing any conclusions from imagining what a legal system might be like for angels, aliens or Hart's giant land crabs[15] (if, that is, it would still be a legal system), some of whom may have telepathic abilities.

Another idea that I will rely on is that statutes (and other written regulatory instruments) and judicial decisions play a significant role in determining legal content.[16]

II. THE EPISTEMIC PROBLEM FOR GREENBERG AND DWORKIN

As is well known, both Greenberg and Dworkin have holistic theories of law. The reader may be familiar with the main outlines of Greenberg's view. According to his Moral Impact Theory, the content of the law is 'the moral impact of certain

[12] In other words, this chapter is not offering a full metaphysical theory about the grounds of law.

[13] This restriction gets complicated when the division between statutory content and constitutional content is blurred, as it may be in Alabama and the UK. I am indebted to Kenneth Ehrenberg for this point. Private correspondence.

[14] Burazin (n 1) has a good discussion of the complications in applying the notion of efficacy to legal permissions and empowerments. For purposes of this chapter, legal permissions and power-conferring laws will be excluded.

[15] HLA Hart (1958) 'Positivism and the Separation of Law and Morals' *Harvard Law Review* 71: 623. Raz writes about a legal system for angels in Joseph Raz (1999) *Practical Reason and Norms*, 2nd edn, Oxford: Oxford University Press, 157–61. Scott Shapiro invites us to consider legal systems in science fiction in Scott Shapiro (2011) *Legality*, Cambridge, MA/London: Belknap, 407, fn 16.

[16] To borrow a point from Hrafn Asgeirsson (2020) *The Nature and Value of Vagueness in the Law*, Oxford: Hart Publishing.

decisions of legal institutions'.[17] That impact is 'that part of the moral profile that obtains in virtue of the actions of legal institutions'.[18] The relevant part of the profile will be a certain subset of all-things-considered moral obligations.[19]

The thing to note is that the determinants of legal content according to the Moral Impact Theory are such that it would be in extraordinary circumstances, not ordinary social conditions, that a sufficient number of lay law persons would use them to know the local legal content. For a law subject must have a high level of moral judgement and understanding to identify all the relevant moral considerations and to draw the appropriate inference to the correct conclusion about his or her all-things-considered moral obligation given the statutes, judicial decisions and so forth. The problem goes well beyond any worry about whether pro tanto moral norms are epistemically accessible to the ordinary person. Let us grant that they are and that ordinary persons are not only capable of perceiving but often do perceive pro tanto moral considerations applicable to a choice of act token (or act type). It is a tall order to require that lay law subjects grasp *all* of the relevant pro tanto moral considerations applicable to the question of what they ought to do given the apparent linguistic meaning of a statute or the disposition of a legal case. It is even taller to require that lay law subjects accurately perform the inference in question; for this involves discerning which of these considerations, if any, exclude others, which outweigh others and so on for every possible logical operation on moral considerations. On these matters moral philosophers, who doubtless have spent more time contemplating the logic of moral considerations than non-philosophers, famously disagree.

The main features of Dworkin's account are familiar to most readers. In other work, I have explained why Dworkin's brand of interpretivism has a problem accounting for epistemic access.[20] My points may be summarised as follows:

1. On Dworkin's theory, no legal text – including the text of statutes – can be counted on to state the law accurately – if at all. This is because the local law is the result of the competing weightings of the principles constituting the best interpretation.
2. Identifying the best interpretive theory and correctly weighing the principles requires a high level of judgement and understanding in identifying the

[17] Mark Greenberg (2017) 'The Moral Impact Theory, the Dependence View, and Natural Law' in *Cambridge Companion to Natural Law Jurisprudence*, eds George Duke and Robert P George, Cambridge: Cambridge University Press, 275–313, 294.

[18] Mark Greenberg (2014) 'The Moral Impact Theory of Law' *Yale Law Journal* 123: 1288–1342, 1341. Several legal philosophers, including Raz, have noted that law can change the moral profile. For an account, see Brian Bix (2014) 'When Law Becomes Morality: Comments on Mark Greenberg's Moral Impact Theory of Law' at https://papers.ssrn.com/sol3/papers.cfm?abstract_id=2434075, 3–4.

[19] Greenberg (n 18) 1290 and 1293–94.

[20] Barbara B Levenbook (2020) 'A Puzzle About Legal Systems and Democratic Theory' in *Jurisprudence*, doi: 10.1080/20403313.2020.1726689.

relevant moral considerations, finding the 'value' and 'point' (as Dworkin puts it) of law, legislation and so on, and in making coherent the various inputs in the best way.

3. As the inputs for interpretation (from which the principles arise) are the members of the historical set of political decisions of the polity (and legal system) in question, the lay law subject lacks the knowledge of the inputs and rarely has the degree of moral judgement and understanding required.

The picture that emerges for familiar existing legal systems is that, for much of law subjects' behaviour directly addressed by law, the determinants of the relevant legal content are not epistemically accessible by the lay law subjects on Dworkin's theory.

Might lay law subjects have epistemic access if the determinants of legal content were accessible by legal experts? An immediate problem is that the lay law subject is in no position to reliably identify which experts, if any, have both the knowledge of the inputs and the degree of moral judgement required. A more profound problem is that it is possible, on Dworkin's view, that at any given time none of the experts do. They may all be mistaken on a particular point of law.

Dworkin contends that in familiar legal systems, judges develop some 'unconscious' or 'unthinking' feel for the Herculean work involved in discovering the local law,[21] and that judges develop 'skills of craft husbandry and efficiency' in the task.[22] (I am assuming he would make the same contention about other legal experts.) It is not clear what would count as evidence of such an ability and, worse, it is not clear that anything would; these claims may not be falsifiable.[23] Therefore, there is no reason to believe Dworkin's contentions on this matter, no reason to believe that legal experts can be relied on for lay epistemic access to the relevant legal content.

III. OFFICIAL INTERPRETIVE CONVENTIONS

This section examines a view found in the works of Raz and Hart. On this view, legal content depends upon the local practices ('conventions') of officials. Raz maintains that any metaphysical theory of content will be thin. The only universal in a theory of legal content is that legal content is established by local conventions of interpretation used by legal authorities.[24] It follows that the

[21] Ronald Dworkin (1986) *Law's Empire*, Cambridge, MA: Harvard University Press, 245 and 256.

[22] ibid, 265.

[23] I am indebted to Robert Mabrito for this point. Personal communication.

[24] Joseph Raz (2009a) 'On the Nature of Law' in *Between Authority and Interpretation*, Oxford: Oxford University Press, 91–125, 120–22. See Joseph Raz (2009b) 'Intention in Interpretation' in *Between Authority and Interpretation*, Oxford: Oxford University Press, 265–98 for the more general claim about the role of conventions. Raz assumes, at least in 'Intention in Interpretation', that the interpreting that counts is the interpreting done by legal authorities – notably, judges.

content of law is entirely metaphysically dependent on officials. Filling in the details will, Raz thinks, be entirely parochial, relative to the legal system in question. Hart comes close to a similar view.[25]

It is clear that, on this theory, lay law subjects are in no position to use the determinants of the content of legal directives. Lay law subjects are not participants in the official interpretive conventions. Using these conventions requires special knowledge – in addition to knowledge of the source material, linguistic conventions, technical definitions and background common knowledge. Given the existence of specialised legal training, there is reason to believe lay law subjects do not typically know the content of the conventions in question. Further, lay law subjects in existing legal systems – even the most conscientiously law-abiding – do not consult the relevant officials to nearly the extent necessary for lay law-compliant behaviour *as a general rule* to be the result of direct application of official conventions.

Though I will not make it my primary objection in this chapter, there are theoretical problems with the interpretive conventions theory of legal content that make it reasonable to search for a better alternative. On this theory, a legal text or a judicial decision can in principle set any legal content whatsoever. (When it sets an unusual content, time and energy must be devoted to communicating in plain language to the lay law public the results of applying the official conventions in order to achieve conduct guidance by law.) It is conceivable on this view that, by enacting a statutory provision reading, 'No one is to Φ', a legislature might actually be requiring its law subjects to Φ. The idea that such legislative double-talk provides a perfect example of the generation of statutory legal content is implausible. The pattern could, in principle, be iterated often in what we are invited to view, given a sufficient educational campaign, as a model legal system (or at least one that is not defective on that count). This idea is absurd.

IV. THE CORRELATION APPROACH

There is one stratagem that proponents of the three theories of legal content might use to explain the possibility of lay epistemic access in existing legal systems. It goes as follows. As a matter of fact in existing legal systems, there is (to the appropriate degree) a correlation between two things: the determinants of legal content (all-things-considered moral obligations, what is justified by

[25] Hart (n 5) ch VI. One caveat: ibid, 111, Hart denies that the rule of recognition itself, the ultimate identifier of (other) *ex ante* law, can be characterised as a convention. (For explicit discussion of conventions and their role in clear cases in the law, see HLA Hart (1967) 'Problems of the Philosophy of Law' repr in HLA Hart (1983) *Essays in Jurisprudence and Philosophy*, Oxford: Clarendon Press, 88–119, 106. There Hart is not writing solely about conventions created by officials, as he mentions conventions of ordinary language.)

the best interpretation of legal data, or the application of official interpretive conventions) and something else.

The first candidate for the second correlate is a belief about the dictates and permissions of morality or some subset of it (eg what it would be fair to permit or require in a certain recurring situation). Lay law subjects, it might be claimed, often rely on this belief as a guide to what the law requires, prohibits and permits.[26] In familiar existing legal systems there is an overlap at the core of the criminal and the most basic tort law between their dictates and the dictates of the local folk morality. Lay law subjects' convergence on folk morality explains why they converge on and can reliably arrive at true beliefs about (this portion of) the legal content.[27] If the law subjects know that using folk morality is a reliable method for arriving at beliefs about legal content, the beliefs are justified.

One drawback of the folk-morality-correlation approach is that it will not explain the possibility of lay epistemic access in existing legal systems to some of the law applying to them to which they seem to conform. I have in mind the local traffic code, airport security regulations and, in some countries, restrictions on the number of persons permitted in a gathering during a pandemic.

There is another candidate for the second correlate when it comes to statutes, regulations and other written regulatory instruments that may be particularly attractive to the official conventions theorist. In many advanced legal systems, official interpretive conventions for statutes (and the like) either privilege linguistic meaning or count it as one of the criteria.[28] In a sufficient number of situations, it may be claimed, the relevant set of official interpretive conventions produces the same content meaning for the texts of these written instruments as whatever linguistic conventions lay law subjects use to understand the texts. The result is a correlation between official interpretive conventions applied to a statutory (or regulatory) text and ordinary linguistic conventions so applied. Once more, if lay law subjects know that relying on the conventions they use to understand this sort of written language is a reliable method to reach the content of (a sufficient number of) statutes (and the like) aimed at them, their beliefs about this legal content will be justified.[29]

[26] There is empirical evidence that many lay persons in some familiar legal systems fashion their ideas about the dictates of their local law (pertaining to their behaviour) on just such a basis. See, eg, Lucas Miotto (2019) 'The Good, The Bad, and The Puzzled: Coercion and Compliance' in *Conceptual Jurisprudence: Methodological Issues, Conceptual Tools, and New Approaches*, eds Jorge Fabra-Zamora and Gonzalo Villa Rosas, Cham: Springer Nature Switzerland AG, citing empirical research from 2004.

[27] Suggestion from James Penner, private correspondence.

[28] For this response, I am grateful to Adam Rigoni, Kenneth Ehrenberg and James E Penner. Private correspondence.

[29] More is necessary for knowledge than justified belief, of course. However, pursuing this topic would take us too far into epistemology. Let us grant, for the sake of argument, that the three theories of legal content might show that the additional epistemic conditions, whatever they are, can be met in real-world situations.

This response faces two immediate challenges. The first is that in many existing legal systems there is only an incomplete ordering of the criteria for statutory interpretation. There are conflicts among the criteria, some of them just where the response needs a determinate order. The second is that the response assumes that the criteria for statutory interpretation are always criteria for determining *ex ante* legal content and never for repair of it; or, if sometimes for one and sometimes for the other, it is clear that the criteria generating the match to lay law subjects' beliefs are for *ex ante* law only.[30] Neither assumption may be correct. However, let us disregard these problems for the sake of argument.

Notice that on the stratagems suggested in this section, the possibility of epistemic access by lay law subjects under real-world conditions depends upon the contingent existence of the relevant correlations. It also depends on knowledge by lay law subjects that their method of reaching (a sufficient amount of) legal content is reliable (even if they do not know why – that is, do not know of the correlation).

V. INTENTION-DEPENDENT THEORIES

Intention-dependent theories are a popular school of thought. They are treated separately in this chapter for reasons that will become apparent. By 'intention-dependent theories of legal content', I mean those theories holding that legal content is entirely determined by content-specific intentions of officials.

Readers may be unfamiliar with an intention-dependent theory of judicial decisions. It will only be addressed briefly here. If one supposes that judicial decisions in common law systems set down rules to guide behaviour, the theory that the content of these rules is determined by the intentions of judges deciding the cases may seem attractive. However, I have defended, in an earlier publication, the idea that judicial decisions in a precedent system ought not to be thought of as paradigmatically laying down rules or norms in the philosophical sense (ie complete standards of behaviour).[31] More precisely, I have argued that the model of precedent as laying down an example (with 'unfinished' or partial categories) has significant advantages over the rule model. I will not repeat my arguments or the advantages here. Where judicial decisions function as examples, there is no canonical linguistic content, and so nothing like an official propositional meaning-intent view is appropriate.

I also considered and criticised in that earlier work a contention by an intention-dependent theorist that official intentions to lay down an example

[30] It is not clear whether the official conventions thesis can offer a principle for distinguishing these situations. Raz, for one, cautions that determining the *ex ante* legal content in interpretation should not be separated from innovative interpretation. Raz (2009a) (n 24) 120–22.

[31] Barbara B Levenbook (2000) 'The Meaning of a Precedent' *Legal Theory* 6: 185–240. Complete standards of behaviour employ whole categories, specifying kinds of action and the like.

determine which example, and so what legal content a precedential decision has. Part of my criticism was the mismatch between such a view and the possibility (and actuality) of epistemic access by lay law subjects under the conditions of existing legal systems. For this reason, I will not repeat my criticisms here and will not further discuss intention-dependent theories of judicial decisions.

Most readers will be familiar with intention-dependent theories applied to statutes. Some of these theories employ the notion of actual (subjective) intention, and some use an imputed (objective) notion. These theories may or may not be founded on some form of speaker-intention theory of linguistic content added to what Greenberg called 'the communicative content theory' of the law,[32] according to which the linguistic content of legal texts (including statutes) is (or in some important sense directly corresponds to[33]) their legal content.[34]

The simplest form of such a theory is the view that actual independent legislative intentions determine the legal content of a statute. I have criticised this view in a previous work[35] on the grounds of its lack of economy in explaining epistemic access by lay law subjects. For this reason, in this section I will concentrate on the most sophisticated version – an imputed-intention version – taking Asgeirsson as the representative proponent.[36] He holds that the legal content of a statute directly corresponds to the content that a reasonable addressee would infer the legislature intended to communicate (assuming, I suppose, that the addressee has access to the text).[37] The primary advantage claimed for this view is that it uses a sophisticated theory of the content of speech acts. This is an advantage, of course, only on the assumption that statutes are legislative speech acts.[38]

Let us set aside the question of whether it would be reasonable to attribute a content-relevant intention to some alleged intention holders (such as a

[32] This is the most discussed prong of a three-prong theory of how law works that Greenberg (2011) calls 'the Standard Picture' ('The Standard Picture and its Discontents' in Leslie Green and Brian Leiter (eds), Oxford Studies in Philosophy of Law vol 1 (Oxford University Press), 39–106). In Barbara B Levenbook (2006) 'How a Statute Applies' *Legal Theory* 12: 71–112, I called the theory that the full linguistic content of statutes is set by the (meaning) intentions of the legislators or legislature (or rational inference to them) 'linguistic intentionalism'.

[33] Asgeirsson (n 16) 7 explains why 'directly corresponds to' might be more appropriate.

[34] One need not be a linguistic intentionalist or a communicative theorist to hold this kind of view. Richard Ekins (2012) *The Nature of Legislative Intent*, Oxford: Oxford University Press may be a case in point. It is difficult to be sure, since he writes about statutory interpretation; and his use of the phrase 'statutory interpretation' plus his proffered theory of legislating blur the distinction between identifying the full linguistic content of a statute and identifying the legal content contributed by that statute. Only by assuming the communicative content theory for statutes can one hold that there is no distinction to blur; and this is an assumption I will not make in this chapter. Ekins appears to reject the communicative content theory for statutes.

[35] Levenbook (n 32).

[36] Unfortunately, in 'How a Statute Applies' (n 32) I was unclear and peremptory in the reply I hereby develop in full, relegating much of it to a footnote (ibid, 80, fn 11).

[37] Asgeirsson (n 16) 34. See also ibid, 41.

[38] Sandro has argued that they should be regarded instead as 'text acts'. (As he acknowledges, the phrase is not original to him.) See Paolo Sandro (2021) *The Making of Constitutional Democracy: From Creation to Application of Law*, Oxford: Hart Publishing, 169–210.

corporate legislature), as distinguished from attributing collective intentional action or collective intentions to enact a particular statute.

If Asgeirsson goes on to maintain that in existing legal systems addressees can have access to the texts of statutes and that addressees can (and do) draw reasonable inferences about legislative (communicative) intentions, can he account for the real possibility of lay epistemic access to the legal content of statutes? One difficulty in answering this question is that whether or not he succeeds cannot be determined in the absence of an account of the conditions for such reasonable inference drawing. Exploring this difficulty will reveal a deeper problem endemic to his theory.

Suppose, for example, that he maintains that in the simplest case, knowledge of the text, competence in the language and some general common ground (held by addressees and legislatures) jointly provide sufficient warrant for the inference in question. Consider, for example, the following text:

> The driver of any vehicle who knows or reasonably should know: (1) that the vehicle which he or she is operating is involved in a crash; and (2) that the crash has resulted in serious bodily injury … or death … shall immediately stop his or her vehicle at the scene of the crash. The driver shall remain with the vehicle at the scene of the crash until a law-enforcement officer completes the investigation of the crash or authorizes the driver to leave and the vehicle to be removed …[39]

In this case, Asgeirsson might maintain, it is reasonable to infer that the legislative intention was to create a duty for drivers involved in accidents that they know or ought to know resulted in serious bodily injury or death to remain at the scene awaiting law enforcement.

Unfortunately, this answer is *ad hoc*. To see this, consider this question: When do law subjects have evidence that makes it reasonable to infer that legislatures do (or do not) intend legal content that matches the surface linguistic meaning of their statutory provisions? One cannot assume that we can import the model of speech act theory to answer this question, using, for example, Grice's maxims as inference rules, on the undefended assumption that statutes are speech acts of legislatures. These maxims are plausible for conversation only because we can have independent evidence of what speakers intend, at least in a good many circumstances.[40] On this basis, we can assign probabilities that when speakers literally say one thing under conditions C, they intend to communicate it; and when they literally say another thing under conditions C (violating, eg, Grice's maxims),

[39] North Carolina General Statutes, § 20-166(a).

[40] As others have pointed out, some conditions Grice sets for his maxims are unmet in the case of statutes and other written regulatory instruments. A statute is not part of a conversation. There is no ' talk exchange' between the legislature and the lay public, and *a forteriori* no 'accepted purpose or direction of the talk exchange' to which Grice's Cooperative Principle, which he holds essential to generating conversational implicatures, applies. See HP Grice, 'Logic and Conversation' repr in Paul Grice (1989) *Studies in the Way of Words*, Cambridge, MA: Harvard University Press, 22–40, 26.

they intend to communicate another. We can gather that information because, as Schauer observes, in a conversational context, there is commonly an 'adaptability'. By this observation, Schauer means that speakers have an opportunity to 'clarify, explain, and embellish' what they say whenever it is necessary to remedy misunderstandings of their intended meaning.[41] Typically, an interlocutor can ask questions and, in the case of a directive, can test hypotheses about the speaker's intention in the presence of the speaker.

However, and contrary to the contentions of some intention-dependent theorists, we do not have the kind and quantity of independent evidence of what legal content corporate legislatures intend that is necessary to assign probabilities, and on that basis, to determine which inferences in the case of statutes are reasonable.[42] For this determination to be possible, and for the probability to be greater than chance, there would have to be some robust, actual intention of corporate legislatures, and we would have to have sufficient evidence (in a good many instances) of its content *independent of reasonable inferences*. That we do not have, and that is the endemic problem. The claim that legislative debates or statements by a bill's sponsor provide such evidence is unconvincing, if not arbitrary. The meaning of the text cannot be sufficient evidence of legislative intention. For if it were, the idea of a robust legislative intention would be eviscerated and the reasonable attribution view would dissolve into a theory of legal content for statutes that uses independent determinants – viz, the determinants of meaning independent of legislative intention.

The problem stems, at least in part, from the fact that the situation with respect to legislation is typically *un*adaptable. Lay law subjects cannot test the hypothesis that the legislature intends a certain content for a particular statutory provision. (This fact is most obvious for law subjects considerably distanced in time from the enacting legislature. Law subjects can choose obedience or disobedience and wait for the reaction of officials, but that will be the reaction of a different set of officials from a different institution.)

The search for evidence may lead some readers to this line of thinking: reading statutes (and other written regulatory instruments) according to full linguistic meaning as a default is a common practice in the courts and other law-applying organs in existing legal systems. Let us suppose that the corporate legislature knows the practice, yet makes no move to pre-empt such a reading of

[41] Frederick Schauer (1991) *Playing by the Rules*, Oxford: Oxford University Press, 40–42. Quoted phrase from ibid, 42. Although Schauer does not mention it, the cues in a conversational situation may include non-verbal communication, such as tone of voice and facial expression.

[42] Probability, of course, depends upon evidence. The probability in the absence of all evidence is 50:50, ie chance. However, as I understand it, it is not reasonable to conclude that the legislature intends a particular content (say, the one lay law subjects would assign on other bases) if the probability is a mere 50% that the legislature intends this content. Alternatively, perhaps it is equally reasonable to conclude that the legislature does and also that it does not intend this content. In this case, Asgeirsson's theory of legal content generates an inconsistent set of legal contents for each statute.

a given statute. Would not an inference that the corporate legislature intends this reading for a given statutory text be reasonable on this basis?

Unfortunately, it would not. Consider the following analogy. I know Uncle Skippy to be touchy and to take certain types of questions or remarks routinely 'the wrong way' (as meaning something insulting). Somehow, I cannot consistently remember when talking to him to avoid these questions, or to preface these remarks with reassurances or disclaimers. Suppose I say, out of curiosity, 'Why did you do that, Uncle?' Suppose that once again he takes my remark as having an impliciture and meaning, in full, 'Why, since it was such a stupid thing to do, did you do that, Uncle?' It is not reasonable to infer that I intended to convey this message. (His taking this intention as reasonably inferred of me is precisely why he is unreasonable.) The same may be said, *mutatis mutandis*, about legislatures having common knowledge of how courts (or, for that matter, lay law subjects) would read statutory provisions.

At this point, some readers will insist that, nonetheless, it seems normally rational to suppose that the enacting legislature intends to communicate the full linguistic meaning of a statute. Fortunately, the persistence of this idea can be explained without reliance on an intention-dependent theory of legal content. One can maintain that the statutory text has an independent meaning. If, in addition, one makes three assumptions that I find questionable but that are fairly common in the literature on this subject – that statutes are communications, that legislatures are rational and that legislatures intend to communicate clearly – it is rational to suppose that by choosing a text, a legislature intends to communicate its independent meaning.

Obviously, this explanation must be rejected by the intention-dependent theorist. Nor can this theorist appropriate the assumption that typically, or as a default, legislatures (in existing legal systems) intend the full linguistic meaning of their statutory provisions to be the legal content (and that in the simplest case, the full linguistic meaning is the apparent or plain meaning). As a contingent claim, it would be *ad hoc*, designed to save the theory.

To escape from this difficulty, the intention-dependent theorist might maintain that *necessarily* typically legislatures intend the full linguistic meaning of their statutory provisions to be the legal content (and in the simplest case, the full linguistic meaning is the apparent meaning). This contention may be asserted as a truth about the 'logic' of this kind of reasonable inference: it is reasonable in the simplest case for lay law subjects to infer that the meaning of directives intended by the legislature directly corresponds to their apparent meaning.[43] On this approach, the determinants of this legislative intention are the same as the determinants of the full linguistic meaning. The idea of a content-relevant legislative intention thus does no independent metaphysical

[43] Alternatively, it might be claimed that the assumption is implied by the conditions for rational comprehension of language.

explanatory work. Reference to it is otiose in an account of epistemic access. There is a more straightforward alternative: appeal directly to the determinants of full linguistic meaning.

VI. PRODUCTS OF THE STREET

It is time for an alternative, and the purpose of this section is to introduce one, or rather a first approximation of one. I should start by making it clear that the court decisions concerning, and directives aimed at, lay law subjects have their own determinants. I am taking their production, in accordance with official procedures, as a given. As I said at the beginning of this chapter, the theory I will elucidate is about the determinants of their content. Understanding the legal content of directives aimed at lay law subjects as epistemically accessible by them (to some unspecified sufficient extent) in an existing legal system is consistent with the desirable goal of describing legal content in such a way as to explain its function in guiding and constraining private conduct.

The heart of the theory I advocate is 'the law of the street'. By this phrase, I do not mean to include everything the lay law subject thinks is the content of the local law, nor even what the vast majority of law subjects in any given jurisdiction think. Nor do I mean to include all the norms law subjects guide themselves by in the name of compliance with the law. One reason is that I am discussing the legal content of the relevant local authoritative pronouncements, such as statutes, judicial decisions and administrative regulations. According to an apocryphal story of several decades ago, Canadian citizens living on the border with the United States watched so much broadcast US crime television, they (erroneously) concluded that they had a Fifth Amendment right against self-incrimination. I am not contending that they did have this right under Canadian law. For there was at the time no Canadian authoritative pronouncement to which that belief attached, either directly or indirectly.

A second reason is that, as legal experts well know, lay law subjects are notoriously inaccurate about the legal content of authoritative pronouncements on various points. This is why legal experts are needed. However, at the core of directive legal content addressed to lay law subjects, a certain kind of social salience about content in existing legal systems does not just fortuitously or as a contingent matter track legal content (because, eg, lay law subjects are so good at reasonable inferences to likely official intentions) but determines it. In spelling out this position, I will sometimes refer to and draw on earlier work.

As I indicated in the previous section, judicial decisions in common law typically set down no rule or standard with propositional meaning.[44] To repeat,

[44] Levenbook (n 31), laid out the position I sketch here, with the exception of my contention about legal content. One familiar view is that legal content, or at least its directive portion, is a set of norms (in the philosophical sense). (See, eg, Raz (n 15) chs 4–5.) On my account, this is stretching

my earlier work advanced the view that judicial decisions that set precedent for courts and lay persons alike are, instead, examples. What follows is an abbreviated version of the position elucidated and defended there, with some small elaboration for present purposes.

Judicial decisions have *exemplar meaning*. That meaning is, in the first instance, socially set. There is, of course, a normative dimension to this meaning: a permitting, protecting or prohibiting of an act token.[45] The act token is an example of the kind of act permitted, protected or prohibited. What is 'on all fours' with the original act token – what is 'the same as' some act, circumstance and legal person in the original case – is determined by social salience.

Social salience, as I am using the term, stands in need of clarification. A socially salient grouping of sameness stands out sharply from among other contenders for the answer to the question 'Doing what (and in what circumstances) would be doing the same thing as the particular party's behaviour adjudicated in this legal case?' A socially salient grouping is a 'the-same-thing-at-bottom' grouping. Groupings are not *socially* salient unless they are the groupings on which the social group does or is disposed to converge in the aforementioned judgment under the right conditions.[46] The right conditions include knowledge of certain facts about the original case and correct relevant background empirical beliefs.[47]

On the approach I advocate in this chapter, the socially salient exemplar meaning (with its normative dimension) is the default legal content of the precedential decision. Since the relevant kind of socially salient grouping is possible under real-world conditions, when the public is given certain facts about a legal case, epistemic access to its legal content is possible under real-world conditions.

matters when applied to common law precedents. For typically the only norm-like thing that emerges from precedential examples is radically unspecific, something like 'Don't behave like this', or 'You may behave like this'. Such an alleged standard seems significantly vacuous just where one would expect categories for the behaviour and the conditions to be specified in a general rule-like way. As I indicated in the previous section of this chapter, they are not specified by the precedent but rather left unfinished, partial or somewhat open.

[45] In Levenbook (n 31), section V, I speculated that the normative aspect may depend upon a special case of social salience.

[46] In my earlier work, I assumed there would be mutual knowledge of this convergence or mutual expectation of it. A socially salient grouping is there characterised as an 'everyone-knows-they're-the-same-thing-at-bottom' grouping. I leave open the possibility that the group must share the belief that the answer on which they converge is *manifestly* correct.

[47] I am indebted to Kenneth Ehrenberg (in private correspondence) for challenging me to think about the case in which the populace is under a false belief about some background empirical condition or fact, and for this reason would converge on behaviour after suitable exposure to a judicial decision. For example, a court for the first time rejects the doctrine of *caveat emptor* for the sale of a product used in the home that proved to be carcinogenic – eg benzene. A consumer is permitted to sue and recover medical expenses from a seller of and a manufacturer of the benzene product. Suppose that there is a widespread belief among the populace that genetically modified corn is carcinogenic, and that belief is false. I do not want to claim that the precedent is a socially salient example for suing a seller of genetically modified corn. On the other hand, if the populace falsely believes that asbestos is not carcinogenic, I do want to claim that the precedent may be a socially salient example for suing and recovering medical expenses from a seller of asbestos for the home.

Precedent (correctly) guides the conduct of lay law subjects in a common law system when enough of the case is known by the law subjects so that the decision serves for these persons as a socially salient example of how to behave or how not to behave (or what one is entitled to do, and so on).

Lay law persons who wish to follow the guidance of a precedential decision and do not or cannot seek legal expertise will act on their best understanding of its conduct implications, especially of what constitutes doing the same thing as the defendant or plaintiff in the original case. Moreover, lay persons often lack ready access to legal experts who might correct these groupings, especially at every instance (regarding every act token) in which law subjects might wish to apply the guidance of a precedent. The best understanding of lay persons will typically be a socially salient grouping. Among the socialised, this is an entrenched grouping.

It follows that the approach to legal content of precedential decisions that I advocate is economical. There is no conceptual room for a correlation between the determinant of legal content of a precedential decision and something else that as a rule lay law subjects rely on to be guided by the decision, or would rely on, given the right conditions. Instead of a correlation, there is identity.

Written statutory and other regulatory texts have *contextual meaning*. It will help to think of contextual meaning as the meaning a statutory text has when it is considered for a vote by the legislature, or for whatever process the legislature uses to enact it. The text must have some meaning in order for consideration, debate and deliberation on its merits to be possible. For statutory provisions, contextual meaning includes pragmatically enriched meaning.[48]

By introducing the idea of pragmatic enrichment, I am not reintroducing a legislative intention theory. It is controversial whether or not there are norms generating pragmatically enriched meaning for this sort of written language; but let us grant, for the sake of argument, that there are. It is obvious that such pragmatic norms cannot refer to actual legislative intentions before a legislative intention can exist, namely, before enactment. Nor can those norms refer to a hypothetical reasonably inferred legislative intention before enactment. For reasons rehearsed in the previous section, this idea is empty without independent standards of what it would be reasonable to infer a legislature will intend if it enacts the bill in question.[49]

Contextual meaning is presupposed by intention-dependent theorists. Consider, first, those who look for actual meaning intentions of legislatures, as opposed to outcome intentions (sometimes called 'purpose'), and who contend

[48] By saying that contextual meaning is pragmatically enriched meaning, I am acknowledging that there can be implicit parts of this meaning. (I call these *statutory implicitures*.) See Levenbook, 'Beyond Legislative Intent' (unpublished ms) for an elaboration and defence of the idea that there can be contextual statutory implicitures.

[49] I have begun to elucidate some norms for pragmatic enrichment of statutory language that make no essential reference to any sort of legislative intentions in 'Beyond Legislative Intent' (n 48).

that the inference to the legislative meaning intention is based on evidence. Contextual meaning is the default, or starting point, of the proposed reasoning. In the case of the inference to meaning intentions, contextual meaning of statutory provisions has an epistemological relationship to legislative intent – viz, prima facie, the legislative intent is to mean the contextual meaning. The text itself is considered evidence of actual legislative intent because of this independent, *ex ante*, contextual meaning.

Second, contextual meaning is presupposed by those who look for what it would be reasonable to suppose is the legislative meaning (or legal content) intention. Assuming inferences to legislative content intentions can be reasonable, if, for example, the statutory text enacted by a legislature (*ex ante*) means that it is forbidden to Φ, an inference to a legislative intention to make it forbidden to Φ is reasonable. Indeed, the fact of this meaning is a weighty epistemic consideration. If the text does not have this meaning, prima facie it is not reasonable to make this inference. At the very least, there is a great epistemic hurdle to overcome for a contrary inference.[50]

I am not convinced that it can be overcome. The reasons are as follows. Enactment is the way that legislatures introduce something into total local legal content. Enactment is always by formal procedure. For these reasons, it is counterintuitive to suppose that a legislative intention that does not correspond to the enacted statutory contextual meaning introduces legal content that fails of such correspondence. There is no mechanism for such introduction, not in the pragmatics of statutory language and not in formal legislative procedures. Instead, if there were a conflicting legislative intention, it misfired incontinently.

Finally, contextual meaning is presupposed by the Gricean model of pragmatic enrichment. It follows that contextual meaning is presupposed by any theory of legal content that accepts the idea that legal content (of regulatory instruments) is the outcome of applying the Gricean model. The official interpretive conventions theory is an example if one of the official interpretive conventions specifies that the content of statutes is presumed to be full linguistic meaning, and the Gricean model of full linguistic meaning is assumed.[51]

Contextual meaning is determined by social salience. Discerning contextual meaning is part of language competence. If there are norms governing the drawing of contextual meaning, they are accessible to and, in some sense, are products of the street. They are accessed by competent speakers of the language in question (including, of course, legislators), whose competence in part consists of grasping these norms and (though this may not be metaphysically inseparable) using them correctly.[52]

[50] If we are presupposing that it makes sense to talk about legislatures intending and choosing, then legislatures choose to enact a text because it bears a meaning *ex ante* (corresponding to what they intend to introduce into the law).

[51] I am indebted to Adam Rigoni for this point. Private correspondence.

[52] There is another possibility, namely that language competence does not consist in grasping *norms*, as I am using the term, but rather in following examples. All prior uses of language would

The directive legal content of a statute may be conceived of as a legal norm, or as the difference the statute makes to the *ex ante* set of legal norms or total legal content. In the simplest or default case, that norm or that difference corresponds to the socially salient normative meaning of the statute – that is, the contextual meaning.

For this reason, in the simplest case, legislators can know what it is they are voting to introduce into law,[53] and lay law subjects can have epistemic access to the legal content of directives aimed at them under real-world conditions. Lay law subjects can have epistemic access when it is possible for them to access the texts of the relevant directives (or accurate paraphrases), since they will tend to have correct beliefs about contextual meanings. These beliefs will be justified if the persons involved are socially and linguistically competent, and perceive and think normally. Existing legal systems typically meet these conditions.

It follows that the reason it is rational for so many legal systems to have, among official conventions of so-called 'statutory interpretation', the default canon that, other things being equal, the statute is to be interpreted in accordance with its 'plain', 'ordinary' or common' meaning, is that it is this meaning that is the default legal content. The driver is the contextual meaning, not the official convention.

As with judicial decisions, lay law persons who wish to follow the guidance of a statutory provision or other written regulatory instrument without the advice of legal experts will act on their best understanding of its meaning. This best understanding will start with the socially salient contextual meaning, which will then be applied to the law subject's circumstances. For guidance by a statute requires applying the statute to one's circumstances, that is, identifying act tokens compliant with the statute.[54] Introduction of the idea of application does not, however, undermine the social salience approach. I have presented a social salience account of statutory application elsewhere[55] and will not rehearse its points or my arguments for them here.

then be examples with varying levels of social salience. (Suggested by Kenneth Ehrenberg, private correspondence.) See also Millikan's claim (at 89) that there are no determinate rules of language, and her account of linguistic conventions in terms of following precedent and the salient in Ruth G Millikan (2008) 'A Difference of Some Consequence Between Conventions and Rules' *Topoi* 27: 87–99.

[53] The knowledge makes it possible for legislators to intend, in the robust sense of 'intend', the specific change they are choosing (or voting against). Such knowledge makes it possible for legislators collectively, in the simplest case to, as Raz puts it, 'make the law they intend to make'. Raz (2009b) (n 24) 275.

[54] Suppose that the law subject can identify some act tokens and knows they would be compliant with local law but nothing more – ie not the contextual meaning. (Suppose, for example, the law subject has not accessed the text but has been tutored with regard to certain act tokens compliant with it.) I regard such a situation as illustrating guidance to a particular extent (and so, to a lesser degree) by the local law.

[55] Levenbook (n 32).

The foregoing account of statutory legal content is as economical as the foregoing account of the legal content of precedential decisions. There is no conceptual room for a correlation between the default determinant of legal content of a statute and something else that as a rule lay law subjects tend to rely on, or would rely on given the right conditions. They are the same.

It remains to point out that what is socially salient, in the linguistic and social contexts, is determined by social practices (and perhaps natural tendencies of mind and perception) that belong to the street. Social salience belongs to the street, in the sense that it is metaphysically produced (in some sense of that tricky word, it is *grounded*) on the understandings or dispositions to understand and group, the habits of conceptualising and methods of reasoning to salience, of the populace in question and the social structure of norms and meanings they help to create and maintain.

VII. A BRIEF LOOK AT THE SECOND STAGE

The previous section discussed the default or simple case. However, the law of a jurisdiction tends to be systematic. Several judicial decisions over time may help to precisify (or even close) the categories of circumstance, act and agent involved in an initial precedential decision. More challenging for the simple picture previously sketched, there is sometimes what Asgeirsson calls a 'gap' between what a statute or other written regulatory instrument appears to introduce into law and what it does introduce into law. That is because of the operation of other legal elements at a second stage.

It will be helpful to categorise the legal elements that operate at the second stage (at a secondary level, one might say) on inputs at a more basic level (primary) to generate what I have elsewhere called 'systematicity'.[56] I will do so by adapting discussion of legal elements mentioned by those who maintain that there is a gap between legal content and what on an intention-dependent theory would be the communicative content of statutory directives, judicial decisions and administrative regulations. These elements fall into three broad categories.[57] The first consists of what Smith calls 'prospectively-operating modifier laws', legal elements that prospectively alter the legal effect of other legal elements (such as statutory provisions). Examples offered include the US Code's Dictionary Act[58] and the common law rule of lenity for criminal offences (which holds that if a statutory provision would otherwise be indeterminate, a court should interpret it in a way most favourable to the defendant).[59] The second consists of what

[56] Levenbook (n 20).

[57] In this typology, I rely heavily on Smith's excellent discussion in Dale Smith (2019) 'The Practice-based Objection to the "Standard Picture" of How Law Works' *Jurisprudence* 10: 502–31.

[58] 1 USC §§ 1–8 (2012). This Act dates back to 1871.

[59] See, on the Dictionary Act and the rule of lenity and other 'closure rules', William Baude and Stephen E Sachs (2017) 'The Law of Interpretation' *Harvard Law Review* 130: 1079–1147.

Smith calls 'retrospectively-operating modifier laws', such as the UK Human Rights Act. The third category consists of common law presumptions such as the mens rea doctrine for criminal offences and other aspects of what is referred to as 'the general criminal law'. The latter includes the presumption against retroactivity and defences such as self-defence.

Knowledge of these elements is not, generally, the province of the street. Not only are lay law subjects usually unaware of these doctrines and statutes and conventions, legislatures cannot be plausibly credited with awareness of them; and paraphrase writers seldom make the effects of such elements explicit in the paraphrases upon which lay law subjects rely. The informed elite, the legal experts, know the elements and their operations. The resulting legal content – when it is *ex ante* legal content – can be contrary to the expectations of the lay law public based on social salience. Accounting for systematicity thus poses a considerable challenge to a social salience account of legal content. In what remains of this chapter, I will only gesture at the solution.

I call my account the *hypothetical law of the streets*. It holds that systemic legal content is what would be socially salient to law subjects if they were fully informed, that is, given the full set of inputs for the systematicity – including relevant legal cases, common law doctrines, presumptions of the general criminal law, modifier statutes and so on. (Of course they would not, then, be *lay* law subjects.) In other words, the notion of 'the right conditions' under which convergence would occur in the account of social salience must be expanded to capture the operation of the second stage.

In many cases in existing legal systems, the systemic legal content of a statute will overlap, in applications, a good deal of the default legal content. Lay law subjects who know applications in this overlap can *to this extent* be guided by the statute. Something similar can be said about the legal content of a judicial decision.

The hypothetical law of the streets explains how the elements of the second stage have content. For instance, a modifier statute has the content that would be socially salient if the modifier statute were common knowledge. A legal practice based entirely on past examples has the exemplar force that would be socially salient if the past examples were common knowledge, and so on.

Note that unlike some hypothetical accounts of other philosophical matters, the hypothetical law of the streets is not a sterile view. Social salience distinguishes in a principled way what legal reasoning results in finding *ex ante* law and what does something else – viz, extends the law or repairs it by determining it where it is indeterminate, by curing ambiguity or by making a vague provision precise. Whether a legal conclusion arising from the second stage is *ex ante* law depends upon the truth of a counterfactual of this form: 'If p and q were common knowledge, the conclusion about legal content in question would be socially salient.' The counterfactual will not always be true.

For example, if the presumption against retroactivity and the rule of lenity were common knowledge, their effects on a criminal statute might be socially salient. Then their operation on a criminal statute results in *ex ante* legal content. (I strongly suspect that the lay law subject in familiar legal systems presumes that criminal statutes are prospective without being told that the presumption is part of the criminal law.) At the other extreme, consider an Australian statute, the Charter of Human Rights and Responsibilities Act, which provides 'So far as it is possible to do so consistently with their purpose, all statutory provisions must be interpreted in a way that is compatible with human rights.'[60] It is one of Smith's examples of a retrospectively-operating modifier law. If, as Smith claims, the rights are not specified and one must resort to moral reasoning to determine them,[61] no one determination may be socially salient. In this situation, an authority, such as a judge, goes beyond discovering antecedent law when applying the Act to a previous statutory provision to determine what human right is involved and precisely how it affects the application of that provision.

It may be indeterminate whether a legal conclusion would be socially salient if all of the relevant inputs were common knowledge. Then it is indeterminate whether it is *ex ante* legal content. I do not think this is a disadvantage of my approach. I am aware of no reason why we should assume that *ex ante* legal content forms a determinate class.

VIII. CONCLUSION

In this chapter, I have advanced and defended on relatively novel methodological grounds a new theory of legal content. The distinctive feature of this account for the law concerning lay law subjects' behaviour is that social salience sets the default legal content. The main points of my position are as follows:

1. In the case of judicial decisions in a common law system, the behaviour that the decision adjudicates and its protection, prohibition or requirement of that behaviour sets a socially salient example of behaviour (for law subjects) that is the default legal content.
2. In the case of statutory directives, the socially salient contextual meaning sets the default legal content.

This approach is superior to rival theories of legal content because it is economical in accounting in the simplest case for the possibility of epistemic access by lay law subjects to legal content pertaining to them in existing legal systems. The other theories of legal content considered can account for the possibility of this epistemic access, if at all, at the expense of economy, rational justification or explanatory significance.

[60] Charter of Human Rights and Responsibilities Act 2006 (Vic), s 32(1).
[61] Smith (n 57).

3

Must Legal Reasons Be General?

FÁBIO PERIN SHECAIRA*

I. INTRODUCTION

THE WORD 'MUST', in the title of this chapter, can be understood in at least two different ways. It can indicate either conceptual necessity or duty. If 'must' is understood in the first way, then the title asks the following question: 'Are Legal Reasons Necessarily General?' If 'must' is understood in the second way, then the title asks instead 'Is There a Duty to Give General Legal Reasons?' In section II, I give a negative answer to the first question: reasons given in support of legal judgments are not necessarily general. In section III, I discuss the second question and focus on the putative judicial duty to ground legal decisions on general reasons. Considering the negative answer to the first question, issuing utterly unjustified legal rulings is not, as some authors seem to assume, the only alternative to giving general reasons for legal decisions. The claim of section III will be that judges ought to give reasons in ways that further the values of accountability and transparency. In some circumstances, the way to do this is indeed to give general reasons, but in other circumstances non-general reasons can be appropriate.

The ambitions of this chapter will become clearer if we briefly consider the following two-part argument, which may appear to be sound to some readers:

1. Judges have a choice to make, between giving and omitting to give reasons for their rulings.
2. To give reasons is a way to further the values of transparency and accountability.
3. Therefore, judges should give reasons for their rulings instead of omitting to give them.
4. Now, reasons given for legal rulings are necessarily general.
5. Therefore, judges should give general reasons for their rulings instead of omitting to give them.

* For helpful comments and discussion, I am grateful to Guilherme de Almeida, Luís Duarte d'Almeida, Svein Eng, Christoffer Eriksen, Mark McBride, James Penner, Adam Rigoni, Veronica Rodriguez-Blanco, Emily Sherwin, Katharina Stevens, Jorgen Stubberud and Noel Struchiner.

Some of the claims that make up this argument require a significant amount of explanation, which will be provided in the sequel. But let it be clear from the outset that only the first inference (from 1 and 2 to 3) is sound. The second inference (from 3 and 4 to 5) is not. It has one false premise (claim 4) and a false conclusion. Section II of this chapter attempts to refute claim 4, and by doing so rejects an important route for reaching claim 5. But since this is not the only known route to claim 5, section III takes up the task of considering and rejecting other prominent arguments that have been used to reach claim 5 by means of the conjunction of claim 3 with other premises pertaining to the duty of judicial impartiality. Section IV concludes the chapter with a brief analysis of a legal judgment that serves to illustrate the view that judges are not duty-bound to ground their rulings on general reasons.

II. GENERALITY AS A FEATURE OF LEGAL REASONS

A. Preliminary Remarks: Reasons and Commitments

In a well-known paper from the 1990s, Frederick Schauer wrote that 'When lawyers argue and when judges write opinions, they seek *to justify* their conclusions, and they do so by offering *reasons*. The reasons they provide, however, are broader than the outcomes they are reasons for.'[1] The thesis that reasons given by legal actors are broader or more general than the conclusions they mean to justify – let us call it *the generality thesis*, or simply GT – has been endorsed by several authors. So, for Michael Dorf, 'To accept reason-giving is to accept that a court can legitimately assimilate the case before it to a more general, in the sense of larger, category of cases.'[2] Similarly, Cass Sunstein states that 'by their very nature, reasons are more abstract than the outcomes they justify'.[3] Abstractness and generality might not seem to be the same attribute, but Sunstein clearly has generality in mind, as he infers from the foregoing statement that 'Reasons may therefore apply to cases that the court, in justifying a particular decision, does not have before it.'[4] The basic idea expressed by GT is thus that reasons given in justification of a judgment in a legal case are general in the sense that they apply to other cases beyond the case under consideration, that is, cases involving similar but not identical facts, acts and/or agents.

To be clear, in this context a general reason is any statement that serves as a premise in a legal argument and articulates a general norm (that is, a norm

[1] Frederick Schauer (1995) 'Giving Reasons' *Stanford Law Review* 47: 633–59, 635.

[2] Michael Dorf (2000) 'Courts, Reasons, and Rules' *Quinnipiac Law Review* 19: 483–503, 486.

[3] Cass Sunstein (1996) *Legal Reasoning and Political Conflict*, Oxford: Oxford University Press, 137.

[4] ibid, 137. I will not pay much heed to the distinction between generality and abstractness, because GT is really about the former. Another subtle distinction that will need to be addressed later in the chapter is that between generality and universality.

about how cases of a certain type ought to be adjudicated). A general reason can amount to the statement of a rule (ie a fairly precise general norm), a standard (ie a fairly vague general norm) or even a principle (ie a general norm that does not apply in 'all-or-nothing' fashion but has a dimension of weight).[5] So, GT may also be described as the view that arguments advanced in support of legal decisions include among their premises at least one general norm that applies to a class of cases extending beyond the specific case under consideration.

Sunstein presents GT as a conceptual thesis, that is, a thesis about a characteristic that reasons *necessarily* have 'by their very nature'. The passages from Schauer and Dorf are more ambiguous in that regard; one might read them as claims about the necessary generality of reasons, or instead about the typical generality of reasons. Considered as a group, Schauer's different writings on this topic are less helpful than they might be. In his paper from the 1990s he does talk about the 'typical' or 'ordinary' generality of reasons; indeed at one point he states emphatically that GT refers to reasons as they are ordinarily given: 'I say "ordinarily" because some reasons might seem less general than the decisions that they support.'[6] In more recent work, however, Schauer refers back to GT as the view that 'a reason is *necessarily* broader than the outcome that it is a reason for'.[7] This is also how Larry Alexander and Emily Sherwin interpret Schauer's position.[8] In what follows, I will discuss and evaluate GT as if it were indeed a conceptual thesis (although alternative interpretations of GT will be briefly considered toward the end of section II).

Before evaluating GT, three preliminary remarks are in order. First, Schauer proposes a neutral concept of *reason*. A reason is the premise of an argument, understood as any attempt (failed or successful) to justify a conclusion. On this understanding of a reason, the expression 'good reason' is not redundant and 'bad reason' is not incongruous:

> For my purposes … 'reason' labels what follows the word 'because' in, 'We reach this result because …' or, 'I find for the plaintiff because …' or, 'You should come to this conclusion because …' Under this definition, a judge who says she has decided for the plaintiff because it is raining in Calcutta offers a reason – 'because it is raining in Calcutta' – even though the reason, unconnected to any sound basis for decision, is a bad one indeed.[9]

[5] Some may think that it is unnecessary to treat principles as a separate category because all legal norms (even the clearest rules of positive law) are defeasible and thus have a dimension of weight. This complication will not be addressed here. I want to show in this section that GT is problematic regardless of the type of general norm (precise or vague, conclusive or defeasible) that one associates with the idea of a general reason.

[6] Schauer (n 1) 641, fn 21.

[7] Frederick Schauer (2009) *Thinking Like a Lawyer*, Cambridge, MA: Harvard University Press, 56 (emphasis added).

[8] Larry Alexander and Emily Sherwin (2008) *Demystifying Legal Reasoning*, Cambridge: Cambridge University Press, 51, fn 35.

[9] Schauer (n 1) 636.

But Schauer sometimes runs the risk of violating his own definition. He appears to abandon it, for instance, when raising doubts about whether analogies unaccompanied by supporting generalisations count as reasons:

> [T]he assertion of an analogy, without an articulated explanation of why the analogy holds, resembles the assertion of a result unaccompanied by any reason for that result. Because the bare statement that a resembles b presupposes some general rule subsuming both a and b, and because the failure to articulate the rule leaves open any number of extensionally divergent rules, the assertion of an analogy, without more, could well be considered another example of a result without a reason.[10]

According to Schauer, a judge in the United States gives a reason to find for the plaintiff if she attempts to ground her decision on the (entirely irrelevant) fact that it is raining in Calcutta. On the other hand, Schauer doubts that a judge gives a reason to rule for the plaintiff if she attempts to ground that decision on the assertion that a different plaintiff with a similar grievance prevailed in a previous case. Perhaps it is true that analogies are not probative when they fail to articulate general criteria for the comparison of the analogues. But even if this is true, it in no way supports the conclusion that crude analogies are not reasons, that is, reasons in the neutral sense that they could follow the word 'because' in an attempted justification of a legal decision.[11]

Second, let us keep in mind that legal conclusions are not necessarily rulings for plaintiffs or defendants with particular grievances. For example, when a court is asked to give an answer to a general legal question of the form 'Is statute S valid according to the Bill of Rights?', as courts authorised to exercise 'abstract' judicial review are often asked to do, its conclusion will inevitably have implications for a number of potential litigants with various grievances. All future cases falling under the scope of S may be affected by the court's decision. Nevertheless, the question stands as to whether the reasons for conclusions about such general questions must be even more general than the conclusions themselves. Must S be deemed (in)valid on the ground that all statutes of a broader category subsuming S are (in)valid under the Bill of Rights? In other words, the truth of GT is open to discussion, regardless of whether we focus on reasons for conclusions about concrete legal disputes or reasons for conclusions about general legal questions, such as the question about the constitutionality of a statute.

[10] ibid, 637–38, fn 11.

[11] I hold the view that, at least from a dialectical point of view, analogical arguments are at their best when they spell out the relevant similarities between analogues. But this view does not entail that terse analogies are not reasons; see Fábio Shecaira (2018) 'The Value of Methodological Deductivism in Argument Construction' *Informal Logic* 38: 471–501. It should also be noted that there is a tendency within argumentation theory to value analogies precisely for their terseness; see eg Trudy Govier (1989) 'Analogies and Missing Premises' *Informal Logic* 11: 141–52, 148 ('The trick about analogies – and their charm as well, I think – is that we are often able to see or sense important resemblances between cases without being able to spell them out exhaustively in just so many words.'). I will return to the topic of analogies in this section.

Third, it must be acknowledged that there is more than one way to 'give' a reason. To begin, a reason may be given explicitly, as it happens when one openly advances conclusion C for reason R. But another way to give a reason is to do so implicitly, as it happens when R is not articulated directly but is still implied by other assertions leading up to or surrounding C. Schauer addresses this question as follows:

> When we provide a reason for a particular decision, we typically provide a rule, principle, standard, norm, or maxim broader than the decision itself, and this is so even if the form of articulation is not exactly what we normally think of as a principle. 'I criticized Mary because she did not write a thank-you note' presupposes (or conversationally implies) that there is a principle pursuant to which people in Mary's situation should write thank-you notes, and that Mary's behavior, falling within the scope of the principle, is open to criticism for not comporting with the principle.[12]

I agree with the basic point that a general norm may be implied even when it is not explicitly articulated in argument. But a commitment to a general norm is not something that we should ascribe to arguers as casually as Schauer does, that is, in the absence of specific clues that might be drawn from the words or context. Indeed, there are situations where failure to articulate a general norm suggests precisely the opposite, that is, that the arguer prefers not to commit to any general norm. Judicial decision making is arguably such a context, especially where the decision is made by a court that has power to set precedent. Where a court has this power, the readers of its judgment will naturally be looking out for the rule – or 'doctrine' – that grounds the ruling. To the extent that the court is aware of this general expectation, it is possible to interpret its occasional omission of a general norm as an implicit refusal to establish a definite doctrine and, thus, as a suggestion for future judges to construct their own doctrine in light of similar cases.

It is true that some future judges may hold that the doctrine developed by them in the context of new cases is harmonious or continuous with the judgment in the precedent case, so that, in a sense, the general norm was already 'lying behind' or motivating the previous judgment. But we should not take this sort of claim literally. Otherwise we might come to interpret GT not as a thesis about what reasons are explicitly or implicitly adduced in legal arguments but about how they are reconstructed by their readers. In other words, on this interpretation GT would not focus on the nature of legal reasons as they are given but on how they are read, or, more accurately, how they are read *into* legal judgments by those who are wont to generalise the non-general claims of others. I doubt that this is what Schauer and other proponents of GT have in mind, considering their interest in understanding the structure of legal judgments and the commitments one makes when proposing a legal argument: GT is a thesis about how legal reasons are given, not about how they are taken.

[12] Schauer (n 1) 641.

It should pay to dwell for a moment on the idea of a commitment.[13] To say that I commit myself to a statement is to say that I attach myself to it in such a way that I am liable to receive criticism if I subsequently contradict or otherwise disregard that statement. It is Schauer's position that to argue is to commit oneself not only to one's explicit premises and conclusions, but also to what they imply or implicate. So, if I argue that 'x, therefore, y' (or 'y because x'), I thereby commit myself to y, to x, and arguably to every other proposition that x and y logically imply or conversationally implicate. To be clear, I do not want to dispute this general view about the relation between arguments and commitments – my point is simply that discerning implicit commitments is a trickier exercise than Schauer suggests.

Consider a hypothetical example outside the legal context. Imagine that I go to dinner with someone for the first time. I pick something out from the menu and state, 'I will have this because it looks healthy.' My dinner companion (even though she knows nothing about my eating habits) may infer that I take myself to have a constant reason to choose healthy dishes at restaurants. That is, she may conclude that I think myself bound to choose healthy dishes at restaurants, or at least that health is a constant concern of mine when eating out. The inference of my dinner companion is not unusual or irrational, but it is based on scant information and is therefore subject to correction. Obviously, I have not explicitly committed myself to any general norm. It is also clear that my statement does not logically entail a general norm, though it could be argued that a general norm is conversationally implicated by what I said. But that, I submit, is a dubious proposition.

Imagine that, on a second dinner date, I choose an unhealthy meal, and my companion reacts with surprise. If asked about my choice, there are many explanations I could give. Naturally, I could say that my concern about health was defeated in this instance by my exceptional craving for greasy food. But I might also reveal something more surprising, namely, that healthy eating had never been a serious concern of mine. I might say that I only made the healthy choice in our previous dinner because I had made a promise to my partner to eat wisely, or (even more contingently) because I was scheduled to take a blood test the next day and was hoping to cover up my high cholesterol. Again, my companion may be surprised to hear these explanations, but she should not feel deceived. My explanation should make it clear that she made a mistake. I never intended to express – and indeed never did express, explicitly or implicitly – any general commitment (not even a defeasible one) to healthy eating. The point is that my dinner companion misunderstood my argument and the scope of the commitments it implied.[14]

[13] This idea is particularly prominent in Schauer's work, but Sunstein and Dorf seem to follow his lead.

[14] Notice that I could hold this position even if I did in fact believe at the time of our first dinner that I had a general reason to eat healthily. The point is that this belief never came out in my argument. We can all (privately) have beliefs to which we do not (publicly) commit ourselves.

The foregoing example does not pertain to legal argumentation and, consequently, could not be used as an argument against GT. The example is meant only to clarify the notion of a commitment made in argument. Let us come back to the legal context now. It should be clear that GT is inter alia a view about argument interpretation, that is, about the commitments we may assign to legal actors based on their arguments.[15] Proponents of GT hold that a judge who adduces a reason in one legal case somehow attaches herself to the idea that the same reason will continue to demand attention in other cases, even if that reason was not formulated in general terms. Much like my dinner companion, jurists often attribute such commitments based on scant evidence. My argument is that this tendency among jurists leads to interpretative mistakes. It often leads jurists (proponents of GT included) to misunderstand legal arguments by attributing to judges a commitment to general reasons that was neither expressed nor implied.

B. The Legal Syllogism and its Limits

We may do well to begin a discussion about the truth of GT by taking up the topic of the (so-called) legal syllogism. Many authors have argued that the legal syllogism plays a prominent role in legal reasoning.[16] By 'legal syllogism' I mean a two-premise argument with the following characteristics: one premise refers to the facts of the case, while the other premise affirms a general norm whose content is supposed to be drawn more or less directly from standard legal materials (statutes or precedents, for example). Here is a hypothetical example:

> The circulation of writings concerning any person ought to be prohibited upon that person's request if the publication affects their honour or respectability, or if the publication has commercial purposes (general normative premise);[17]
>
> Smith has requested the prohibition of the circulation of a biography that discusses intimate aspects of Smith's life and was written by Jones with the purpose of publication for profit (factual premise);
>
> therefore, the circulation of Jones's biography on Smith ought to be prohibited (ruling).

[15] I say 'inter alia' because some proponents of GT may think that it in some sense captures the 'true' nature of legal reasons – ie that legal reasons, correctly understood, are general (regardless of what any particular judge thinks about the nature of reasons). I have doubts about this theory of reasons (see section II.D), but my main target is the interpretative aspect of GT. The mistake I attribute to proponents of GT is that of thinking not that their philosophical understanding of the nature of legal reasons is correct, but that it is shared or inadvertently adopted by legal arguers whenever they seek to justify a ruling.

[16] See eg Robert Alexy (2010) *A Theory of Legal Argumentation*, Oxford: Oxford University Press, 221–86; Neil MacCormick (2005) *Rhetoric and the Rule of Law*, Oxford: Oxford University Press, ch 4; and Jerzy Wróblewski (1971) 'Legal Decision and its Justification' *Logique et Analyse* 53–54: 409–19.

[17] This is a simplified version of Art 20 of the Brazilian Civil Code, whose constitutionality was recently questioned before the Supreme Federal Tribunal (ADI 4815/DF).

It would be a happy world for rule-of-law enthusiasts if judicial decision making rested exclusively on such straightforward syllogisms.[18] But real cases often give rise to controversial questions of law and fact. Standing in the way of simple syllogisms are such common obstacles as conflicts between apparently valid norms, vagueness or ambiguity in canonical legal texts, as well as uncertainty about the facts of the case. To be more precise, the following is a list of relatively common circumstances that may give rise to doubts about the soundness of proposed legal syllogisms:

(a) The standard sources of law establish conflicting norms, but the conflict cannot be resolved by appeal to any simple maxim, such as *lex posterior derogat priori*.
(b) The standard sources of law are subject to different interpretations either because they are vaguely worded, or because there is divergence in the legal community about the proper method of interpretation with which to approach them, for example textualism, originalism, purposivism, etc.
(c) There is conflicting or sparse evidence about the facts of the case, and the resulting uncertainty cannot be resolved by the application of any authoritative presumption or standard of proof.

In the foregoing circumstances, legal actors tend to invoke other forms of argument that do not necessarily share the syllogism's straightforward 'general-to-specific' structure. For instance, circumstance (a) usually calls for balancing or proportionality reasoning. Circumstance (b) invites analogical reasoning (particularly in the face of vagueness, where borderline cases need to be compared to central cases of the disputed concepts) and different types of interpretative argument. Circumstance (c) usually calls for abduction or inference to the best explanation. In the following subsection I will give examples of these argument types in order to show that, as they often appear in legal practice, they cannot be described as resting on reasons that are more general than their conclusions. Sometimes these arguments contain obscure premises that count at best as inchoate norms with no clear implications for futures cases; at other times, they contain no premise at all (explicit or implicit) that could be described as general.[19]

To be clear, the current section discusses primarily whether general reasons are necessarily a part of legal arguments, not whether they are desirable.

[18] MacCormick (n 16) 54, '[R]ecourse to the legal syllogism is a necessary part of the rhetoric of legal justification, on the ground that respect for the Rule of Law requires respect for the rules of law.' I will not argue here that this view of the central role of the syllogism in legal judgment is correct. My point will be that GT is false even on the assumption that the legal syllogism is a necessary part of legal argument.

[19] An inchoate norm is not the same as a vague standard. Vague standards leave numerous cases unsettled, but they do provide guidance with respect to some (core) cases. An inchoate norm is one to which the arguer appears to be alluding but whose content we cannot identify with any confidence.

The desirability of general reasons is the topic of section III. But although the analysis provided in this section is not primarily normative, it does not limit itself to searching for counterexamples to GT. It also compares the counterexamples with problematic arguments that do conform to GT. The contrast will be useful for explaining the occasional judicial reluctance to use general norms as premises of legal arguments. Understanding this reluctance is an important step toward the normative points that will be made in section III. Although jurists who are sympathetic to GT may instinctively reject legal arguments that lack general premises, they should be reminded from the outset of the price there often is to pay for indulging in generalisations.

C. Counterexamples to GT

Let us begin with balancing and the variety of ways in which it can be done. Although courts often balance conflicting norms by means of complex, layered proportionality tests, one should not be surprised to encounter simpler legal arguments such as this:

> Tortfeasors are liable to pay full reparative damages to those whom they tortiously injure;
>
> Adams tortiously injured Edwards to the tune of $100;
>
> but the tort was also the breach of a contract between Adams and Edwards;
>
> the contract provided for maximum reparative damages of $50 for any breach;
>
> contracts and the limits on damages they set are legally binding as between parties to the contract;
>
> *and it is unjust to let someone avoid a legally binding contractual limit on damages by instead suing the other contracting party in tort*;
>
> therefore, Adams is liable to pay Edwards only $50 in reparative damages.[20]

The claim that it is unjust to let someone avoid a legally binding contractual limit on damages by suing the other party in tort is the statement of a general norm that has implications for other cases beyond that of *Adams v Edwards*. This means that the above argument moves from general to specific (it has at least one premise that is more general than the conclusion). Notice, however, that an actual court might have avoided the formulation of a generic norm; especially if the court at issue were not an appellate court or for some other reason

[20] This hypothetical argument was formulated by John Gardner (2012) *Law as a Leap of Faith*, Oxford: Oxford University Press, 187. I have only altered the names of the parties.

did not have to attend to the expectation of setting precedent. Indeed, avoiding the formulation of a generic norm could be a wise course of action in the face of objections likely to be raised in respect of the over-inclusiveness of the norm. If, on the one hand, it is unjust to allow someone to avoid a contractual limit on damages by suing in tort, on the other hand it would also be unjust to allow someone to rely on a strict contractual limit on damages in order to avoid the liability resulting from a premeditated tort.

One may also wonder if the court's views about the just course of action would vary depending on the nature of the contract and the extent of the tortious injury (imagine that the court were comparing not $100 to $50, but $500 to $50). Doubts such as these may understandably lead a court to avoid a generic doctrine, keeping instead to the facts of the case. So, consider a different version of the argument:

> Tortfeasors are liable to pay full reparative damages to those whom they tortiously injure;
>
> Adams tortiously injured Edwards to the tune of $100;
>
> but the tort was also the breach of a contract between Adams and Edwards;
>
> the contract provided for maximum reparative damages of $50 for any breach;
>
> contracts and the limits on damages they set are legally binding as between parties to the contract;
>
> *and it is unjust to let Edwards avoid the legally binding contractual limit on damages by instead suing Adams in tort*;
>
> therefore, Adams is liable to pay Edwards only $50 in reparative damages.[21]

Whether this version of the argument, which does not have definite implications for other cases, is less probative or for some other reason less commendable than the previous version of the argument is something we have yet to consider. Notice for now that this is a realistic legal argument: it gives reasons (in a neutral sense) for a ruling on the extent of Adams' liability. It is not a form of argument that we should be surprised to see judges using in real cases. In any event, it will pay to consider an example taken from an actual judgment.

[21] The premise in italics is not general. One might be tempted to think that it implies the defeasible principle that suing the other party in tort is made *pro tanto* unjust by the fact that it is a means to avoid a contractual limit on damages. But the foregoing argument makes no such claim and is compatible with the view that Edward's act is only unjust because of the peculiar circumstances of the case (there is no reason to think the tort was premeditated, the damages are relatively low, etc). In any case, there will be more in this section on the matter of reading defeasible principles into arguments that do not explicitly formulate them.

In ADI 4983/CE (2016), a case judged by the Supreme Federal Tribunal of Brazil, Justice Marco Aurélio Mello denied the constitutionality of a statute admitting the practice of the '*vaquejada*' in the Brazilian state of Ceará. The '*vaquejada*' is a traditional spectacle in which horse riders attempt to dominate bovine animals by pulling and twisting their tails. According to Mello, it was necessary to balance two conflicting constitutional rights in this case, one pertaining to the well-being of animals, and the other to the protection of local customs and traditions. After describing the ways in which horses and oxen are harmed in the rodeos, Mello glibly asserts that 'the intrinsic cruelty of the vaquejada does not allow the [conflicting] cultural good to prevail as a result desired by the system of fundamental rights of the 1988 Charter'. In other words, *this* practice is too cruel to receive protection on the ground that it has cultural value. There is no general explanation about what makes a rodeo (or any other spectacle involving animals) too cruel to be legally admitted. Nor is there any instruction about how to assess the significance of practices that, albeit harmful to animals, might still be excused on cultural grounds. Aurélio's argument is not a general one about how to assess cruelty against animals in relation to the value of tradition. It is an argument that applies specifically to the subject matter of the statute *sub judice*.

The general points that I have made about balancing can also be made in relation to analogies, namely, not every argument of this type contains a general premise, and there are understandable reasons why arguers would sometimes want to avoid general premises. Let us begin by considering four possible schematic representations of analogical arguments in law and elsewhere (where A and B refer to the acts or facts being compared; x, y, z are specific features of those acts or facts; and W refers to the way in which the acts or facts are to be treated, for example as legally permissible or impermissible):

(1)
A is W;
B is just like A;
therefore, B is W.

(2)
A has x, y, z;
B has x, y, z;
A is W;
therefore, B is W.

(3)
A has x, y, z;
B has x, y, z;
A is W;
it is in virtue of x, y, z that A is W;
therefore, B is W.

(4)
A has x, y, z;
B has x, y, z;
A is W;
all things that have x, y, z are W;
therefore, B is W.[22]

[22] These schemes are taken from Govier (n 11).

Scheme 4 is the only one of the four schemes that explicitly includes a general norm (in the fourth line). Scheme 1 clearly does not include such a norm. Schemes 2 and 3, on the other hand, may give rise to interpretative dispute. Since scheme 1 is sometimes instantiated in the legal domain, examples of it would suffice to show that GT is false in respect of legal analogies. Interestingly, proponents of GT have acknowledged that terse analogies are a common feature of legal reasoning. Sunstein, for instance, recognises that in practice, 'Sometimes the creative dimensions of analogical thought are downplayed, as people simply announce that case A is analogous to case B, when an unarticulated supplemental judgment [ie a normative principle] is necessary and not defended.'[23] There are at least two ways to reconcile Sunstein's claim that principles are 'necessary' in analogies with his other claim that sometimes analogies fail to articulate principles. First, we might take the word 'necessary' to refer not to conceptual necessity, but to some normative notion of rational or practical necessity. Alternatively, we might interpret Sunstein to mean that sets of propositions fitting something like scheme 1 are not real or genuine arguments by analogy. Both alternatives are problematic. The first would obviously divert our attention from GT, which has been understood so far as a conceptual thesis. The second would involve rejecting Schauer's suggestion that we understand reason giving in a neutral sense. When I say that (i) case B should be treated like case A *because* (ii) the two cases have (unspecified) shared features, then I adduce (ii) as a reason for (i), even if that reason is not ultimately a good one. In other words, I argue by analogy even if I do so poorly.

Perhaps jurists will find schemes 2 and 3 more familiar than scheme 1, so it should pay to comment on their structure as well. Let us begin by considering a simple argument by analogy: 'Since we allow people to smoke tobacco, we should also allow them to smoke marijuana. One is *just like* the other.' If pressed, the author of such a terse argument might try to explain in what respects tobacco and marijuana are similar: they are prejudicial to the smoker's health, yet they do not cause imminent risk of death, they do not induce violent behaviour towards others, and so on. By specifying the similarities between the analogues, the arguer approximates something like scheme 2, where the relevant features of the analogues appear in the first two premises. It could be argued that scheme 3 simply exposes a premise – 'it is in virtue of x, y, z that A is W' – that is already implicit in arguments fitting scheme 2. Moreover, if that premise is interpreted as being equivalent to the fourth premise in scheme 4 – 'all things that have x, y, z are W' – then schemes 3 and 4 are only different ways of representing the same argument pattern. Such would be the case made by someone who holds that every analogy is (implicitly) based on a general proposition so long as it specifies relevant similarities between analogues. In other words, it could

[23] Sunstein (n 3) 72–73.

be argued that there is a slippery slope leading the author of an analogy that fits scheme 2 straight to scheme 4.[24]

The problem with this view is twofold. First, it is not clear that the fourth premise in scheme 3 is indeed implicit in scheme 2. This is so because there are different ways to interpret the claim that '*it is in virtue of x, y, z* that A is W'. If it means that the combination of x, y, and z *always counts in favour* of the conclusion that something is W, then it should be distinguished from the loose thought expressed in scheme 2, namely, that x, y, and z are grounds for approximating A and B – but not necessarily for approximating other cases to A or B. A third case, C, could have additional features not present in A or B, features that serve to block or even change the valence of x, y and z, making them count *against* the conclusion that C is W. Second, it is not clear that the fourth premise in scheme 3 is equivalent to the fourth premise in scheme 4. Even if the former is thought to mean that x, y, and z always count in favour of the conclusion that something is W, it is still weaker than the absolute norm that *all things* that have x, y, z are W.

Let me illustrate these points with an example of a legal argument from analogy provided by Schauer:

> [P]rohibition on same-sex marriage is similar to a prohibition on interracial marriage because both prevent people who want to be married from marrying solely because of their immutable personal characteristics. The prohibition on interracial marriage was properly struck down. Therefore, following this logic, the prohibition on same-sex marriage should be struck down as well.[25]

This analogy arguably fits into scheme 2. It states the similarities between the analogues and recommends that they receive the same treatment. Does the analogy also fit schemes 3 and 4? Let us consider the latter possibility first. It might be thought that the general reason implicit in the analogy states that the law cannot prevent people from being married because of their immutable personal characteristics. But as soon as this norm is formulated, one should become aware of the risk of over-inclusion. Does the norm allow father and daughter to be married? Does it allow individuals with severe mental disability to be married? A general norm resembling the fourth line of scheme 4 would apply equally to these problematic cases.

How about scheme 3? Again, that depends on how we interpret the 'in virtue of' relation. Considering the problematic cases alluded to above (incestuous relationships, for example), we may come to think that there is reason *not* to allow marriage between people who have certain immutable characteristics. In that case it would be a mistake to commit even to a defeasible principle to the

[24] I advanced this argument myself in the past but have come to doubt it. See, for my original position, Fábio Shecaira (2013) 'Analogical Arguments in Ethics and in Law: A Defence of a Deductivist Analysis' *Informal Logic* 33: 406–37. I am no longer confident that scheme 2 implicitly contains a general norm.

[25] Schauer (n 7) 86–87 (reference omitted).

effect that the law is *pro tanto* prohibited from preventing people from being married based on immutable personal characteristics.

Concerns about the formulation of an appropriately qualified general norm may lead the proponent of an analogy like the one discussed above to avoid committing to any general norm. One may prefer to indicate simply what features of the specific cases under consideration render them similar for legal purposes, which is arguably all that arguments fitting scheme 2 really do. Any judge should be aware of the perils involved in committing to broad principles that may have problematic implications for future cases. The point, again, is that courts can understandably refrain from including general principles in their analogies. That is to say: they may understandably stop at scheme 2 for fear of the implications of arguments fitting schemes 3 and 4.

We can continue to pursue this line of reasoning as we consider additional forms of argument that are common in legal practice and that tend to appear in cases where the legal syllogism does not suffice. I mentioned earlier that legal actors do not always converge in employing the same methods for the interpretation of legal texts.[26] Even when considered individually, legal actors do not always exhibit consistency, as they will read texts literally in one case only to disregard literal meaning in the next case for the sake of authorial intent or some vaguer notion of 'purpose'.[27] Although comparative lawyers have found some broad patterns in judicial interpretative practices,[28] judges who make use of different methods often do so without committing to any theory about how legal interpretation ought to be done. They amass evidence of authorial intent or speculate about the true purpose of a legal text in order to justify *this* interpretation of *this* piece of legal text, while allowing their audience to wonder about how they might go about interpreting other legal texts. Their goal is often to justify the major premise of a particular legal syllogism, or explain, in the context of abstract review, how a particular legal text should interpreted; but they do not commit in the process to any general principle of interpretation. Consider another Brazilian example.

In HC 824242/RS (2004), the Supreme Federal Tribunal was charged with the task of determining whether a writer and publisher of books with anti-Semitic content should be convicted of 'racism' – a crime, according to the Brazilian Constitution. Moreira Alves, one of the members of the Tribunal, advanced (inter alia) the argument that anti-Semitism is not a form of racism, as far as

[26] For an influential discussion about how appellate judges diverge about the right way to read statutes, see Karl Llewellyn (1950) 'Remarks on the Theory of Appellate Decision and the Rules or Canons about How Statutes Are to Be Construed' *Vanderbilt Law Review* 3: 395–406.

[27] For discussion of this practice, see Brian Leiter (2009) 'Explaining Theoretical Disagreement' *University of Chicago Law Review* 75: 1215–50, 1242–43.

[28] Stefan Vogenauer (2006) 'Statutory Interpretation' in *Elgar Encyclopedia of Comparative Law*, ed Jan Smits, Cheltenham: Edward Elgar, 677–88, 684.

the relevant constitutional provision is concerned. He analysed the legislative history and reproduced in his opinion speeches by members of the Constituent Assembly in which the provision on racism was discussed. Moreira Alves noted that these speeches made exclusive reference to the problem of discrimination against black individuals. All the judge offers by way of interpretative 'theory' is an elliptical remark to the effect that, given a relatively young Constitution, it is 'important' to have recourse to a 'historical' (ie originalist) method of interpretation. He expresses scepticism about methods that may force a premature 'evolution' of the Constitution but does not say that the historical method is to be used to the exclusion of all other methods. Indeed, at a different point he also endorses the 'systematic' method of interpretation.

If I were to put Moreira Alves's argument in standard form, it would look something like this:

> It is permissible to use a historical method of constitutional interpretation as well as other methods that do not force the premature evolution of the Constitution;
>
> the historical method of interpretation, given the records of the Constituent Assembly, indicates that 'racism', for constitutional purposes, includes discrimination against black individuals but not anti-Semitism;
>
> therefore, 'racism', for constitutional purposes, may be interpreted as including discrimination against black individuals but not anti-Semitism.

This argument apparently moves from general to specific. The first general premise is my tentative reconstruction of a few obscure lines in which Moreira Alves attempts to justify his approach. (Other readers of the opinion may get less from these lines than I did.) The general premise offers some – but not much – guidance as to how constitutional interpretation should be undertaken.[29] The historical approach is deemed appropriate but not obligatory, other approaches being permissible. Notice that this is a prominent case decided by the highest court in the country (indeed, a leading case among the court's recent decisions on the limits of freedom of speech.) Other judges in Brazil are wont to have recourse to different interpretative methods without even sketching out their general theories of interpretation. In other words, they will not make use of anything like the first premise of Moreira Alves's argument. They will state the method of interpretation that strikes them as adequate in the case at hand and will not give an interpretative argument resting on general reasons.

Moreira Alves uses another type of argument in his opinion that is common among judges in Brazil and elsewhere: he attempts to corroborate

[29] This general premise states a vague standard. So, strictly speaking, my reconstruction of Alves' argument is not a counterexample to GT.

his interpretation of the law by appeal to the learned authority of scholars. Arguments from scholarly authority sometimes exhibit the following structure:

> Scholar S says p;
>
> S is authoritative on such things;
>
> therefore, p.[30]

The second premise is a general one, though its vagueness makes it a limited source of guidance for future cases. On what exactly is S an authority: the specific issue under dispute (the crime of racism, for example) or the broader themes that subsume it (for example, criminal and/or constitutional law)? In legal practice, judges often omit the second premise altogether. We see judges treat scholars as authorities, but we are given no information about the extent of the scholar's authority. To be clear, I do not mean anything special by the word 'authority' in this context. A scholar is treated as an authority if her 'say-so' is used to reinforce a legal judgment independently of the merits of the scholar's underlying arguments (which are not spelled out, much less evaluated in the judgment). So, when Lord Denning explains his position on a matter of law and adds that he is 'glad to see that Professor Winfield in this country (55 Law Quarterly Review, 514) and Professor Williston in the United States of America (Contracts I S. 82, 239) take the same view', he is arguing from authority in the relevant sense of the word.[31] It is also important to note that, in failing to give us anything like the second premise of the aforementioned scheme, Denning's argument serves as a counterexample to GT.[32]

Here is another example from the Supreme Court of Canada. In *R v Morgentaler*, Justice Wilson found that a criminal statute prohibiting abortions at all stages of pregnancy failed the proportionality test pertaining to section 1 of the Canadian Charter of Rights and Freedoms. She reinforces her position by referring to a scholar whose argument she does not discuss. His credentials, which Justice Wilson does not fail to mention, indicate that he should know what he is talking about. What Justice Wilson does not clarify is the extent of his authority (philosophical matters? ethical matters? constitutional matters? abortion laws?). This is the type of argument one might regard as resting on an inchoate general norm. Wilson mentions Sumner's professional position

[30] The scheme is taken, with some changes, from Edwin Coleman (1995) 'There Is no Fallacy of Arguing from Authority' *Informal Logic* 17: 365–83 (who discusses arguments from authority generally, not scholarly authority in particular).

[31] *Entores Ltd v Miles Far East Corporation* [1955] EWCA Civ 3.

[32] It might be thought that Denning is not really giving an argument in the quoted passage but simply making a side remark about his contentment with the fact that two authors agree with him. This interpretation is implausible, because it takes Denning to be making a gratuitous remark that would be no different from mentioning that, say, his physician, his father-in-law or some other layperson agrees with his viewpoint. One thing is clearly implicit in the above passage: Denning refers to two specialists for support. What is not clearly implicit, however, is the class of cases in respect of which those authors have authority.

but does not provide us with enough information to discern the scope of his purported authority:

> [I]n balancing the state's interest in the protection of the foetus as potential life under s 1 of the Charter against the right of the pregnant woman under s 7 greater weight should be given to the state's interest in the later stages of pregnancy than in the earlier. The foetus should accordingly, for purposes of s 1, be viewed in differential and developmental terms: see Sumner LW (1981), Professor of Philosophy at the University of Toronto, Abortion and Moral Theory, pp 125–128.[33]

So far, I have only discussed arguments concerning questions of law. What about arguments concerning questions of fact? Are they not also within the purview of GT, understood as a general claim about the nature of legal reasoning? As suggested earlier, inference to the best explanation is an important tool for dealing with factual questions in the legal process.[34] Juries do not ordinarily articulate their inferences, but judges do. To the extent that they do, it could be argued that judges' arguments about factual matters fit something like the following scheme:

> F is a set of facts in need of explanation;
>
> hypothesis H is the best available explanation of F;
>
> therefore, H is true.

It is not difficult to come up with illustrative examples: 'When a detective [or a lawyer] puts the evidence together and decides that it *must* have been the butler, he is reasoning that no other explanation which accounts for all the facts is plausible enough or simple enough to be accepted.'[35] The point I want to make is that arguments such as this do not rest on general reasons: the premises of arguments fitting the scheme given above do not have implications about what hypothesis best explains the facts of other cases. Things would of course be different if typical inferences to the best explanation took another, more elaborate form:

> F is a set of facts in need of explanation;
>
> hypothesis H is the best available explanation of F according to criteria C1, C2 … Cn;
>
> the correct criteria for comparing hypotheses are C, C2 … Cn;[36]
>
> therefore, H is true.

[33] *R v Morgentaler* [1993] 3 SCR 463, para 257.

[34] See eg Amalia Amaya (2009) 'Inference to the Best Legal Explanation' in *Legal Evidence and Proof*, eds Hendrik Kaptein, Henry Prakken and Bart Verheij, Farnham: Ashgate, 135–59.

[35] Gilbert Harman (1965) 'The Inference to the Best Explanation' *The Philosophical Review* 74: 88–95, 89.

[36] These criteria might include simplicity, coherence, depth, etc. The typical inference to the best explanation does not attempt to articulate these criteria but rests on an intuitive comparison of the available hypotheses.

D. Whence the Mistake?

We have seen various examples of real or at least realistic legal arguments that either contain no general premise or only some inchoate general premise with no clear implication for cases apart from the one *sub judice*. In other words, we have seen various counterexamples to GT. Have proponents of GT simply ignored these counterexamples? How could they hold on to GT given the variety of legal arguments that deviate from the pattern of 'general-to-specific'?

There are probably two related reasons behind the tendency to overlook counterexamples to GT. One is the previously mentioned tendency to generalise that may lead some readers of legal judgments to automatically and casually read a general norm into legal arguments that do not articulate any such norm. The other reason is that some authors who hold GT, when referring to non-general reasons, can think only of the most objectionable examples of such reasons:

> The norms of judging demand a reason that is broader than the particular case at hand – one cannot decide a case in favor of John Doe on the unique ground that 'I think John Doe should prevail here.' Some reasons of greater breadth must be given, and the greater breadth will sweep in at least some future cases which will presumptively be decided in like fashion.[37]

'The court rules in favour of John Doe because John Doe should prevail here' is an argument based on an entirely redundant non-general premise. It is even less informative than saying, for example, 'The court rules in favour of John Doe because deciding in favour of John Doe is the equitable thing to do here' – which at least gives one a sense of the sort of considerations the court has in mind (ie moral considerations, as opposed to legalistic ones). At this point someone could say that the reason the latter argument is not redundant is precisely that it contains an implicit commitment to a general norm. On this view, if a judge rules based on equity in one case then she commits at least to the principle that judges should make equitable decisions *generally*. Notice that the hypothetical court did not provide criteria for assessing the equity of a decision, which means that it did not provide instructions about how to assess future cases based on equity. But still, the argument continues, the court has committed to the general (if vague) standard that, in the legal process, one should always make the equitable decision. That is also a dubious proposition, however, since it is equally plausible to interpret the court as holding that the equitable decision is the right decision *other things being equal* – that is, in the absence of countervailing considerations (such as rule-of-law considerations). But even that interpretation

[37] Theodore Ruger (2006) 'The Chief Justice's Special Authority and the Norms of Judicial Power' *University of Pennsylvania Law Review* 154: 1551–74, 1559 (reference omitted).

may be contested. The court could have a particularistic outlook about equity according to which one does not have even a defeasible reason to decide based on equity in every context.

These alternative understandings of the relevance of equity to judicial decision making – from generalism to particularism – may not be equally plausible as a matter of normative theory. But the point is that they are equally plausible as interpretations of the view of equity underlying the terse statement, 'The court rules in favour of John Doe because deciding in favour of John Doe is the equitable thing to do here.' If a court opts for this kind of terseness, then a reader of the court's opinion may not be justified (in the absence of additional clues derived from context) in holding that the court has *given* a general norm in support of its ruling. Lawyers, with their tendency to generalise, are often too quick to attribute general commitments to judges who have (probably advisedly) omitted to give general norms.[38]

Section II has presented examples of legal arguments with non-general premises that are by no means redundant in the way that the premise imagined by Ruger is redundant ('… because John Doe should prevail here'). In fact, GT would be less vulnerable to counterexamples if put forward as the view that legal arguments necessarily contain *non-redundant* premises. But then the focus of discussion would cease to be on the generality of reasons, understood as the fact that a reason for the present judgment is necessarily a reason for deciding other cases in the same way.

III. DO JUDGES HAVE A DUTY TO GIVE GENERAL REASONS FOR THEIR DECISIONS?

A. Preliminary Remarks

To refute a conceptual claim, one must confront it with counterexamples. That is what I attempted to do in the previous section. Against GT – understood as a claim about the necessary generality of reasons – I offered some examples of legal arguments that do not move from general to specific. In fact, there is a possibility that the reader will find the examples of the previous section so familiar that she will also come to entertain doubts about the truth of a weaker version of GT, namely, that legal reasons are *ordinarily* more general than the

[38] Let me insist that the critique of GT in section II does not depend on the correctness of particularism. For the sake of argument, we could even assume that the best justifications of legal decisions are those that refer to general norms (an issue to which I return in section III). A judge will still fail to commit to a general norm if she writes an opinion that neither expresses nor implies such a norm. We cannot settle the interpretative question (what did *this* judge commit to in *this* opinion?) by reference to abstract normative theory.

conclusions they mean to justify. In any case, the previous section meant only to establish that legal reasons are not necessarily general. It is now time to discuss whether they *ought to be* general. The previous section focused on a conceptual question; this section takes up a normative one.

The general normative question whether legal reasons ought to be general can be interpreted in a variety of ways, for example as an epistemic, dialectical, rhetorical or moral/political question. Let us compare these four different interpretations of the normative question:

1. Epistemic interpretation: Do legal reasons have more evidentiary value (or do they only have such value) when they are general?
2. Dialectical interpretation: Is the use of general legal reasons more apt to lead the parties in a legal debate to rational agreement (as opposed to mutual incomprehension or intractable dissent)?
3. Rhetorical interpretation: Are legal reasons more persuasive (to the typical legal audiences) when they are general?
4. Moral/political interpretation: Is there a moral or political duty for legal actors (eg judges) to use general reasons?

These questions are only relatively independent from one another. The answer that we give to one question may affect the plausibility of our responses to the others. Even with this caveat in mind, however, it should be clear that these questions are too numerous for just one paper. Questions 1 and 2 will be put to the side.[39] The focus of the remainder of this chapter will be question 4, which has a particularly noteworthy connection with question 3. One of the implications of the current 'culture of justification'[40] is that judges in democracies ought to attempt to render their judgments legitimate through argument. The forcefulness of argument takes precedence over the authority of the judicial office and the coerciveness of the legal apparatus. To obtain legitimacy through argument, judges ought to design their reasoning so that, even if not actually persuasive to all their audiences (parties, counsel, other judges, concerned citizens, etc), the reasoning will be of a kind that can in principle persuade all rational or reasonable audiences (whatever the adequate definition of rationality or reasonableness may be). This connection between the moral/political and the rhetorical will not be developed here, but it should become apparent in the forthcoming discussion of an argument by John Bell.[41]

[39] I have addressed the dialectical question, and to some extent the epistemic question, elsewhere; see Shecaira (n 11).

[40] The term is used by Etienne Mureinik (1994) 'A Bridge to Where? Introducing the Interim Bill of Rights' *South African Journal on Human Rights* 10: 31–48.

[41] I have discussed these connections at greater length elsewhere; see Fábio Shecaira and Noel Struchiner (2019) 'Audience Diversity and the Rhetorical Value of Public Reason' *Rechtstheorie* 50: 225–40.

To begin, let us recall the two-part argument presented in section I:

1. Judges have a choice to make between giving and omitting to give reasons for their rulings.
2. To give reasons is a way to further the values of transparency and accountability.
3. Therefore, judges should give reasons for their rulings instead of omitting to give them.
4. Now, reasons given for legal rulings are necessarily (more) general (than the conclusions they mean to justify).
5. Therefore, judges should give general reasons for their rulings instead of omitting to give them.

Let me say something about each of the claims that compose this argument. Claim 1 should be qualified in order to account for the fact that, in some jurisdictions, judges are bound by constitutional or statutory law to justify their decisions.[42] In these countries, the length and style of judicial reasoning may vary significantly, but utterly unjustified decisions are not a legally permitted option. This qualification is given limited emphasis in this chapter because it engages mostly with the ideas of legal theorists from common law jurisdictions, where traditionally there is no formal legal duty for judges to give reasons.

Again, claim 2 is not some idiosyncratic assumption of mine. Current political theory is deeply concerned with the quality of public deliberation and with authorities' democratic duty to engage citizens as rational and autonomous agents. Accordingly, one prominent debate in current political theory pertains to the kinds of reasons judges and other legal officials should give to the public. May judges give reasons based on their personal moral outlook, or should they give more ecumenical, 'public' reasons?[43] May judges engage in lofty theorising, or should they try to give reasons at a moderate level of abstractness?[44] Although theorists disagree about what kinds of reasons judges should give, they tend to agree that not giving reasons at all would be undemocratic or otherwise prejudicial to the autonomy of law subjects.

Admittedly, transparency and accountability are not the only relevant moral/political values in this context. They do recommend judicial reason giving, but sometimes they run across other values, such as efficiency, which may recommend just the opposite.[45] For instance, it is impractical to demand that judges justify every interlocutory decision.[46] Claim 3 should thus be read as affirming a

[42] Mathilde Cohen (2015) 'When Judges Have Reasons not to Give Reasons: A Comparative Law Approach' *Washington & Lee Law Review* 72: 483–571.

[43] See eg John Rawls (1997) 'The Idea of Public Reason Revisited' *University of Chicago Law Review* 64: 765–805.

[44] See eg Sunstein (n 3).

[45] Cohen (n 42) 514–25.

[46] Jason Bosland and Jonathan Gill (2014) 'The Principle of Open Justice and the Judicial Duty to Give Public Reasons' *The Judicial Duty to Give Public Reasons* 38: 482–524, 502–05.

defeasible duty for judges to give reasons. So qualified, claim 3 follows from the conjunction of 1 and 2.

On the other hand, the inference from 3 and 4 to 5 is not sound because, as I have argued, claim 4 is false. This is not enough to show, however, that claim 5 itself should be rejected. Others, without going through claim 4, have tried to establish a duty to give general reasons by reference to judges' responsibilities as public officials. Claim 5 should not be rejected before this alternative approach is assessed.

B. A Putative Judicial Responsibility to Generalise

There are probably many different versions of the type of argument I want to consider – and refute – in this section. They are all attempts to establish a connection between generality in judicial reasoning and a family of related ideals, such as fairness, even-handedness and impartiality. For the sake of brevity, I will consider two versions of this kind of argument here in the hope that they will be found representative, even if they are not exhaustive of all plausible alternatives. Let us begin with an argument by MacCormick:[47]

> [L]egal deliberation once matters come to court is (with a tiny handful of exceptions) a public process. In that public process, because of the public responsibility of judges, they are required (sometimes by law, sometimes simply by custom and usage) to state publicly what they are doing and why it is right to decide as they are deciding. … [T]his stating of reasons as public reasons by officials committed to even-handed justice in all cases necessarily partakes of universality, albeit defeasibly so. In a certain carefully explained sense, one can perhaps conceive of 'ethics without principles'; the same does not go for law.[48]

In assessing MacCormick's argument, it is important to begin by noticing his reference to 'universality'. MacCormick writes about universal reasons instead of general reasons. Though related, universality and generality are not identical concepts. Reasons can be more or less general, but universality does not come in degrees. Consider three different claims, from most general to least general: (i) all biographies are legally permitted; (ii) all authorised biographies are legally permitted; and (iii) the biography on Smith by Jones is legally permitted. Claim (i) is more general than claim (ii), since the category of biographies is larger, so to speak, than that of authorised biographies; but – in contrast to claim (iii) – they are equally universal, in the sense that they apply to all objects fitting some generic category.

[47] To be followed by a similar argument by John Bell (2006) 'The Institutional Constraints on Particularism' in *The Universal and the Particular in Legal Reasoning*, eds Zenon Bankwoski and James MacLean, Farnham: Ashgate, 41–51.

[48] MacCormick (n 16) 100 (reference omitted).

Since the concepts of generality and universality are not identical, some legal arguments may satisfy MacCormick's condition of having a universal premise while failing the condition of having a premise that is more general than its conclusion. Think, for example, of cases concerning abstract legal questions. The arguments pertaining to such cases will have general premises as well as general conclusions serving as answers to abstract legal questions. Granted that possibility, there is still a significant class of arguments – namely, those that have conclusions formulated in particular terms – that could only live up to MacCormick's expectations by the inclusion of premises that are more general than their conclusions. By claiming that reasons should be universal, MacCormick commits himself to the view that, in the relevant class of cases, reasons should also be more general than the conclusions they mean to justify.

We can now distinguish three claims that MacCormick combines in his argument, namely, that judges ought to justify their decisions publicly and that they ought to show the public that they are deciding as 'even-handed justice' requires, which in turn is supposed to lead to the conclusion that judges ought to ground their judgments on universal reasons. The first two claims are plausible, but the third does not seem to follow from either of them (nor from the conjunction of the two). So, let us consider the question whether the requirement of publicity and/or that of justice really entails a duty to argue with general reasons.

To the extent that justice has to do with 'treating like cases alike', it could be argued that justice requires decision making grounded on general reasons (or at least general reasons of a defeasible kind, as MacCormick indicates). In hard cases – where simple syllogisms are insufficient and other forms of argument are called upon – judges do not have clear-cut posited rules on which to ground their rulings. Nevertheless, they do have the ability to articulate general norms that encompass the instant case as well as similar cases expected to arise in the future. By articulating such norms, they contribute prospectively to the coherence and even-handedness of case law as they introduce norms on which other judges will be able to rely for the adjudication of similar disputes.[49]

It is thus plausible to think that 'even-handed justice' supports the (prospective) use of general reasons. This is not enough, however, to establish a *duty* for judges to use such reasons. As I argued in section II, doubts involved in the formulation of appropriately qualified general norms are part of the explanation why judges sometimes prefer to give non-general reasons for their decisions. They sacrifice opportunities to contribute to judicial consistency across cases, and they do so for fear of bad outcomes in the future. Justice competes against other values that also deserve judicial attention. Think, for instance, of the value of 'humanity', understood as the goal of forestalling harm that would result

[49] The articulation of precise rules (as distinct from vague standards) might also have prospective rule-of-law benefits related to predictability and facilitation of coordination. This is not MacCormick's argument, but it could be used to strengthen the case for rule-based reasoning.

from the application of a general norm to individuals in especially urgent or difficult situations.

But even this may be to concede too much to MacCormick. To say that justice competes with other values is not exactly to deny that judges have a stable, justice-related reason to use general reasons. MacCormick could thus insist that judges have a defeasible, but still general, justice-related duty to argue with such reasons. But even that (I think) is a dubious proposition. As is well known, justice is not unidimensional; it has both formal and substantive aspects.[50] In a formal sense, justice may indeed require recourse to general norms. In a substantive sense, however, it requires fair allocation of benefits and burdens among individuals – which is something that general norms often fail to do. If a judge is uncertain about what general norm would ensure fair allocation of benefits and burdens in the instant case and in future cases, might she not justifiably defer to the judgment of the future judges, who will be better acquainted with the particularities of the individual cases?

Of course, I do not want to make the implausible suggestion that MacCormick ignores the distinction between formal and substantive justice. His position could be taken to be that judges ought to pursue substantive justice *within the limits* of formal justice. In other words, judges ought to promote the fair allocation of benefits and burdens between litigants, but they must always ground their views about fair allocation on general norms that would cover similar cases. The trouble with this position is that it fails to acknowledge that, when faced with difficult moral questions, judges may justifiably refrain from articulating general norms precisely in order to preserve substantive justice. It is a mistake to think that judges never face the challenge of having to sacrifice one aspect of justice for the sake of the other.

So, the view that judges have a justice-related duty to give general reasons is a dubious one. In fact, justice (substantively understood) may sometimes require the opposite. Moreover, we should also resist the temptation to think that a duty to give general reasons somehow follows directly from judges' duty to respect the public, that is, to be transparent in their rationales and open to criticism. True, judges should not hide their assumptions (when they have in fact relied on such assumptions) behind terse opinions. On the other hand, judges hide nothing by refusing to commit to general reasons for *avowed* fear of bad decisions in the future. It is a mistake to accuse a judge of being coy or resisting accountability if she admits to preferring a terse form of argument on the ground that it is perilous to posit a broad norm instead of allowing a judicial doctrine to develop piecemeal in the light of future cases. Thus, what transparency and accountability require is something that varies according to the nature of the judge's predicament. The use of non-general reasons may be a way to exercise

[50] See HLA Hart (1994) *The Concept of Law*, 2nd edn, Oxford: Oxford University Press, ch 8.

sensible parsimony; it need not come of a wish to hide one's commitments or avoid democratic dissent. (I will return to this point in the final section.)

John Bell has an argument that resembles MacCormick's while giving special emphasis to the (putative) connections between universality and the values of accountability and impartiality. Judicial accountability, says Bell, is peculiar insofar as a judge's position requires her to address the concerns of various audiences. In Bell's words, judges 'engage in various levels of accountability: to the parties and their lawyers, to the legal community and to the general public'. This means that judges open their 'decisions to inspection [in a way that] forces some considerations of how the particular features of the case fit into a universal standard'.[51] So, Bell thinks there is an important relation between the requirement of universality of reasons and the recognition of diversity in the audiences to which judicial reasons are given. A judge must consider the perspectives of diverse groups, relinquishing any biases toward specific members of her audiences, be they rich or poor, male or female, black or white, etc. In a word, judges must be impartial. But to argue in a way that is truly impartial, Bell thinks, judges must rely on universal reasons.[52]

Bell's argument, then, is that reasons given to diverse audiences must be universal to ensure that all audiences are given their due. But how does decision making grounded on universal reasons come to serve as a check on partiality? Imagine a judge committed to consistently enforcing apartheid laws to *all* cases in her jurisdiction. Is she 'impartial' in any morally relevant sense? Genuine impartiality pertains to the substantive correctness of a legal decision, not to the mere fact that it can be subsumed under some general norm.[53]

It could be that there is a contingent connection between universal reasons and impartiality, since the very effort to elaborate sound general norms may help to offset biases that go unnoticed when a judge allows herself to decide on particularistic grounds. For instance, a legal decision against a female plaintiff may reveal itself as prejudiced when a male judge realises that he can think of no plausible general principle to ground his decision that does not discriminate against women. But if that is true, then we have at best an impartiality-related reason to recommend that judges *attempt* to articulate general reasons. The value is in the exercise, or the process, not in the product. The attempt to elaborate a general norm may still be given up when it becomes clear that there

[51] Bell (n 47) 46.

[52] Bell is not alone in deriving a judicial duty of impartiality from the fact of audience diversity in the law. But jurists who do so do not necessarily go on to associate the judicial duty of impartiality with a demand that judges adduce universal reasons. There is often talk of a judicial duty to address the 'universal audience' (in Chaim Perelman's sense of the term) but that is a different matter. For more on this point, see Fábio Shecaira and Noel Struchiner (2018) 'Legal Audiences' *Argumentation* 32: 273–91.

[53] For a detailed critique of the alleged connection between rule-governed decisions and impartiality, see David Lyons (1993) *Moral Aspects of Legal Theory*, New York: Cambridge University Press, 32–37.

is some non-prejudiced general norm that would imply the judge's preferred decision but has the separate flaw of being likely to have bad (eg inhumane, or iniquitous or utility-reducing) consequences in futures cases. For instance, as discussed earlier, the norm that one may not avoid a contractual limit on damages by suing in tort is probably over-inclusive. In the absence of an alternative norm that probably is not over-inclusive, the judge may be allowed to give up the attempt to ground her decision on a general norm altogether. The point is that she may do so without qualms about prejudice or bias, for those are not the reasons for her concerns about the candidate norms.

I submit that MacCormick and Bell fail in their respective attempts to connect universality with such values as fairness, accountability and impartiality. Recall that although they refer more often to universality than generality, there is sufficient overlap between these notions for their arguments to be relevant to a discussion about GT. One might worry that this overlap is illusory, because MacCormick and Bell could have in mind some Kantian notion of universality that is definable in terms of the *possibility* of generalising a premise to other cases without thereby arriving at a contradiction or some other kind of intellectual absurdity. If this were the case, then MacCormick's and Bell's contributions would indeed have little to do with GT, which is a claim about the actual generality of reasons, not about the theoretical possibility of their generalisation. I leave this interpretation to the side, not only because I doubt that it captures the authors' intentions correctly, but also because it would hardly contribute to our assessment of GT.

IV. CONCLUSION

In *Re A (Children)*, Ward LJ concludes his opinion about the surgical separation of the conjoined twins Mary and Jodie in the following way:

> Lest it be thought that this decision could become authority for wider propositions, such as that a doctor, once he has determined that a patient cannot survive, can kill the patient, it is important to restate the unique circumstances for which this case is authority. They are that it must be impossible to preserve the life of X without bringing about the death of Y, that Y by his or her very continued existence will inevitably bring about the death of X within a short period of time, and that X is capable of living an independent life but Y is incapable under any circumstances, including all forms of medical intervention, of viable independent existence. As I said at the beginning of this judgment, this is a very unique case.[54]

Ward LJ articulates a general norm in terms of X and Y. Worried about the implications that the norm might be taken to have, he makes sure it is tightly

[54] *In Re A (Children)* [2001] Fam 147, 204–05.

connected to the 'very unique' features of *Re A*. As Fernando Atria has put it, the connection is so close that one might even suspect that Ward's proposition does little more than 'replace the words, "Mary" and "Jody", by letters, "x" and "y"'.[55] Indeed, this is a case where the judges showed misgivings about articulating a general reason.

I submit that the Ward LJ could have avoided general reasons altogether. For example, the judgment might have used a more particularistic form of balancing of the rights or interests in conflict. If Ward LJ did not resort to particularistic reasoning in this case, that is perhaps because of the pressure to generalise or, in other words, to establish 'doctrine'. But omitting to give general reasons in circumstances of doubt is not simply a conceptual possibility; it can also be permissible considering the values of judicial accountability and transparency. Although the use of non-general reasons in *Re A* could be criticised on various grounds (for instance, as a missed opportunity to establish a new and broader doctrine of necessity), it should not be denounced as a sign of partiality, disingenuousness or aversion to dissent. After all, Ward LJ begins his opinion with a candid acknowledgement of his doubts:

> In this case the right answer is not at all easy to find. I freely confess to having found it exceptionally difficult to decide – difficult because of the scale of the tragedy for the parents and the twins, difficult for the seemingly irreconcilable conflicts of moral and ethical values and difficult because the search for settled legal principle has been especially arduous and conducted under real pressure of time.[56]

He might have said that it was difficult not only to find a settled principle, but also to articulate an original principle unlikely to generate harm in future cases. This, I have tried to argue, is a predicament that calls for sympathy, not suspicion.

[55] Fernando Atria (2006) 'Adjudication and the Particular' in Bankwoski and MacLean (eds) (n 47) 69–82, 79. See also Nicola Lacey (2006) 'Thoughts on MacCormick's "Particulars and Universals"' in Bankwoski and MacLean (eds) (n 47) 247–50, 249–50 (arguing that the opinion in *Re A* focuses very narrowly on the circumstances of Mary and Jodie due to a reluctance to enlarge the scope of the necessity defence in criminal law).

[56] *In Re A (Children)* (n 54) 155.

4

The Factor Model and General Jurisprudence

ADAM RIGONI

I. INTRODUCTION

THIS CHAPTER EXAMINES some of the jurisprudential implications of the factor model, or, perhaps more accurately, the factor model as I understand it, which is essentially a model where ratios are default rules that can be defeated in certain circumstances. In doing so, some of the model's strengths and weaknesses are revealed. Further, as a methodological matter, some in jurisprudence think legal reasoning reveals a great deal about the nature of law itself. My analysis shows that this is not the case with the factor model, as it is largely compatible with a number of different theses of general jurisprudence.

I begin, as much modern scholarship in legal philosophy does, with a discussion of legal positivism and the Hart/Dworkin debate. I will show that the model is compatible with positivism and offers a compelling solution to Dworkin's problem of 'hard cases'. Further, I will argue that it can approximate Dworkin's interpretivism in many, but not all, respects. Second, I consider approaches, very similar to Dworkin's, that involve the construction of the best theory that explains certain case results. Next, I show how the factor model relates to the recently influential legal theory of pragmatism. Finally, I briefly explain the relationship between the factor model and substantive theories of law.

To begin, a brief summary of the factor model is in order. The factor model provides a theory of precedent in common law judicial reasoning. Informally, we can think of it as starting with a judge trying to decide a current case against the background of a past case. From the past case she extracts a rule (or rules), which has a set of reasoning favouring the prevailing party (eg the plaintiff) as the antecedent and a judgment for that party as the consequent. She also extracts the complete sets of reasons for the losing party as discussed in the opinion. This information yields a weighing of reasons, namely, that the set of reasons in the antecedent of the rule outweighs the complete set of reasoning favouring the losing party. This weighing is the precedential force of the case; to alter it would be to overrule the past case."

More elaborate versions of the model introduce factor hierarchies[1] and sub-rules. These allow the model to represent the reasoning in greater deal.[2] For example, a factor hierarchy and sub-rules can represent the reasoning from the presence of an offer, consideration and acceptance to the conclusion that an agreement has been made.[3] The offer, consideration and acceptance are all sub-factors that are required to infer the presence of the factor 'agreement'. The sub-rule is one that says you can defeasibly infer an agreement from those sub-factors. The presence of an 'agreement' is itself a sub-factor required to infer the existence of a 'legal contract'.[4] Roughly, non-legal facts sit at the bottom of the hierarchy, and inferences regarding abstract legal entities like contracts, negligence and ultimately who prevails in the case sit at the top. Factor hierarchies give portions of the past case precedential force. For example, the sub-rule used to establish the existence of an agreement could bind the current court's determination of whether an agreement is present, regardless of the outcome of the past case. Essentially, the hierarchy treats each inference (or some subset of them) in the opinion as its own little case, with reasons and a rule.

Of course, giving precedential force to more aspects of the past case puts pressure on the distinction between ratio and dicta. The factor model gives no single answer to the question of to what extent sub-rules should be considered precedential. What is important for this chapter is just the understanding that the factor model *can* accommodate an expansive account of precedent, beyond just aggregating reasons for the final outcome. A reader interested in the details is encouraged to review the referenced work in artificial intelligence and Law.[5]

II. RULES, PRINCIPLES AND THE HART/DWORKIN DEBATE

In his article, 'The "Hart-Dworkin Debate": A Short Guide for the Perplexed', Scott Shapiro notes:

> For the past four decades, Anglo-American legal philosophy has been preoccupied – some might say obsessed – with something called the 'Hart-Dworkin' debate.

[1] The original source is CATO. See Vincent Aleven (1997) *Teaching Case-Based Argumentation Through a Model and Examples*, unpublished dissertion, University of Pittsburgh.

[2] They also keep opposing reasons and undercutting reasons distinct. The opposing reasons are weighed on one level of the hierarchy, while the reasons for or against (undercutters) those reasons are weighed on the lower level. Thanks to Katarina Stevens for discussion of this distinction in the factor model.

[3] See American Law Institute, The Restatement (Second) of Contracts (1981).

[4] ibid.

[5] See Katie Atkinson et al (2013) 'Argumentation Schemes for Reasoning about Factors with Dimensions' in *Proceedings of 26th International Conference on Legal Knowledge and Information Systems*, ed Kevin D Ashley, JURIX, 39–48; Alison Chorley and Trevor JM Bench-Capon (2005) 'An Empirical Investigation of Reasoning with Legal Cases Through Theory Construction and

> Since the appearance in 1967 of 'The Model of Rules I,' Ronald Dworkin's seminal critique of HLA Hart's theory of legal positivism, countless books and articles have been written either defending Hart against Dworkin's objections or defending Dworkin against Hart's defenders.[6]

The profession's fixation on this debate is not without reason. It pitted two of the field's best and brightest against each other on questions about the very nature of law, with consequences for 'judicial discretion, the role of policy in adjudication, the ontological foundations of rules, the possibility of descriptive jurisprudence, the function of law, the objectivity of value, the vagueness of concepts, and the nature of legal inference'.[7]

A. The Positivist Position

Since the conceptual scope and sheer volume of participants makes entering the debate a daunting task, I adopt a more modest course of action. I offer two theses taken from Hart's *The Concept of Law*[8] – (i) the rule of recognition; and (ii) the difference between good and legal – which I take to characterise the core of positivism with respect to legal reasoning.[9] Even this will likely strike some as controversial, but it offers a stable and, in my view, accurate picture of positivism's core commitments. Positivism, like Dworkin's interpretivism, is first and foremost a theory about the concept of 'law'. Still, it (like interpretivism) is not completely independent of one's theory of legal reasoning, because the rule of recognition is sensitive to the practices of a society's legal sector. For example, a positivist could not hold that legal reasoning answered to divine revelation without evidence of this in the practices of a society's legal actors.

In contrast, the factor model is first and foremost a theory of legal reasoning. Yet it, too, is not entirely independent of one's theory of law. As I will show, however, it is largely compatible with the major theories of law found in the literature. In this section, I will show how it is compatible with (i) and (ii) to

Application' *Artificial Intelligence and Law* 13: 323–71; Latifa Al-Abdulkarim, Katie Atkinson and Trevor JM Bench-Capon (2015) 'Factors, Issues and Values: Revisiting Reasoning with Cases' in *Proceedings of the 15th International Conference on Artificial Intelligence and Law* 3–12; Trevor JM Bench-Capon and Giovanni Sartor (2003) 'A Model of Legal Reasoning with Cases Incorporating Theories and Values' *Artificial Intelligence* 150: 97–143.

[6] Scott J Shapiro (2007) 'The "Hart-Dworkin Debate": A Short Guide for the Perplexed' in *Ronald Dworkin*, ed Arthur Ripstein, Cambridge: Cambridge University Press, 22–55, 22.

[7] ibid, 23–25 (citations omitted).

[8] HLA Hart (2012) *The Concept of Law*, 3rd edn, Oxford: Oxford University Press, Clarendon Law, 204.

[9] In this section I assume, contra critics like Posner, that common law reasoning is consistent with positivism. See Richard A Posner (1996) 'Pragmatic Adjudication' *Cardozo Law Review* 18: 1, 3–18.

establish its consistency with positivism. Then I can turn to Dworkin's criticisms in 'The Model of Rules I'[10] in section II.C.

As mentioned above, I sketch positivism as composed of two commitments: (i) the rule of recognition; and (ii) the difference between good and legal. Commitment (i) holds that where there is a society with a legal system, there must be a standard (a rule), evident in the practice of those within the legal system and the obedience of the citizenry, that determines the acceptable sources of law.[11] For example, the standard might recognise the pronouncements of the king or legislative body as sources of law. These sources themselves can create subordinate sources, for example, the US Constitution is a source of law that created the US Congress, which is also a source of law. Laws made by Congress are then subordinate to the law of the Constitution itself. Likewise, State constitutions create common law State courts, which can then create law through rulings in cases. A judge extracts the law from these sources and applies it to the case before him. Things are much more complicated in actual practice, as Hart himself knew,[12] but this is the general picture. As the factor model focuses on common law judicial reasoning, the relevant source of law is the opinions written by past judges. Note that the ratios within the factor model are not rules of recognition; they are rules whose status as law can be traced to a source, such as judicial custom, that meets the requirements of the rule of recognition.

There is a distinction between two sorts of positivism with respect to (i) as well as (ii). Inclusive or soft positivism is committed to (i).[13] Exclusive or hard positivism is committed to the stronger thesis that the rule of recognition cannot make use of moral terms, that is, the law can be identified using only social (amoral) facts.[14] In what follows I try to note whenever a difference between the two types of positivism matters to the factor model.

[10] Ronald Dworkin (1967) 'The Model of Rules' *University of Chicago Law Review* 35: 14–46. Reprinted in Ronald Dworkin (1978) 'The Model of Rules I' in *Taking Rights Seriously*, London: Duckworth. I use 'The Model of Rules' because it is the clearest and most self-contained of Dworkin's criticisms of positivism and hence the easiest through which to guide a reader. Dworkin has offered additional criticisms, such as his 'semantic sting' argument, in later works, but I do not think they are relevant to the issues I address here. See Ronald Dworkin (1986) *Law's Empire*, Cambridge, MA: Harvard University Press; Ronald Dworkin (2008) *Justice in Robes*, Cambridge, MA: Belknap Press.

[11] See Hart (n 8) 204.

[12] HLA Hart (1958) 'Positivism and the Separation of Law and Morals' *Harvard Law Review* 71: 593–629.

[13] See Leslie Green (Fall 2009) 'Legal Positivism' in *The Stanford Encyclopedia of Philosophy*, ed Edward N Zalta, at http://plato.stanford.edu/cgi-bin/encyclopedia/archinfo.cgi?entry=legal-positivism; Jules L Coleman (1982) 'Negative and Positive Positivism' *The Journal of Legal Studies* 11: 139–64.

[14] Green (n 13). Himma provides a perhaps confusing discussion of this issue. He writes, '[Exclusive positivists] deny that ostensibly moral provisions in a rule of recognition succeed in incorporating moral content in to the validity criteria. Instead, they argue that such provisions, if part of the law, must be construed as directions that courts consider moral norms under certain circumstances.' Kenneth Einar Himma (2002) 'Inclusive Legal Positivism' in *The Oxford Handbook of Jurisprudence and Philosophy of Law*, eds Jules Coleman and Scott Shapiro, Oxford: Oxford

The second positivist commitment is (ii), the difference between good and legal. It deals with the relationship between morality and legality and comes in two strengths. In its weaker form it says that '[there *could* be a legal system in which the] legality of a norm does not depend on any of its moral properties'.[15] It asserts that there is no conceptual connection between legality and morality. This captures the view of soft positivists.[16] Hard positivists say that there *could not* be a legal system in which the legality of a norm depends on any of its moral properties.[17] They assert a necessary/conceptual gulf between legality and morality. I use (ii) to mean the weaker thesis.

Having explained in a preliminary way the two central theses of positivism, we can see whether they comport with the factor model. Commitment (i) poses no problems for the factor model. It depends on taking precedent as a form of law, which requires treating past court opinions as valid sources of law. Nothing in (i) conflicts with this. Commitment (ii) raises greater concerns. Since the factor model is just a theory of common law judicial reasoning and not a complete theory of all legal reasoning, let alone all possible legal reasoning, it does not rule out any sort of legal system. Non-common law legal systems are obviously possible, as they dominate Continental Europe. Thus, even if the factor model incorporates some moral elements, it is compatible with the possibility of legal systems and modes of legal reasoning without such elements, which is all (ii) requires.

Still, it is worth asking whether the factor model incorporates such elements. The answer depends on the manner of extracting rules of precedent and the related weighing of reasons,[18] on which I have tried to remain scrupulously

University Press, 125–65, 140. But this is strange, since, as Himma points out, the exclusive positivist Raz explicitly says that the rule of recognition is not part of the law: ibid, 133; hence Himma's 'if part of the law' condition is never satisfied according to Raz. Himma claims that the treatment of moral language as directives for discretional law making allows exclusive positivists to the avoid the problem posed by 'the obvious fact that written constitutions often contain clauses that are expressed in moral language': ibid, fn 32. However, the exclusive positivist response to those cases should be to point out that the language of the Constitution itself is not the rule of recognition; the Constitution is a source (perhaps the source) granted authority by the rule of recognition. That is, the rule of recognition says something like 'something is valid law if and only made in according with the Constitution'. That rule has no moral language, though it refers to a document with moral language. In a footnote, Himma gets it right, saying 'the Source Thesis [a part of exclusive positivism] precludes incorporation of moral content into the rule of recognition … [though it is compatible with incorporating] moral principles as first order rules': ibid, fn 31. The language, including moral language, of a constitution forms first order rules. The exclusive positivist may still need to treat the moral language of these first order rules as directives for discretional law making in order to maintain strict separability between law and morals, but that is outside my point regarding the rule of recognition.

[15] Shapiro (n 6) 23.

[16] See Leslie Green (1996) 'The Concept of Law Revisited' *Michigan Law Review* 94: 1687–1717; Coleman (n 13).

[17] See Green (n 13).

[18] One could separate these two and have distinct methods of extracting the weighing of reasons and the rule. I ignore that possibility here.

silent. In the discussion of Dworkin's views in section II.B, I offer some methods of extraction that involve norms of political morality. Additionally, even more traditional methods of extraction may still depend on morality. For example, one could hold that the current judge (the extractor) reads the opinion looking for facts that she believes are reasons favouring one party or the other. She then extracts the rule and the weighing of reasons using these reasons. This introduces a conceptual connection to morality, insofar as the identification of which facts are reasons is conceptually connected to morality. Here the looming issue is whether all reasons are moral reasons.

However, methods of extraction that minimise the role of moral judgments are available, namely, treating rule extraction as a search for what the prior judge, in the opinion, took to be reasons in favour of her decision.[19] This process reduces the influence of the moral views of the current judge, since she cannot extract what she takes to be the reasons present in the past case. However, if precedent is to function as a significant constraint, then the extractors should be (judiciously) charitable in interpreting the past court as having treated as reasons what they (the extractors) take to be the actual reasons. Otherwise, they will increase the potential for finding novel reasons in the present case that allow it to be distinguished. Note that this strategy allows a judge to distinguish on the basis of a fact acknowledged in the past case if she thinks the past judge did not treat that fact as a reason. This does limit the power of precedent,[20] but it also allows courts to adapt to new information.

For example, carriers of highly explosive materials are typically subject to the highest standard of care for the purposes of tort claims.[21] Hence, in a tort suit, where the plaintiff was harmed by the explosion of such material, the fact that the defendant was transporting highly explosive material is a reason in favour of the plaintiff. Suppose a judge has a suit in tort before her in which the plaintiff is suing for damages caused by the explosion of the defendant's truck carrying Chemical X. There is a very similar past case involving Chemical X that held for the defendant. However, at the time that case was decided it was not known that Chemical X was highly explosive. Now this fact is well known. My approach allows the current court to distinguish the current case on the basis of Chemical X's being highly explosive, even though that fact was present in the past case as well. We can say that, although that fact obtained, the past court failed to treat or recognise it as a reason, and hence it is a novel reason in this case.

[19] As we shall see in section II.C and section III, other methods of rule extraction are available as well. While I hope to show why I prefer this approach to extraction to an alternative focused on the actual reasons present, I do not dream that I have established that this approach bests all the alternatives.

[20] As I have discussed previously, the force of precedent depends on some agreement amongst judges on what count as reasons, or simple reasons, or relevant facts, etc. Adam Rigoni (2015) 'An improved factor based approach to precedential constraint' *Artificial Intelligence Law* 23: 133–60.

[21] See Restatement (Second) of Torts, 519, 520 (1979).

Extracting rules in this way limits the role of the current judge's normative (and potentially moral) commitments in common law judicial reasoning but does not eradicate it completely. Distinguishing is permitted in the presence of a novel reason, that is, a reason or set of reasons that was not present in the past case and favours the party that lost in the past case. Whether a particular factual difference is a novel reason can depend on moral considerations; for example, the effect this factual difference has on overall happiness may determine whether it is a reason in favour of some party. If there is a novel reason, the judge has discretion (more on this later) to determine whether the novel reason is sufficient to outweigh the opposing reasons. This determination may be a species of moral reasoning. The factor model does not attempt to describe or justify that process; rather, it explains when common law systems permit the judge to engage in it.

Here I must distinguish two claims: (i) the theory is silent regarding the right weighing of the reasons; and (ii) the theory entails that there is no right weighing of the reasons. Critics like Holton attack the factor model because they think that (ii) is true of it, but it is only committed to (i).[22] The theory is compatible with any account of how the judge should weigh the reasons –particularists, utilitarians, Kantians, contractualists, etc are all welcome. Any one of these will endorse some weighings and reject others. Given the right/best/correct account, we can then determine when a judge acts wrongly in exercising this sort of discretion. Hence the factor model is entirely compatible with thinking that in some cases judges weigh novel reasons wrongly.[23]

The weighing a judge produces in exercising this discretion is in some sense a change in the law. For soft positivists, the proper weighing may have been part of the law prior to the judge's decision. For hard positivists, the judge is literally making new law, as the weighing only becomes part of the law once the judge performs it. But both accounts largely agree with the factor model that once the judge makes the decision in a common law system, the weighing gets a status it did not have before: it becomes precedent. The hard-positivist view is that this weighing becomes precedent at the same time it becomes law, and a soft positivist could take the same position. When it comes to novel reasons that allow for distinguishing, the two positions can diverge. A hard positivist is committed to saying that the question of a whether a moral reason is sufficiently strong

[22] Richard Holton (2011) 'Modeling Legal Rules' in *Philosophical Foundations of Language in the Law*, eds Andrei Marmor and Scott Soames, Oxford: Oxford University Press, 165–83, 180–83.

[23] One might ask whether the judges' error is still a legal error on my view of the factor model The answer is that it can be, since the factor model does not exhaust the realm of legal reasoning. On the soft-positivist picture, legal reasoning can incorporate moral reasoning, so the error is still straightforwardly legal. On the hard-positivist picture, the law can require the application of extra-legal norms. Although the reasoning about the extra-legal norms is not legal reasoning on this view, the failure to apply the right norms is still a legal error since it is a failure to do as the law requires. Either way, the error is a still a legal error. The only difference is that a soft-positivist might see the factor model as a less complete theory of legal reasoning than the hard-positivist.

to distinguish a case (to trump the ratio of the past case) is not settled by the law, that is, it is discretionary. The inclusive positivist *could* hold that the law includes an account of all moral reasons that are sufficient to distinguish various ratios, which leaves judges no discretion on that issue. This peculiar inclusive positivist position is not immediately compatible with the factor model, because it requires that court case merely to follow or fail to follow the law, while the factor model holds that cases create law by weighing reasons. That is, the factor model gives judges (at least) possible discretion.

The discretion the factor model gives judges looks compatible with the general commitments of positivism. An example using Hart's influential treatment of discretion is helpful.[24] Hart thought judges had discretion just in cases where the legal rule was indeterminate or legal rules conflicted.[25] For example, a legal source might say 'No operating vehicles in the park.' Some things, like taxicabs, are clearly within the extension of 'vehicles' in the statute. Other things, like trees, are clearly outside the extension. But for a third class of things it is not clear whether they are vehicles. Hart uses the example of a toy motor car.[26] He says the judge has discretion to determine if the toy is a vehicle. In making this determination, she is making law.

Hart's treatment of discretion comes into contact with the factor model at two points. Consider the judge's determination regarding the toy car. Suppose she holds that it is a vehicle and therefore decides for the plaintiff. This can be given precedential force via sub-rules. We can operationalise the prohibition on vehicles with this rule:

R1: If defendant is operating a vehicle in the park, then rule for the plaintiff.

Rule R1 treats 'the defendant is operating a vehicle in the park' as a reason in favour of the plaintiff. Let us label that reason 'R^p_1'. We want to characterise the judge as using R1 to hold for the plaintiff. One strategy is to use the vehicle's being a toy as a reason in favour of the defendant (call it 'R^d_1'), and then the force of the ruling is that R1 trumps a rule involving R^d_1 and the other pro-defendant reasons. But this strategy will not work if the court finds that the toy is a vehicle but an exception applies so the defendant still prevails. Sub-rules in a factor hierarchy allow an independent representation of the determination regarding the toy. They say that the reasons favouring treating the toy as a vehicle (call them 'R^v_1') outweigh those opposing such treatment (call them '$R^{\sim v}_1$'). We then get the sub-rules:

SR1: $R^v_1 \rightarrow R^p_1$

SR2: $R^{\sim v}_1 \rightarrow \neg R^p_1$

24 HLA Hart (2013) 'Discretion' *Harvard Law Review* 127: 652–65.
25 Hart (n 8) 130–33.
26 Hart (n 24) 662.

with the ordering that SR1 trumps SR2 (SR1 > SR2). This ordering is part of the new law that the judge makes via her decision, because prior to her decision judges were not bound by precedent to give SR1 priority over SR2.

The factor model also gives an explicit representation of cases in which established rules of precedent conflict. Suppose the current case involves this set of reasons $\{R^{d}_{1}, R^{d}_{2}, R^{p}_{1}, R^{p}_{2}\}$, where the superscript 'd' denotes a reason for the defendant and the superscript 'p' denotes a reason for the plaintiff. Further, suppose we have the following rules from past cases, where 'P☺' means the plaintiff wins and 'D☺' means the defendant wins:

R2: $R^{p}_{1} \rightarrow$ P☺

R3: $R^{d}_{1}, R^{d}_{2} \rightarrow$ D☺

R4: $R^{p}_{2} \rightarrow$ P☺

Also suppose the following ordering: R3 > R4. Now the case triggers conflicting rules, since R2 and R4 are inconsistent with R3. Here the judge has discretion to rule for the plaintiff using R2 or using a new rule, R5: $R^{p}_{1}, R^{p}_{2} \rightarrow$ D☺. These are distinct options: the first adds R2 > R3 to the precedential ordering, while the second adds R5 > R3 instead. Again, the judge's decision will make new law as the precedential ordering will be changed.

I think I have established the compatibility of the factor model with positivism, broadly understood. Further, I have shown that the factor model nicely complements the treatment of judicial discretion offered by the Arch-Positivist, HLA Hart. I now turn to the most prominent alternative to positivism.

B. Dworkin's Doctrine

In opposition to the positivist position sits Dworkin's influential doctrine of interpretivism. Dworkin takes the concept of 'law' to be interpretive. To determine what the law is in a community requires interpreting the past history of certain political institutions in that community. This interpretative process involves constructing the theory – composed of weighed principles – that *best justifies* the institutional history. 'Best justifies' here is explicitly understood as involving the values of political morality. Hence Dworkin rejects my second thesis of positivism, as for him the law is inextricably bound up with morality. Similarly, he rejects the first thesis insofar as it countenances an amoral rule of recognition.[27]

[27] He also rejects (i) on the grounds that it is incompatible with certain types of disagreement about the content of law, but that is irrelevant to the present treatment. See Dworkin (1986) (n 10) 45–86.

In discerning whether the factor model is compatible with Dworkin's view, the first question must be whether Dworkin's theory permits precedential constraint, because the inquiry ends there if it does not. Dworkin can accommodate a constraint akin to but distinct from the factor model's view of precedential constraint. The process of interpretation must be sensitive to the results in past cases, as those are part of the institutional history. For example, suppose a judge is deciding a case and the institutional history includes a case, C1, with a pro-plaintiff result. The judge thinks C1 was wrongly decided. The laws given by the best interpretation of this institutional history prescribe a decision in the present case for the plaintiff. Let C2 be the decision that the judge thinks C1 should have been. Suppose further that if we replace C1 with C2 in the institutional history, then the best interpretation of the resultant counterfactual institutional history favours a decision in the present case for the defendant. Then we can say that the judge is compelled by C1 to decide the present case contrary to what she thinks would be best in the absence of precedent.

The factor model can understood as roughly following Alexander and Sherwin in defining precedential constraint as involving a judge in following a rule solely in virtue of its status *qua* rule and not due to systematic concerns.[28] What I mean is that on the factor model, the reasons come from the specific facts of the case, not from further facts about how that case relates to other cases or aspects of the legal system. The model itself is meant to show how those local, case-specific facts interact with past cases. Once those reasons have been weighed in a particular way, the judge is understood as bound to follow the weighing; the model has no place for the justification for the judge's being so bound, and hence no room for the judge to avoid being bound because a justification is lacking. Within the model the rule is simply followed.

In contrast, the force of precedent on Dworkin's interpretivism is entirely due to systematic concerns regarding how it fits with the rest of the relevant history and political morality. Nevertheless, both the factor model and Dworkin's model can require a judge to follow the result in a past case despite her thinking that that result was incorrect. One might wonder if the factor model could be modified to handle this weaker form of precedential influence. The answer is, 'not quite'. One attempt would be to allow reasons of the following form, called DR for 'Dworkinian Reason':

> $DR^{d/p}{}_n$: The best interpretation of relevant political practices favours a ruling for the defendant/plaintiff.

This would seem to give the process of interpretation a central role in determining the result of a case as well as when a case can be distinguished. But DRs are not the sort of reasons that can be weighed. Once a judge has determined that a DR favours one party, according to Dworkin her decision is made: that party

[28] See Adam Rigoni (2014) 'Common-Law Judicial Reasoning and Analogy' *Legal Theory* 20: 133–56.

must prevail. A DR is the conclusion of judicial reasoning, hence there is no point in trying to make DRs a part of some further reasoning. This would be like allowing reasons such as 'ruling for the plaintiff is the right result' into the factor model. The point of the model is to model how the judge establishes that; we do not want to treat the desired output as another input.

Ultimately, Dworkin's theory is incompatible with the factor model because he does not require that a past ratio must be followed unless the present case involves a novel reason.[29] If the past ratio conflicts enough with political morality, then a court, lacking the power to overrule it, may distinguish it regardless of the presence of a novel reason. In these instances, lower courts are effectively given the power to overrule in the guise of distinguishing. On the factor model, lower courts can try to bury a disliked precedent by distinguishing on the basis of decreasingly significant reasons, stacking new rules atop the old one in the ordering. Yet this burial will always be incomplete; the lower courts cannot remove the old rule completely and insert a new one.

Still, the factor model can approximate Dworkin's view in many respects, especially his theory of legal principles. Dworkin's famed criticism of positivism in the 'Model of Rules' concisely illustrates his understanding of legal principles and his argument that they are incompatible with positivism.[30] The next section reviews this criticism, demonstrating that the factor model provides one kind of positivist response and revealing how closely it can mimic interpretivism.

C. Dworkin's Criticism in 'The Model of Rules' and Accommodating Interpretivism

Dworkin's 'The Model of Rules' attacks positivism on a number of fronts,[31] but I will focus on his charge that positivism fails because it is committed to a conception of the law as composed solely of all-or-nothing rules[32] or 'strict rules'. I do this despite the fact that the critique was not particularly effective. As Hart notes, 'But I certainly did not in my use of the word "rule" claim that legal systems comprise only "all or nothing" standards or near conclusive rules.'[33] Rather, I focus on this part of Dworkin's attack because the factor model answers it directly, while the rest of his criticisms only obliquely affect it. That is not to imply that those criticisms are unimportant, just that the factor model offers no new insights regarding them. If those criticisms convinced you of the truth of interpretivism, the rest of this section will not change your mind.

[29] Perhaps more fundamentally, he does not require that cases be treated as having ratios rather than results.

[30] Dworkin (1967) (n 10).

[31] See generally ibid.

[32] ibid, 24.

[33] Hart (n 8) 263.

In his essay Dworkin argues, using *Riggs v Palmer*[34] and *Henningsen v Bloomfield Motors, Inc*[35] as examples, that cases are decided using legal 'principles' rather than 'rules'.[36] In these hard cases, we can discern that judges are not merely applying all-or-nothing rules. Rules, per Dworkin, cannot conflict, nor can they have a dimension of weight or importance.[37] When triggered, they necessitate a particular outcome.[38] Principles, on the other hand, can conflict and are accorded varying weights. They do not necessitate any particular outcome; they simply 'state a reason that argues in one direction'.[39] An example is helpful: 'if the defendant was voluntarily intoxicated, then rule for the plaintiff' is a rule, while 'voluntary intoxication should not excuse reckless behaviour' is a principle. The former necessitates a result, a ruling for the plaintiff, while the latter simply supports ruling against the defendant if he was voluntarily intoxicated. The latter can be defeated by a weightier opposing principle.[40]

The factor model rejects all these claims. Its rules can conflict and be weighed through the process of prioritising the rules. They do mirror the form of Dworkin's rules, specifying a particular result in the consequent. However, some of them fail to 'necessitate'[41] a result, precisely because they can be trumped by higher-priority rules. Given the complete collection of defaults and priorities, we could identify the set of all rules that are not trumped by any other rules – call these the 'highest-priority rules'. Even these rules will not 'necessitate' a result in every case in which they are triggered, because the judge will have the option of distinguishing the rule (introducing a new rule with a higher priority) in cases with novel reasons. The default logic underlying the factor model formalises just the sort of rules that Dworkin thinks impossible.[42]

[34] *Riggs v Palmer*, 22 NE 188 (NY 1889).

[35] *Henningsen v Bloomfield Motors, Inc*, 161 A2d 69 (NJ 1960).

[36] Dworkin (1967) (n 10) 23–31.

[37] ibid, 23–29.

[38] ibid, 26.

[39] John F Horty (2012) *Reasons as Defaults*, Oxford: Oxford University Press offers an account of default rules doing exactly this.

[40] A note on the language of principles is in order here. I have tried to hew closely to Dworkin's language regarding principles and their formulations, but this may not square with ordinary usage. James Penner has pointed out that we often think of the principles of a particular area of the law as those general norms of contract law that admit of no exception or adjustment, rather norms that may be violated in cases of conflicts. I am sympathetic to this concern, but I have retained Dworkin's terminology because I think it has become entrenched in the discourse on this issue for too long to reformulate matters.

[41] Dworkin (1967) (n 10) 27.

[42] I am setting aside the issues created by Dworkin's 'right answer thesis', which is logically distinct from his criticisms in 'The Model of Rules'. Compare Dworkin (1967) (n 10) with Ronald Dworkin (1986) 'Is There Really No Right Answer in Hard Cases?' in *A Matter of Principle*, Oxford: Oxford University Press, 119–45. The right answer thesis would be equivalent to a factor model where, for any two opposing sets of reasons, there is an established weighing that favours only one of them. In such a system there are no novel reasons, so judges are always subject to a unique legally required outcome. The peculiar inclusivist positivist position I sketch in section II.A is similarly committed to legally required weighing involving novel reasons.

This raises the question of whether the factor model's rules can play the role of Dworkin's principles, whether it offers a formalisation of his theory with a change in terminology. Again, the answer is 'not quite'. One problem is the generality of Dworkin's principles. He gives the example 'no one should be permitted to profit … from his own wrong'[43] from *Riggs*. We must convert this into two rules to preserve the standard form:

> R5: If the defendant committed a wrong and will profit if he prevails, then rule for the plaintiff.

> R6: If the plaintiff committed a wrong and will profit if he prevails, then rule for the defendant.

We need two rules because the principle is applied to both plaintiffs and defendants. For example, suppose the plaintiff and defendant were engaged in illegal gambling and the plaintiff is suing to collect a debt the defendant incurred. The principle from *Riggs* favours the plaintiff, because otherwise the defendant benefits from the wrong of refusing to uphold an obligation freely entered. But it also favours the defendant, because the plaintiff stands to benefit from the wrong of illegal gambling.[44] Thus, Dworkin's principles cannot be converted into my rules without doing some violence to their form and perhaps content. Nonetheless, R5 and R6 seem to nicely operationalise the force of the *Riggs* principle, namely, that the law forbids plaintiffs and defendants from profiting from their wrongs.

The extraction of the principles poses a larger problem. On the factor model, rules are extracted locally from individual past cases: a case either restates a past rule or introduces a new one. Dworkin extracts his principles globally,[45] from the mass of legal history and political values, which include justice, fairness and, above all, integrity.[46] Principles explain cases, but they need not be expressed within any one case. A prima facie solution is to introduce a limited form of interpretivism at the ground floor, in the extraction of rules from past cases. That is, let the rules and weighings (the precedential import) of a past case be themselves a function of the best interpretation of past political practices. Instead of focusing on what the past judge took to be reasons, or on what the

[43] Dworkin (1967) (n 10) 23.

[44] The standard result in such cases is a ruling for the defendant. See Reporter Andrew Kull, Restatement (Third) of Restitution and Unjust Enrichment §§ 62, 63 (2011).

[45] A technical note: one might wonder whether altering the properties of the weighing relation, >, can allow for a more global extraction of rules. In all present versions of the factor model the relation is asymmetric but non-transitive following Horty's initial presentation of it. See John F Horty (2011) 'Rules and Reasons in the Theory of Precedent' *Legal Theory* 17: 1–33, 8, 15–17. Making the relation transitive, creating a strict partial order over legal rules, strengthens the force of precedent. This allows a global influence on rule priorities, but the content of the rules themselves is still entirely locally determined. Finessing the > relation can make precedent less localised in a sense, but not in the manner Dworkin requires.

[46] Dworkin (1986) (n 10) 225.

actual reasons in that case were, the judge looking back on a past case extracts the rules and weighings that best cohere with the rest of the (interpretivist) law.

It is not clear how far this solution will take us, as much depends on the workings of the interpretive process. On Dworkin's picture, one starts with a pre-theoretical notion of the relevant data and of how closely a theory must 'fit' with the data to count as an interpretation of them.[47] Then, via the process of interpretation guided by political morality, he constructs a theory justifying these data. Finally, with his theory in hand, he can refine the set of relevant data by expanding it, contracting it or re-interpreting members of it.[48] Thus there is no fixed set of data to be explained by an interpretation. While one starts with a set of data, any member of it could be removed in the final stage and anything could be added to that set. Hence, prior to interpretation, no single point of data must be explained and every event is potentially a datum.[49]

In the interpretation of cases, presumably the text of the opinion is a datum of some importance.[50] If fit with the text of the opinion is highly valued, the interpretation of past cases will yield rules similar to those involved in my version of the factor model. The factor model is compatible with this type of interpretivism in rule extraction. Still, a problem arises if this is the *only* method of extracting rules. If the judge interprets the past cases once then the factor model can take over and build on this interpretation by adding new rules and priorities, which have their content determined in a non-interpretivist manner.[51] However, if this interpretive process is the only manner of extracting rules then it must be performed after each new case is decided. For example, suppose a judge interprets the past history to decide a case at a time, *t1*. Then at a later time, *t2*, she must decide another case. During the time between *t1* and *t2*, cases were decided, new laws were enacted and so on, so that the institutional history at *t2* differs from that at *t1*. This change could alter the rules and priorities extracted

[47] ibid, 65–68.

[48] Nothing prevents the process from iterating and hence further refining the set of relevant data.

[49] As Nicos Stavropoulos puts it, 'interpretivism claims that neither question – what are the data and what justifies them – can be answered in a non-normative manner … values select, from among all the facts that could conceivably be determinants of legal duty, the ones that are such determinants, by providing an account that justifies the impact that each precise determinant has on our rights and duties'. Nicos Stavropoulos (Fall 2008) 'Interpretivist Theories of Law' in *The Stanford Encyclopedia of Philosophy*, ed Edward N Zalta, at http://plato.stanford.edu/archives/fall2008/entries/law-interpretivist/. It is difficult to conceive how this would work using the value of integrity, because integrity itself seems to require data. One cannot demonstrate integrity without some fixed point to which one can cohere. Nonetheless, I will not try to work out my misgivings here. Perhaps other values, like justice, can provide the fixed point.

[50] Though Dworkin himself seems to think the result is what really matters. See Ronald Dworkin (1978) 'Hard Cases' in *Taking Rights Seriously*, rev edn, Cambridge, MA: Harvard University Press, 81–131, 113, 115, 118–19; Dworkin (1986) (n 10) 247–48. Thanks to James Penner for pointing this out.

[51] This is very similar to the synthesis of Bench-Capon and Sartor (n 5) with John F Horty and Trevor JM Bench-Capon (2012) 'A Factor-Based Definition of Precedential Constraint' *Artificial Intelligence and Law* 20: 181–214 offered in the latter article.

from any number of cases, hence the judge must begin anew in extracting rules and priorities. She cannot just append rules and priorities from the intervening cases to old rules and priorities (from *t1*), because the intervening cases can alter the old rules and priorities. Thus, there is no method of incrementally building up the case base. On this view, the factor model amounts to cataloging the results of past interpretations.

On the other hand, if fit with the opinion is not highly valued, the interpretation of past cases will yield rules that may vary wildly from the opinion. They may not look at all like rules created using what the past judge took to be reasons. One could treat these rules as defaults in the factor model, but it is hard to see the point in chronicling rules from cases when the cases themselves are largely irrelevant to the content of the rules. The vast majority of legal reasoning on this view is done without examining a case, leaving the model marginalised in the extreme.

To put this another way, this type of interpretivism makes ratios nearly infallible, since they will rarely conflict with the demands of the best theory of the remaining legal materials, as that theory itself is determining the ratios. I will call the situation where ratios are infallible 'complete theoretical success'. In that situation, the 'data' are ensured to cohere with the theory. Cases will never exert precedential constraint, even in the Dworkinian sense of the term discussed previously, because the law given the result in a past case and the (counterfactual) law given a different result in that case are identical. We can move away from complete theoretical success by emphasising the text of the opinion to a greater degree. Situations of nearly complete theoretical success will marginalise case-based reasoning.

Hence, we can see that the factor model is incompatible with Dworkin's interpretivism. How well the model can imitate interpretivism depends heavily on what kind of interpretivism we are using. Some strains of interpretivism will be nearly indistinguishable from the current factor model, but others will differ greatly. I now turn to a different reading of Dworkin's view, one that the factor model can more easily accommodate.

D. Accommodating Dworkin's (per Hurley) Coherentism and Hard Cases

Note that the interpretivism I attribute to Dworkin differs from the coherentist approach offered by theorists like SL Hurley,[52] who herself attributes a coherentist approach to Dworkin. As Hurley correctly points out:

> While, concerning any particular settled case [ie an actual or hypothetical case on which the legal community does or would agree on the proper result], it is possible

[52] SL Hurley (2006) 'Coherence, Hypothetical Cases, and Precedent' in *Exploring Law's Empire: The Jurisprudence of Ronald Dworkin*, ed Scott Hershovitz, Oxford: Oxford University Press, 69–103.

> that the best theory of settled cases may show that it is mistaken, if theoretical coherence overall with settled cases is the standard, then it is not possible for all settled cases to be mistaken; hence coherentist consistency involves a certain element of conservatism.[53]

I take Dworkin's theory to be more thoroughly interpretivist, following Stavropoulos,[54] but it is worth exploring this alternative. I will discuss the differences between the two approaches below, and then address how the factor model fits with coherentism.

Interpretivism allows for what I will call 'complete legal failure', in that political morality – justice, fairness, etc – may fail to endorse any of the society's political practices at all; there may be no justifying theories available for those data and hence no best (or set of best) interpretations. This could happen if the society is profoundly immoral, for example.

In comparison, Hurley's coherentism is incompatible with complete legal failure. Her theory requires that some cases (whether actual or hypothetical) are settled correctly, although these correctly settled cases could all be hypothetical. To explain, Hurley's coherence account includes both actual and hypothetical cases. Hypothetical cases matter, because for Hurley the dispositions of legal decision makers regarding how to decide such cases are a part of the society's political practice. The important hypothetical cases are the settled hypothetical cases: cases with results upon which the legal community *would* agree (if they considered them), which function as data for the law to fit.[55] Coherentism is compatible with all the actual cases being mistaken, but interpretivism allows for even the hypothetical cases to be mistaken.

Further, coherentists do not allow the data to be determined by coherence, while interpretivism allows the data themself to be revised in light of the interpretation.[56] The process of revision threatens to trivialise the interpretivist project, since the data around which the theory is supposed to be moulded can now be moulded around the theory. Therefore, coherentism differs from interpretivism by presupposing a divide between the theory and the data, and by precluding complete legal failure. The views will look very similar if, as any reasonable interpretivist will insist, the notion of fit and norms of political morality highly value the text of the opinion. Thus, interpretivists and coherentists may reach the exact same results through similar routes, although the approaches are fundamentally different.

The relationship between coherentism and interpretivism reveals a way one might incorporate some of Dworkin's views into the factor model. Namely, one could treat Dworkin's theory as a theory of judicial discretion, operating

[53] ibid, 89.

[54] Stavropoulos (n 49).

[55] In a somewhat positivist vein, these hypothetical cases reduce to matters of social fact, namely, the dispositions amongst legal decision makers as how to decide them.

[56] See n 49.

only when the case does not fall within a binding rule. Dworkin's theory then explains the reasoning judges use to decide what priority to fix between conflicting rules from past cases, whether to distinguish a case that presents a novel reason, what ratio to establish when writing an opinion and whether a decision should be overruled. This approach hews closer to the broad sort of principles Dworkin writes about, which seem better suited to explain (rather than abbreviate) the more specific rules the factor model uses.

Importantly, this approach involves a limited coherentism, not interpretivism. The content of the past cases (results and ratios) is fixed and the judge is looking for the best theory that explains that content. The data are thus distinct from the theory, as coherentism but not interpretivism demands. Further, the past cases are treated as settled (to establish the lack of a binding rule needed to make discretion possible in the factor model), meaning some actual cases must be correct. This rules out complete actual theoretical failure. In fact, this approach is stricter than Hurley's, because some actual (not merely hypothetical) cases must be treated as correct. The factor model is entirely compatible with this sort of coherentism-as-discretion for the same reasons that it is compatible with a variety of moral approaches to how to weigh reasons. Once the coherentism is safely isolated to solely discretionary reasoning, it will not conflict with the model.

Before concluding the discussion of Dworkin and interpretivism, I should be explicit about what my understanding of the factor model says about the so-called 'hard cases'. Hard cases, on my view, can be explained as instances either of conflict between well-entrenched rules, or of conflict between a well-entrenched rule and an important novel reason. I read *Riggs*[57] as the former, involving a conflict between a rule from the wills statute and a rule of unjust enrichment regarding whether a murderer can inherit from his victim, and *Henningsen*[58] as the latter, involving a conflict between a rule of contract requiring privity between plaintiff and defendant and the novel reasons presented by automobiles sold exclusively through dealers but mass-marketed by manufacturers. In such cases the judges must decide which rule trumps the other, or whether the novel reason is sufficiently strong to distinguish the existing rule. The factor model is consistent with the decisions in each case.

My reading of *Riggs* merits a brief comment, since it is slightly at odds with Dworkin's. Dworkin reads it as an exemplary case dealing with a conflict between a statute and a moral principle. I read it as a confused opinion that failed to appreciate the doctrine surrounding constructive trust.[59] This is more

[57] See *Riggs v Palmer* (n 34).

[58] *Henningsen v Bloomfield Motors, Inc* (n 35).

[59] I struggle to see how Dworkin can use the case as an exemplar when he must ignore much of the opinion to reach his desired reading: the first argument the court endorses is that principles of statutory interpretation focused on law makers' intentions require reading the statute of wills as disinheriting the slayer. See *Riggs v Palmer* 115 NY 506, 509–11. The principle Dworkin fixates on only appears in the majority's second argument: ibid, 511.

or less the approach adopted by the New York Court of Appeals, the same court that decided *Riggs*, in *Ellerson v Westcott*,[60] and the approach argued in a series of articles by JB Ames from the 1890s.[61] The gist is that the will statute required the passage of legal title, and then common law doctrines of equity, such as unjust enrichment, which had at this point become merged with law in New York, require that the slayer hold that money in constructive trust for the rest of the heirs. The heirs were then within their rights to compel him to give up the money. In my view, equitable doctrines like constructive trust and unjust enrichment are themselves positive law, not direct applications of political morality.[62] The 'hard' issue in *Riggs*, if there is one, is a matter of the conflict (or seeming conflict) between the rule of constructive trust and the rule of the statute of wills.

* * *

In sum: the previous section demonstrated the incompatibility of the factor model with Dworkin's interpretivism. I showed how the factor model directly addresses one of the criticisms levelled against positivist theories in 'The Model of Rules'. This suggested that interpretivism might be partially assimilated within the factor model, or vice versa. I examined the results of allowing interpretivism to determine the content of past cases, concluding that this makes sense only if the norms of interpretation place a high priority on fit with the text of past opinions and interpretation (in Dworkin's sense) is not the sole method of rule extraction. I then highlighted the distinctions between coherentism and interpretivism, which led to a second possible assimilation: using coherentism as a theory of judicial discretion. The factor model can accommodate that proposal fairly easily, as should be expected, since it is not a theory of judicial discretion. Finally, I discussed how the factor model can identify hard cases and how it allows for their resolution.[63]

[60] *Ellerson v Westcott*, 42 NE 540 (NY 1896).

[61] JB Ames (1891) 'Note: Can a Murderer Acquire Title by His Crime?' *Harvard Law Review* 4: 394–95; JB Ames (1897) 'Can a Murderer Acquire Title by his Crime and Keep it?' *American Law Register* 45: 225–38.

[62] Here I follow Reporter Andrew Kull in the Restatement (Third) of Restitution and Unjust Enrichment, esp §1 of that document, in opposition to some, like Wolcher, who treats unjust enrichment as essentially connected to morality. See Louis E Wolcher (2011) "Intent to Charge for Unsolicited Benefits Conferred in an Emergency: A Case Study in the Meaning of 'Unjust' in the Restatement (Third) of Restitution & Unjust Enrichment" *Washington & Lee Law Review* 68: 911–47. I have argued for an even narrower, more exclusively positivist characterisation of unjust enrichment than Kull offers. Adam Rigoni (2011) 'A Sin of Admission: Why Section 62 Should Have Been Omitted from the Restatement (Third) of Restitution & Unjust Enrichment' *Washington & Lee Law Review* 68: 1203–26.

[63] In the computer science literature, coherentist approaches are often called 'theory construction approaches', for obvious reasons. For examples of such approaches, see Bench-Capon and Sartor (n 5); Alison Chorley and Trevor Bench-Capon (2005) 'An Empirical Investigation of Reasoning with Legal Cases Through Theory Construction and Application' *Artificial Intelligence and Law*,

III. POSNER'S PRAGMATISM

The most prominent theory of law after positivism and Dworkin's view is probably legal pragmatism, which has been revived largely due to the influence of Judge Richard Posner.[64] The pragmatist picture of legal reasoning that Posner offers is in some ways a strange creature. In its earlier iteration it was opposed to 'positivism'; more recently, Posner characterised the opposition (more accurately) as 'legalism'.[65] Posner's legalism is the view that judges merely apply the law as it is found in past decisions, statutes and other authorities.

Posner characterises a pragmatist judge thus:

> [He] always tries to do the best he can do for the present, unchecked by any felt duty to secure consistency in principles with what other officials have done in the past … [He] does not regard the maintenance of consistency with past decisions as an end in itself but only as a means for bringing about the best results in the present case.[66]

Yet he also claims that the pragmatic judge would determine the best result 'and only then examine … [past cases] to see whether they might block, by operation of the doctrine of *stare decisis* the decision that would be best'.[67] It is hard to square these positions, since *stare decisis* seems to require consistency with past decisions as an end in itself, and it looks as if *stare decisis* can block the best result. Posner makes similar remarks elsewhere about precedent and other constraints on judges.[68] The best interpretation is that Posner treats *stare decisis* as shorthand for considerations of predictability, stability and future influence, which are important considerations in determining the decision with the best result.[69] These considerations can block what would *otherwise* be the best result.

Pragmatism is not a substantive theory of law. It does not purport to establish criteria for what results are best, though we are told '[t]hey are not what is

vol. 13, no 3–4, pp 323–71; B Roth and B Verheij (2004) 'Cases and Dialectical Arguments – an Approach to Case-Based Reasoning' in *OTM Workshops, Lecture Notes in Computer Science*, eds R Meersman, Z Tari and A Corsaro, Heidelberg: Springer, 634–51. Horty and Bench-Capon give an excellent and detailed discussion of the relationship between these theories and theories that extract defaults prioritised based on fixed weighings of reasons. Horty and Bench-Capon (n 51) 203–11.

[64] See Richard A Posner (2008) *How Judges Think*, Cambridge, MA: Harvard University Press; Posner (n 9).

[65] Compare Posner (2008) (n 64) to Posner (n 9).

[66] Posner (n 9) 3, 5.

[67] ibid, 7.

[68] See Posner (2008) (n 64) 220 (explaining '[the successful advocate] will have to show that the position does not violate settled law … [s]o precedent … [acts] as a constraint on [his] efforts'). See also Posner (n 9), 7.

[69] He acknowledges the effect defying precedents can have on a judge's long-term power – the more often judges defy precedent, the less influential their own decisions become. He treats deference to precedent as a strategy for a repeated game. Posner (2008) (n 64) 144. Although Posner abandons exclusively economic approaches (ibid, 237, 246), it should be noted that his 'best results' usually aim at maximising aggregate welfare.

best for the particular case without consideration of the implications for other cases'.[70] However, Posner seems to imply that a pragmatist must accept the values generally accepted by his legal community, writing, 'Pragmatism will not tell us what is best but, provided there is a fair degree of value consensus among judges … it can help judges seek the best results unhampered by philosophical results.'[71] In his most recent book on pragmatism he continues, 'the wider the agreement on what kind of consequences are good and what kind are bad (and how good and how bad), the greater the guidance that pragmatism will provide'.[72] This is a bit puzzling, but according to the overall picture, the pragmatic judge is a particularist, suspicious of overarching moral theories as well as his weaker intuitions. He proceeds in a piecemeal fashion, balancing competing interests, cautiously trying to reach the right local result.

Further complicating matters are Posner's claims that 'most American judges are legalists in some cases and pragmatist in others; for remember that legalism is a pragmatic tactic'[73] and 'legal pragmatism incorporates … legalism'.[74] Hence legalism, introduced as in opposition to pragmatism, is subsumed within pragmatism. Additionally, Posner often treats pragmatism as a matter of degree, for example, 'English judges can afford to be … less pragmatic than our [American appellate] judges.'[75]

To make sense of this, let us start by distinguishing pragmatism writ large, legal pragmatism and pragmatic adjudication. Posner never explicitly defines these, so what follows is my own interpretation. Pragmatism writ large is simply making decisions based on their short-term and long-term consequences. Legal pragmatism is the application of pragmatism writ large to legal institutions. For Posner, all (or nearly all) judges are pragmatic writ large and hence legal pragmatists in virtue of their position in the legal system. Legalism and pragmatic adjudication are two possible methods of adjudication. Legalism focuses on applying or extending the rules/results of past cases and legal authorities such as statutes without much regard for the consequences of the decision. Pragmatic adjudication is making judicial decisions with a focus on the consequences, treating non-legal sources of information about these consequences, such as social science, as equally important as legal authorities.

According to Posner, a legal pragmatist will, in some situations, endorse legalism in the same way that an act-utilitarian will, in some situations, endorse a rule-utilitarian decision procedure. Within some legal systems, such

[70] Posner (n 9), 16; see also Posner (2008) (n 64) 245–49.
[71] Posner (n 9), 18.
[72] Posner (2008) (n 64) 241.
[73] ibid, 230.
[74] ibid, 246.
[75] Posner (n 9), 19.

as unicameral parliamentary systems, judges do better trying to follow rules instead of trying to work out the best result in each case.[76] In these systems, legal pragmatism endorses legalism. In other political systems, such as the system in the United States, judges will do best if they explicitly focus on the consequences of the decision. Here, legal pragmatism endorses pragmatic adjudication.[77]

However, for Posner, a judiciary cannot be completely legalist because there is too much indeterminacy in even very detailed laws, and in some instances the results of legalism are intolerable.[78] Hence legalism and pragmatic adjudication are a matter of degree, even within systems that clearly favour one or the other. This clarifies Posner's comment that judges can be more or less pragmatic: some may pore over the intricacies of legalist sources and only take a hard look at consequences when those resources are completely inadequate, while other judges may give the legal doctrine only a cursory look before focusing on the consequences.[79]

It also explains how judges can be legalists in some cases and pragmatic in others: in some cases the legalist materials are conclusive, in others they are woefully inadequate. Posner himself admits that (even in the United States) judges in most cases behave as legalists, writing:

> [M]any, indeed most, judicial decisions really are the product of a neutral application of rules not made up for the occasion to facts fairly found. Such decisions exemplify what is commonly called 'legal formalism,' though the word I prefer is 'legalism.'[80]

The approach that emerges from all this discussion is two-tiered, although ultimately justified by legal pragmatism. The judge first applies legalist methods. Then, should they fail to produce any result or produce an unacceptable one,[81] she applies pragmatist methods.

So how does the factor model fit with Posner's pragmatism? On one hand, much like Dworkin, Posner's approach to precedent is that it should be followed only when the judge thinks doing so is best. The factor model is not made to capture that view of precedential constraint. However, the model can still find a place within the pragmatist's framework as a representation of legalist reasoning. The factor model can serve as a model for the reasoning performed in routine cases. When the rules fail to address the present case, pragmatism explains the

[76] ibid, 18–20. Posner thinks this follows from unicameral parliaments' ability to quickly pass laws addressing recent issues.

[77] Posner (2008) (n 64) 9.

[78] See Posner (n 9) 13; Posner (2008) (n 64) 199–200, 214–16 (discussing the absurdity doctrine in statutory interpretation).

[79] Note that the legal sources still take priority. Pragmatism is not committed to this, but Posner admits it is descriptively accurate – only the non-routine cases go beyond the legal sources.

[80] Posner (2008) (n 64) 370.

[81] Just what makes a result unacceptable is unclear. Posner describes it as similar to the doctrine of absurdity in statutory interpretation. See Posner (n 9) 13; Posner (2008) (n 64) 199–200, 214–16.

judge's discretionary reasoning. The pragmatist must add one caveat: pragmatic adjudication can override the conclusions drawn by the factor model when the result is egregious.[82]

I must stress that explaining routine cases is no meagre feat. Legal theorists tend to be enamoured with appellate adjudication.[83] It is symptomatic of this myopia that Posner, in *How Judges Think*, can acknowledge that in most cases judges are legalists but then devote nearly the entirety of the book to the remaining cases in which judges use pragmatic adjudication. Posner has a better excuse than most theorists for focusing on the non-routine cases: as a federal appellate judge, he was more likely to see these cases.

Indeed, the influence of legalism goes deeper than determining results in most cases. In the same vein as the passage quoted above, Posner writes:

> [M]ost cases are routine (and would not be litigated at all if lawyers were better at predicting juridical outcomes), rather than residing in that uncomfortable open region in which judges are at large … The routine case is dispatched with least fuss by legalist methods. It is in such a case that the virtues of such methods shine; [the judge] feel[s] no need to go beyond those methods to decide the case satisfactorily.[84]

Posner is talking about data from Cross,[85] showing a high rate of affirmation of federal district court decisions by federal courts of appeal, but note the parenthetical remark. A tremendous portion of legal claims are settled before final judgment,[86] including roughly 95 per cent of automobile claims[87] and 67 per cent of all federal civil cases across all districts in 2005.[88] As both parties become more certain of the same outcome at trial, settlement becomes increasingly likely to avoid the deadweight loss of trial costs.[89] The routine, legalistic cases will be more likely to settle than the non-routine. Thus, the predicted results of legalistic reasoning govern the outcome in many settled cases.

That means that legalist reasoning, which the factor model aims to explain, covers an even larger range of legal disputes than the Cross data show. If we think a (or the) purpose of a legal system is to adjudicate disputes in a manner acceptable to society at large, then trials and appeals are an increasingly small

[82] See Schauer's Presumptive Positivism in Fred Schauer (1988) 'Formalism' *Yale Law Journal* 97: 509–48.

[83] I am just as guilty as the rest. See Rigoni (n 20).

[84] Posner (2008) (n 64) 46.

[85] Frank Cross (2005) 'Appellate Court Adherence to Precedent' *Journal of Empirical Legal Studies* 2: 369–405.

[86] See discussion in Theodore Eisenberg and Charolette Lanvers (2009) 'What is the Settlement Rate and Why Should We Care?' *Journal of Empirical Legal Studies* 6: 111–46.

[87] H Laurence Ross (1980) *Settled Out of Court: The Social Process of Insurance Claims Adjustment*, Piscataway, NJ: Transactions Publishers, 285.

[88] Kevin M Clermont (2009) 'Litigation Realities Redux' *Notre Dame Law Review* 84: 1919–74, 1954–55.

[89] See John P Gould (1973) 'The Economics of Legal Conflicts' *The Journal of Legal Studies* 2: 279–300.

part of the enterprise.[90] Although a judge is only the final decision maker in this small percentage of disputes, predictions of how she will or would reason resonate throughout the system. Therefore, an account of legalist reasoning is very important, even to those who share Posner's goal of 'transcend[ing]' it.[91]

IV. ANALYTIC, NORMATIVE AND SUBSTANTIVE THEORIES OF LAW

I turn now to theories that are more focused on the actual law, rather than the concept of law or legal reasoning, although, as Dworkin shows, theories often touch on all three. I call such theories 'theories of substantive law'. Examples of such theories include the corrective justice theory of tort law and the promissory theory of contract law.[92] Substantive theories can encompass both analytic and normative theories. The analytic theories attempt to interpret and explain an area of law.[93] Normative theories of an area of law attempt to justify or reform features of that area of law. The analytical theories are closer to what we might call pure descriptions of the law, but they go beyond merely stating the relevant black-letter law to explaining which aspects of the law are central to the specified field (torts, criminal law, etc) and how these aspects relate to each other. The normative theories are less tied to results of cases or the text of statutes, in that they may suggest significant reform or justify the existence of an area of law, for example, a justification of why we ought to have criminal law.

Analytical and normative theories are not mutually exclusive. A normative theory must have or presuppose an analytical aspect that determines which norms and features make up the area of law it seeks to justify or reform. An analytic theory will have difficulty identifying norms and features as central and offering an interesting explanation of their relationship without recourse to normative notions such as the values furthered by the relevant field.

Within the factor model, the analytic aspect of a substantive theory guides the interpretation of past opinions and ratios. It provides a way of constructing the set of reasons, rules and weights to be used by the model. For example, a law and economics adherent will extract rules and ratios centred on efficiency, per the analytic claims of that theory. The normative aspects of the theory

[90] Marc Galanter (2004) 'The Vanishing Trial: An Examination of Trials and Related Matters in Federal and State Courts' *Journal of Empirical Legal Studies* 1: 459–570. Contrast this with Posner's assertion that the kingdom of legalism 'has shrunk and greyed': Posner (2008) (n 64) 1.

[91] Posner (2008) (n 64) 252.

[92] Jules L Coleman (2003) *The Practice of Principle: In Defence of a Pragmatist Approach to Legal Theory*, Oxford: Oxford University Press; Charles Fried (2015) *Contract as Promise: A Theory of Contractual Obligation*, Oxford: Oxford University Press.

[93] Jules Coleman and Gabriel Mendlow (Fall 2010) 'Theories of Tort Law' in *The Stanford Encyclopedia of Philosophy*, ed Edward N Zalta, at http://plato.stanford.edu/archives/fall2010/entries/tort-theories/; Antony Duff (Summer 2010) 'Theories of Criminal Law' in *The Stanford Encyclopedia of Philosophy*, ed Edward N Zalta, at http://plato.stanford.edu/entries/criminal-law/.

attempt to govern discretionary decision making, that is, they govern the judge's weighing of reasons in cases where she is not bound by precedent. The force of precedential constraint will depend on the concept of law the theorist adopts, not the substantive theory.

V. CONCLUSION

I have examined the relationship between the factor model and prominent theories of the nature of law. The examination revealed that it fits most comfortably with the positivist conception of law because of its use of binding (contra the pragmatist) rules of precedent that are extracted from individual cases (contra the coherentists and interpretivists). Still, I showed that it can coexist with aspects of interpretivist, coherentist and pragmatist theories, mainly by treating those theories as theories of judicial discretion.

Further, I demonstrated that the factor model is amenable to different substantive theories of law, as it should be. As a theory that tries to approximate the reasoning of actual judges, who frequently disagree about substantive theories, it would be a mark against the theory if it settled these disputes. In sum, the factor model is amicable to many insights from diverse jurisprudential perspectives regarding both the concept and content of law, though its core notions of precedential constraint and extracting a rule (or rules) from an individual case best fit with positivism.

Part II

Rules and Reasons

5

No Reasons

MARK McBRIDE*

IDENTIFYING THE ROLE of *precedent* in law, and the conditions under which a judge may permissibly *distinguish* precedent, is a central task for any account, or theory, of legal reasoning. Unsurprisingly, different accounts, or theories, of precedent abound. My focus in this chapter is on an intriguing, and prima facie appealing, relatively recent effort to identify the role of precedent in law, offered by Grant Lamond.[1] My modest aim is threefold:

(1) To point out that Lamond's account of Joseph Raz's seminal so-called *rules* account of precedent[2] is inaccurate in important ways.
(2) To claim that Lamond fails to see that the *core* of his so-called *reasons* account of precedent is *extensionally equivalent* to Raz's account.[3] Moreover, Lamond reaches extensional equivalence with Raz by means of several contestable assumptions not needed by Raz.
(3) To argue that the (only) portion of Lamond's account that genuinely goes beyond Raz – *viz* Lamond's *extension* of his core to account for the development of *legal doctrine* – is, whilst fascinating, mistaken.[4]

While the core aims in this chapter may be termed *negative*, negative verdicts on an interesting theory can be valuable. The core of the reasons account is no different (extensionally) from the (simpler) rules account; and the extension of the reasons account beyond its core is flawed. The reasons account of precedent is either nothing new (its core), or, if new (its extension), faulty.

Before commencing, an acknowledgement: John Horty has already forcefully made an equivalence claim between these two models of precedential

* Thanks to Andrew Halpin and Adam Rigoni for stimulating discussion.

[1] Grant Lamond (2005) 'Do Precedents Create Rules?' *Legal Theory* 11: 1–26.

[2] Joseph Raz (1979) 'Law and Value in Adjudication' in *The Authority of Law*, Oxford: Oxford University Press, 180–209.

[3] And the failure in (2) *might* be so (in part) *because of* the inaccuracy in (1).

[4] John Horty (2011) 'Rules and Reasons in the Theory of Precedent' *Legal Theory* 17: 1–33, fn 22, has somewhat anticipated point (3), though I put things slightly differently from Horty.

constraint – *viz* rules and reasons.[5] But two points are in order. First, Horty reaches his equivalence claim by an utterly different method from me: it can be salutary for two philosophers to independently reach the same result for different reasons. Second, and perhaps more importantly, Horty goes on to provide reasons to prefer the reasons model over the rules model (in spite of their extensional equivalence). By contrast, I go the other way: the spareness and austerity of the rules account, in comparison with the reasons account, is a pro tanto strike in its favour.

I. MISREPRESENTING RAZ

Though what follows will be fairly abstract at times, we shall attempt to anchor things by tracing a toy example through the chapter – a version of the well-worn 'no vehicles in the park' case. Lamond[6] sketches what he calls a 'conventional view of precedent', on which 'precedent is a form of "rule-based" decision-making'. And though Lamond has other theorists in mind, falling within this so-called *conventional* picture, time and again it is clear that Raz[7] is the exemplar of this rule-based account. It is both fair and apposite, then, to take the following as Lamond's[8] representation of Raz on precedent and distinguishing:

> If the *ratio* is:
>
> $$R = \text{If } \{J, K, L\}, \text{ then } C$$
>
> Then (1) the later court must alter R only by adding a new element to $\{J, K, L\}$ (or by substituting a subcategory of J, or K, or L, for that element),[9] thereby *narrowing* the scope of R; and (2) the amended rule must not be inconsistent with the *result* in the precedent case. So if the facts of the case are:
>
> $$F_1 = \{g_1, h_1, i_1, j_1, k_1, l_1\}$$
>
> then R can be altered by adding some novel factor M but it cannot be altered by adding $\sim G$ or $\sim H$ or $\sim I$, since the modified *ratio* would no longer support the result in the precedent.

(Given the focus of this chapter is on Lamond, and consideration of his core and extended theses, it is best to present Lamond's structure and to weave

[5] John Horty (2015) 'Constraint and Freedom in the Common Law' *Philosophers' Imprint* 15: 1–27.

[6] Lamond (n 1) 5.

[7] Raz (n 2).

[8] Lamond (n 1) 10–11.

[9] My note: I take this to be a welcome addition to, or refinement of, Raz's account. Let 'J' be: x acts negligently. A later court can clearly narrow R by substituting *J** for *J*, where '*J**' is: x acts *grossly* negligently. And this permissible narrowing cannot be captured by the addition of a *new element* to R, but only by introduction of a subcategory – *viz J**.

consideration of Raz into that structure.) We can think of (1) and (2), jointly, as Lamond's effort to capture Raz's *formal* constraints on distinguishing.[10]

Before interrogating (1) and (2) as such an effort, let's introduce our toy example to tether things. Transposing Raz's taxonomy[11] to Lamond's structure, we can let '*J*' = x is a vehicle and 'j_1' = x is a car, '*K*' = x is in the park and 'k_1' = x is in Hyde Park, and '*L*' = x is motorised and 'l_1' = x is a V6, and 'C' = x is prohibited (where, throughout, x receives the same interpretation).[12]

So, what of (1) and (2) as an effort to capture Raz? Put briefly, while (1) is accurate, (2) is inaccurate, in virtue of being too *weak*. *Raz's* condition (2) is not *merely* that, as Lamond puts it, the amended rule must 'not be inconsistent with' – or, as Raz puts it,[13] 'be compatible with' – the result in the precedent case. Raz's condition (2) does require this (rather weak constraint); but it requires more. The amended rule must, for Raz,[14] moreover 'justify' the result in the precedent case. (Any amended rule justifying the precedent result, is compatible with that result; but the converse entailment doesn't hold.) We need to get very clear on the justification/compatibility distinction for Raz, and what is thereby *permitted/forbidden* for a distinguishing judge.

It is best to build up to justification (our target) by way of consideration of compatibility (what justification entails). A constraint that an amended rule be compatible with the result in the precedent case is really incredibly weak. All that is required for an amended, or modified, rule to be compatible with the result in the precedent case is that it 'does not require a contrary decision'.[15] So Lamond is right, using his template above, that it is impermissible to alter R by adding ~*G* or ~*H* or ~*I*. But this is *not* because so adding to R would be *inconsistent*, or *incompatible*, with the result in the precedent case (but rather, as we'll see, because it would *fail to justify* that result).[16]

[10] Presumably, implicit in (1) is that the facts in the later case fall *outside the scope* of the narrowed rule (but cf n 27). They – the formal constraints – are supplemented by what we might refer to as Raz's two *non-formal* constraints on distinguishing. Though my focus in this chapter is on formal matters, we can note that, while Lamond ((n 1) 11) includes Raz's ((n 2) 188) non-formal constraint that the new rule must preserve the 'fundamental rationale' of the original rule, he appears to omit Raz's ((n 2) 187) other non-formal constraint that the distinguishing court has an 'obligation … to … best improve the rule'. We can think of a putative act of distinguishing failing the initial hurdle of the formal constraints as a *failed* act of distinguishing. And we can think of such an act meeting the formal, but then failing the non-formal, constraints as a *bad* act of distinguishing.

[11] Raz (n 2) 183.

[12] So, upper-case letters are 'general properties of facts' (ibid), such that, for example, j_1 is an instance of *J*. Pretty clearly, one could go *higher up* and *lower down* in generality, here: x is an inanimate object, and x is a Ford Fiesta, respectively. And presumably in virtue of some legal relationship obtaining between the object in question and an agent, some legal consequence attaches to the agent in question (eg a penalty, compensatory obligations, etc).

[13] ibid, 187.

[14] ibid, 186–87.

[15] ibid, 187.

[16] Insofar as Lamond's 'support', as is plausibly the case, is equivalent to 'justify', Lamond's final explanation of this impermissibility in his template above is correct; but the point remains that his statement of Raz's second formal condition is (importantly) inaccurate.

Let us focus on ~*I* (the point carries directly over to ~*G* or ~*H*). Let '~*I*' = x is noisy[17] (and so '*I*' = it's not the case that x is noisy). And presumably, as a putative act of distinguishing, the instant case is an *i*-case. As a formal matter, adding ~*I* to R is perfectly *compatible* with the result in the precedent case: it does *not require* a *contrary* decision; it merely *fails to require* – fails to 'justify', in Raz's use of that term – the *same* decision. This putative modification of R, leads to R*:

$$R^* = \text{If } \{\sim I, J, K, L\}, \text{ then } C$$

The facts of the precedent case – $F_1 = \{g_1, h_1, i_1, j_1, k_1, l_1\}$ – *fail* to satisfy the antecedent of R*, and thus R* fails to *require* the same result in F_1.[18] But this is importantly short of establishing that R* requires a contrary decision. To think that it does is to commit the fallacy of *denying the antecedent*. As Raz notes, '[a]ll *rationes* can be formulated as setting sufficient conditions'.[19] This is to say, any *ratio* is of the (conditional) form: If *A* (antecedent), then *C* (consequent). But we commit the foregoing fallacy by inferring from the fact that F_1 fails to satisfy the antecedent of R* (ie from ~*A*), that ~*C* (ie that it's not the case that x is prohibited). And it's only if the new rule (here R*) would entitle us to infer ~C that that new rule flouts the (weak) compatibility constraint.

(All of the foregoing can respect Brewer's point[20] that pragmatic features of legal systems give rise to a background assumption, or default rule, to the effect that, in any particular cause of action, satisfying the antecedent of the ratio in question is the *only way* to establish its consequent. Of course, if such a default rule is in operation, and is not defeated, then we *could* legitimately infer ~C from ~A. But it is in the nature of pragmatic features that they can be cancelled; and we'll shortly see how this can be in the case at hand. I think this is the context within which to interpret Raz's remark that (transposed to Lamond's structure) 'A decision that the absence of [*J*] is sufficient to show that the action must be dismissed establishes that [*J*] is a necessary condition for such an action to succeed.'[21] The decision that established R may have done this; but it need not (for reasons given above) have done so.)

[17] ~*I* can be rendered more definite by supposing it is satisfied by the emission – or, the capacity to emit – noise over a certain fixed number of decibels. This assignment to '~*I*' relies on a plausible assumption to be made explicit shortly (cf n 38). But we could just as readily have made our point without this assumption by, more *positively*, letting '*I*' = x is quiet (and so ~*I* would be: it is not the case that x is quiet).

[18] And *satisfying* the antecedent of the *ratio* is, we'll see, the nub of Raz's idea of 'justifying' the result in the precedent case. This use of 'justify', whilst perfectly kosher, can be prone to mislead readers into importing some moral notion of justification into the idea of distinguishing – something alien to Raz's purposes.

[19] Raz (n 2) fn 13.

[20] Scott Brewer (1996) 'Exemplary Reasoning: Semantics, Pragmatics, and the Rational Force of Legal Argument by Analogy' *Harvard Law Review* 109: 923–1028, fn 215.

[21] Raz (n 2) fn 13.

Without more, this logical point is sufficient to establish that R* *doesn't* flout the (weak) compatibility constraint on distinguishing.[22] But it is instructive to consider how R could be modified to R*, consistently with the same result *in fact* being reached in the precedent case. The key here is to draw upon the (legal) possibility of *multiple ratios bearing on* any case (here: F_1), without *(explicitly) being invoked* in the case in question.[23] So let us suppose, in our structure, that, in addition to R – the *ratio* bearing on and (explicitly) invoked in F_1 – there is also a *ratio* R** bearing on, but *not (explicitly) invoked* in F_1:

$$R^{**} = \text{If } \{H, J, K, L\}, \text{ then } C$$

(And, for completeness we can suppose that the instant case is a ~*h*-case.)[24] Let '*H*' = x is heavy.[25] If all this is so, we are in a position to move beyond the bare logical point, and see a live situation where R is modified by R*, and the same result is – or, would be – in fact reached in F_1 in virtue of R**: F_1 *is* an *h*- (and *j*-, *k*-, *l*-) case.[26]

It's worth closing our discussion of this compatibility constraint by considering how exactly it *would* be flouted. For any constraint to be a genuine normative constraint it must be floutable; and to understand it fully we need to see the (paradigmatic) circumstances under which it is flouted. So, returning to our basic structure, let '*G*' = x is environmentally-friendly (and assume that the instant case is a *g*-case).[27] Here, then, is a modification of R that flouts the compatibility constraint:

$$R^{***} = \text{If } \{G, J, K, L\}, \text{ then } {\sim}C$$

So, R*** is a narrowing of R by adding an element to its antecedent (*viz G*), but it is *incompatible* with the result in the precedent case: applying R*** to the precedent case mandates a contrary decision.[28]

Let's take stock: so it is indeed, as Lamond asserts, impermissible (on Raz's picture) to alter R by adding ~*G* or ~*H* or ~*I*. But this is the case not for the

[22] Recall: this weak constraint is entailed by the operative 'justify' constraint.

[23] The notion of multiple *ratios* bearing on a case is nothing especially novel; in fact it is the root of core accounts of reasoning by analogy in law. But, differently from our present structure, those explanations of analogical reasoning in law have two (or more) ratios *pointing in different directions* – that is, mandating different decisions.

[24] And to be perfectly complete, we can also assume that no *further ratio* bears on the instant case, such that the instant court can legitimately infer ~C from ~*A*, with respect to R**.

[25] Again, *H* can be rendered more definite by supposing it is satisfied by the object in question weighing over a certain fixed number of kgs.

[26] And we are now in a position to be explicit that the antecedent of a *ratio is* constituted by necessary elements of *a* sufficient set for its consequent.

[27] Again, *G* can be rendered more definite by supposing it is satisfied by the object in question's *carbon footprint* – ie emitting less than a fixed amount of CO_2. The parenthetical assumption is due to the unusualness of the modified rule's consequent (cf n 28).

[28] The comparative *strangeness* of R*** *qua* modification of R affirms the weakness of formal constraint (2): we need to consider rather outré cases (here: ~C as a consequent) to see constraint (2) flouted.

failure of *inconsistency* (constraint (2), as set out by *Lamond*), but rather for the failure of Raz's *justification* condition on distinguishing (constraint (2), as set out by *Raz*). And it is clear from the examples given by Raz[29] fleshing out what acts of distinguishing are permitted/forbidden by this justification constraint, that it means no more nor no less than that *the modified rule, when applied to the precedent case, has its antecedent satisfied thereby* (and its consequent is the result of the precedent case). There is nothing moralised about this bare, formal notion of justification. So far then, Lamond has micharacterised Raz's constraint. But that mischaracterisation has resulted in no misdiagnoses by Lamond with respect to what acts of distinguishing are permitted/forbidden according to Raz's picture. We might say Lamond has accurately represented Raz *extensionally*, but not *intensionally*.

It remains in this section to consider *M*. Lamond asserts 'R can be altered by adding some novel factor *M*'[30] (and assume that the instant case is a ~*m*-case). Let '*M*' = x is operational (where, by 'operational' I mean (capable of) being operated).[31] Now on the face of it, this modified rule:

$$R^{****} = \text{If } \{M, J, K, L\}, \text{then } C$$

does *not* justify the result in the precedent case. The facts on the record in the precedent case do not report it as an *m*-case. As we shall come to see (section II), if we were to look for a paradigmatic modification of R *permissible* on Raz's account, it would be the following already encountered rule (where, recall, '*H*' = x is heavy, and our assumption is that the instant case is a ~*h*-case):

$$R^{**} = \text{If } \{H, J, K, L\}, \text{then } C$$

(Assume, now, that R** is *not* a ratio – explicit or implicit – in the precedent case, P_1.[32]) That is, the record in the precedent case explicitly reported it as an *h*-case, albeit *H* did not feature in its *ratio*. Thus, applying R** – a narrowing of R – to the precedent case, we justify the result in the precedent case: the facts of F_1 satisfy the antecedent of R**. But modifying instead with R**** (Lamond's putative exemplar of a permissible act of distinguishing on Raz's view) does not straightforwardly generate the foregoing result. So, to say the least, Lamond's selection of R**** as a paradigmatic example of Razian distinguishing is *odd*. Despite its oddity, we can still profitably ask whether R**** is a permitted/forbidden modification of R on the Razian account. Raz remarks (with required

[29] Raz (n 2) 186–87.

[30] Lamond (n 1) 10.

[31] So if, as in our example, the object in question is a motorised vehicle, for it to be operational would be for it to have a motor (capable of) being operated. Thus, 'operationality' wouldn't be satisfied were the object to be a war memorial tank with a defunct motor. The antecedent of R is satisfied when a motorised vehicle is in the park, but this leaves open both (i) its motor's being incapable of being operated, and (ii) its motor's being capable of being operated but not in fact being operated.

[32] That R** was such a ratio was our prior assumption to generate multiple ratios (in the precedent case).

transposition) 'There is no record whether it was a case of [*M*] or of [~*M*] and the latter court is normally allowed the benefit of the doubt in such cases.'[33] Now to be sure, Raz's example involves a distinguishing court's moving from there being no public record in the precedent case whether *M* or ~*M*, to modifying the *ratio* in question by adding ~*M*. And there may seem something more kosher about moving from no record with respect to *M* in the precedent case, to asserting *M*'s *absence* (as Raz's example does),[34] than moving from no record with respect to *M* in the precedent case, to asserting M's *presence* (as Lamond's example implicitly does).

At this point we need to interrogate some underlying assumptions of Raz's (and Lamond's) account. To begin, note that 'x is operational' is clearly a permissible substituend for '*M*' for Raz (and Lamond). That fact – *viz* 'x is operational' – is, on any reckoning, a positive fact, containing, as it does, a positive property – *viz* operationality – being predicated of an object.[35] Now, given this, and given Raz (and Lamond) regularly invokes *negations* of (positive) facts in his account of legal reasoning, it is clear that Raz (and Lamond) does not (cf Horty)[36] restrict representations of legal reasoning to *positive factors*.

Now, even if core cases of an instant court taking advantage of the 'benefit of the doubt' point involve assuming the *non-presence* of *M* from no record with respect to *M*, our current example may be a case in which the opposite assumption is more rational, *viz* assuming the *presence* of *M* from no record with respect to *M*. Suppose the object in question is a fresh-off-the-lot Ford Fiesta. Even if there is no (explicit) information on the record bearing on the Ford Fiesta's operationality, it is likely rational to assume, at the very least, that the Ford Fiesta has a motor capable of being operated. Certainly, in this context, this seems more rational than any opposite assumption (cf Horty).[37]

Indeed, more generally, I think drawing any important distinction here between positive and negative factors would be misplaced. This can be readily seen by noting that we could instead have let '*M*' = (i) *it's not the case* that x is operational, or (ii) x is *un*operational[38] (and it now follows, on our prior

[33] Raz (n 2) 187.

[34] This is licensed by so-called *closed-world reasoning* (familiar in computer science): reasoning from 'the absence of positive information to the presence of negative information' (cf Horty (n 4) 26–27).

[35] Positive facts/properties (a category whose contrast-category is negative facts/properties) will undoubtedly be a category with borderline cases, but I operate here with paradigmatic cases.

[36] Horty ((n 4) 26–27) is explicit that his account does operate with this restriction, but in the next breath expresses (apt) concerns about whether such a restriction is sufficiently faithful to legal practice.

[37] ibid, 27.

[38] On (i) we would be letting '*M*' (an atomic variable) be the negation of a positive factor, while on (ii) '*M*' would be a fact predicating a negative property of an object. Either way, I take it '*M*' would *effectively be* a negative factor. Now one could make stipulations precluding these as substituends for '*M*': something to the effect that only negated variables can *function* as negative factors. But I think any such assumption would be ad hoc; moreover, Lamond's worked example (Lamond (n 1) 12) following his schema indicates he doesn't make any such assumption.

assumption, that the instant case becomes an *m*-case). Now, in the instant case, when a judge distinguishes by instead adding ~*M* to R we have the structural analogue of Raz's example: moving from no record with respect to *M* in the precedent case, to asserting *M*'s absence. But we achieved this structural identity without substantively altering Lamond's example. All just to say, any fishiness about Lamond's example (vis-à-vis Raz's) is ostensible rather than genuine.[39] Thus, in conclusion with respect to *M*, while Lamond's picking R**** (rather than, for example, R**) as a paradigmatic permissible rule modification for Raz is odd, it is not *clearly* mischaracterising Raz to say R**** is a permissible modification of R.

II. THE CORE OF THE REASONS ACCOUNT INVOLVES CONTROVERSIAL ASSUMPTIONS AND IS EXTENSIONALLY EQUIVALENT TO THE RULES ACCOUNT

Taking stock, we've so far established that Lamond *misrepresents* Raz's *formal constraints* on distinguishing, but no *clear* misrepresentation as to the *acts* of distinguishing that Raz's account permits/forbids has yet occurred. And in the process of establishing this we got a little clearer on Raz's account itself. It now falls to prosecute my second claim, *viz* the core of Lamond's reasons account of precedent is (extensionally) the same as Raz's rules account.

To prosecute this second claim, I need to reproduce the core of Lamond's reasons account[40] (an account putatively distinct from, and putatively an improvement on, the rules account):

> In the precedent case (P_1), the facts may be:
>
> $$F_1 = \{g_1, h_1, i_1, j_1, k_1, l_1\}$$
>
> and the grounds sufficient for the result may be:
>
> $$R_1 = \text{If } \{J, K, L\}, \text{ then } C$$
>
> If there was a case F_n with the facts:
>
> $$F_n = \{g_n, h_n, i_n, j_n, k_n, l_n\}$$
>
> then the court would regard *C* as the justified result in F_n as well … There are two aspects to what the court decided. The first is that the presence of features $\{J, K, L\}$ provided a sufficient reason to conclude *C*. The second is that the presence of the

[39] So, as a *formal* matter, I venture tentatively that the judge may, in the abstract, permissibly distinguish both by adding *M*, and by adding ~*M* (though not at the same time). Consistently with this, in the context of any particular case, one or the other may be more appropriate. And as noted in the main text, any objection to this finding drawing on a load-bearing distinction (such that there be) in this context between *positive* and *negative* fact(or)s/properties, would seem to me to be a red herring. Finally, exploring further the conditions under which this benefit of the doubt (presumably, a default rule) is cancelled would be an interesting route of enquiry.

[40] Lamond (n 1) 15–16.

> other features $\{G, H, I\}$ did not defeat the reason provided by $\{J, K, L\}$ … Take the case P_2 with the following facts:
>
> $$F_2 = \{\sim g_2, h_2, i_2, j_2, k_2, l_2, m_2\}$$
>
> In this case, unlike the precedent case, feature G is absent, but additional feature M is present … [T]he *later court* … must consider how strong the reason provided by $\{J, K, L\}$ for C really is and whether it is defeated by any reason(s) based on the absence of G and the presence of M.

Herein lies the core of Lamond's reasons account. (And Lamond is up front that a natural way of explicating it further draws upon Razian *protected reasons.*[41]) Clearly, Lamond's account can, here, be distilled into two claims. First, that 'features $\{J, K, L\}$ provided a sufficient reason to conclude C'. And second, that 'features $\{G, H, I\}$ did not defeat the reason provided by $\{J, K, L\}$'. And a Razian can – will – happily agree to all this.

The issue is what happens next. For Lamond, then – the (interim) conclusion he wants to get to – one can't add either $\sim G$, $\sim H$, or $\sim I$ (or any combination thereof) to the rule, R_1; for to do so would be to say, respectively, that G, H, or I *defeats* the reason provided by $\{J, K, L\}$. Lamond – **implicit assumption 1** – clearly assumes that *each member* of the set $\{G, H, I\}$ has (what I call) *uniform polarity.*[42] (That assumption continues.) If one doesn't assume this, we could only infer that *the set* $\{G, H, I\}$ doesn't defeat the reason provided by $\{J, K, L\}$, and couldn't assume that *each member* of the set doesn't defeat that reason. (I explain why this is so, with a worked example, shortly.) I take it, though this assumption isn't explicit in Lamond, it's necessary to get his project up and running. What, then, exactly is uniform polarity? It means that – in this instance – each member of the set $\{G, H, I\}$ *points in the same direction*, in the sense of favouring the same result in the case at hand, brought under this norm. Perhaps, better (to account for the possibility of *neutrality*,[43] it means that – in this instance – it's not the case that any members of the set $\{G, H, I\}$ *point in different directions*, in the sense of favouring a different result in the case at hand, brought under this norm.

Why, then, this assumption? Well, we can get to this answer by picking up on the (prima facie admissible) assignments of values to variables G, H, and I employed thus far: recall, 'G' = x is environmentally-friendly, 'H' = x is heavy, and 'I' = it's not the case that x is noisy. These were employed as values to make intuitive points along the way. But note that, plausibly, they are not all of uniform polarity. Whereas, plausibly, G and I point *against* a prohibitedness finding (suppose part of the rationale for the norm is 'environmental friendliness' and

[41] ibid, fn 31.
[42] Cf Horty ((n 4) 8), for whom uniform polarity is a defining feature of (legal) *reasons*.
[43] Cf n 48.

part is 'quietude'), plausibly, *H* points in *favour* thereof (suppose part of the rationale is 'safety', and suppose further there is an inverse relation between weight of vehicles and safety).[44] This fact – multiple underlying rationales for a rule – is commonplace. Now compatibly with the fact that *the set* {*G, H, I*} *doesn't* defeat the reason provided by {*J, K, L*}, it could be that *one or more members* of that set – here, plausibly, *G and/or I* – *does* defeat that reason. We can suppose that were *G and/or I* to have occurred *without H*, features {*J, K, L*} *would no longer* provide a sufficient reason to conclude *C*. And to get to the (initial) conclusion that *no member* of the set defeats the reason in question, from the true premise that *the set* doesn't, we need **implicit assumption 1** – the uniform polarity assumption: with, and only with, it, it a fortiori follows that no member of the set defeats from the (true) premise that the set doesn't defeat.

Now that **implicit assumption** 1 is clear, and its role in getting Lamond's project off the ground is apparent, we need to note just how big – nay, unsustainable – it is *qua* assumption. For one thing, it would preclude the (prima facie admissible) assignments of values to variables *G*, *H*, and *I* I've employed thus far: plausibly they *aren't* of uniform polarity. More generally, it simply cannot be true that the facts on the record yet not mentioned in *rationes* of judgments are, as a general matter, of uniform polarity. No account of precedent, therefore, should make such an assumption.[45]

But let us suppose – with the help of **implicit assumption 1** – Lamond gets to the proposition that neither the set {*G, H, I*}, nor any of its members, defeats the reason provided by {*J, K, L*} to conclude *C*. To now get to the (interim) conclusion he wants to get to – *viz* one can't add either ~*G*, ~*H*, or ~*I* (or any combination thereof) to the rule, R_1 – one needs a further **implicit assumption 2.** That is the assumption of *invariant polarity*: *viz within the scope of a particular legal norm*,[46] facts necessarily favour one side (or the other).[47] I take it that Lamond needs a general, or universal, assumption, such as **implicit assumption 2**, to ensure polarity doesn't *switch* between the time of P_1 and the time of P_2. The basic point is that for Lamond to get to conclusions about permissible uses of (~)*G*, (~)*H*, or (~)*I* in *subsequent cases* from the role they play in P_1, their role – in particular, their polarity – cannot vary across time.

[44] The foregoing suppositions are contingent; let's grant them for now, before coming back to interrogate reasons not to make the uniform polarity assumption (indeed, their very contingency is part of the issue).

[45] We'll shortly see how Raz's account doesn't. Note also that Horty ((n 4) 8), for whom uniform polarity is a defining feature of (legal) *reasons*, assuredly *does not* make **implicit assumption 1**: for him, the polarity of such facts not mentioned in *rationes* of judgments need not – typically, will not – be uniform (cf n 42).

[46] The assumption of invariant polarity needs *this* restriction: it's not even remotely plausibly the case that invariant polarity could obtain absent this restriction. Regrettably this restriction is rarely made explicit.

[47] Or neither. Strictly it requires a further, distinct assumption to rule out facts favouring neither side, to which I shall come shortly (n 48).

Now that **implicit assumption** 2 is clear, and its role in keeping Lamond's project off the ground is apparent, we need to note just how big – potentially, unsustainable – *it* is *qua* assumption. It would seem to rule out the following (piggy-backing on our use of *G* as environmentally-friendly, above). Suppose at the time of P_1, part of the rationale of the rule in question was 'environmental friendliness', such that the presence of *G* in P_1 counted *against* a prohibitedness finding, but not *sufficiently so* to defeat the reason for prohibiting. A way of making this real is to suppose that, while environmental issues were part of the rationale for the 'no motorised vehicles in the park' rule, the court in P_1 wanted to satisfy the environmentally-friendly rationale *indirectly*, and not via a clear environmentally-friendly criterion in the *ratio* itself. This is all perfectly plausible. But now suppose that, between P_1 and P_2, the 'environmental friendliness' rationale *disappears* (leaving only the 'safety' and 'quietude' rationales). It is not, now, that being environmentally-friendly counts *in favour* of prohibition; it is simply *neutral* thereon.[48] To shift from favouring prohibitedness to being neutral is a shift in polarity – a shift from having one to having none.[49] It would seem, then, that **implicit assumption 2** counterintuitively precludes the natural foregoing shift (and the point generalises).[50] No account of precedent, therefore, should make such an assumption.[51]

To complete matters on the core of Lamond's account of precedent (a final conclusion), we should note that one can, *as a formal matter*, for Lamond, add *G* and ~*M* (in the sense that a subsequent court, P_2, can, if it assesses the reasons thus and so, distinguish on these bases). Now, given the natural substituends for *G* and *M*, which we utilised above to make certain points, any act of distinguishing on the basis of *G* (environmentally-friendly) and ~*M* (unoperational) would be substantively odd (check for yourselves), but the point remains that Lamond's formal machinery would permit any such act of distinguishing (albeit it might

[48] One might – Horty ((n 4) 4–5) would – object to this point by relying on a further assumption that legal fact(or)s necessarily favour one side or the other, *and are not neutral thereon*. I don't know where Lamond exactly stands here, but this strikes me as an unwarranted assumption. In our example here, the court in P_2 may wish to mention 'environmental friendliness' simply to reflect its change in status from having a polarity to being neutral.

[49] A more paradigmatic, and sweeping, shift in polarity would be a shift from pointing in one direction to pointing in the other direction (cf n 48). But it is hard to play this out realistically with our present worked example. An upshot of all this is the following (on my taxonomy): (i) the *uniform* polarity assumption is *not* infringed by one fact with one polarity and one fact with neutrality (but is rather infringed by one fact with one polarity and one fact with another); (ii) the *invariant* polarity assumption, meanwhile, *is* infringed by one fact shifting from one polarity to neutrality. The combination of (i) and (ii) is a little awkward, but is necessitated by my not coming up with a realistic example of one fact shifting from one polarity to another across time.

[50] The precise mechanics of how such a shift in rationale occurs (eg what *determines* it?) can be safely bracketed here; it just needs to be natural, aka plausible. Moreover, the foregoing traded on what I take to be a natural distinction between an *enduring* legal rule and *unenduring* rationales for said rule. Likewise, this can be prosecuted without committing on precise individuation conditions for rules and rationales.

[51] We'll shortly see how Raz's account doesn't. Note also that Horty ((n 4) 4–5) *does* (explicitly) make **implicit assumption 2.**

be a bad such act). Given P_1's conclusion that *G* doesn't defeat the reasons for prohibition provided by {*J*, *K*, *L*}, and given P_1's silence with respect to *M*,[52] it is open to the court in P_2 to add *G* and/or ~*M* to the rule or reason that {*J*, *K*, *L*} provides for the conclusion *C*.

In sum, then, the foregoing sets out the core of Lamond's theory of precedent (before getting to his extension to account for the development of legal doctrines). We might think of the end point as a kind of dilemma for Lamond. Either he avoids making the foregoing (**implicit**) **assumptions**, at the (severe) cost of rendering his core inferential moves invalid; or he secures their validity by means of some rather questionable (**implicit**) **assumptions**.

In line with this, I want to now show that Lamond's reasons account is *extensionally equivalent* to Raz's rules account, in the sense that what is formally permitted/forbidden for the subsequent judge seeking to distinguish seems identical for Lamond and Raz. Moreover, Raz reaches the same point as Lamond without making any of the foregoing questionable assumptions. In a sense, then, the core of Lamond's reasons account is nothing new; and, moreover, it has been proposed before – Raz's rules account – without Lamond's baggage.

We have already, in section I, done the hard yards in seeing how Raz's account *forbids* the subsequent judge from distinguishing on the basis of ~*G*, ~*H*, and ~*I*. And we noted that Raz's account forbids such a move not for the *inconsistency* reasons canvassed by Lamond, but rather because any such act would fail to *justify* the result in the precedent case.[53] In the context of what is forbidden, it remains to show how Raz gets to this result *without making* Lamond's (**implicit**) **assumptions**. A way into this is to recapitulate that Raz can happily agree with Lamond that, in our running example, 'features {*G*, *H*, *I*} did not defeat the reason provided by {*J*, *K*, *L*}'. But at this point Raz would stop happily agreeing with Lamond's reasoning. To reach the conclusion that the subsequent judge is forbidden from distinguishing on the basis of ~*G*, ~*H*, and ~*I*, Raz has no need of **implicit assumption 1** (that is, he, happily, need not infer from *the set's* failure to defeat that *none of its members* defeats, and thus has no need to invoke uniform polarity); and has no need of **implicit assumption 2** (that is, he, happily, need not preclude *shifting rationales*, and thus has no need to invoke invariant polarity). All Raz needs is the simple, bare formal fact that none of these putative acts of distinguishing *justifies* the finding in the precedent case (in his formal sense of justify, ie the facts of the precedent case don't satisfy the antecedent of the modified rule).

It remains to show that Raz's account, as with Lamond's, *permits* distinguishing on the basis of *G* and ~*M*.[54] *G* is perfectly straightforward, as a narrowing of

[52] See our discussion above, with respect to Raz, of the subsequent court's benefit of the doubt concerning unmentioned fact(or)s when interpreting the precedent case. Lamond is here piggybacking on this Razian point.

[53] Recall, justification entails consistency; but the converse entailment doesn't hold.

[54] Albeit, we've noted, any such acts would be substantively odd, given our substituends therefor.

the precedent rule, and a narrowing that would justify the result in the precedent case. ~*M* is somewhat more interesting. We already saw in section I how Raz's account, plausibly, permits distinguishing on the basis of *M*. Interestingly, his account would seem, as a formal and *a priori* matter, to permit distinguishing on the basis of both *M and* ~*M* (though not simultaneously). As a *formal* matter, and even more straightforwardly than the permissibility of distinguishing on the basis of *M*, the subsequent court, on Raz's account, is permitted to infer from the *absence* of any record in the precedent case whether *M* or ~*M*, that ~*M*. Once the subsequent court does that, distinguishing on the basis of ~*M* becomes straightforward.

Now, establishing the *foregoing* extensional equivalences between Lamond's reasons account and Raz's rules account is hardly to establish equivalence *across the board*. But it is enough to entitle me to venture the following claim: the accounts *are* extensionally equivalent. (I can simply invite counterexamples, but I'm fairly confident there are none.) Moreover, Raz reaches his conclusions based on none of Lamond's required and controversial **implicit assumptions**. Raz's rules account is therefore, to this extent, to be favoured over Lamond's reasons account.

III. LAMOND'S PROBLEMATIC EXTENSION TO DOCTRINE

Our last task is to show that Lamond's extension beyond the foregoing core – to account for the development of legal doctrine – is, while provocative, ultimately also unsuccessful. (And it is to be noted that Raz himself devotes no energies to accounting for legal doctrine.) Here is Lamond's extension in a nutshell:

> After cases P_1 to P_{10}, the legal position may be expressed in the following way:
>
> $$\text{Doctrine} = \text{If } \{J, K, L, {\sim}M, {\sim}N\}, \text{ then } C$$
>
> while the facts considered insufficient to defeat the doctrine now amount to:
>
> $$\{a, b, c, d, e, f, g, h, i, o, p, q, r, s\}$$
>
> … If the court decides in case P_{12} that the presence of feature *U* distinguishes the case, then the doctrine could be restated as follows:
>
> $$\text{Doctrine}^* = \text{If } \{J, K, L, {\sim}M, {\sim}N, {\sim}U\}, \text{ then } C$$
>
> Where $P_{12} = \{j_{12}, k_{12}, l_{12}, {\sim}m_{12}, {\sim}n_{12}, u_{12}\}$[55]

The basic idea, then, is clear enough. As a series of cases accretes within a body of law, with precedent cases being *followed*, more and more facts are added – in a *linear* and *aggregative* fashion – to the set of facts insufficient to defeat the developing doctrinal rule. And as a result of this *fewer facts* are a permissible

[55] Lamond (n 1) 20ff.

basis on which to distinguish any subsequent case. One of the especially interesting features of Lamond's account is how it brings out that *following* (and not just *distinguishing*) a precedent case involves a *change* in the law. This account, then, is not only clear, but also fairly appealing as a picture of the way in which legal doctrine develops.

In critiquing Lamond's extension to legal doctrine, we can be refreshingly brief, as John Horty has, in essence, beaten us to it.[56] As I've noted, doctrine, for Lamond, develops in a linear, aggregative manner. So, result R_1 gave us that the set $\{G, H, I\}$ didn't defeat the rule in R_1. Between R_1 and P_{10}, we could have had a case not involving (a) the set $\{G, H, I\}$, but involving (for the first time) (b) the set $\{O, P\}$, and which followed the doctrine. As I understand it, Lamond's account needs us to be able to legitimately infer from this that the set $\{G, H, I, O, P\}$ doesn't defeat the rule in R_1 (and, moreover, that no construction of a set out of a subset of (a) and a subset of (b) defeats that rule). I simply (like Horty) don't see how this can be done. Suppose the set $\{G, H, I, O, P\}$ now arises (for the first time) *in combination*. None of Lamond's machinery (even granting his **implicit assumptions**)[57] prevents a finding that that set, *in the aggregate*, defeats the rule in R_1.

IV. CONCLUSION

So, Lamond's account ultimately fails. With Horty's help, we've just seen that the extension to legal doctrine is inadequate. But there is a deeper problem at source. Only by making some questionable assumptions – and thereby holding himself hostage to several fortunes – does Lamond's project get off the ground. And Raz's seminal rules account can deliver the same verdicts as Lamond's reasons core with no such assumptions. No reasons exist to prefer the reasons account of precedent (over Raz's).[58]

[56] Horty (n 4) fn 22.

[57] Given we're granting these assumptions, we cannot redeploy the substitutends for these variables from our running toy example (one of the points of the selection of these substituends was to question Lamond's assumptions). But we don't really need any toy example to see the rudimentary operative point here.

[58] It would be an interesting next step to see whether the bare, formal machinery of Raz's account *could* be extended to account for the development of bodies of legal doctrine. But that is a task for another day.

6

Revisiting the Reasons Account of Precedent

GRANT LAMOND*

THE DOCTRINE OF precedent is central to the operation of case law in the common law. The doctrine holds that courts are bound by the decisions of courts higher in the judicial hierarchy, and usually also by their own earlier decisions. Precedents are fundamental to the constitution of case law, and courts and lawyers cite and rely on precedents in establishing the law on some topic. This is not to say that precedent is all there is to case law. Cases can also serve as persuasive authorities; they can play a role in establishing legal principles; and they form the basis for the analogical extension of the law. But the role of cases as binding precedents is the most fundamental feature of the common law.

How should the operation of precedent in the common law be understood? The standard account, which represents both a lawyerly and theoretical orthodoxy, is that precedents operate by creating rules that bind later courts. Those rules are to be found in the rationes decidendi of decided cases – the rulings authoritatively established in the judgments of the case. Courts create rules in deciding cases, therefore, just as legislatures create rules by enacting statutes. The methods for creating rules differ, but the outcome is nonetheless the same. This view, which may be described as the rule-based view of precedent, has been defended in a number of forms.[1]

Some years ago I argued that the rule view of precedent was inadequate and could not happily account for the practice of distinguishing, which is a central

* I would like to thank Adam Rigoni, John Horty and Mark McBride for their helpful comments on an earlier draft of this chapter. I would also like to thank Mark McBride for suggesting I return to this topic and reconsider my earlier views.

[1] See eg Neil MacCormick (1994) *Legal Reasoning and Legal Theory*, rev edn, Oxford: Oxford University Press, 213–28; Joseph Raz (2011) *The Authority of Law*, rev edn, Oxford: Oxford University Press, ch 10; Fred Schauer (1991) *Playing by the Rules*, Oxford: Oxford University Press, 181–87; Larry Alexander (1989) 'Constrained by Precedent' *Southern California Law Review* 63: 1–64.

aspect of case law reasoning.[2] The practice of distinguishing permits later courts to decline to follow a precedent, even though the ratio of the precedent applies quite clearly to the case at hand. Courts can decline to follow a precedent on the basis that there is a material difference between the facts of the current case and the facts of the precedent case, a material difference that supports a different outcome in the current case. What is more, distinguishing can be done by courts *lower* in the judiciary hierarchy, that is, courts that have no power to overrule the decisions they are distinguishing. Instead of understanding precedents as creating rules in their rationes, I proposed that precedents should be understood instead as decisions on the balance of reasons. Courts make decisions about the balance of reasons on the facts before them. These decisions have an impact on later courts not because they lay down rules to be applied in later cases, but because they establish that certain facts provide sufficient reason for an outcome. Where the same types of facts are present in a later case, the later court must consider whether there are any factual differences that provide a basis for defeating the decision in the earlier case. This view I called the 'reasons' view of precedent. It involves case-by-case reasoning, rather than rule-based reasoning.

The proposal to understand precedents in terms of reasons has been developed in a modified form by some theorists.[3] Others have defended the rule-based view of precedent against it.[4] In this chapter I revisit the original proposal and consider whether it requires modification or rejection in light of the criticisms of others. My conclusion will be that some aspects of my original account were over-simplified and require revision. But I will argue that it provides a better understanding of precedent than rule-based accounts, and that the form in which it was originally presented is essentially sound, and has certain advantages over other versions that have been developed from it.

I. THE REASONS ACCOUNT OF PRECEDENT

As noted, the reasons account of precedent grew out of a dissatisfaction with the rule-based account of precedent, in particular with the way in which the rule-based account dealt with the practice of distinguishing. Rules are, of course, an important feature of institutionalised decision making. It is common for organisations to govern their own operations and the behaviour of their members through a system of rules, and to establish bodies to adjudicate on breaches of those rules. Rules are normally chosen in preference to simply deciding each

[2] Grant Lamond (2005) 'Do Precedents Create Rules?' *Legal Theory* 11: 1–26.

[3] eg John Horty (2011) 'Rules and Reasons in the Theory of Precedent' *Legal Theory* 17: 1–33; John Horty (2015) 'Constraint and Freedom in the Common Law' *Philosophers' Imprint* 15: 1–27; Adam Rigoni (2015) 'An improved factor based approach to precedential constraint' *Artificial Intelligence and Law* 23: 133–160; and Rob Mullins (2020) 'Protected Reasons and Precedential Constraint' *Legal Theory* 26: 40–61.

[4] eg Larry Alexander and Emily Sherwin (2008) *Demystifying Legal Reasoning*, Cambridge: Cambridge University Press, chs 2–4.

question on its merits for a number of reasons. Given human limitations – limitations of information, reasoning and partiality – rules, at least if they are well formed, have a number of advantages. They can be easier to follow and apply than assessing each situation on its full merits, and leave less scope for disagreement over what result should be reached in a particular situation. As a result, it is easier for members of an organisation (including decision makers themselves) to rely on rules for the purposes of guiding their conduct. It is also easier to determine if the rules have been violated, and for members of an organisation to be assured that the rules have been applied consistently by decision-making bodies. Of course rules per se do not guarantee these advantages, since a system of rules can be unduly complex, vague, internally inconsistent or difficult to understand. Nor do rules, even if they are well formed, guarantee better outcomes overall than deciding each issue on its merits: that depends on how well the rules serve the underlying values and interests at stake. Rules involve making decisions on the basis of a selection of features (including proxy features), rather than on the basis of all of the relevant considerations. So rules tend to be imperfect – both under- and over-inclusive of cases that merit the outcome determined by the rule. A rule that produces too many sub-optimal outcomes may be worse than not using rules at all to determine particular issues.[5]

From this rule-based perspective, it is difficult to discern the rationale for the doctrine of distinguishing in the common law. The doctrine can be represented in the following way. Let us say we have an initial case, P1, with following facts:

$$\mathrm{F1} = \{g_1, h_1, i_1, j_1, k_1, l_1\}$$

where the court decides that the general features J, K and L warrant the outcome S, that is, that the ruling (or ratio) in P1 is:

$$\mathrm{R1} = \text{If } \{J, K, L\} \text{ then } S$$ [6]

According to the rule model of precedent, R1 lays down a general rule that is binding on later courts. The doctrine of distinguishing, however, permits a later court in P2 to decline to follow R1, even when R1 is applicable. Let us say that the facts in P2 are:

$$\mathrm{F2} = \{g_2, h_2, i_2, j_2, k_2, l_2, m_2\}$$

R1 applies straightforwardly to these facts, since features $\{J, K, L\}$ are present. But P2 can distinguish R1 by pointing to the presence of feature M in P2 (and the absence of M in P1), and conclude:

$$\mathrm{R2} = \text{If } \{J, K, L, M\} \text{ then } {\sim}S$$

[5] See eg Schauer (n 1) ch 5; Alexander and Sherwin (n 4) ch 1.

[6] These symbols are used for the sake of clarity, not to represent the claims in any type of logic. The upper-case letters stand for general features, whereas lower-case letters stand for particulars that satisfy the general feature (so *J* stands for some general features, whereas *j* stands for a particular with that feature). In addition, the symbols can be used to cover both a 'positive' state of affairs and a 'negative' state: for example, in representing the doctrine that a bona fide purchaser for value

That is, given the presence of the novel feature *M*, the court can find that it is not the case that *S*. Since P1 was considered by the court in P2, the decision in P2 has the further implication that the legal doctrine based on R1 and R2 is now:

$$\text{Doctrine } \{\text{R1, R2}\} = \text{If } \{J, K, L, \sim M\} \text{ then } S$$

The practice of distinguishing as it is normally understood is subject to at least two constraints:

(a) it can only depart from the result in R1 by adding an *additional* feature to the ratio (here *M*), thereby narrowing the scope of R1; and
(b) the developed doctrine {R1, R2} must still be applicable to P1 and justify the same result that was originally reached in that case (ie *S*).

There are two common ways in which a later court may distinguish an earlier precedent. The first is where there are additional facts present in the later case that were not present in the precedent case. For instance, the English doctrine of duress in criminal law held that a defendant could rely on threats of death or serious injury to avoid liability for the commission of some crimes.[7] A later case, however, held that where the defendant had knowingly joined a violent criminal gang, they had no defence of duress when they committed a crime following threats by members of that gang.[8] The earlier precedents had said nothing about joining a violent criminal gang, but the later court was able to distinguish those precedents. The second common way in which distinguishing occurs is where some fact in the earlier case that was not included in the ratio is relied upon by a later court. For instance, a precedent might hold that a party who has entered a contract relying on an innocent misrepresentation from the other party can avoid the contract. A later case might involve similar facts, except in this case it is accepted that the party who relied on the misrepresentation would have entered the contract even had the misrepresentation not been made. The misrepresentation was one factor, but not a decisive factor in entering the contract. Here the later court might hold that where the misrepresentation has not made a causal difference to the formation of the contract, the contract is not voidable. In the earlier case, by contrast, the misrepresentation *did* make a causal difference, so the result in the precedent is still supported by new decision.

The practice of distinguishing is puzzling from the rule perspective. It sacrifices many of the advantages of rule-based decision making, because the rule is always subject to revision at the time of application by the later court. Someone trying to guide themselves by a precedent rule must decide whether the rule will be distinguished in their case – a far more difficult task than ascertaining

without notice can acquire good legal title to trust property, the element of 'without notice' can be represented as *J*, and the presence of notice can be represented as ~*J*.

[7] *Graham* (1982) 74 Cr App R 235 (CA), endorsed by the House of Lords in *Howe* [1987] AC 417.

[8] *Sharp* [1987] 1 QB 853 (CA).

whether the rule simply applies to their case. And to carry out that task they need to know not just the rule in the precedent case but the full facts, since those facts will limit the possibility of distinguishing. The practice of distinguishing is also puzzling because the way in which it is constrained by the facts in the precedent case makes its operation quite haphazard. A later court cannot distinguish on the basis of a fact that was also present in the precedent case, even though the precedent court did not regard that fact as forming part of the ratio, that is, did not regard it as crucial to the decision. Why give later courts a limited power of just this kind to amend earlier rules? Would it not be better to simply dispense with distinguishing, and restrict the power of amendment to those courts with the power to overrule?[9]

It was worries of this kind about the rule model of precedent that suggested that precedents do not create rules of the kind that statutes create, and that precedent should not be thought simply as an alternative means of creating legal rules.[10] This led to the development of the *reasons* model of precedent as an alternative to the rule account. The reasons model starts from the same basic outline as above. So let us say that precedent P1 has the facts:

$$F1 = \{g_1, h_1, i_1, j_1, k_1, l_1\}$$

The ratio of the decision is:

$$R1 = \text{If } \{J, K, L\} \text{ then } S$$

How should we understand this? We should understand it as a form of *case-by-case* decision making, rather than rule-based decision making.[11] There are a number of important aspects to this:[12]

1. First of all, $\{J, K, L\}$ are the features of the case that the court believed provided a *sufficient reason* for the outcome S. So $\{J, K, L\}$ provide a justification for holding S. For example, a misrepresentation relied upon by a party in entering a contract provides a justification for the contract's being voidable by that party.
2. The other features of the case – $\{G, H, I\}$ – are also important because they were not regarded as providing grounds *defeating* the justification for S. For instance, perhaps the party making the misrepresentation honestly believed it was true, or had no reasonable way of discovering that it was not true. Nonetheless the court might decide that the sufficient reason for S provided by $\{J, K, L\}$ was not defeated by $\{G, H, I\}$. The court concluded, therefore, that on the balance of reasons S was justified.

[9] This is indeed the one of the conclusions that Alexander and Sherwin reach in defending a strict rule-based view of precedent: (n 4) 83–87 and 122–24.
[10] For a more detailed analysis of distinguishing, see Lamond (n 2) 9–15.
[11] ibid, 1–4.
[12] For more detail, see ibid, 15–24.

3. The result in the case is *context dependent*, that is, it settles the dispute between the plaintiff and the defendant on the facts of the case before the court (ie $\{g_1, h_1, i_1, j_1, k_1, l_1\}$). It does not purport, therefore, to settle the outcome of disputes that involve different sets of facts.
4. On the other hand, later courts, if they are not entitled to overrule P1, must treat it as *correctly decided* on its facts. So later courts are bound to accept that $\{J, K, L\}$ *does* provide sufficient reason for *S*, and that $\{G, H, I\}$ does *not* provide any grounds defeating that reason. This is the cornerstone of the common law doctrine of precedent. Later courts, unless they are entitled to overrule a precedent, must treat it as correctly decided on its facts.
5. Where the facts of a later case fall under the ratio of P1, that is, where features $\{J, K, L\}$ are present, the later court is under a disjunctive obligation to *either* follow *or* distinguish P1. So if in P2 the facts are:

$$F2 = \{g_2, h_2, i_2, j_2, k_2, l_2, m_2\}$$

   the court must consider P1, and must either follow P1 and conclude *S*, or distinguish P1 in order to conclude ~*S*.
6. For the court in P2 to distinguish P1, it must adduce some difference in the facts between P1 and P2 that the court assesses *does* defeat the reason provided by the ratio in P1 (ie that does defeat the sufficient reason provided by $\{J, K, L\}$). So in the case of duress, the later court held that knowingly joining a violent criminal gang did defeat the reasons for allowing a defendant who acted under duress to be relieved of criminal liability.
7. In addition, to distinguish the decision in P1, the court in P2 must rely on some difference in the facts that either:

   (a) provides a type of defeating consideration different from that provided by $\{G, H, I\}$; or
   (b) provides a better defeating consideration of the same type as $\{G, H, I\}$.

8. Where a later court in P2 distinguishes a precedent P1, it further elaborates the legal doctrine based on P1, so that the doctrine can now be stated, in part, as:

$$\text{Doctrine } \{P1, P2\} = \text{If } \{J, K, L, \sim M\} \text{ then } S$$

9. Where a later court P3 *declines* to distinguish P1, that is, where P3 *follows* P1, it also elaborates the legal doctrine based on P1, although it does not alter the positive part of the doctrine based on the ratio of P1. Decisions like P3 that follow P1 alter the law by adding to the features that do *not* defeat the reason provided by the doctrine. Let us say that the facts of P3 are:

$$F3 = \{g_3, h_3, i_3, j_3, k_3, l_3, n_3\}$$

and that P3 declines to distinguish P1 on the basis of feature *N*. Then after P1, P2 and P3 the doctrine can be represented as:

Doctrine {P1, P2, P3} =

(a) If {*J*, *K*, *L*, ~*M*} then *S*

and

(b) {*G*, *H*, *I*, *N*} do not defeat {*J*, *K*, *L*, ~*M*}

10. So a legal doctrine emerges from a series of cases that either follow or distinguish a precedent. The doctrine is altered both by cases that distinguish the precedent *and* by cases that follow the precedent, though it is altered in different ways by each.

The reasons account of precedent has a number of advantages over the rule-based account. To begin with, it makes better sense of the format and content of common law judgments. Judgments have a standard set of elements. They provide a detailed account of the facts of the case and identify the legal issue(s) that are in dispute between the parties and that would affect the outcome of the case. Judgments will cite any relevant earlier authorities that bear on the issue in dispute, and will use those authorities, as well as considerations about the merits of the dispute, to provide a justification for the resolution of the issue(s). It will then apply that resolution to the case before it, and hold for the plaintiff or the defendant.[13] The discursive recitation of facts in common law judgments is necessary in order for future courts to understand the nature of the dispute before the court, and the considerations that bore on either side. The facts establish the context for the court's resolution of the issue(s), and are crucial for later courts to understand the significance of the decision. The citation of earlier authorities, particularly any binding precedents, is necessary for the court to justify either following or distinguishing those precedents.

In addition to making better sense of the format of common law judgments, the reason-based account of precedent integrates distinguishing into the doctrine of precedent, rather than seeing it as an exception to it. Precedents are not laying down general rules to be followed in later cases but settling the basis on which later courts must decide whether to follow or distinguish the precedent. There is no presumption in favour of following, but simply a decision to be made as to whether the facts in the later case merit following or distinguishing.

Finally, the reason-based account makes sense of the distinction between the ratio decidendi of a case, and obiter dicta. Only some parts of a judgment are binding on later courts, namely those that were necessary to resolve the issue(s)

[13] The parties are described in different terminology in criminal cases and some public law cases, but the basic points still hold.

in dispute before the court. The court may choose to make other statements about the law, and about how certain questions of law should be answered, but these statements are not binding on later courts (though they may have important persuasive influence[14]). Why is this? If the precedent is laying down rules to guide future courts, why should a court not take the opportunity to resolve other questions that have been raised or argued before it for the benefit of later courts? Because the court is settling a particular issue on the facts before it, not issuing general rules. The settlement of that dispute binds later courts, whereas observations about other issues lack a determinate context for being resolved.

The reason-based account of precedent, then, conceptualises precedents as decisions on the balance of reasons in the context before the court. The decision constrains future courts because (absent the legal power to overrule the precedent) they are obliged to treat the case as correctly decided, that is, to treat the ratio as laying down facts that provide a sufficient justification for the outcome *S*, and to treat the other facts in the case as not providing considerations that defeat the justification for *S*.

II. EVALUATING THE REASONS ACCOUNT

There are a number of criticisms that have been raised, directly or indirectly, against the reason-based account. In the remainder of this chapter I will consider some of the most significant criticisms, and explain where I think the account needs to be revised, but also why it retains advantages over the both the rule-based account and other reason-based accounts that have been developed from it. I will divide the discussion into three broad sections, dealing in turn with: (i) whether the reason-based account is a version of the rule-based account, rather than an alternative to it; (ii) whether the original account is over-simplified and in need of revision; and (iii) whether it would be better to cast the reasons model of precedents in terms of factors rather than facts.

A. Is the Reason-Based Account of Precedent Simply a Version of the Rule-Based Approach?

One key argument for thinking that the reason-based account is a version of the rule-based account of precedent grows out of work on defeasible rules in non-monotonic logic. In monotonic logic, a rule is a universal, and if it applies to a state of affairs it determines the outcome on those facts. Rules in monotonic logic can be amended, or changed, by adding new exceptions or conditions

[14] On this role, see Grant Lamond (2010) 'Persuasive Authority in the Law' *Harvard Review of Philosophy* 17: 16–35.

to them, but this in essence involves replacing the original rule with a new rule. The new rule, just as much as the original rule, determines the result of cases that fall within its scope. Hence the general view among rule-based theorists that distinguishing amounts to a legal power to amend the ratio of the precedent case at the moment of application of the precedent. But common lawyers do not conceptualise the practice of distinguishing as an exercise in *replacing* an original rule with a new rule. They see it, instead, as a process of determining that the original decision does not, after all, control the outcome on the new set of facts, despite those facts falling within the scope of the ratio of the original decision.

In non-monotonic logic, on the other hand, rules can be defeasible.[15] Two rules can apply to the same fact situation, and one rule can override the other rule in that situation. To take our earlier cases, P1 and P2. On this approach, P1 holds:

$$\text{R1} = \text{If } \{J, K, L\} \text{ then } S$$

while P2 holds:

$$\text{R2} = \text{If } \{J, K, L, M\} \text{ then } {\sim}S$$

Obviously, any case to which R2 applies will also be one to which R1 applies, and the two rules support conflicting outcomes. But this conflict between R1 and R2 can be resolved by treating R2 as defeating, or overriding, R1. Wherever a case has facts $\{j_n, k_n, l_n, m_n\}$ R2 overrides R1 and determines the result of the case. But where a case has facts $\{j_n, k_n, l_n, {\sim}m_n\}$ then R2 is inapplicable, and the case will be determined by R1. On this approach, what is happening in cases of distinguishing is that later courts such as P2 are laying down new rules that defeat the rule in P1 (and are themselves subject to being defeated by decisions in later cases). It is not that the original rule is amended or replaced; rather, it is superseded in certain circumstances by another rule. This provides a more satisfactory analysis of the practice of distinguishing.[16]

Although the account of precedents in terms of defeasible rules has certain merits, there are two main reasons for resisting this assimilation of the reason-based account to the rule-based account. The first concerns the way that a defeasible rule account conceptualises common law doctrine. According to this approach, common law doctrines consists in a series of rules, each in turn defeating an earlier rule. So after three cases, there are three rules. The second precedent may distinguish the first, and the third may in turn distinguish the

[15] For discussion, see Katharina Stevens (2018) 'Reasoning by Precedent – Between Rules and Analogies' *Legal Theory* 24: 216–254, 226–30. A more complex account of distinguishing in terms of default rules can be found in Horty (2011) (n 3) 6, 7, 11–12, 17–19.

[16] Such an approach will also provide an account of when and why R2 defeats R1. My concern is not with that dimension of the approach but with the use of rules in non-monotonic logic.

second (or distinguish the first in a way different from the way that the second distinguished it). From this perspective, the common law consists of an elaborate and ever-expanding system of rules, adding more and more complexity as more cases are decided. But this is not the way in which common lawyers understand common law doctrine. Common law doctrine is cumulative, that is, it grows out of a series of cases but does so by adding to a more detailed account of a doctrine, not by amassing a series of rules. In addition, common lawyers regard the ratio of a precedent as representing an assessment by the court that those facts provide a sufficient reason supporting a particular conclusion (eg that the defendant cannot rely on duress, or that the contract is voidable by the innocent party). So it is not just a logical relationship between the ratio and the conclusion, it is a substantive reason-based relationship. Finally, legal doctrine is not just constituted by rationes: as argued above, it is also constituted by the facts that have been held *not* to defeat the reasons provided by the ratio. This is particularly clear in the case of later decisions that *follow* an existing precedent. Here, there is no additional rule defeating an earlier rule: instead, there are additional features that do not defeat the original rule. Now it may of course be useful for some purposes to represent precedent in terms of defeasible rules, but it is not the most perspicuous way to capture how common lawyers think about precedent.[17]

The second main reason for resisting the assimilation of the reason-based account of precedent to a rule-based account concerns the relationship between precedent and statute.[18] The language of 'rules' seems entirely apt in the case of legislation, since legislation is (normally) aimed at establishing general rules to govern some area of conduct.[19] The idea that law is a system of rules has a long and influential pedigree.[20] But one of the main points of the reason-based view of precedent is to emphasise how *unalike* precedent is to statute, that is, how it is a process of case-by-case decision making. There are a number of key differences. One is that statutes are presented in a canonical verbal formulation, and the way in which it is formulated in a particular statute is meant to make a difference to the law created by that statute. Precedents, although presented in a verbal form, do not attach such significance to the particular wording of the ratio. Indeed, courts rarely enunciate their rationes in an easily identifiable

[17] Of course sophisticated accounts of precedent in terms of default rules do address some of these further issues. But to the extent that they do, their classification as 'rule'-*based* theories seems unhelpful.

[18] This was the gravamen of the argument that precedents do not create rules: they do not create rules akin to statutory rules: see Lamond (n 2) 6–9, 19–20.

[19] There are of course numerous exceptions, where legislation is designed to deal with a one-off situation. But legislation is standardly used to lay down general rules.

[20] HLA Hart (2015) *The Concept of Law*, 3rd edn, Oxford: Oxford University Press; MacCormick (n 1); Schauer (n 1); Alexander and Sherwin (n 4).

form: the ratio is something to be constructed from the reasoning in the judgment and the conclusion reached by the court. It is the substance of the decision that matters, rather than the form in which it is presented. Second, as has been discussed already, precedents are distinguishable by later courts, whereas statutes are not. Third, statutes are generally prospective in operation, whereas precedents are both prospective and retroactive in their effect. Why do statutes and precedents differ in these ways? Fundamentally, it grows out of the basic institutional functions and competences of legislatures and courts. One of the key functions of legislatures is to establish general bodies of rules to govern future conduct in particular areas of community life. Such rules are relatively context-independent: they abstract from the details of particular concrete situations and determine how a class of situations should be treated. In the process they seek to achieve the virtues associated with rule-based decision making that were discussed earlier. Legislatures also have the resources and time to gather information and make assessments of the likely impact of such changes to the law, as well as assessing how a new system of rules will work. The basic function of courts, on the other hand, is to settle questions of the legal effect of the specific conduct of the parties in the case before the court. Courts make law incidentally as they decide how the existing law applies to the cases before them. In addition, they have very limited information available to them on the likely broader impact of a decision. It makes sense, then, to circumscribe the effects of individual decisions.

There are, naturally, also some important similarities between legislation and case-based law. Both create authoritative decisions that must be followed and used by courts, regardless of the courts' assessment of the merits of those decisions. Consequently legislation and precedent can alter the decisions of courts. The courts may reach a decision that is different from the decision it would have reached in the absence of the authoritative decision, or it may reach the same decision it would have reached, but for different reasons. Nonetheless, it is misleading to think of statutes and precedents as both constituting rule-based decision making. The process of relying on a precedent is so different from the application of a statute that it is appropriate to describe them in different terms.

B. Limitations of the Original Reason-Based Account of Precedent

The original exposition of the reason-based account of precedent presented a very basic case of a precedent. Case P1 involved:

Facts F1 = $\{g_1, h_1, i_1, j_1, k_1, l_1\}$

Ratio R1 = If $\{J, K, L\}$ then S

And $\{G, H, I\}$ did not provide grounds defeating $\{J, K, L\}$.

It would have been clearer to have stated that the effect of the ratio as follows:

Ratio R1 = {*J*, *K*, *L*} provides a sufficient reason for *S*

The common law doctrine of precedent has the following features:

1. Later courts that lack the power to overrule P1 must treat the case as correctly decided, that is:
   (a) they must treat {*J*, *K*, *L*} as providing a sufficient reason for *S*; and
   (b) they must treat {*G*, *H*, *I*} as not providing grounds that defeat the sufficient reason for *S*.
2. Consequently, later courts dealing with cases involving the facts $\{j_n, k_n, l_n\}$ must either follow P1 and decide *S*, or they must distinguish P1 to conclude ~*S*.
3. Finally, in distinguishing P1, later courts must rely on some feature that defeats the reason provided by {*J*, *K*, *L*}, and in doing so cannot rely on grounds based on {*G*, *H*, *I*}.

The basic case P1 was over-simplified in a number of ways. At least four aspects of the analysis require modification in the light of more complex cases. The first aspect is this.[21] The original discussion of P1 implied that if a fact did not form part of the ratio of the case (R1) then it was a consideration *against* the conclusion *S*. But this is not necessarily the case. That {*G*, *H*, *I*} did not provide grounds defeating {*J*, *K*, *L*} does not mean that each of *G*, *H* and *I* must have been considerations *against S*. For example, it could have been that *G* was neutral, or even in favour of *S*. Why does this matter? Recall the earlier case where the party to a contract relied upon an innocent misrepresentation from the other party in entering the contract. Then, in a later case P4, a party relied upon such a misrepresentation in entering the contract but would have entered the contract even if the misrepresentation had not been made. So:

$$F4 = \{\sim g_4, h_4, i_4, j_4, k_4, l_4\}$$

Here *G* is the fact that the party would not have entered the contract without the innocent misrepresentation. The court in P4 may conclude that this makes a difference. The misrepresentation was, after all, innocent: the party making the representation believed it was true, although it was in fact false. Here the court might decide that because the misrepresentation was innocent and because it did not make the crucial difference between entering the contract or not, it does not render the contract voidable.[22] So P4 concludes:

R4 = {~*G*, *J*, *K*, *L*} leads to ~*S*

[21] This issue is raised by Mark McBride, 'No Reasons', ch 5 of this volume, section II, and indirectly by Horty (2011) (n 3) 22–26.

[22] It might still be a ground for damages against the party making the misrepresentation, but not for avoiding the contract.

that is, the absence of *G* defeats the reason(s) for *S*. By implication the legal doctrine is now:

Doctrine {R1, R4} = {*G*, *J*, *K*, *L*} is a sufficient reason for *S*

Applying this doctrine to the facts of P1 (the original precedent) would still support the result in P1, that is, it would still show that P1 was correctly decided on its facts, since the facts in P1 included g_1. And relying on an innocent misrepresentation still provides a sufficient reason for avoiding a contract, except where it can be shown that the contract would have been entered even without the misrepresentation.[23] The upshot of all of this is that it would be wrong to think that any feature of a case that does not form part of the ratio is a feature that counts *against* the outcome of the case. The features may be neutral, or they may support the outcome but be regarded as superfluous by the precedent court.

A second way in which the basic analysis of the reason-based view was oversimplified was the way it dealt with those features in the case that *do* count against the outcome. Take the new case P3, whose facts are:

$$F3 = \{g_3, h_3, i_3, j_3, k_3, l_3, n_3\}$$

P3 follows P1, that is, it does not distinguish P1, and holds that {*J*, *K*, *L*} is not defeated by the novel feature *N*. So in P1, the court held that {*J*, *K*, *L*} was not defeated by {*H*, *I*} (assuming now that *G* was a factor in favour of *S*, rather than against *S*). The original reason-based analysis claimed that later courts could not rely on *H*, *I* or (after P3) *N*, to defeat {*J*, *K*, *L*}.[24] But this was inaccurate in implying that later courts cannot rely on *H* or *I* or *N* (or some combination of these features) in *conjunction* with a novel feature to defeat {*J*, *K*, *L*}.[25] Take the following case P5, with the novel fact o_5:

$$F5 = \{g_5, h_5, i_5, j_5, k_5, l_5, n_5, o_5\}$$

Here, despite P1 and P3, P5 might distinguish P1 by holding that features *H* and O taken *together* defeat {*J*, *K*, *L*}, that is:

R5 = {*H*, *O*, *J*, *K*, *L*} leads to ~*S*

and consequently:

Doctrine {P1, P3, P5} = {*J*, *K*, *L*, ~*H*, ~*O*} is a sufficient reason for *S*

For instance, *H* might be the fact that the misrepresentation was innocent, and O might be the fact that other information provided by the defendant made it obvious that the representation was inaccurate. So although the court in P5 could not have decided that P1 was distinguishable on the basis of *H* alone, and

[23] Of course, a later court might instead reinterpret P1 as having really held {*G*, *J*, *K*, *L*}, ie that P1 did in fact require a but-for causal connection. But that is not the possibility being explored here. See below for further discussion of this point.

[24] Lamond (n 2) 16.

[25] Horty raises this criticism ((2011) (n 3), 21 fn 22).

despite O alone not providing grounds for distinguishing P1, the two features in conjunction *did* provide grounds for distinguishing. Similarly, consider case P6, which has facts:

$$F6 = \{j_6, k_6, l_6, p_6\}$$

P6 follows rather than distinguishes P1, that is, it holds that feature *P* does not defeat {*J, K, L*}. Despite P1 holding (inter alia) that *H* does not defeat {*J, K, L*}, and P6 holding that *P* also does not defeat {*J, K, L*}, it would still be open in a new case for the court to hold that the (novel) conjunction of *H* and *P* do provide grounds defeating {*J, K, L*}.

Thus it is more accurate to say that later courts can only distinguish a precedent on the basis of either (i) a novel *feature* (on its own, or in conjunction with existing features) or (ii) a novel *combination* of features that are already present separately in the case law. So when later courts are bound to treat earlier decisions as correctly decided, they are only bound to accept that no combination of the features in the precedent case defeated the reason(s) for the result (*S*). They are not required to totally disregard those features in future cases.

This issue also suggests that it would be more perspicuous to separate the defeating features from the features that establish a sufficient reason for *S*, and to indicate that the conjunction of certain features is crucial. So in the case of P5, it would be more helpful to state the ratio as:

$$R5 = \{J, K, L\} \ \& \ \{H, O\} \text{ result in } {\sim}S$$

And similarly the implication of R5 is that:

$$\text{Doctrine } \{P1, P3, P5\} = \{J, K, L\} \ \& \ {\sim}\{H, O\} \text{ is a sufficient reason for } S$$

This is also significant because when a doctrine is set out by courts in their judgments, the initial focus is on the constitutive elements of the doctrine, rather than on any defeating conditions. If the constitutive elements are not present in the facts of the case then the doctrine is simply inapplicable. But where it *is* applicable, there is the further question of whether any defeating conditions exist.

The third way in which the original reason-based account needs to be extended is this. The presentation of {*J, K, L*} as the features providing a sufficient reason for *S* covers cases where the combination of features provides one consideration supporting *S*. But of course there can be cases where there is more than one consideration in favour of the outcome. It might be, for example, that {*J, K*} provided a consideration in favour of *S*, and {*L*} provided a separate consideration to that effect. In which case it would be more accurate to present the ratio as follows:

$$R1^* = (\{J, K\} \ \& \ \{L\}) \text{ provide a sufficient reason for } S$$

thereby indicating that there are two relevant considerations, not just one.[26]

[26] A further complication, which I will not try to address, involves cases where the court explicitly presents more than one basis for the outcome, eg where it states that {*J, K*} was a sufficient reason for *S* and that {*L*} was also a sufficient reason for *S*. In effect the court provides two rationes for the decision.

A fourth way in which the original reason-based account of precedent can be improved concerns facts not present in the precedent case. A later court can distinguish a precedent on the basis of a novel feature, that is, a feature that was not present in the precedent case. It cannot distinguish simply on the basis of a feature that was present in the case. Whether a feature was present or not depends upon the recitation of facts in the precedent's judgment (indeed, what matters is not the true facts of the case but the facts as recorded in the judgment.) The original presentation of the reason-based account stated that it could be assumed that a feature was absent from the precedent if it was not mentioned or implied by what was said in the judgment.[27] But what was meant by some facts not being 'implied' by the judgment was not considered.

A better question, suggested by McBride, is to ask whether it is more rational to suppose that the unstated fact was absent or present in that context.[28] Many things will go without saying in certain contexts because they are part of the normal conditions for such a situation. In addition, one would expect the court to highlight the unusual absence or presence of some fact in that situation. So if a case significantly involves a car, it can usually be assumed that the car has an engine, and seating, since the absence of these aspects would be so unusual as to merit comment (unless of course the state of the car is irrelevant to the legal question). When a later court relies on a distinguishing feature of the later case, it assumes that the distinguishing feature is not sufficiently standard in such a context that it would have gone unremarked by the precedent court. In addition, that the feature provides an arguable ground for distinguishing means that it might have been expected that the precedent court would have mentioned it in the original case, had it been present.

A good example of these points is the earlier case of innocent misrepresentation. Let us say that the precedent court said nothing about whether the party would have entered the contract even if the misrepresentation had not been made, that is, that the facts as reported were $\{h_n, i_n, j_n, k_n, l_n\}$. If it was assumed that the failure to mention a fact was equivalent to the *absence* of that fact, it would have to be assumed in the original precedent that it was not the case that the party would have entered the contract had the representation not been made, that is, that the facts were $\{\sim g_n, h_n, i_n, j_n, k_n, l_n\}$, and that the court had decided that it was irrelevant whether the representation had a but-for effect. But it is more rational to think that parties *are* influenced by representations, and that they are critical to the decision to enter a contract. So absent evidence to the contrary, it would be reasonable to assume that in the earlier case the misrepresentation *did* make a difference to the party's decision, and thus that the new decision would still support the conclusion in that case. So reading the *presence* of g_n into the earlier case is the rational view, despite its presence going unreported in the judgment.

[27] Lamond (n 2) 16

[28] McBride (n 21) section I. See also the comments by Horty (2011) (n 3) 26–27.

The question of which facts were present in the precedent, and whether they were relevant to the resolution of the question of law, points to a further complication in the practice of distinguishing that my original presentation of the reason-based view did not address. When the later court in P4 (with facts $\{\sim g_4, h_4, i_4, j_4, k_4, l_4\}$) distinguishes P1 by holding that:

$$R4 = \{\sim G, J, K, L\} \text{ leads to } \sim S$$

there are two things that P4 might be doing. It might be arguing that, contrary to initial appearances, the true ratio of P1 just was:

$$R1^{**} = \{G, J, K, L\} \text{ is a sufficient reason for } S$$

and so R1 was never actually applicable to P4, and hence *S* could not be justified on these grounds. Recall that the ratio of a case is rarely expressly stated by the precedent court; and even if it is stated, it is the *substance* of the decision, not the formulation of the ruling, that is ultimately binding. The ratio is something that must be constructed from the judgment in P1 – on the basis of what it expressly says about the question of law in dispute, from the justifications it gives for that ruling and from the facts that it highlights in its characterisation of the case. The process of restating the ratio of P1 as R1** might be described as 'reinterpreting' the precedent.[29] It is claiming that R1** represents the genuine import of P1, and that *G* was simply not emphasised in the existing understanding of P1's judgment because *G* went without saying or was not in the forefront of the submissions before the court, or for some other reason.[30] On this approach, then, the true basis for the voidability of a contract always lay in the innocent representation having made a causal difference to the contract's being formed, and this had simply been overlooked in previous accounts of the decision in P1.

Alternatively, P4 might be recognising a new ground for distinguishing the decision in P1. On this view it *is* enough that a party relied on an innocent misrepresentation for a contract to be voidable: they do not also have to prove that they would not have entered the contract without it. On the other hand, if the party making the misrepresentation *can* positively establish (on the balance of probabilities) that the contract would still have been entered even if the misrepresentation had not been made, then the contract is not voidable on this ground.[31] This consideration defeats the basis for avoiding the contract. If this is the case, the more accurate way to represent P4 is:

$$R4^{*} = \{J, K, L\} \,\&\, \sim\{G\} \text{ results in } \sim S$$

[29] See Lamond (n 2) 8–10.

[30] Raz (n 1) 188 suggests something along these lines as the underlying rationale for distinguishing, but this seems better suited to reinterpretation (what Raz calls the 'tame view' of distinguishing: ibid, 185) rather than distinguishing proper.

[31] In practice, it will often not be possible to establish this fact either way.

that is, instead of *G*'s being a constitutive element of the reason for *S*, it is ~*G* that is a defeating condition for {*J*, *K*, *L*}.

When a later court distinguishes an earlier decision on the basis of some fact that is already present in the earlier case, therefore, it can be unclear whether the court is distinguishing or reinterpreting the earlier decision. Indeed the language of 'distinguishing' is often applied to what I have described as 'reinterpreting' the ratio. And for most legal purposes it does not matter which is the proper analysis of what the later court has done. For this reason, the clearest category of distinguishing arises when there is a novel feature in the later case that was absent in the earlier case, such as the duress case discussed earlier.

C. Features and Factors

One significant variation on the reason-based account outlined previously has been developed by John Horty and others over the last decade.[32] It focuses not on the features of the case – the general types of facts that are mentioned in rationes – but with *factors*, that is, considerations in favour of the plaintiff (π) or the defendant (δ) in a particular case. I will provide a brief summary of this approach, omitting some of the details that are incidental to the points I wish to raise. In this section I will refer to Horty's approach as the 'factor-based' account, and to my own approach as the 'feature-based' account.

The standard notation for such a factor-based approach is as follows:

$$f_1^{\pi} = \text{a factor in favour of the plaintiff}$$

$$f_1^{\delta} = \text{a factor in favour of the defendant}$$

A case may have many factors in favour of the plaintiff or the defendant. Whether a factor favours the plaintiff or the defendant can be described as the *polarity* of the factor. Now sets of factors with the same polarity generate reasons in favour of the plaintiff or the defendant, for example:

$$\{f_1^{\pi}, f_2^{\pi}\} \text{ provides a reason in favour of } \pi$$

and

$$\{f_1^{\delta}, f_2^{\delta}\} \text{ provides a reason in favour of } \delta$$

[32] See Horty (2011) (n 3); and Horty (2015) (n 3) esp 4–7 and 10–13. See also John Horty and Trevor JM Bench-Capon (2012) 'A factor-based definition of precedential constraint' *Artificial Intelligence and Law* 20: 181–214; Rigoni (n 3) 133, Adam Rigoni (2018) 'Representing dimensions within the reason model of precedent' *Artificial Intelligence and Law* 26: 1–22, and Gabriel L Broughton (2019) 'Vertical precedents in formal models of precedential constraint' *Artificial Intelligence and Law* 27: 253–307.

Let us say in one case P(i) the factors are as follows:

$$\text{Factors(i)} = f_1^{\pi}, f_2^{\pi}, f_3^{\pi}, f_1^{\delta}, f_2^{\delta}$$

And the court decides in favour of π, making the following ruling:

$$R(i) = \{f_1^{\pi}, f_2^{\pi}\} \rightarrow S$$

The factors $\{f_1^{\pi}, f_2^{\pi}\}$ lead to the ruling *S*. The ruling has another implication, namely:

$$\{f_1^{\pi}, f_2^{\pi}\} > \{f_1^{\delta}, f_2^{\delta}\}$$

that is, the reason for π provided by $\{f_1^{\pi}, f_2^{\pi}\}$ outranks the reason in favour of δ provided by the set of *all* of the reasons in favour of δ in the case. By contrast, the ratio need not include every factor in favour of the prevailing party. Here in case P(i), for example, factor f_3^{π} does not form part of the ratio. The ratio R(i) amounts to a defeasible rule that is applicable to any later case that includes factors f_1^{π} and f_2^{π}.

But the analysis says more than just this. From the ranking:

$$\{f_1^{\pi}, f_2^{\pi}\} > \{f_1^{\delta}, f_2^{\delta}\}$$

it follows that:

$$\{f_1^{\pi}, f_2^{\pi}\} > \{f_1^{\delta}\} \text{ or } \{f_2^{\delta}\}$$

that is, if $\{f_1^{\pi}, f_2^{\pi}\} > \{f_1^{\delta}, f_2^{\delta}\}$, then it follows that $\{f_1^{\pi}, f_2^{\pi}\}$ also outranks the individual factors f_1^{δ} and f_2^{δ}. It also follows that any set of factors in favour of π that includes both f_1^{π} and f_2^{π} must outrank a set of any or all of $\{f_1^{\delta}, f_2^{\delta}\}$. So a single case creates a partial ranking of at least some of the factors in the case.

Another attraction of this analysis lies in the way that it can provide an elegant account of distinguishing. Let us say that there is a second case, P(ii), with the following elements:

$$\text{Factors(ii)} = f_1^{\pi}, f_2^{\pi}, f_3^{\pi}, f_1^{\delta}, f_2^{\delta}, f_3^{\delta}$$

that is, there is a new factor f_3^{δ}. Now given P(i), the court in P(ii) cannot distinguish P(i) on the basis of either (or both) f_1^{δ} or f_2^{δ}, since both factors were already present in P(i), and P(i) has already held that:

$$\{f_1^{\pi}, f_2^{\pi}\} > \{f_1^{\delta}, f_2^{\delta}\} \text{ (or } \{f_1^{\delta}\} \text{ or } \{f_2^{\delta}\})$$

On the other hand, P(ii) differs from P(i) because of the presence of the new factor f_3^{δ}. The court in P(ii) can rule, distinguishing P(i), that:

$$R(ii) = f_3^{\delta} \rightarrow \sim S$$

The implication of this ruling is that:

$$\{f_3^\delta\} > \{f_1^\pi, f_2^\pi, f_3^\pi\}$$

that is, the reason provided by $\{f_3^\delta\}$ outranks the reason provided by $\{f_1^\pi, f_2^\pi, f_3^\pi\}$ (ie *all* the factors in favour of π in P(ii), not just the factors in the ratio of P(i)).[33] Consequently, the legal doctrine based on P(i) and P(ii) is now:

$$\text{Doctrine } \{P(i), P(ii)\} = \{f_1^\pi, f_2^\pi\} \ \& \sim\{f_3^\delta\} \rightarrow S$$

In addition, P(ii) has the following implications. If:

$$\{f_3^\delta\} > \{f_1^\pi, f_2^\pi, f_3^\pi\}$$

that is, if $\{f_3^\delta\}$ outranks the set of all of $\{f_1^\pi, f_2^\pi, f_3^\pi\}$ then it is also true that it must outrank any of the individual factors:

$$\{f_3^\delta\} > \{f_1^\pi\} \text{ or } \{f_2^\pi\} \text{ or } \{f_3^\pi\}$$

and also outrank any combination of those factors:

$$\{f_3^\delta\} > \{f_1^\pi, f_2^\pi\} \text{ or } \{f_1^\pi, f_3^\pi\} \text{ or } \{f_2^\pi, f_3^\pi\}$$

Equally, if:

$$\{f_3^\delta\} > \{f_1^\pi, f_2^\pi, f_3^\pi\}$$

then any set of factors in favour of δ that includes f_3^δ must outrank any combination of $f_1^\pi, f_2^\pi, f_3^\pi$. So a case of distinguishing adds new information to the body of case law (cases P(i) and P(ii)). Later decisions must be consistent with both the decisions and the priority rankings in this body of law, either in following the decided cases or in distinguishing them.

The significance of this account is that it provides a partial ordering of different sets of factors that then bind later courts. To illustrate how this works, let me take one of Horty's (non-legal) examples.[34] Imagine a family with two parents and two children. One child is 9 years old, one is 13 years old. One night the 9-year-old wants to stay up to watch television. Parent$_1$ decides that children aged 9 or over may stay up late to watch television. The following night, the 13-year-old also wants to stay up late. The 13-year-old, however, has failed to finish their dinner and also failed to do their homework. Parent$_2$ does not agree

[33] Of course, the court might instead have ruled that it was the *combination* of f_1^δ, f_2^δ and f_3^δ (or the combination of f_1^δ, and f_3^δ or the combination of f_2^δ and f_3^δ) that led to $\sim S$. New factors can combine with some or all of the existing factors to outrank the conflicting set of factors. I am just taking the simplest situation for ease of exposition.

[34] Horty (2015) (n 3) 2–3, 19–21.

with the decision made by parent$_1$ (ie that children aged 9 or over may stay up late to watch television), but thinks that it is important to be consistent when dealing with their children. Parent$_2$ could say that children who have not finished their dinner may not stay up late. But in fact the 9-year-old had not finished their dinner the previous night. To say that the 13-year-old could not stay up because they failed to finish their dinner would be inconsistent with the previous decision, even though it was not the basis on which the first decision was made. On the other hand, the 9-year-old had finished their homework, so parent$_2$ could decide that a failure to finish homework means a child cannot stay up late. The decision by parent$_2$ distinguishes the decision made by parent$_1$ but also upholds it, implying that a child who is 9 or older and has finished their homework may stay up late, as was the case with the 9-year-old.

The scenario has the following elements:

$$\text{Factors} = f_1^{\pi}, f_1^{\delta}, f_2^{\delta}$$

where

f_1^{π} = being 9 years or older

f_1^{δ} = having not finished dinner

f_2^{δ} = having not finished homework

Now the decision of parent$_1$ P(i) amounts to:

$$\text{Factors(i)} = f_1^{\pi}, f_1^{\delta}$$
$$\text{R(i)} = \{f_1^{\pi}\} \rightarrow S$$
$$\{f_1^{\pi}\} > \{f_1^{\delta}\}$$

Whilst the decision of parent$_2$ P(ii) amounts to:

$$\text{Factors(ii)} = f_1^{\pi}, f_1^{\delta}, f_2^{\delta}$$
$$\text{R(ii)} = \{f_2^{\delta}\} \rightarrow {\sim}S$$
$$\{f_2^{\delta}\} > \{f_1^{\pi}\}$$

which has the following implication:

$$\text{Doctrine } \{\text{P(i)}, \text{P(ii)}\} = \{f_1^{\pi}\} \& {\sim}\{f_2^{\delta}\} \rightarrow S$$

The analysis in terms of factors provides an economical and precise way in which to capture the effect of precedent and distinguishing. The factor-based and the (revised) feature-based views of precedent are not incompatible, that is, they support the same outcome in the same cases. So are there any reasons for preferring the feature-based view? There are, I think, two main advantages the feature-based account has in comparison to the factor-based view. These advantages do not show that the factor-based account is flawed, but they do point to areas where it would need to be supplemented.

The first point about the factor-based view is simply that it begins with factors, rather than facts.[35] The factors are considerations that count in favour of the plaintiff or the defendant in the case. The approach can be extended to building up doctrinal detail rather than simply supplying factors directly favouring one party or the other.[36] But one limitation of this analysis is that it starts with the *factors* that the court in P(i) used to settle the case. Some facts of the case are relevant to the existence of those factors, but others are not. Take P1. It identifies the facts in the case as follows:

$$F1 = \{g_1, h_1, i_1, j_1, k_1, l_1\}$$

The same case, from the factor point of view, might be this:

$$F(1) = f_1^{\pi}, f_1^{\delta}, f_2^{\delta}$$

So there are three factors based on the six facts, one factor in favour of the plaintiff, two in favour of the defendant. But not all of the facts need be relevant to the factors identified by the court in P1. The court might regard f_1^{π} as grounded on $\{J, K, L\}$, f_1^{δ} as grounded on $\{H\}$, and f_2^{δ} as grounded on $\{I\}$. But the court might regard feature *G* as irrelevant, contributing to neither a factor in favour of the plaintiff nor a factor in favour of the defendant. Nevertheless, it is not the case that a later court is only restricted in distinguishing P1 on the basis of factors f_1^{δ} and/or f_2^{δ}. The later court is also not permitted to distinguish P1 on the basis of feature *G*, even if it regards *G* as providing a consideration (ie a factor) in favour of the defendant that the court in P1 did not mention. Let us call the factor based on *G* f_3^{δ}, and the view of the court in P2 as being that $\{f_3^{\delta}\}$ defeats $\{f_3^{\pi}\}$. Despite this, the court in P2 is *not* permitted to distinguish P1 on the basis of $\{f_3^{\delta}\}$, because that factor is based exclusively on a feature already present in P1. It is irrelevant that it is a novel *factor* vis-à-vis the analysis of the court in P1. Consider again the case of the child staying up late. It does not matter whether parent$_1$ simply regarded not finishing dinner as irrelevant to giving permission, and that it did not feature in their decision making as a consideration for or against staying up. Parent$_2$ may think that it *should* have mattered, and that it is a good reason for refusing permission to stay up. But parent$_2$ is not free to introduce a new factor $\{f_3^{\delta}\}$ to distinguish the decision by parent$_1$. To take that view would be inconsistent with the decision on the facts in the original case. So parent$_2$ is bound by the facts of the case, not just by the factors identified and relied upon by parent$_1$.

[35] Horty (2011) (n 3) 4–5; and Horty (2015) (n 3) 4–5.
[36] Rigoni (n 3).

What this case highlights is that later courts do not necessarily take the same view of the factors presented by the features in a case as did the original court. Nor do they have to: they are free to re-examine the case. Of course, factors are grounded on features of the case, for example in P1 factor f_1^π is grounded on features $\{J, K, L\}$. But what later courts are bound to accept is that features $\{J, K, L\}$ provided a sufficient reason for *S*, even if they take a different view as to *why* those features provide a reason for *S*. The later court might, for instance, regard $\{J, K, L\}$ as providing *two* factors in favour of the plaintiff, that is, f_1^π and f_2^π, not just f_1^π.[37]

This leads to a second point about the factor-based analysis. In some cases, a court will hold that there were two considerations in favour of the decision. Let us say in P7 that the facts are:

$$F7 = \{b_7, c_7, d_7, e_7, f_7, g_7\}$$

And the court rules that:

$$R7 = (\{B, C\} \ \& \ \{D, E\}) \text{ are sufficient reason for } S$$

On the factor-based analysis this would seem to cash out as:

$$R(vii) = \{f_4^\pi, f_5^\delta\} \rightarrow S$$

But the court might instead hold that it is the *conjunction* of $\{B, C\}$ and $\{D, E\}$ that is sufficient for *S*, that is, that neither would have been sufficient on their own. In that case it seems that the factor-based analysis would analyse the situation as:

$$R(vii)^* = \{f_6^\pi\} \rightarrow S$$

As far as I can tell, factors are always sufficient for the conclusion *S* unless they are defeated by some consideration for the other party.[38] Now it is also possible that the court in P7 might hold as follows. It might say that the conjunction of features $\{B, C\}$ and $\{D, E\}$ were *at least* sufficient for *S*, but leave it open to later cases to decide whether either (or both) would have been sufficient on their own. In such a case it is unclear how the factor-based analysis can represent this position. Is it just R(7)*, that is, is the factor f_6^π? But then consider a later case P8, holding:

$$R8 = \{B, C\} \text{ is a sufficient reason for } S$$

Presumably $\{B, C\}$ is factor f_4^π, leading to:

$$R(vii) = \{f_4^\pi\} \rightarrow S$$

[37] As noted earlier, a court may regard the proper analysis of the case as involving $(\{J, K\} \ \& \ \{L\})$, not simply $\{J, K, L\}$.

[38] See Horty (2011) (n 3) 4–7; and Horty (2015) (n 3) 4–7.

But if P9 now arises, with the facts:

$$F9 = \{b_9, c_9, d_9, e_9, f_9, g_9, h_9\}$$

Given that features $\{B, C, D, E\}$ are all present, what should the court say the factors in favour of π are in P9? Are the factors $\{f_4^\pi, f_6^\pi\}$, or just $\{f_6^\pi\}$? The first option – $\{f_4^\pi, f_6^\pi\}$ – seems a case of double counting, since $\{B, C\}$ is counted in both f_4^π and f_6^π, but the second option – $\{f_6^\pi\}$ – disregards the decision in P8, which it should not on the factor-based approach.

The underlying issue here with the factor-based approach is the idea that factors must always be sufficient to justify S (so long as they are undefeated). But it seems more attuned to our ordinary understanding of considerations in support of an outcome that some are sufficient, and others lend support without being sufficient in and of themselves. What a court is saying when it rules that both $\{B, C\}$ and $\{D, E\}$ are necessary for holding S, is that both sets are considerations in favour of S but neither is sufficient in itself. It is also saying that there are *two* considerations at play, not just one, that together provide sufficient support. When the court rules, on the other hand, that *at the least* the combination of $\{B, C\}$ and $\{D, E\}$ was sufficient for S, it is leaving it open to later cases to determine whether either or both considerations would be individually sufficient. So the factor-based analysis does not have the resources, in its current form, to capture these distinctions.[39]

In conclusion, what is to be said in favour of the feature-based approach to precedent over the factor-based? The first point is that an analysis in terms of sets of features providing a sufficient reason for a legal position reflects the way in which common lawyers think about case law. Which features are necessary for such a reason is a critical question, and it is a question finessed by the factor-based approach. The factor-based account seems to presuppose the feature-based account, since factors are grounded on features. So to that extent the feature-based approach is more informative than the factor-based approach. The second point is that sets of features can capture what is expressed in terms of factors, that is, those considerations that provide a justification for the result of the case. The factor-based analysis does not add any additional element that is missing from the (revised) feature-based account, though it expresses some points in a more economical form.[40] Third, the feature-based account can easily accommodate considerations that courts regard as supporting an outcome but not on their own justifying that conclusion. So one set of features might strengthen the case for an outcome without itself justifying the outcome, and two sets of features might be sufficient in combination without being sufficient

[39] It might be that the added complexity in building up factors in Rigoni (n 3) could help address this issue.

[40] Of course, this is not surprising: the revisions to the feature-based account outlined above are due in large part to points raised by the factor-based accounts: the factor-based account is superior in a number of ways to the original feature-based account in Lamond (n 2).

on their own. Identifying features of this kind is helpful for understanding the approach of the common law. Fourth, the facts of a case are the stable aspect of case-law reasoning. It is with reference to the reported (and implied) facts that courts decide whether there is a sufficient reason for some outcome, and whether there are grounds for distinguishing an earlier precedent. By contrast, the factors that those features give rise to are subject to revision and refinement by later courts.

There may of course be contexts where the factor-based approach has advantages over the feature-based approach, such as the computational representation of precedent. But the feature-based approach better captures the use of precedent as it is understood in the practice of common lawyers.

III. CODA: RULES AND REASONS IN DISTINGUISHING

One final point. It has been argued by some theorists that the rule-based account is extensionally equivalent to the reason-based account. Any distinguishing that the reason-based account would permit would also be permitted by the rule-based account (and vice versa).[41] However, it is not the case that that every distinguishing that would be permitted by the rule-based account would be permitted by the reason-based account (at least on a common interpretation of the rule-based account[42]). Let us go back to P1. The facts are:

$$F1 = \{g_1, h_1, i_1, j_1, k_1, l_1\}$$

The ratio is:

$$R1 = \text{If } \{J, K, L\} \text{ then } S$$

Now according to the rule-based account, distinguishing P1 is subject to two constraints:

(a) a new case can only alter R1 by adding an *additional* feature to the ratio, thereby narrowing the scope of R1; and
(b) the amended rule ($R1^{\dagger}$) must be applicable to P1 and justify the same result that was originally reached in that case.

These two 'formal' constraints on distinguishing, however, would permit the following. Take the case yet again of the children being allowed to stay up late. The 9-year-old has been allowed to stay up late on the basis that they are 9 years or older, despite not finishing their homework. A few days later the 13-year-old wishes to stay up. Parent_2 does not believe that children should be allowed to stay up during the school week whether or not they are 9 years or older. But that

[41] Horty (2015) (n 3) 7–13; McBride (n 21).

[42] eg Raz's account in *The Authority of Law* ((n 1) 185–87); and Alexander and Sherwin (n 4) 83–87.

is what $parent_1$ has decided. In the interests of consistency, $parent_2$ is willing to accept the original decision. But on the night in question the 13-year-old has come home from visiting a friend. $Parent_2$ distinguishes the decision by $parent_1$ on the basis that there is a difference between the two cases. In the 9-year-old's case, they had not been visiting a friend. So $parent_2$ decides that the 13-year-old cannot stay up late because they visited a friend. This decision adds a new feature, narrowing the original decision, and it still justifies the original decision, since the 9-year-old did not visit a friend. The decision is also (in parent2's view) an improvement on the original decision, because the best rule would be to generally prohibit staying up late on school nights. But this is *not* an acceptable distinction to draw, unless $parent_2$ also think that visiting a friend is a *consideration* against being allowed to stay up late (eg because the child will be tired from the visit, or has already been given special treatment that night). It is not sufficient that it is a condition that narrows the original ruling whilst still supporting the result in the original case. Nor is this simply a case of an unpersuasive or unconvincing distinction.[43] It is not a permissible distinction at all unless $parent_2$ claims that visiting a friend is a *reason against* being allowed to stay up late.[44] So the rule-based constraints on distinguishing needs at least a third condition:

(c) the feature rendering R1† inapplicable to the new case is said to provide a reason against *S*.

This is not a purely formal constraint, as it depends upon the substance of the consideration in R1†.[45] In this situation there is a difference between the reason-based and the rule-based account of distinguishing. A distinguishing feature on the reason-based account must provide a consideration that defeats the sufficient reason for *S*, that is, it must be a consideration *against* the conclusion *S*.

Having said this, it would be a mistake to think that the argument in favour of the reason-based account of precedent relies on its better capturing when distinguishing is permissible in the common law. Instead, the reason-based account is superior because it makes better sense of the practice of distinguishing, that is, in explaining *why* a decision-making process would include just such a practice.[46]

[43] Horty (2015) (n 3) 21–23.

[44] Of course it will normally be the case that a later court claims that the feature is a reason against the applicability of R1 because it genuinely believes this to be the case. But a later court might not actually believe this: it might simply see the case as an opportunity to narrow the application of R1 by adding a further restriction. But it must at least claim that the feature is a reason against applying R1.

[45] Horty's account of the rule model ((2015) (n 3) 7–10) avoids this problem because the rule model is cast in terms of *factors* that necessarily favour either π or δ. But the standard account of the rule model (eg Raz's) is in terms of *features*, not factors.

[46] Lamond (n 2) 3.

IV. CONCLUSION

The common law is a process of case-by-case decision making,[47] which differs in fundamental ways from rule-based decision making, at least from the type of rule-based decision making that characterises statutory law. The reason-based account of precedent provides a model of such case-by-case decision making. The original formulation of the reason-based account presented a simple, basic case for analysis. In this chapter I have suggested some ways in which it can be extended to cover more complex situations and be presented in a more informative manner. But I have resisted the appeal to recast the model in terms of factors rather than features. The differences between the (revised) feature-based and the factor-based accounts of precedent are not great, since the factor-based account builds on the original feature-based model, and many of the improvements to the feature-based model are due to reflection upon the factor-based account. But the feature-based model has the advantage of capturing certain aspects of common law reasoning that the factor-based model does not address, and of presenting it in a more intuitive manner.

[47] ibid, 1–4, 15–24.

7

Grant Lamond's Account of Precedent: A Personal Encounter

JOHN HORTY*

I. INTRODUCTION

Ever since reading Aristotle as an undergraduate, I have been intrigued by the particularist idea – which I believe to be correct – that normative generalisations cannot be formulated carefully enough to apply properly in every situation: there will always be circumstances in which the straightforward application of a normative generalisation, no matter how finely articulated, will yield the wrong result. How can we live in a world like this? Except by appealing to normative generalisations, how can we justify our own actions, or evaluate the actions of others? Questions like these have recently received sustained attention in moral philosophy due, especially, to the work of Jonathan Dancy, who argues for an extreme version of particularism according to which generalisations have no role at all to play in the moral justification or evaluation of actions.[1]

Several years ago, I wrote a book that provided, as I thought, a sensible response to Dancy's extreme version of particularism, arguing that moral justification and evaluation could be provided by defeasible generalisations, and sketching a logic for reasoning with these generalisations.[2] Even if this response was successful in deflecting Dancy's broad-scale assault on normative generalisations, however, it did not address the more detailed problem of explaining how our moral justifications or evaluations could actually be guided, or constrained, by generalisations that might, at any moment, allow for exceptions.

* I am grateful for comments from Ilaria Canavotto, Mark McBride and Adam Rigoni on an earlier draft of this chapter.

[1] For a canonical statement of the argument, see Jonathan Dancy (2004) *Ethics Without Principles*, Oxford: Oxford University Press.

[2] See John Horty (2012) *Reasons as Defaults*, Oxford: Oxford University Press; previous appeals to defeasibility in response to Dancy's argument can be found in Mark Lance and Margaret Little (2004) 'Defeasibility and the normative grasp of context' *Erkenntnis* 61: 435–55; Mark Lance and Margaret Little (2007) 'Where the Laws Are' in *Oxford Studies in Metaethics*, vol 2, ed Russ Shafer-Landau, Oxford: Oxford University Press, 149–71.

It struck me – as it has many people – that we might begin to understand how normative constraints could be derived even from generalisations that allow for exceptions by looking carefully at the patterns of reasoning at work in systems of common law. Here we find a stable institution in which, on a daily basis, courts confront new situations against a background of constraints derived from precedent decisions. These constraints are sufficiently firm that decisions in most situations are a matter of routine, but also flexible enough that courts have the freedom to respond to fresh circumstances in creative ways. How, in the common law, is this balance between constraint and freedom achieved?

With this question in mind, I embarked on a haphazard study of the literature on common law reasoning – which is, of course, vast and contentious, touching on central problems in legal theory. As I sifted through this literature, I found that it was helpful to bear in mind the perspective adopted by Larry Alexander and Emily Sherwin.[3] Although Alexander and Sherwin set out a broader taxonomy of positions – or *models*, as they say – concerning precedential constraint, they are particularly focused on the opposition between two central positions.

Both of these positions are based on the observation that a precedent case normally contains not only a factual description of some situation as well as a decision on the basis of that description, but also some rule through which that decision is justified; and both suppose that the constraints derived from a precedent case depend, in some sense, on this rule. Where the two positions differ is in the exact way this rule leads to constraints. According to the first position – which Alexander and Sherwin advocate, and which they describe as the *rule model* – the rule formulated in a precedent case governs any later situation to which it applies, unless the court in the later case wishes to overrule that earlier decision and has the authority to do so. According to the second position – which Alexander and Sherwin do not explicitly label, but which I refer to as the *standard model* – courts have the power of *distinguishing* the present case from previous cases in which a rule was formulated or applied; the power, that is, of identifying important, or material, differences between the facts of these cases, and so modifying the rule set out earlier in order to avoid an inappropriate application of that rule to the present situation.[4] The idea that later cases can

[3] See Larry Alexander (1989) 'Constrained by Precedent' *Southern California Law Review* 63: 1–64 for an initial statement, and then Larry Alexander and Emily Sherwin (2001) *The Rule of Rules: Morality, Rules, and the Dilemmas of Law*, Durham, NC: Duke University Press and, esp, Larry Alexander and Emily Sherwin (2008) *Demystifying Legal Reasoning*, Cambridge: Cambridge University Press for later and more substantial development.

[4] I refer to this model as 'standard' because of its prevalence among legal theorists; versions have been advocated by Edward Levi (1949) *An Introduction to Legal Reasoning*, Chicago, IL: University of Chicago Press; AWB Simpson (1961) 'The *ratio decidendi* of a case and the doctrine of binding precedent' in *Oxford Essays in Jurisprudence*, ed AG Guest, Oxford: Oxford University Press, 148–75; Joseph Raz (1979) *The Authority of Law*, Oxford: Oxford University Press; Melvin Eisenberg (1988) *The Nature of the Common Law*, Cambridge, MA: Harvard University Press; Frederick Schauer (1989) 'Is the Common Law Law? *California Law Review* 77: 455–71; and Frederick Schauer (1991) *Playing by the Rules: A Philosophical Examination of Rule-Based Decision-Making in Law*

be distinguishing, in this sense, can be seen as the common law response to the particularist view that generalisations formulated in earlier cases may not apply properly to new situations.

The contrast between these two positions on precedential constraint, the rule model and the standard model, can be illustrated with a domestic scenario: Suppose that Jack and Jo are the parents of two children – Emma, who has just turned 9, and Max, age 12 – and that they have agreed to respect each other's decisions concerning the children, treating these decisions, in effect, as binding precedents. And imagine that, one night, Emma, who has completed her homework and finished her chores, but did not finish dinner, asks Jo if she can stay up and watch TV. This is like a legal case: a situation is presented to an authority, Jo, who must make a decision and, ideally, provide a rationale for her decision. Suppose that Jo resolves the case by granting the request, stating that Emma can stay up to watch TV since she is now 9 years old. This decision can be seen as introducing a household version of a common law rule – perhaps, 'Children age 9 or greater can stay up and watch TV' – fashioned in response to a particular set of circumstances, but applicable to future situations as well.

Now imagine that, the next day, Max, who has likewise finished chores, but neither finished dinner nor completed homework, asks Jack whether he can stay up to watch TV. And suppose that Jack views the fact that Max, unlike Emma, has not completed homework as a material difference between the two situations, providing strong support for the conclusion that he should not be allowed to stay up and watch TV. On the other hand, Max is also, like Emma, at least 9 years old, so that the rule formulated by Jo in the previous case applies to Max as well. It therefore follows from the rule model that, in spite of his own preference, Jack is nevertheless required to apply the previous rule to the current situation, and conclude that Max can stay up and watch TV. According to the standard model, by contrast, Jack can arrive at his preferred decision by distinguishing the two cases, arguing that the previous rule should not apply to the new case of Max, since this new case, unlike the previous case of Emma, presents the additional feature that the child in question has not completed his homework. An effect of Jack's decision would then be that the rule set out by Jo in the previous case of Emma is now modified – perhaps reading, 'Children age 9 or greater can stay up and watch TV, unless they have failed to complete their homework.'

In their formulation of the rule model, Alexander and Sherwin suppose that a common law rule must behave like a rule from ordinary logic, entailing its consequent, without fail, whenever its premise is satisfied – so that, for example, Jo's original rule entails that a child must be allowed to watch TV whenever that

and Life, Oxford: Oxford University Press, along with many others. Of course, even according to the standard model, rules cannot be modified entirely at will; acceptable modifications must be subject to conditions that I describe as the *Raz/Simpson* conditions, after two prominent advocates, and explore at length in John Horty (2015) 'Constraint and Freedom in the Common Law' *Philosopher's Imprint* 15(25): 1–27.

child is at least 9 years old. They therefore miss the possibility that these rules might be thought of as defeasible – so that Jo's rule could be taken as entailing that a child should, as a default, be allowed to watch TV whenever that child is 9 years old, unless there is some particular reason for overriding that default. Logics governing defeasible rules like this had already been applied, very successfully, within the field of artificial intelligence and law, primarily in the analysis of common law argumentation.[5] I was convinced that a useful treatment of common law constraint could likewise be developed within the framework of these logics, and was in the process of working out the details of a proposal.

It was at this point that I came across Grant Lamond's 'reasons account' of precedent.[6] Lamond's paper seemed to contain that rare thing – not a development, an application, a response to criticism, a move in a debate, but a genuinely new idea. The idea, as I see it, is this: common law constraint can be understood as depending not on rules at all, whether ordinary or defeasible, but on relations among reasons. As soon as I read this paper, I realised that exactly the proposal I was trying to develop using a complex logic of defeasible rules could be stated much more simply without any appeal to rules at all, but directly in terms of a relation among reasons, just as Lamond recommends. The result was my first paper on the topic, setting out what I described as the *reason model* of constraint.[7]

Like many important philosophical proposals, Lamond's idea allows for multiple interpretations. There is my own interpretation, which has been applied within artificial intelligence and law by Trevor Bench-Capon, refined, improved and compared to arguments from analogy by Adam Rigoni, limited in scope by Gabriel Broughton and explored from a formal perspective by Henry Prakken.[8] There is also a new interpretation by Robert Mullins, which I feel is much closer to Lamond's own views, and which also connects more closely with some of the traditional literature from legal theory.[9]

[5] For the starting point in this very large body of research, see Henry Prakken, and Giovanni Sartor (1998) 'Modelling reasoning with precedents in a formal dialogue game' *Artificial Intelligence and Law* 6: 231–87.

[6] See Grant Lamond (2005) 'Do precedents create rules?' *Legal Theory* 11: 1–26 and then Grant Lamond, 'Revisiting the Reasons Account of Precedent', ch 6 of this volume, for more recent reflections.

[7] See John Horty (2011) 'Rules and reasons in the theory of precedent' *Legal Theory*, 17: 1–33. I use the phrase 'reason model', rather than Lamond's 'reasons account', primarily to fit the view into Alexander and Sherwin's taxonomy of models, but it is also useful to have two different phrases to distinguish my account, which I think of as a particular implementation of Lamond's general idea, from that general idea itself.

[8] See John Horty and Trevor Bench-Capon (2012) 'A factor-based definition of precedential constraint' *Artificial Intelligence and Law* 20: 181–214; Adam Rigoni (2014) 'Common-law judicial reasoning and analogy' *Legal Theory* 20: 133–56; Adam Rigoni (2015) 'An improved factor based approach to precedential constraint' *Artificial Intelligence and Law* 23: 133–60; Gabriel Broughton (2019) 'Vertical precedents in formal models of precedential constraint' *Artificial Intelligence and Law* 27: 253–307; and Henry Prakken (forthcoming) 'A formal analysis of some factor- and precedent-based accounts of precedential constraint' *Artificial Intelligence and Law*.

[9] See Robert Mullins (2020) 'Protected reasons and precedential constraint' *Legal Theory* 26: 40–61; interestingly, Mullins also shows that his alternative interpretation is, in a precise sense, equivalent to my own.

Rather than consider any of this more recent work, I want to return to my original version of the reason model and try to set it out as simply and clearly as I can. Why do this? Because I have noticed that, in several recent papers, the original account has been misunderstood. This is a matter for which I take responsibility. In my first presentation of the reason model, I had not, in my mind, fully separated the reason model itself from its connections to defeasible logic, with the result that some readers have concluded that rules play an essential role in my formulation of the reason model. In later presentations, I was concerned either with exploring connections between the reason model and other models, or else with developing the reason model in a richer environment, with the result that the presentation of the reason model itself was tangled up with other complexities.[10] There has not yet been a simple, clear statement of the reason model itself, without unnecessary connections to defeasible logics, or to other theories. That is what I hope to provide.

I begin, in the next section, by reviewing the framework within which the reason model is developed. Section III then defines the reason model itself. Section IV shows how the reason model can be seen as an interpretation of Lamond's proposal, and discusses a few additional points.

II. BASIC CONCEPTS

A. Factors and Fact Situations

We will suppose that a situation presented to a court for decision can usefully by represented as a set of *factors*, where a factor is a legally significant fact or pattern of facts bearing on that decision. In our domestic scenario, the legal, or quasi-legal, issue at hand is whether a child can stay up and watch TV, and the factors involved might reasonably include those already considered – whether the child has reached the age of 9, completed chores, eaten dinner, finished homework – as well as countless others.

But the factor-based representation of legal situations is not restricted to everyday examples of this kind. In fact, this style of representation has been used to analyse case-based reasoning in a number of complex legal domains within the field of artificial intelligence and law, where it originated in the work of Edwina Rissland and Kevin Ashley.[11] Cases in different areas of the law will

[10] See Horty (n 4); John Horty (2016) 'Reasoning with Precedent as Constrained Natural Reasoning' in *Weighing Reasons*, eds Errol Lord and Barry Maguire, Oxford: Oxford University Press, 193–212; and John Horty (2019) 'Reasoning with dimensions and magnitudes' *Artificial Intelligence and Law* 27: 307–45, for connection between the reason model and, respectively, the standard model and a defeasible rule model, and for development of the model in a richer environment.

[11] The analysis of legal cases in terms of factors was first introduced by Edwina Rissland and Kevin Ashley (1987) 'A case-based system for trade secrets law' in *Proceedings of the First International Conference on Artificial Intelligence and Law (ICAIL-87)*, New York: The Association for Computing

be characterised by different sets of factors, of course. In the domain of trade-secrets law, for example, where the factor-based analysis has been explored most extensively, a case typically concerns the issue of whether the defendant has gained an unfair competitive advantage over the plaintiff through the misappropriation of a trade secret; and here the factors involved might turn on, say, questions concerning whether the plaintiff took measures to protect the trade secret, whether a confidential relationship existed between the plaintiff and the defendant, whether the information acquired was reverse-engineerable or in some other way publicly available, and the extent to which this information did, in fact, lead to a real competitive advantage for the defendant.[12]

Many factors can naturally be taken to have polarities, favouring one side or another. In our domestic example, being older than 9 or completing chores strengthens the child's claim, as plaintiff, that he or she should be allowed to stay up and watch TV; failing to finish dinner or homework strengthens the parents' claim, as defendants, that the child should go to bed immediately. In the domain of trade-secrets law, the presence of security measures likewise favours the plaintiff, since it strengthens the claim that the information secured was a valuable trade secret; reverse-engineerability favours the defendant, since it suggests that the product information might have been acquired through legitimate means. As a simplification, we will assume here not just that many, or even most, factors have polarities, but that all factors are like this, favouring one particular side. In addition, we rely on the further simplifying assumption that the reasoning under consideration involves only a single step, proceeding at once from the factors present in a situation to a decision – directly in favour of the plaintiff or the defendant – rather than moving through a series of intermediate legal concepts.

Formally, then, we start by postulating a set F of legal factors bearing on some particular issue. We will let $F^{\pi} = \{f_1^{\pi}, \ldots, f_n^{\pi}\}$ represent the set of factors favouring the plaintiff and $F^{\delta} = \{f_1^{\delta}, \ldots, f_m^{\delta}\}$ the set of factors favouring the defendant. Given our assumption that each factor favours one side or the other, the entire

Machinery Press, 60–66; see Kevin Ashley (1990) *Modeling Legal Argument: Reasoning with Cases and Hypotheticals*, Cambridge, MA: MIT Press for a canonical treatment, Edwina Rissland (1990) 'Artificial intelligence and law: stepping stones to a model of legal reasoning' *The Yale Law Journal* 99: 1957–81 for an overview of research in artificial intelligence and law that places this work in a broader perspective, and Edwina Rissland and Kevin Ashley (2002) 'A note on dimensions and factors' *Artificial Intelligence and Law* 10: 65–77 for later reflections on factor-based representation of legal information.

[12] The most detailed analysis in this domain is presented by Vincent Aleven (1997) *Teaching Case-Based Argumentation Through a Model and Examples*, PhD thesis, Intelligent Systems Program, Pittsburgh, PA: University of Pittsburgh, who analysed 147 cases from trade-secrets law in terms of a factor hierarchy that includes five high-level issues, 11 intermediate-level concerns, and 26 base-level factors. The resulting knowledge base is used in an intelligent tutoring system for teaching elementary skills in legal argumentation, which has achieved results comparable to traditional methods of instruction in controlled studies; see Vincent Aleven, and Kevin Ashley (1997) 'Evaluating a learning environment for case-based argumentation skills' in *Proceedings of the Sixth International Conference on Artificial Intelligence and Law (ICAIL-97)*, New York: The Association for Computing Machinery Press, 170–79.

set of legal factors will be exhausted by those favouring the plaintiff together with those favouring the defendant: $F = F^{\pi} \cup F^{\delta}$. As this notation suggests, we take π and δ to represent the two sides in a dispute, plaintiff and defendant, and where s is one of these sides, we let $\overline{s}$ represent the other: $\overline{\pi}=\delta$ and $\overline{\delta}=\pi$.

Given this collection F of factors, a *fact situation* X, of the sort presented to the court for judgment, can then be defined simply as some particular subset of these factors: $X \subseteq F$. And where X is a fact situation of this kind, we let X^s represent the factors from X that support the side s, so that: $X^{\pi} = X \cap F^{\pi}$ and $X^{\delta} = X \cap F^{\delta}$ Of course, any interesting situation will contain factors favouring both sides of a given dispute. For example, the situation $X_1 = \{f_1^{\pi}, f_2^{\pi}, f_1^{\delta}, f_2^{\delta}\}$ contains two factors each favouring the plaintiff and the defendant, with those factors favouring the plaintiff contained in $X_1^{\pi} = \{f_1^{\pi}, f_2^{\pi}\}$ and those favouring the defendant contained in $X_1^{\delta} = \{f_1^{\delta}, f_2^{\delta}\}$.

B. Reasons and Rules

When presented with a fact situation, the court's primary task is to reach a decision, or determine an outcome. Given our assumption that reasoning proceeds in a single step, we can suppose that the *outcome* of a case is a decision either in favour of the plaintiff or in favour of the defendant, with these two outcomes represented as π or δ respectively.

In addition to deciding for one side or the other, we generally expect the court to supply a rule, or principle, to serve as justification for its decision. Rules of this kind will be characterised in terms of reasons, where a *reason for a side* is some set of factors uniformly favouring that side; a *reason* can then be defined as a set of factors uniformly favouring one side or another. To illustrate: $\{f_1^{\pi}, f_2^{\pi}\}$ is a reason favouring the plaintiff, and so a reason, while $\{f_1^{\delta}, f_2^{\delta}\}$ is a reason favouring the defendant, and so likewise a reason; but the set $\{f_1^{\pi}, f_1^{\delta}\}$ is not a reason, since it contains factors favouring opposite sides. Reasons are to be interpreted conjunctively, so that, for example, the reason $\{f_1^{\pi}, f_2^{\pi}\}$ represents the conjunction of the propositions represented by the factors f_1^{π} and f_2^{π}, and the reason $\{f_1^{\pi}\}$ carries the same meaning as the factor f_1^{π}.

Since reasons, like fact situations, are sets of factors, we can stipulate that a reason U *holds* in a situation X just in case each factor from U belongs to X, so that U is a subset of X, or $U \subseteq X$. And we can also define a relation of strength among reasons for a side according to which, where U and V are reasons for the same side, then *V is at least as strong a reason as U for that side* just in case U is a subset of V, or $U \subseteq V$. To illustrate: we can see, first, that the reason $\{f_1^{\pi}\}$ holds in the previous fact situation $X_1 = \{f_1^{\pi}, f_2^{\pi}, f_1^{\delta}, f_2^{\delta}\}$, since $\{f_1^{\pi}\} \subseteq X_1$. And we can see that, of the two reasons $\{f_1^{\pi}\}$ and $\{f_1^{\pi}, f_2^{\pi}\}$, the second favours the plaintiff at least as strongly as the first, since $\{f_1^{\pi}\} \subseteq \{f_1^{\pi}, f_2^{\pi}\}$.

Given this notion of a reason, a *rule* can now be defined as a statement of the form $U \rightarrow s$, where U is a reason supporting the side s. For convenience, we introduce two auxiliary functions – *Premise* and *Conclusion* – picking out the premise and conclusion of a rule, so that, if r stands for the rule just mentioned, we would have $Premise(r) = U$ and $Conclusion(r) = s$. And we will say that a rule is *applicable* in a situation whenever the reason that forms its premise holds in that situation. To illustrate: the statement $\{f_1^{\pi}\} \rightarrow \pi$ is a rule, since $\{f_1^{\pi}\}$ is a reason supporting the plaintiff. If we take r_1 to stand for this rule, we would have $Premise(r_1) = \{f_1^{\pi}\}$ and $Conclusion\ (r_1) = \pi$. And r_1 is applicable in the situation X_1 above, since $Premise(r_1)$ holds in this situation.

The rules defined here are to be interpreted as defeasible, telling us that their premises entail their conclusions not as a matter of necessity, but only by default. Continuing with our illustration: What the rule $r_1 = \{f_1^{\pi}\} \rightarrow \pi$ means, very roughly, is that, whenever the premise $\{f_1^{\pi}\}$ of the rule holds in some situation, then, as a default, the court ought to decide that situation for the conclusion π of the rule – or perhaps more simply, that the premise of the rule provides the court with a pro tanto reason for deciding in favour of its conclusion.

C. Cases

Given the concepts introduced so far – fact situations, rules, outcomes – a *case* can now be defined as a situation together with an outcome and a rule through which that outcome is justified: such a case can be specified as a triple of the form $c = \langle X,r,s \rangle$, where X is a situation containing the factors presented to the court, r is a rule, and s is an outcome.[13]

To aid our discussion of cases, we introduce three more auxiliary functions – *Facts*, *Rule*, and *Outcome* – mapping cases into their component parts, so that, in the case c above, we would have $Facts(c) = X$, $Rule(c) = r$, and $Outcome(c) = s$. And in order for the concept of a case to make sense, we impose two coherence conditions: first, that the rule of the case is applicable to the fact situation of that case, or equivalently, that the reason for the decision must hold in that fact situation, and second, that the conclusion of the case rule must match the outcome of the case itself.

The various concepts and conditions can be illustrated with the case $c_1 = \langle X_1,r_1,s_1 \rangle$, where the fact situation of this case is the familiar $X_1 = \{f_1^{\pi}, f_2^{\pi}, f_1^{\delta}, f_2^{\delta}\}$, where the case rule is the familiar $r_1 = \{f_1^{\pi}\} \rightarrow \pi$ and where

[13] Our representation of cases embodies the simplifying assumption that the particular rule underlying a court's decision is plain, ignoring the extensive literature on methods for determining the ratio decidendi of a case; and we suppose, as a further simplification, that a case always contains a single rule, ignoring situations in which a court might offer several rules for a decision, or in which a court reaches a decision by majority, with different members of the court offering different rules, or in which a court might simply render a decision in a case without setting out any general rule at all.

the outcome of the case is $s_1 = \pi$, a decision for the plaintiff. Evidently, the case satisfies our two coherence conditions. The case rule is applicable to the facts, since $Premise(r_1) \subseteq X_1$ and the conclusion of the case rule matches the case outcome, since $Conclusion(r_1) = \pi$. This particular case, then, represents a situation in which the court, when confronted with the fact situation X_1, decided for the plaintiff by applying or introducing the rule r_1, according to which the presence of the factor f_1^{π} – that is, the reason $\{f_1^{\pi}\}$ – leads, by default, to a decision for the plaintiff.

Finally, with this notion of a case in hand, we can now define a *case base* as a set Γ of precedent cases. It is a case base of this sort – a set of precedent cases – that will be taken to represent the common law in some area, and to constrain the decisions of future courts.

III. CONSTRAINT BY REASONS

How do the cases from a case base constrain future decisions? According to the reason model, what matters about a precedent case is the precedent court's assessment of the relative importance of the reasons presented by that case for each of the opposing sides; this assessment can be represented as a priority ordering on reasons. Later courts are then required to reach decisions that are consistent with the priority ordering derived from the decisions of earlier courts, thereby respecting the assessment of relative importance among reasons determined by these earlier, or precedent, courts.

A. Priority Ordering on Reasons

In order to develop this idea, we need to explain how a priority ordering on reasons can be derived from the decisions of earlier courts, and then what it means for the decision of a later court to be consistent with that ordering.

To begin with, then, let us return to the case $c_1 = \langle X_1, r_1, s_1 \rangle$ – where $X_1 = \{f_1^{\pi}, f_2^{\pi}, f_1^{\delta}, f_2^{\delta}\}$, where $r_1 = \{f_1^{\pi}\} \rightarrow \pi$, and where $s_1 = \pi$ – and ask what information is carried by this case; what is the court telling us with its decision? Well, two things. First of all, with its decision for the plaintiff on the basis of the rule r_1, the court is registering its judgment that $Premise(r_1)$, the reason for its decision, is more important – or has higher *priority* – than any reason for the defendant that holds in X_1, the fact situation of the case.[14] How do we know this?

[14] When comparing the relative importance of reasons, it is more common to say that one carries greater weight than the other, or that one is weightier than the other. I prefer to speak in terms of priority, rather than weight, for two reasons: first, the priority ordering on reasons to be defined here is non-linear, while the concept of weight tends to suggest linearity; second, the ordering to be defined here allows only ordinal comparisons among reasons, while the concept of weight suggests that cardinal comparisons must be available as well.

Because if the court had viewed some reason for the defendant that held in the situation X_1 as more important, or higher in priority, than *Premise*(r_1), the court would have found for the defendant on the basis of that reason, rather than for the plaintiff on the basis of *Premise*(r_1). And second, if the court is telling us explicitly that the reason *Premise*(r_1) itself has higher priority than any reason for the defendant that holds in X_1, then the court must also be telling us, at least implicitly, that any other reason for the plaintiff that is at least as strong as *Premise*(r_1) must likewise have a higher priority than any reason for the defendant that holds in this situation.

We can recall that a reason U for the defendant holds in the situation X_1 just in case $U \subseteq X_1$. And a reason V for the plaintiff is at least as strong for the plaintiff as the reason *Premise*(r_1) just in case *Premise*$(r_1) \subseteq V$. If we let the relation $<_{c_1}$ represent the priority ordering on reasons derived from the particular case c_1, then, the force of the court's decision in this case is simply that: where U is a reason favouring the defendant and V is a reason favouring the plaintiff, we have $U <_{c_1} V$ just in case $U \subseteq X_1$ and *Premise*$(r_1) \subseteq V$. To illustrate: consider the reason $\{f_1^\delta\}$ for the defendant and the reason $\{f_1^\pi, f_2^\pi, f_3^\pi\}$ for the plaintiff. Here, we have $\{f_1^\delta\} \subseteq X_1$ as well as $Premise(r_1) \subseteq \{f_1^\pi, f_2^\pi, f_3^\pi\}$. It therefore follows that $\{f_1^\delta\} <_{c_1} \{f_1^\pi, f_2^\pi, f_3^\pi\}$ – the court's decision in the case c_1 entails that the reason $\{f_1^\pi, f_2^\pi, f_3^\pi\}$ favouring the plaintiff is to be assigned a higher priority than the reason $\{f_1^\delta\}$ favouring the defendant.

Generalising from this example, we reach the following definition of the priority ordering among reasons derived from a single case:

> **Definition 1 (Priority ordering derived from a case)** Let $c = \langle X, r, s \rangle$ be a case, and let U and V be reasons favouring the sides $\overline{s}$ and s respectively. Then the relation $<_c$ representing the priority ordering on reasons derived from the case c is defined by stipulating that $U <_c V$ if and only if $U \subseteq X$ and *Premise*$(r) \subseteq V$.

Once we have defined the priority ordering on reasons derived from a single case, we can introduce a priority ordering $<_\Gamma$ derived from an entire case base Γ by stipulating that one reason has a higher priority than another according to the case base whenever that priority is supported by some particular case from the case base:

> **Definition 2 (Priority ordering derived from a case base)** Let Γ be a case base, and let U and V be reasons. Then the relation $<_\Gamma$ representing the priority ordering on reasons derived from the case base Γ is defined by stipulating that $U <_\Gamma V$ if and only if $U <_c V$ for some case c from Γ.

And using this concept of the priority ordering derived from a case base, we can now define a case base itself as inconsistent if its derived ordering yields conflicting information about the priority among reasons – telling us, for some pair of reasons, that each has a higher priority than the other – and consistent otherwise:

> **Definition 3** (**Inconsistent and consistent case bases**) Let Γ be a case base with $<_\Gamma$ its derived priority ordering. Then Γ is inconsistent if and only if there are reasons U and V such that $U <_\Gamma V$ and $V <_\Gamma U$, and consistent otherwise.

B. Constraint

We now present the reason model of constraint itself, building on the concept of case base consistency. The guiding idea, once again, is that, in deciding a case, a constrained court is required simply to preserve the consistency of the background case base. Suppose, more exactly, that a court constrained by a consistent background case base Γ is confronted with a new fact situation X. Then what the reason model requires is that the court should reach a decision in the situation X that is itself consistent with Γ – that is, a decision that does not introduce inconsistency into the background case base.

The reason model applies, in the first instance, to the rules on the basis of which a court can justify its decisions:

> **Definition 4** (**Reason model constraint on rule selection**) Let Γ be a consistent case base and X a fact situation confronting the court. Then the reason model of constraint on rule selection requires the court to base its decision in the situation X on some rule r supporting an outcome s such that the case base $\Gamma \cup \{X,r,s\rangle\}$ is consistent.

But of course, once this constraint on rule selection is in place, the reason model can naturally be interpreted as requiring a decision for a particular side just in case every rule satisfying the constraint on rule selection supports that side:

> **Definition 5** (**Reason model constraint on decision**) Let Γ be a consistent case base and X a fact situation confronting the court. Then the reason model of constraint on decision requires the court to reach a decision in the situation X for the side s if and only if every rule satisfying the reason model constraint on rule selection supports the side s.

These definitions can be illustrated by imagining that the background case base is $\Gamma_1 = \{c_1\}$, containing as its single member the familiar case $c_1 = \langle X_1, r_1, s_1\rangle$ – where, again, $X_1 = \{f_1^\pi, f_2^\pi, f_1^\delta, f_2^\delta\}$, where $r_1 = \{f_1^\pi\} \rightarrow \pi$, and where $s_1 = \pi$. Suppose that, against this background, the court confronts the fresh situation $X_2 = \{f_1^\pi, f_2^\pi, f_1^\delta, f_2^\delta, f_3^\delta\}$ and considers finding for the defendant in this situation on the basis of the reason $\{f_1^\delta, f_2^\delta\}$, leading to the decision $c_2 = \langle X_2, r_2, s_2\rangle$, where X_2 is as above, where $r_2 = \{f_1^\delta, f_2^\delta\} \rightarrow \delta$, and where $s_2 = \delta$. Can the court carry through with this plan of action, according to the reason model?

Well, as we can see, $Premise(r_1)=\{f_1^{\pi}\}$, the reason for the decision in the initial case, holds in the new situation X_2 as well, since $\{f_1^{\pi}\}\subseteq X_2$. And of course, the new reason $Premise(r_2)=\{f_1^{\delta},f_2^{\delta}\}$ favours the defendant at least as strongly as itself – that is, $Premise(r_2) \subseteq Premise(r_2)$, or $Premise(r_2)\subseteq\{f_1^{\delta},f_2^{\delta}\}$. It therefore follows from Definition 1 that c_2, the court's envisaged decision, would assign the reason $\{f_1^{\delta},f_2^{\delta}\}$ for the defendant a higher priority than the reason $\{f_1^{\pi}\}$ for the plaintiff – that is, $\{f_1^{\pi}\}<_{c_2}\{f_1^{\delta},f_2^{\delta}\}$. But Γ_1 already contains the case c_1, from which, in a similar fashion, we can derive the priority relation $\{f_1^{\delta},f_2^{\delta}\}<_{c_1}\{f_1^{\pi}\}$, telling us exactly the opposite. Since the augmented case base

$$\begin{aligned}\Gamma_2 &= \Gamma_1\cup\{c_2\}\\ &=\{c_1, c_2\}\end{aligned}$$

resulting from the court's envisaged decision contains both these cases, we would then have both $\{f_1^{\delta},f_2^{\delta}\}<_{\Gamma_2}\{f_1^{\pi}\}$ and $\{f_1^{\pi}\}<_{\Gamma_2}\{f_1^{\delta},f_2^{\delta}\}$ by Definition 2, so that, by Definition 3, this augmented case base would be inconsistent. By Definition 4, then, we can conclude that the court is not permitted to carry through with its plan of deciding for the defendant in the situation X_2 on the basis of the rule r_2, since c_2, the resulting decision, would introduce an inconsistency into the background case base, but the reason model requires decisions to preserve case base consistency.

Of course, it does not follow from the fact that the court cannot decide for the defendant in the situation $X_2=\{f_1^{\pi},f_2^{\pi},f_1^{\delta},f_2^{\delta},f_3^{\delta}\}$ on the basis of the particular rule r_2 that it cannot decide for the defendant in this situation at all. Suppose, for example, that the court appeals to the reason $\{f_1^{\delta},f_3^{\delta}\}$ to justify its decision for the defendant, leading to the case $c_3 = \langle X_3, r_3, s_3\rangle$, where $X_3 = X_2$, where $r_3=\{f_1^{\delta},f_3^{\delta}\}\rightarrow\delta$, and where $s_3 = \delta$. The augmented case base

$$\begin{aligned}\Gamma_3 &=\Gamma_1\cup\{c_2\}\\ &=\{c_1,c_2\}\end{aligned}$$

resulting from this decision would then be consistent. As before, the previous case c_1 supports the priority $\{f_1^{\delta},f_2^{\delta}\}<_{c_1}\{f_1^{\pi}\}$, and the new decision c_2 would now support the priority $\{f_1^{\pi}\}<_{c_2}\{f_1^{\delta},f_3^{\delta}\}$, so that we would then have both the case base priorities $\{f_1^{\delta},f_2^{\delta}\}<_{\Gamma_3}\{f_1^{\pi}\}$ and $\{f_1^{\pi}\}<_{\Gamma_3}\{f_1^{\delta},f_3^{\delta}\}$. But there is nothing inconsistent about this pair of priorities, as we can see, informally at least, with another homely example: one can easily imagine a teenager thinking, and thinking consistently, that going to the movies is more fun than going to the beach with her parents, but that going to the beach with her friends is more fun than going to the movies.

Suppose the court does, in fact, decide the situation X_2 in this way, supplementing the background case Γ_1 with the new decision c_3, leading to the augmented case base $\Gamma_3=\Gamma_1\cup\{c_3\}$. According to the reason model, this decision would then represent a step in the normal development of a legal system, which proceeds more generally as follows: A court confronts a new situation X against the background of a consistent case base Γ, with an associated ordering $<_\Gamma$ on reasons. The court is required to base its decision on some rule r supporting an outcome s such that the case base $\Gamma' = \Gamma \cup \{\langle X,r,s\rangle\}$ is consistent, with the result that the background case base is augmented with this new decision. The next court confronting the next new situation Y must then work against the background of the augmented case base Γ', which gives rise to the strengthened ordering $<_{\Gamma'}$ on reasons. This new court is likewise required to base its decision on some rule r' supporting an outcome s' such that the case base $\Gamma'' = \Gamma' \cup \{\langle Y, r', s'\rangle\}$ is consistent, thus further augmenting the case base, further strengthening the underlying priority ordering on reasons, and the process continues.

The hypothesis of the reason model is that this is how the common law develops in the normal, incremental case – by building up a stronger and stronger priority ordering on reasons through a series of decisions that are, at each stage, consistent with the existing case base.

C. The Domestic Scenario

All of this has been very abstract. For a more concrete illustration of legal development according to the reason model, we return to the domestic example set out in the Introduction. The example centered around a situation in which Jack and Jo have two children: Emma, who has just turned 9, did her chores, failed to finish dinner, but completed her homework, and Max, age 12, who also did his chores, but neither finished dinner nor completed homework. Both children wanted to stay up and watch TV. We imagined that Emma first asked Jo, who granted the request to watch TV, justifying her decision with the rule, 'Children age 9 or greater can stay up and watch TV.' Next, we imagined, Max asked Jack, who denied the request to watch TV, distinguishing this case from that of Emma by appeal to the fact that Max failed to complete his homework, and introducing the new rule 'Children who have not completed their homework cannot stay up and watch TV.'

With Max and Emma as plaintiffs, and with Jack and Jo functioning – as parents do – both as defendants and as adjudicators, or courts, this scenario can be cast in our framework by letting the factor f_1^π represent the fact that the child in question is at least 9 years old, by letting f_2^π represent the fact that the child in question completed chores, and then letting f_1^δ and f_2^δ represent, respectively, the facts that the child failed to finish dinner and failed to complete homework. The initial situation presented by Emma to Jo can then be represented as $X_4 = \{f_1^\pi, f_2^\pi, f_1^\delta\}$, which Jo then decided for Emma on the basis of the rule $r_4 = \{f_1^\pi\} \rightarrow \pi$, leading to the decision $c_4 = \langle X_4, r_4, s_4\rangle$, where X_4 and r_4 are as above, and where $s_4 = \pi$. As a result of this initial decision, the case base representing the common law of the household, at least as it pertains to staying up and watching TV, is $\Gamma_4 = \{c_4\}$, with $<_{\Gamma_4}$ as its associated ordering on reasons.

Next, the situation presented by Max to Jack can be represented as $X_5 = \{f_1^\pi, f_2^\pi, f_1^\delta, f_2^\delta\}$. In keeping with our story, we can suppose that Jack would like to decide against Max on the basis of the rule $r_5 = \{f_2^\delta\} \rightarrow \delta$, leading to the decision $c_5 = \langle X_5, r_5, s_5 \rangle$, where X_5 and r_5 are as above, and where $s_5 = \delta$. Can he do so, according to the reason model, against the background of the case base Γ_4? The answer is Yes. From Jo's earlier decision, we can conclude that the reason $\{f_1^\pi\}$ is to be assigned a higher priority than the reason $\{f_1^\delta\}$ – that $\{f_1^\delta\} <_{c_4} \{f_1^\pi\}$, so that $\{f_1^\delta\} <_{\Gamma_4} \{f_1^\pi\}$ as well. And Jack's decision would force us to conclude also that the reason $\{f_2^\delta\}$ must be assigned a higher priority than the reason $\{f_1^\pi\}$ – that $\{f_1^\pi\} <_{c_4} \{f_2^\delta\}$. But there is no conflict between this priority statement and the previous priority statement, derived from Jo's decision – a reasonable individual might, for example, prefer chocolate ice cream to vanilla and vanilla to strawberry. And because the background case base Γ_4 currently contains only Jo's decision, it follows that Jack's decision in the case of Max is consistent with this case base as well. The reason model thus allows Jack to carry through with his decision, resulting in

$$\begin{aligned} \Gamma_5 &= \Gamma_4 \cup \{c_5\} \\ &= \{c_4, c_5\} \end{aligned}$$

as the updated case base now representing the household common law, with $<_{\Gamma_5}$ as its strengthened ordering on reasons.

IV. DISCUSSION

I now discuss the relation of the reason model of constraint to Lamond's original account, try to clear up what might be some misunderstandings of the reason model, and address some related issues.

A. Defeat and Consistency

First, what is the relation of the reason model to Lamond's original 'reasons account'? My view is that the reason model provides one particular interpretation of Lamond's account, arrived at by defining the key concept of consistency in one particular way.

Let us begin with Lamond's initial statement of his position:

> The starting point for a reason-based account, then, is a reflection upon what is, in truth, the fundamental requirement of the common law doctrine of precedent, namely, that later courts treat earlier cases as correctly decided on their facts. What flows from this requirement is the necessity of reaching a decision in a later case that is consistent with the correctness of the earlier decision. The question is what sort of 'consistency' does this entail? The conventional view interprets consistency in

> terms of the use of the same 'rule' as that relied upon in the precedent case. Those who demur on the significance of rationes interpret it as entailing the application of the same set of principles that justified the preceding case(s). The reason-based view requires that later courts accept the correctness of the precedent court's assessment of the balance of reasons on the facts of the precedent case.[15]

There is a lot going on here: precedent requires later courts to regard earlier cases as correctly decided, and what this comes to is simply that later courts are required to reach decisions that are consistent with the decisions reached in earlier cases. Consistency is to be interpreted not in terms of rules or principles, but as acceptance of the precedent court's assessment of a certain relation among reasons.

This passage by Lamond is so interesting and innovative that it seems churlish to note that it does not provide a precise definition of what it means for a later decision to be consistent with an earlier decision. Nevertheless, that is what I want to call attention to, since it is exactly this gap that the reason model fills, and fills in a particular way.

In order to see how, we turn first to Lamond's characterisation of the meaning of a particular decision. He imagines – using slightly different notation than that employed here – that a court faced with a fact situation of the form

$$\{g_1,h_1,i_1,j_1,k_1,l_1\}$$

reaches a decision for C on the basis of the rule

$$\textit{If } \{J,K,L\}, \textit{ then } C,$$

and then describes the significance of this decision as follows:

> What the court decided was that in the context of $\{g_1,h_1,i_1,j_1,k_1,l_1\}$, the features $\{J,K,L\}$ justified the conclusion C. There are two aspects to what the court decided. The first is that the presence of features $\{J,K,L\}$ provided a sufficient reason to conclude C. The second is that the presence of the other features $\{G,H,I\}$ did not defeat the reason provided by $\{J,K,L\}$.[16]

[15] Lamond (2005) (n 6) 3.

[16] ibid, 15–16. There are two differences between Lamond's notation and that employed here. The first is that, for Lamond, situations are described in terms of particular facts, or tokens, while rules are described in terms of kinds of particular facts, or types. Thus, for example, a situation might contain x_i to represent the fact that the particular child Emma, say, has not finished dinner, while a rule might contain X to represent the general fact that the arbitrary child in question has not finished dinner – this notation, which is similar to that used in Raz (n 4), is then governed by the convention that the token x_i falls under the type X. By contrast, in the current framework, the same factors occur in both situations and rules; the assumption is that situations are already described in terms of types, rather than tokens – that degree of abstraction is assumed to precede our analysis. This first notational difference is, I believe, inconsequential. The second is more significant: Lamond's situations are described in terms of facts that do not, intrinsically, favour one side or the other; he refers to these in Lamond (2021) (n 6) as 'features'. In the current framework, by contrast, situations are described in terms of factors with a polarity, favouring some particular side – again, it is assumed that the classification of a mere feature as a factor, favouring a particular side, precedes our analysis. We return to this second difference below.

What does it mean to say that one reason defeats another? In philosophy, there are two central notions of defeat, a contrast due to John Pollock but more familiar in legal theory from the work of Joseph Raz.[17] There is, first of all, *rebutting* defeat, which occurs when a reason for one action or conclusion is defeated by a stronger, or more important, reason for an inconsistent action or conclusion. To illustrate: suppose I promise to meet Emma for lunch but encounter a drowning child along the way. Then my promise, which provides a reason for having lunch with Emma, is rebutted by the fact that there is a drowning child, which provides a stronger reason to rescue the child instead, an action that is inconsistent with meeting Emma for lunch. In addition to rebutting defeat, however, there is also, as Pollock points out, the phenomenon of *undercutting* defeat – or in Raz's terminology, *exclusionary* defeat – which occurs when what would ordinarily count as a reason for an action or conclusion is taken out of consideration, or deprived of its force, by another reason. To illustrate: imagine that Max contracts to deliver 150 bales of hay to a local farmer. Generally, such a contract would be taken as a reason to deliver the hay. But suppose it is discovered that Max is 14 years old and so a minor. The fact that Max is a minor does not, of course, provide any reason for him not to deliver the hay. But, since minors cannot enter into contracts, it takes the contract out of consideration – it undercuts, or excludes, the contract – as a reason to deliver the hay.

The reason model set out here can be seen as resulting from Lamond's general description in two steps. First, we suppose that, in examples such as that set out by Lamond above, the kind of defeat involved is rebutting defeat, rather than undercutting or exclusionary defeat. On Lamond's view, recall, what the decision he considers tells us is that $\{J,K,L\}$ provides a reason for C, and that this reason is not defeated by $\{G,H,I\}$. Now, if the notion of defeat involved is rebutting defeat, then $\{G,H,I\}$ defeats $\{J,K,L\}$ just in case $\{G,H,I\}$ provides a stronger reason for the opposite conclusion, say $\neg C$. So, if we can suppose that $\{G,H,I\}$ is, in fact, a reason for the opposite conclusion – and otherwise, how could it defeat $\{J,K,L\}$ at all – then what we can conclude from the fact that $\{G,H,I\}$ does not defeat $\{J,K,L\}$ is simply that $\{G,H,I\}$ does not provide a stronger reason for $\neg C$ than $\{J,K,L\}$ provides for C – in other words, and given certain natural assumptions about the ordering relation, that $\{J,K,L\}$ is stronger, or has higher priority, than $\{G,H,I\}$. On this view, then, what we derive from a precedent decision is a priority ordering on reasons, exactly as in Definition 1 of the current reason model.

So that is the first step in moving from Lamond's general description to the specific interpretation provided by the reason model: taking the kind of defeat

[17] See, eg, John Pollock (1970) 'The Structure of Epistemic Justification' in *Studies in the Theory of Knowledge*, American Philosophical Quarterly Monograph Series, no 4, Oxford: Basil Blackwell Publisher, Inc, 62–78; and Joseph Raz (1975) *Practical Reason and Norms*, London: Hutchinson and Co (2nd edn with new Postscript printed in 1990 by Princeton University Press, and reprinted by Oxford University Press in 2002); the distinction received its first formal treatment in John Pollock (1987) 'Defeasible Reasoning' *Cognitive Science* 11: 481–518.

involved as rebutting defeat, so that a previous decision can be understood as generating a priority ordering on reasons. The second step is even simpler. We can at last define a precise notion of consistency to fill the gap in Lamond's account: using the priority just introduced, a new decision can be characterised as consistent with a previous set of cases just in case the priority ordering derived from the new decision does not conflict with that derived from any of the previous cases – just in case, that is, there are no two reasons *U* and *V* such that the new decision assigns *U* a higher priority than *V* while some previous case assigns *V* a higher priority than *U*. Evidently, just as our first step runs parallel to Definition 1 of the current reason model, this second step runs parallel to the current Definitions 2 and 3. The requirement that new decisions preserve consistency is now captured in Definitions 4 and 5.

I have traced one interpretative path, leading from Lamond's account to my own reason model of constraint, which results from treating the idea of defeat as rebutting defeat, and then using the associated priority ordering to define consistency. But there are other paths as well. In particular, Mullins' interpretation, mentioned above – which he describes as a *protected* reason model, to distinguish it from the present *prioritised* reason model – can be arrived at in a similar fashion, except that it is based on the notion of undercutting or exclusionary, rather than rebutting, defeat, and then defines a different notion of consistency based on those ideas.

B. Reasons and Rules

I have argued that Lamond's central idea is that precedential constraint can be defined entirely in terms of relations among reasons, without any appeal to rules, and also that my reason model is an interpretation of Lamond's account. Yet the reason model presented here is constructed on the bases of a formal representation of cases as containing rules: for example, the case $c_1 = \langle X_1, r_1, s_1 \rangle$ considered earlier containes the defeasible rule $r_1 = \{f_1^{\pi}\} \rightarrow \pi$. How, then, can I say that the reason model does not depend on rules?

To this question I have a simple answer, and then a qualification. The simple answer is that, although rules are indeed present in the representation of cases, they do absolutely no work in our definition of the reason model. With suitable adjustments elsewhere in our series of definitions, the case c_1, for instance, could just as easily have been represented as $c_1' = \langle X_1, \{f_1^{\pi}\}, s_1 \rangle$ containing the reason that forms the premise of the rule r_1, in place of the rule itself. It is now natural to ask: If case rules are not actually used in the definition of the reason model, why are they present in our representation of cases at all? The answer is that, although rules are not used in the definition of the reason model itself, they can, in fact, play an illuminating rule in further development of the theory. It can be shown, for example, that when case rules are actually put to use as rules, the reason model of constraint can then be reconstructed within a defeasible logic, and also that the reason model is equivalent to a version of the standard model, based on rule modification.[18]

So that is the simple answer: rules play no essential role. The reason model can be formulated in terms of reasons alone. The qualification – which I hesitate to mention, but will – is that, in other work, I have argued that reasons themselves can be identified as the premises of appropriate default rules.[19] What does it mean to say that my promise to have lunch with Emma is a reason for doing so? It means that my reasoning – or the proper evaluation of my reasoning – is guided by a rule according to which, if I promise to have lunch with Emma then, by default, I ought to do so. Why would my reasoning, or the proper evaluation of my reasoning, be guided by such a default? Either because I take, or because I should take, promising to have lunch with Emma as a reason for doing so.

C. Features, Factors, Disjunction, Negation

I want to close by mentioning two other issues that come up in Lamond's more recent discussion.

First, in contrasting his reasons account of precedent with my reason model, Lamond emphasises as a significant difference that his own account starts with 'features' of situations while the present reason model starts with 'factors' – where features are mere factual aspects of a situation, and factors are legally significant patterns of facts that are taken to favour one side or the other.[20] Lamond emphasises that important legal reasoning is involved in understanding a situation, presented as a set of features, in terms of factors. I agree. Indeed, I wrote in my initial presentation of the reason model that

> the mere ability to understand a case in terms of the factors it presents itself requires a significant degree of legal expertise, which is presupposed here. Our theory thus starts with cases to which we must imagine that this expertise has already been applied, so that they can be represented directly in terms of the factors involved; we are concerned here only with the subsequent reasoning.[21]

The reason model, then, is entirely concerned with issues that arise 'downstream' of the representation of a situation as a particular set of factors, and not with issues involved in arriving at the appropriate representation – and this holds not just of the reason model, but of the entire body of work in artificial intelligence and law that takes for granted the factor-based representation of legal information.

[18] See Horty (2016) (n 10) for a reconstruction of the rule model within a defeasible logic; and Horty (n 4) for connections between the rule model and the standard model.

[19] See the Introduction to Horty (n 2).

[20] See Lamond (2021) (n 6) section 2.3.

[21] Horty (n 2) 5.

I do feel, though, that Lamond raises an important question here, and that is whether the overall process of legal understanding, argumentation and decision can legitimately be divided into an 'upstream' part that is devoted to arriving at an appropriate factor-based representation of the set of features present in some situation, and then a downstream part that is devoted to arriving at an appropriate decision, supported by appropriate arguments, based on that representation. It may well be, as Lamond suggests, that treating these two stages of the overall reasoning process as entirely separate modules – in the way that the factor-based approach suggests – forces us to ignore important interactions between these two modules.

A second issue that Lamond mentions concerns the representation, within accounts such as the reason model, of disjunctive and negative information.[22] This is a problem I have thought about as well, with little to show for it. My own lack of progress is due to two obstacles: I am not sure, first, exactly how to represent information like this within the reason model framework and, second, I wonder about the extent to which we can do so consistent with the traditional common law distinction between ratio decidendi and obiter dicta.[23]

To illustrate the problem, let us return to the situation presented by Emma to Jo. As we recall, in representing this situation, we took the factor f_1^{π} to represent the fact that the child in question is at least 9 years old, the factor f_2^{π} to represent the fact that the child in question completed chores, and the factor f_1^{δ} to represent the fact that the child failed to finish dinner. Since Emma had reached the age of 9 and completed chores, then, but did not finish dinner, we imagined that the situation she presented to Jo was $X_4 = \{f_1^{\pi}, f_2^{\pi}, f_1^{\delta}\}$. Now suppose, as before, that Jo wants to decide for Emma. What are her options for justifying her decision? According to the reason model, she has three options. She can justify her decision on the basis of the fact that Emma is 9 years old, on the basis of the fact that Emma has completed chores, or on the basis of the fact that Emma is 9 years old and has completed chores – on the basis, that is, of the reasons $\{f_1^{\pi}\}$, $\{f_2^{\pi}\}$, or $\{f_1^{\pi}, f_2^{\pi}\}$.

Suppose, however, that what Jo thinks is that either Emma's age or her completion of chores would justify a decision in her favour. With a rule, this would be easy to express, as, say,

$$\{f_1^{\pi}\} \vee \{f_2^{\pi}\} \rightarrow \pi,$$

where $\vee$ is the standard logical symbol for disjunction. But within the reason model, this is a much more difficult idea to express. One option would be to

[22] See Lamond (2021) (n 6) sections 2.2 and 2.3.

[23] See Rupert Cross and JW Harris (1991) *Precedent in English Law*, 4th edn, Oxford: Oxford University Press, ch 2, for a discussion of this distinction in traditional terms; then Karl L Branting (1993) 'A reduction-graph model of ratio decidendi' in *Proceedings of the Fourth International Conference on Artificial Intelligence and Law (ICAIL-93)*, New York: ACM Press, 40–49, for an analysis within artificial intelligence and law.

liberalise the ways in which Jo, through her judgments, can modify the background case base. Perhaps Jo could register her disjunctive judgment by supplementing the existing case base, not just with a single new case but with both the new cases $c_6 = \langle X_6, r_6, s_6 \rangle$ and $c_7 = \langle X_7, r_7, s_7 \rangle$, where $X_6 = X_7 = X_4$, where $r_6 = \{f_1^{\pi}\} \rightarrow \pi$ and $r_7 = \{f_2^{\pi}\} \rightarrow \pi$, and where $s_6 = s_7 = s_4$. As the reader can verify, this would then have the effect of prioritising both the reason $\{f_1^{\pi}\}$ and the reason $\{f_2^{\pi}\}$ over the opposing reason $\{f_1^{\delta}\}$.

Or suppose what Jo thinks is that Emma's age justifies a decision in her favour but that, taken on its own, her completion of chores does not. It is easy enough to express the idea that Emma's age justifies a decision in her favour – the previous $c_4 = \langle X_4, r_2, s_4 \rangle$ did that – but even if we allow Jo to supplement the background case base with multiple new cases, how could she express the negative information that $\{f_2^{\pi}\}$ itself does not have higher priority than $\{f_1^{\delta}\}$? Jo might try to express this information with the case $c_8 = \langle X_8, r_8, s_8 \rangle$, where $X_8 = \{f_2^{\pi}, f_1^{\delta}\}$, where $r_8 = \{f_1^{\delta}\} \rightarrow \delta$, and where $s_8 = \delta$. As the reader can verify, once again, this would allow us to conclude that $\{f_1^{\delta}\}$ is assigned a higher priority than $\{f_2^{\pi}\}$. But that seems too strong. Jo's intention is only to deny that $\{f_2^{\pi}\}$ carries a higher priority than $\{f_1^{\delta}\}$, not necessarily to affirm that $\{f_1^{\delta}\}$ carries a higher priority than $\{f_2^{\pi}\}$.

Or suppose what Jo wants to express is that Emma's age justifies a decision in her favour, but also – perhaps anticipating the case later presented by Max to Jack, and hoping to block Jack's decision – that Emma's age would still justify such a decision even if she had not done her homework. Again, the positive component of Jo's judgment could be carried by the previous $c_4 = \langle X_4, r_2, s_4 \rangle$, but the negative component would have to draw on factors not even present in the situation presented by Emma to Jo.

These examples are meant to illustrate the technical problems that arise in representing disjunctive or negative information within the reason model, but I hope that they illustrate the conceptual problems as well. The negative information involved in our second two examples seems to force us to consider situations other than that presented by Emma to Jo, and although the distinction between ratio and dicta is notoriously hard to formulate, it is generally agreed that judgments concerning hypothetical situations, not explicitly before the court, are to be classified as dicta.

V. CONCLUSION

My primary goal in this chapter has been to present, as simply and clearly as possible, the reason model of precedential constraint, which I developed as an interpretation of Lamond's idea that precedent in the common law could usefully be understood without any appeal to rules at all. This idea of Lamond has given rise to other interpretations as well, and suggests a number of new paths for research.

I close simply by mentioning one of these, which arises when we reflect on the process of common law development – as the reason model invites us to do – from the standpoint of social choice theory. What the common law yields, according to the reason model, is a social ordering on reasons, constructed as a result of decisions by individual courts, presumably on the basis of their own individual orderings on reasons, their own preferences. The common law can thus be seen as the realisation of a particular kind of preference aggregation procedure – a particular way of aggregating individual preferences, or priorities, among reasons into a group preference. Unlike the preference aggregation functions usually studied in social choice theory, however, the procedure realised by the common law does not simply take a collection of individual preferences as inputs and output a group preference all at once. Instead, the common law constructs its group preference ranking on reasons through a procedure that is piecemeal, distributed and responsive to particular circumstances. Especially given the challenges to common law reasoning that have been advanced over the years, it will be interesting to explore the extent to which the preference aggregation procedure realised by the common law can justified using tools and ideas from social choice theory.[24]

[24] For some initial explorations, see John Horty and Eric Pacuit (2021) 'The common law as a solution to a social choice problem' (unpublished manuscript).

8

How to Govern Conduct

LARRY ALEXANDER AND EMILY SHERWIN

THE FORM OF law is controversial in its own right, apart from the law's substance. Formal variations affect the allocation of decision-making power among law makers, judges and private actors; the point in time at which decisions are made; the degree to which law supports coordinated activity; and the law's capacity to settle moral and practical controversy. Accordingly, choice of form should take account of the expertise of the various decision makers involved, and the importance of coordination and settlement in particular contexts.

Legal directives commonly are typed as rules or standards, although alternative characterisations have been proposed and may be more accurate for some purposes.[1] Following the traditional divide, a rule provides determinate guidance, using language that is readily and uniformly understood by those it governs. Typically the terms of a rule are morally neutral, although a directive phrased in moral terms can operate as a rule if its audience converges on what the language requires. A standard, in contrast, is phrased in relatively vague terms that describe a range of possible conduct with no distinct boundaries, or in terms whose meaning is controversial among members of the audience. Of course, the categories 'rule' and 'standard' are not fully distinct: variations in the indeterminacy and the controversiality of legal language are a matter of

[1] For discussion of the distinction between rules and standards, see, eg, Isaac Erlich and Richard A Posner (1974) 'An Economic Analysis of Rulemaking' *Journal of Legal Studies* 3: 257–86, 261–71; Louis Kaplow (1992) 'Rules Versus Standards: An Economic Analysis' *Duke Law Review* 42: 557–629, 560–62. See also Kevin M Clermont (2020) 'Rules, Standards, and Such' *Buffalo Law Review* 68: 751–804 (preferring a distinction between binary and scalar terminology in legal directives, leads to different forms of logical reasoning). We have referred to this distinction in earlier work, but have focused primarily on the difference between rule-based decision making and natural decision making, meaning decision making on the basis of all-things-considered reasoning. See, eg, Larry Alexander and Emily Sherwin (2008) *Demystifying Legal Reasoning*, Cambridge: Cambridge University Press, 9–15; Larry Alexander and Emily Sherwin (2001) *The Rule of Rules: Morality, Law, and the Dilemmas of Law,* Durham, NC: Duke University Press, 28–32. Here we look more carefully at the role of standards in law.

degree. And a single legal norm may comprise both rule elements and standard elements. In many cases, however, it is possible to say that the language of a directive has a significant core of meaning accessible to most legal actors, making it a rule, or lacks that core, making it a standard.

In the pages that follow we will briefly review what we have said on previous occasions about the uses and advantages of rules in law and about the relationship between rule following and rationality. We will also consider the nature and functions of legal standards. Briefly, in the case of a standard, the role of the law maker is to orient and circumscribe later decision making by actors or judges, rather than to prescribe allowable conduct or choices.

I. RULES AND STANDARDS

By a 'rule' we mean a legal directive that has, as we have said, determinate meaning for most people who are subject to the rule, in most of the situations the rule governs.[2] Relatedly, rules must be general in the sense that they prescribe results for categories of cases and apply equally to all instances that fall within their predicate terms. The rules we are concerned with are also authoritative: they are not simply guides to conduct but requirements imposed by appropriate rule-making authorities.[3]

Rules of this kind purport to create exclusionary reasons for action. An exclusionary reason combines a first-order reason for action (in our case, enactment of the rule) with a second-order reason not to consider a range of first-order reasons that might otherwise influence the actor's choice of what to do.[4] Reasons that might have entered into an actor's all-things-considered deliberation about what to do in the absence of a rule are now disqualified and replaced by the prescription set out in the rule. In this way the rule settles controversy over what to do, at least within the ordinary range of its meaning. We will say more shortly about the function of determinate rules in the legal system.

[2] For an excellent and wide-ranging discussion of the nature of rules and the process of rule following, see Fred Schauer (1991) *Playing By the Rules: A Philosophical Examination of Rule-Based Decision-Making in Law and Life*, Oxford: Clarendon Press. Our discussion assumes that words can convey the meaning their users intend, even if their meaning is unclear in some applications: they have what Schauer calls 'semantic autonomy': ibid, 55–57. See generally Kent Greenawalt (1992) *Law and Objectivity*, New York: Oxford University Press, 34–89; HLA Hart (1961) *The Concept of Law*, Oxford: Clarendon Press, 122–38; Jules L Coleman and Brian Leiter (1992) 'Determinacy, Objectivity, and Authority' *University of Pennsylvania Law Review* 142: 549–638; Lawrence B Solum (1987) 'On the Interminacy Crisis: Critiquing Critical Dogma' *University Chicago Law Review* 54: 462–503.

[3] Another way to put this is that the direction given by the rule is binary and reasonably clear: given general agreement about what counts as A, do A rather than not-A. See Clermont (n 1).

[4] See Joseph Raz (1986) *The Morality of Freedom*, Oxford: Oxford University Press, 57–62; Joseph Raz (1979) *The Authority of Law*, Oxford: Oxford University Press, 16–19, 22–23, 30–33. But cf Heidi M Hurd (1991) 'Challenging Authority' *Yale Law Journal* 100: 1611–78 (arguing that laws do not and cannot have exclusionary effects). For doubts about whether reasons can be exclusionary, see Larry Alexander (1990) 'Law and Exclusionary Reasons' *Philosophical Topics* 18: 5–22.

In past work, we have distinguished between a 'rule model' of legal decision making, as just described, and a 'natural model' of legal decision making. Within the natural model, courts and other actors base their decisions about what to do on an unconstrained combination of moral and empirical reasoning.[5] Moral reasoning typically follows the method of wide reflective equilibrium, in which the reasoner makes a tentative judgment about the problem at hand, formulates a principle to support the initial judgment, then tests the principle by examining its application to other known or imagined cases. The reasoner then adjusts the initial judgment, the principle, or both to obtain a morally satisfying resolution. Empirical reasoning enters in to clarify the likely consequences of a course of action or the best means for implementing a principle. Posited law, in this approach, has no direct impact on reasoning apart from the expectations it may have generated among actors.

There is also a hybrid form of governance, accomplished by means of legal standards. A legal standard is a form of posited law that sets a framework for decision making but does not dictate an outcome. Standards take a variety of forms: their common features are a delegation of decision-making authority to actors or judges within a defined zone, combined with some degree of guidance on the type of reasons decision makers should take into account.

Legal standards share with rules the characteristic of generality, but they deliberately avoid determinacy. The terms they employ may be scalar or otherwise vague, or they may refer to moral considerations about which those who apply the standard may disagree. The standard itself – the posited law – performs two legal functions. First, it describes the scope of its own application, usually in fairly determinate terms. Second, it refers to objectives or values the law maker wants later decision makers to take into account. A standard does not, however, prescribe what actors should do, or what outcomes judges should reach in particular contexts. Instead, law in the form of a standard delegates further decision making to those who must act on the standard or apply it to assess the behaviour of others in concrete settings. Sometimes the standard invites the final decision makers to engage in unconstrained moral and empirical reasoning, within the boundaries it describes. Sometimes it directs them to engage in moral and empirical reasoning about how to promote a given set of aims or values. Sometimes it lists criteria to be considered in reasoning, requiring the reasoner to treat all other potentially relevant criteria as of no consequence – or, to put the same point differently, as in equipoise. In each case, the law maker does not attempt to settle controversy, but only to guide deliberation within a zone of controversy.[6]

[5] See John Rawls (1971) *A Theory of Justice*, Cambridge, MA: Harvard University Press, 14–21, 43–53, 578–82; Howard Klepper (1995) 'Justification and Methodology in Practical Ethics' *Metaphilosophy* 26: 201–19, 205–06; Norman Daniels (1979) 'Wide Reflective Equilibrium and Theory Acceptance' *Journal of Philosophy* 76: 256–82; John Rawls (1951) 'Outline of a Decision Procedure for Ethics' *The Philosophical Review* 60: 177–97 (1951).

[6] See Larry Alexander (2013) 'The Objectivity of Morality, Rules, and Law: A Conceptual Map' *Alabama Law Review* 65: 501–18, 506.

Consider, for example, a standard governing liability for losses caused by accidents. The standard might refer to a type of activity, then provide for compensation if one person's failure to exercise 'reasonable care' results in injury to another person. The zone of activity covered, and the requirement of compensation, likely will be fairly determinate, but assessments of reasonableness are left to the judgment of the future actors, judges and jurors who apply the standard to particular cases.[7] At most, the law will refer decision makers to objectives such as efficient risk management, or moral duties owed by one actor to another, or the rights of those who are harmed.

Benjamin Zipursky has outlined a variety of ways in which 'reasonableness' standards operate in law.[8] Depending on surrounding language and context, a reasonableness standard might be understood as referring to instrumental reason. For example, one understanding of the requirement of reasonable care in accident cases is that it deters actors from taking risks that are not justified in terms of overall welfare: the actor is liable for harm if the risk of harm exceeded the cost of prevention.[9] Alternatively, a reasonableness standard might be understood as requiring an epistemic judgement: a standard that refers to 'reasonable expectation' or 'reasonable mistake' can be understood as asking whether the actor has, or had, adequate grounds for believing that something would happen, or for forming a mistaken belief. Another understanding of reasonableness is that it requires an actor or legal decision maker to make a socially informed judgement about whether some action meets standards of behaviour generally accepted in the relevant time and place.[10] Thus, reasonableness in a nuisance dispute might depend on what sort of interferences landowners are accustomed to tolerate in a particular area. Zipursky also discusses instances of reasonableness within relationships: in some contract settings, for example, reasonableness may depend on the nature or history of a particular contractual relationship, or on customs in a trade.[11] In each case, the nature of the standard – instrumental, epistemic or conventional, or some combination of the three – may be more or less evident from the wording of the standard or the history of its prior applications.

Standards, such as that of 'reasonableness' in determining negligence, may also call for moral judgement. For example, the fiduciary duty of loyalty can be

[7] Application of some standards may become more determinate or 'rulified' over time as a body of precedent decisions develops; but application of others, if dependent on one-off jury verdicts, may not – as with 'reasonableness' determinations of negligence.

[8] See Benjamin C Zipursky (2015) 'Reasonableness In and Out of Negligence Law' *University of Pennsylvania Law Review* 163: 2131–70.

[9] See *United States v Carroll Towing Co*, 159 F2d 169, 173 (2d Cir 1947) (Hand, J stating a formula for negligence); Richard A Posner (1972) 'A Theory of Negligence' *Journal of Legal Studies* 1: 29–96. This is not a reading that Zipursky would endorse. Zipursky's example of instrumental reasonableness is a test for statutory validity that requires a rational relationship between the statutory requirements and statutory ends. See Zipursky (n 8) 2142.

[10] See Zipursky (n 8) 2149–50 (discussing normative and descriptive versions of reasonableness and suggesting that many standards fall in between these markers).

[11] See ibid, 2142–43.

understood as a standard that incorporates or borrows from moral principles.[12] Unconscionability standards in commercial law can be read as based on social or commercial conventions, but they are also susceptible to a moral reading.[13] Equitable defences such as 'unclean hands' also suggest that courts, in enforcing contracts, should at times pass moral judgement on the behaviour of parties.[14] Another obvious example of a morally grounded standard is a standard permitting jurors to award punitive damages when a defendant has acted outrageously.[15]

Legal standards authorise, guide and delimit natural decision making by actors and judges. There are limits, however, on the types of directions a standard can impose on decision makers without losing moral coherence. Suppose, for example, that a legal provision governing commercial transactions states that a contract in which one party agrees to exchange a valuable commodity for an unconscionably low consideration is invalid, provided, however, that if the agreed price is more than one-half of the market value of the commodity at the time the parties finalised their contract, the transaction should be enforced. Comments indicate that the term 'unconscionability' should be understood to express a moral principle that it is wrong to take financial advantage of unsophisticated parties, while recognising that some unconscionable transactions should nevertheless be upheld in the interest of commercial stability.

The problem with this combined directive – do not bargain unfairly, but prices above one-half of market value will be tolerated even if unfair – is that, judged by the stated standard of behaviour, the cut-off is morally arbitrary.[16] The unconscionability provision is deontological in nature: advantage-taking is wrong. In contrast, the safe haven for prices above one-half of market value does not rest on a conclusion that the transaction is no longer unconscionable: it rests on a separate, consequentialist concern about what outcome will best protect the reliability of completed contracts. It is a rule that limits the standard. If both halves of the provision were consequentialist, the cut-off would simply be a judgement about the point at which one type of negative consequence outweighs another. If both were deontological, it might represent a judgement that one

[12] See, eg, Andrew S Gold (2016) 'Accommodating Loyalty' in *Contract, Status, and Fiduciary Law*, Oxford: Oxford University Press, 185–212 (discussing different views on the relation between fiduciary standards of loyalty and morality, and suggesting that fiduciary law should be understood as accommodating rather than incorporating extra-legal morality).

[13] See generally Arthur A Leff (1982) 'Unconscionability and the Code: The Emperor's New Clause' *University of Pennsylvania Law Review* 115: 485–559 (sharply criticising the moral and social underpinning of the Uniform Commercial Code's (UCC's) unconscionability provisions).

[14] See, eg, *Panco v Rogers*, 87 A 2d 770 (NJ Ch 1952) (refusing to enforce a contract of sale by injunction when the buyer should have realised that the seller was making a mistake); *Carmen v Fox Film Corp*, 269 F 928 (1920) (refusing to enforce by injunction a sophisticated minor's legal right against tortious interference with a contract).

[15] See, eg, *Taylor v Superior Court*, 598 P2d 854 (Cal S Ct 1979).

[16] For more in-depth discussion of problems of this type, see Larry Alexander (2008) 'Scalar Properties, Binary Judgments' *Journal of Applied Philosophy* 25: 85–104; Anthony Ellis (1992) 'Deontology, Incommensurability, and the Arbitary' *Philosophy & Phenomenological Research* 52: 855–75.

kind of wrong is worse than another. But when, as here, a deontological limitation gives way at some point to independent consequentialist considerations, the cut-off can only be arbitrary, by the terms of the standard.[17] Advantage taking still occurs, and continues to be wrong, but is tolerated on grounds that have nothing to do with its wrongfulness. Of course, a law maker can do this, but to the extent the law purports to rest on moral grounds, the law maker is placing its subjects in a position of moral incoherence. Yet this is what rules do: their determinacy is at war with moral coherence, as we shall see.

II. REASONS TO GOVERN BY RULE

As noted in section I, the distinguishing characteristic of rules is their determinacy. They apply in like manner to defined situation types and prescribe conduct in terms that have a widely understood meaning in most of their applications. These characteristics lead to several important advantages, particularly when they are used to govern private transactions.

If the law maker has special expertise or access to empirical data, its rules may outperform the case-by-case judgements of less well-informed private actors. If not, the law maker at least has a long-term, generalised perspective on the question what should be done in a particular type of case, and is less likely than private actors to favour particular outcomes. The general terms of its rules may be affected by politics, but not by the type of personal bias or short-sightedness likely to influence individual reasoners deciding without guidance what action to take.

Supposing that the law-making authority has no reasoning advantage over ordinary actors, general, determinate and authoritative rules nevertheless serve a vital role in settling practical and moral controversy within a community.[18] Even when members of the community agree in a general way about the basic values they want to promote or protect, they need a political authority to settle what those values require in practice. An effective political authority must not only resolve disputes as they arise, but also provide guidance for future actors in specific types of cases. Very often the authority can do this most effectively by means of general and determinate legal rules that translate widely accepted values into prescriptions for action in particular types of cases.

Settlement by means of general, determinate rules also enables actors within a community to manage and coordinate their conduct.[19] If the language of

[17] See, eg, Larry Alexander (2000) 'Deontology at the Threshold' *San Diego Law Review* 37: 893–912.

[18] See Alexander and Sherwin (2008) (n 1) 10–11, 13–14; Alexander and Sherwin (2001) (n 1) 11–14, 21–25.

[19] See Alexander and Sherwin (2001) (n 1) 45, 58–61; Schauer (n 2) 163–66; Raz (1986) (n 4) 49–50; Gerald J Postema (1982) 'Coordination and Convention at the Foundation of Law' *Journal of Legal Studies* 11: 165–204.

the rule is uncontroversial and the rule is regularly enforced, private actors can anticipate how courts will respond to their interactions. Regular enforcement also makes it likely that the rule will be widely followed, which in turn enables actors to anticipate what others will do in circumstances governed by the rule and to adjust their own conduct in response.

Settlement and coordination are valuable only to the extent that the authority's rule is a good rule. A rule passes this test if universal compliance with the rule will produce a better sum of results, judged by relevant moral and instrumental standards, than unregulated private choice. In the discussion that follows, we assume that the rules under consideration are good rules in this sense; if not, they should be eliminated or amended.

Many ordinary rules can be justified fairly easily on the grounds just described. A well-designed and widely obeyed speed limit, or a rule against texting while driving, is likely to avoid more harm than it causes because drivers who decide on their own what to do tend to focus on immediate personal objectives rather than background statistics about the probability of harm.[20] A 'mailbox rule' for accepting contractual offers may not be intrinsically superior to a rule holding that acceptance is final upon receipt, but once the rule is in place it creates a convention that can head off costly misunderstandings.

These are very simple examples. They generalise, however, to many types of legal directives designed to bring conduct in line with a broad principle such as welfare maximisation, or with some combination of practical and moral principles. A direction to 'maximise welfare' or 'do what is right' has no immediate effect on behaviour because it is subject to many interpretations. Nor does it enable actors to pursue the goal in concert, because they have no basis for predicting what others will do. A determinate rule can further these ends in most cases, even if some of its outcomes are unsatisfactory.

III. PROBLEMS OF GOVERNANCE BY RULE

The main difficulty with governance by rule is that any general and determinate rule, even a very good one, will produce some bad outcomes in cases that fall within the rule's terms. There may be cases in which a driver has a very good reason to send a text, one that appears to outweigh the danger involved: there is no stopping place and the driver's child is in difficulty. The mailbox rule may result in a contract that is grossly unfair, if the mailer uses it knowingly to obtain a freak advantage. The very determinacy that gives rules their advantage in guiding conduct and settling controversy produces applications that are morally arbitrary or iniquitous.

[20] See generally, Daniel Kahneman, Paul Slovic and Amos Tversky (eds) (1982) *Judgment Under Uncertainty: Heuristics and Biases*, Cambridge: Cambridge University Press, 163; Daniel Kahneman, Paul Slovic and Amos Tversky (eds) (2002) *Heuristics & Biases: The Psychology of Intuitive Judgment*, Cambridge: Cambridge University Press.

Outcomes of this type put significant pressure on the rule and may lead actors to conclude that, all things considered, it is better to break the rule than to follow it.[21] Sometimes they will be wrong, because they have failed to consider not only the immediate consequences of following the rule but also the negative effects that the example of a violation will have on the long-term benefits of the rule. Other times, following the rule will actually *be* wrong, by the same moral or instrumental standards that support the rule. Either way, from the point of view of the authority that promulgated the rule, the reasoner subject to the rule should treat it as an exclusionary rule and follow it without reflection on first-order reasons for action. If all actors do this in all cases, the sum of outcomes over time will be better than the sum of outcomes were all actors to follow their all-things-considered judgement.

The issuance of a rule, however, has no magic power to limit reasoning or control conduct. The rule is just the expression of a norm that is chosen to produce good outcomes in most cases.[22] A threat of sanctions may persuade some actors to follow the rule when they have reason to disobey it, but judges will have similar all-things-considered reasons not to impose sanctions for disobedience. The judicial role – 'it is my duty as a judge to enforce the rules' – may alter some judges' calculations, but role definition has no more exclusionary power than the rule itself.

We can make a similar point in terms of rationality.[23] Practical rationality requires an agent to choose actions that are calculated to further the agent's ends.[24] Assume that the rule-making authority and the agent subject to the rule agree that the rule is a good rule: taking into account the settlement and coordination benefits of the rule, regular rule following will advance shared ends more effectively than unregulated choice of action. It follows that from the rule maker's perspective, the practically rational choice is to issue the rule and insist on compliance in every case. By definition, however, a good rule will produce some bad results, as judged by the same shared ends. Thus, from the perspective of an actor assessing what to do in a particular case, it may appear that compliance with the rule will yield the wrong result. In some cases personal bias or lack of information may cause the actor to misjudge, but in some cases the actor will be correct.

[21] Sometimes, of course, absurd or iniquitous results show that the rule the law maker intended is not what the literal application of its linguistic formulation would produce. For example, a sign declaring 'no cell phone use is permitted in the public library' would not be understood to forbid a patron's use of her cell phone to call paramedics to deal with someone's heart attack. It is not that the rule is justifiably broken in such a case. It is that the true rule – what was intended to be the rule – was not intended to apply to this situation.

[22] As we say in the preceding footnote, the rule – the norm – is expressed by its formulation but is not identical to its formulation applied literally.

[23] For a more complete version of this discussion, see Emily Sherwin (2018) 'Exclusionary Rules' in *Moral Puzzles and Legal Perplexities: Essays on the Influence of Larry Alexander*, ed Heidi M Hurd, Cambridge: Cambridge University Press, 286–302.

[24] Whether rationality imposes any constraint on ends is a debated point. See John R Searle (2001) *Rationality in Action*, Cambridge, MA: MIT Press, 10–11.

This suggests that, for the actor, it may not be rational to follow the rule. A standard approach to practical rationality equates practical rationality with responsiveness to current reasons for action as they appear at the time of choice.[25] On this view, if an actor believes, after taking into account his or her own cognitive imperfections and the effect that violating the rule will have on public values such as coordination and settlement, that following the rule is a mistake in a particular case, the actor cannot rationally follow the rule.[26]

A number of writers have taken a different approach, arguing in one way or another that practical rationality extends over time.[27] A particularly promising theory of temporally extended practical rationality comes from Michael Bratman.[28] Bratman's argument is based on the role of intentions in deliberation and action. Action is based on intentions, which are not simply aggregations of belief and desire but independent mental states that lead to action. An actor is rational in forming an intention if the intention furthers the actor's ends and is consistent with rational intentions the actor formed in the past and has not abandoned. The actor is rational in retaining the intention over time if, in doing so, the actor is guided by dispositions toward previously-formed intentions that generally serve the actor well. The actor can revise or reject an intention at any time, but if the intention remains in place at the time of action, it will generate the intended action without any further deliberation by the actor. If the actor is rational in retaining the intention, the actor is also rational in proceeding to perform the action. It follows that unreflective action based on a past assessment of the action's consequences may be rational even if a fresh assessment at the time of action might differ.[29]

Applying this reasoning to the problem of rules, the actor might conclude at time T1 that, given her own propensity to err in judging what action is best in a particular case, she will obtain better results by following a given rule in all cases than she would obtain by reconsidering the question what to do in each

[25] See Edward F McClennen (1997) 'Pragmatic Rationality and Rules' *Philosophy & Public Affairs* 26: 210–58 (calling the standard view, which he ultimately rejects, the 'Separability' principle). Heidi Hurd appears to take this view, though her position is not explicit. Heidi M Hurd (1999) *Moral Combat*, Cambridge: Cambridge University Press, 69–94.

[26] We are assuming a conception of rationality that rests on the actor's reasonable assessment of the relation between potential actions and ends. See, eg, Michael Bratman (1987) *Intentions, Plans, and Practical Reason*, Cambridge, MA: Cambridge University Press, 62 (focusing on agent rationality).

[27] See generally ibid; David Gauthier (1998) 'Intention and Deliberation' in *Modeling Rationality, Morality, and Evolution*, ed P Danielson, Oxford: Oxford University Press; David Gauthier (1998) 'Assure and Threaten' *Ethics* 104: 690–721; McClennen (n 25); Edward F McClennen and Scott J Shapiro (1998) 'Rule-Guided Behavior' in *New Palgrave Dictionary of Economics and the Law*, vol III, ed Peter Newman, New York: Stockton Press, 363–69: 367; Scott J Shapiro (2011) *Legality*, Cambridge, MA: Harvard University Press, 122–24; Scott J Shapiro (1998) 'The Difference that Rules Make' in *Analyzing Law: New Essays in Legal Theory*, ed Brian Bix, Oxford: Clarendon Press, 33–62.

[28] Bratman's understanding of rationality, and of the role of intentions in guiding rational action, is set out Bratman (n 26).

[29] See ibid, 15–16, 64–65, 81–83.

case. Accordingly, she might form a rational intention to follow the rule in all future cases. In the extended sense of practical rationality proposed by Bratman, she will then be practically rational in following the rule consistently, without further deliberation at the time of action.

This is a plausible answer to the problem of practical rationality that affects rule following. Yet there is also an epistemic side to rationality. Epistemic rationality is rationality of belief. By most accounts, it aims at beliefs that are true, and requires either that the agent's beliefs match her current evidence or that they were formed through processes that are likely to produce beliefs that are currently true.[30] Epistemic rationality, in other words, requires that beliefs be supported at the time of belief. Epistemic rationality is also best understood as requiring some degree of responsiveness to available evidence, at least when the agent confronts evidence that appears to contradict a current belief.[31] If so, then an agent who acts on a prior intention, without reflecting on evidence that poses an obvious challenge to the agent's existing beliefs about what to do, is epistemically irrational even if she is practically rational in an extended sense. Taking epistemic rationality into account, a rational and well-intentioned rule-making authority can demand universal compliance, but compliance by actors and judges may not be a fully rational response.

IV. TURNING FROM RULES TO STANDARDS

Although general, determinate rules perform important functions in law, there are various reasons why a law-making authority might sometimes turn to standards as a method of governance. The circumstances in which an authority might choose a standard are of two types. First, the authority might state an authoritative prescription in the form of a standard of behaviour when coordination and settlement are relatively unimportant and other considerations favour delegation of decision-making power to future actors. Second, the authority might approve a standard authorising leniency in enforcement of rules when they produce harsh outcomes. The authority, in other words, might stand behind the rule but decline to require its judicial agents to enforce it in all cases.

Within the first category, a standard may be preferable to a rule when the law maker lacks expertise and believes both that competent extra-legal norms are in place and that actors will be able to coordinate around these norms.

[30] Compare, eg, Earl Conee and Richard Feldman (2004) *Evidentialism: Essays in Epistemology*, Oxford: Oxford University Press, 57, 83, 178, 232 (describing and defending an evidential internalist approach) and Thomas Kelly (2003) 'Epistemic Rationality as Instrumental Rationality: a Critique' *Philosophy and Phenomenological Research* 66: 612–40 (expanding on evidentialism) with Alvin Goldman (1979) 'What is a Justified Belief?' in *Justification and Knowledge*, ed Gearge Pappas, Dordrecht: Springer, 89–104 (defending process reliabilism).

[31] See Richard Feldman (2004) 'Ethics of Belief' in Conee and Feldman (n 30) 166–96, 178, 186–88 (indicating that epistemic rationality includes a responsibility to take account of evidence that presents an obvious challenge to the agent's current beliefs).

For example, the authority may enact a legal standard that refers to conventional norms of behaviour, such as customs in a trade.[32] Similarly, when an activity is changing rapidly, the authority may conclude that general, determinate rules are not an effective means of regulation, and choose instead to rely on broader standards of behaviour.

A standard may also be appealing when the situations that fall within the purview of a law are too diverse to capture in the determinate language of a rule. In negligence law, for example, some types of conduct may be amenable to 'per se' rules of liability, but a standard of reasonableness is needed to capture the full range of acts that fall below the line of acceptability.[33] In response, the law maker may simply delineate an area of behaviour and then impose either a general standard of reasonableness, or a standard that refers to some form of instrumental, epistemic or customary sense of reasonable behaviour.

Another traditional use of standards in private law is the application of equitable defences based on various forms of hardship or advantage taking.[34] Defences of this kind developed in the days of separate courts of equity, and traditionally served as grounds for denying equitable remedies such as injunctions without affecting the plaintiff's claim to legal relief. The equity court might deny an injunction based on deceptive or opportunistic behaviour by a plaintiff, or on the hardship the remedy would impose on the defendant.[35] Technically, a damages remedy was still available, but whatever features of the case made injunctive relief desirable usually rendered a monetary remedy inadequate to vindicate the plaintiff's rights. The practice of recognising special defences to equitable relief continued long after the merger of law and equity, possibly because it proved useful as a means of softening the impact of general, determinate rules.[36]

The attraction of equitable defences is that, carefully used, they can provide equity in the Aristotelian sense. A rule is in place that may in general be a good rule but dictates a result that appears mistaken or morally unsatisfactory in a particular case. Application of an equitable defence allows the court to soften,

[32] See UCC § 1-303(c).

[33] See Zipursky (n 8).

[34] See Restatement (Second) of Contracts § 364 (1979) (describing special defences to the remedy of specific performance). For a helpful discussion of equitable defences, see Edward Yorio (1989) *Contract Enforcement: Specific Performance and Injunctions*, Boston, MA: Little, Brown, 73–126.

[35] Some examples include *Carmen v Fox Film Corp* (n 14) (sophisticated minor entered into incompatible contracts, then sought relief against interference with contractual relations); *McKinnon v Benedict*, 157 NW2d 665 (Wisc 1968) (unsophisticated borrower agreed to oppressive restrictions on land use); *Panco v Rogers* (n 14) (seller signed an agreement to sell his home for low price in circumstances suggesting buyer may have been aware that the price was a mistake); *Patel v Ali* [1984] 1 Ch 283 (seller encountered substantial personal difficulties after agreeing to sell her home); *Ryan v Weiner*, 670 A2d 1377 (1992) (alcoholic plaintiff facing foreclosure signed an agreement transferring title to his house for minimal consideration).

[36] Cf Yorio (n 34) 96–99 (explaining the modern survival of equitable defences to specific performance on the ground that these defences permit compromise when the facts do not support full enforcement of a bargain).

and often to nullify, the effects of the rule in the problem case without explicitly modifying the rule's terms.[37]

Equitable defences typically take the form of standards: the court denies an equitable remedy on the ground that the plaintiff has 'unclean hands', that the remedy will impose 'disproportionate hardship' on the defendant, that the plaintiff has engaged in some form of 'constructive fraud' or that the plaintiff's conduct was simply 'unconscionable'. When a court grants an equitable defence, its focus is backwards toward a particular set of events rather than forwards to similar future cases. The indeterminacy of the governing standards invites the court to engage in all-things-considered reasoning, incorporating morality, compassion and changing community values.

In this way, equitable defences allow decision makers to disregard legal rules and substitute a more fully reasoned response to the particular facts of the case, after those facts have emerged, without altering or challenging the ongoing validity of the rule. This shadow form of decision making is made possible by the traditional remedial distinction between law and equity, and the relative obscurity of equity and equitable remedies. Even among those trained in law, the prospect that some future decision maker might limit available remedies in a particular future controversy, on the basis of vague criteria, may not loom large in planning or coordination at the time of the transaction. As long as equitable defences remain to some extent 'acoustically separate' from the legal rules they modify – playing a role in legal decisions but not prominent in the minds of parties at the time of action – they provide a partial solution to the problem of rules.[38] Rules can serve their coordinating role among actors, even as courts provide some relief from their bad consequences in particular cases.

The system of law that results from a combination of determinate rules and indeterminate defences is certainly not ideal. Judges may be swayed by salient facts of the cases before them and consequently overlook potential harm to the coordination and settlement values of the rule. Even when judges accurately spot deserving cases, a legal system that purports to enforce a set of rules but allows its judges to override them in non-obvious ways might be thought to show a lack of candour toward those it governs. Another difficulty is that a legal system of this kind may not be stable: the corrective role of equitable defences is dependent on their comparative obscurity. If the exceptions become more prominent, they

[37] This account of equitable defences assumes that the rule in question covers the case but leads to a harsh result. Such a case should be distinguished from situations in which, because of the harsh result, the rule maker would deny that its rule was intended to apply to such a situation. A rule that proscribes patrons' using cell phones in the public library could be said not to apply to the case in which a patron uses a cell phone to call 911 to report a heart attack or an act of terrorism. It is not that applying the rule to the patron is too harsh; rather, it is that by pragmatic implication, the rule is not intended to apply at all. See, eg, Alexander and Sherwin (2008) (n 1) 143–44.

[38] The term 'acoustic separation' is attributable to Meir Dan-Cohen, who used it to describe the sometimes inconsistent messages sent by rules of conduct and rules of decision in criminal law. Meir Dan-Cohen (1984) 'Conduct Rules and Decision Rules: On Acoustic Separation in Criminal Law' *Harvard Law Review* 97: 625–77.

could potentially undermine the values of settlement and coordination associated with rules.

And in fact, the wave of Legal Realism that swept through US law in the twentieth century significantly altered the role of equity and equitable defences, in a way that threatens the traditional compromise between general, determinate rules and satisfying results in particular cases.[39] Realism has changed the dynamic of law and equity, not by doing away with equity but by moving equitable standards into a position of prominence in legal decision making. Perhaps the best-known example of this change is the explicit adoption of 'unconscionability' as a legal defence in the Uniform Commercial Code.[40]

Most Legal Realists were sceptical of general determinate rules, believing that rules do not and cannot effectively guide judicial decision making. Their argument was not that language lacks determinate meaning but that legal rules are not the source of legal decisions.[41] In most cases, rules are subject to interpretation, or are matched by other, contradictory rules.[42] This leaves judges free to choose an outcome for each case, based their assessment of the facts and their judgements or intuitions about fairness and instrumental desirability.[43]

Although Realism has its sceptics,[44] it has had a significant impact on attitudes to law, particularly in the United States. As a result, decisional criteria that were once confined to a relatively obscure corner of legal decision making now compete more openly with general, determinate rules. This is turn makes

[39] Brian Leiter has described and defended Legal Realism on a number of occasions. See, eg, Brian Leiter (2010) 'American Legal Realism' in *The Blackwell Companion to Philosophy of Law and Legal Theory*, 2nd edn, ed Dennis Patterson, Oxford: Wiley-Blackwell, 249–66; Brian Leiter (2020) 'What is a Realist Theory of Law?' *Journal of Institutional Studies* 6: 334–45; Brian Leiter (2015) 'Legal Realism and Legal Doctrine' *University of Pennsylvania Law Review* 163: 1975–84.

[40] See UCC § 2-302. For strong, and entertaining, criticism of the Code's unconscionability provision, see Leff (n 13) 504–07.

[41] See, eg, Jerome Frank (1930) *Law and the Modern Mind*, New York: Brentano's, 276 ('law is what happened or will happen in particular cases'); Karl N Llewellyn (1930) *The Bramble Bush: Some Lectures on the Law and Its Study*, New York: Oceana, 2–4 ('to my mind the main thing is seeing what officials do … and seeing that there is a certain regularity in their doing – a regularity which makes possible prediction').

[42] See, eg, Llewellyn (n 41) 64–69 ('every single precedent, according to what may be the attitude of future judges, is ambiguous, is wide or narrow at will') (emphasis omitted); Brian Leiter (2010) (n 39) 253–54 (discussing 'rational' indeterminacy).

[43] See, eg, Joseph C Hutcheson (1929) 'The Judgment Intuitive: The Function of the "Hunch" in Judicial Decision' *Cornell Law Quarterly* 14: 274–88, 278 ('I, after canvassing all the available material … wait for the feeling, the hunch – that intuitive flash of understanding that makes the jump-spark connection between question and decision'); Frank (n 41) 111 ('[t]he peculiar traits, dispositions, biases and habits of the particular judge will, then, often determine what he decides to be the law); see also Leiter (2010) (n 39) 257 ('the Core Claim of realism' is that 'judges respond primarily to the stimulus of the underlying facts of the case'); Llewellyn (n 41) 69 (advocates must build an inductive case for their desired result); Herman Oliphant (1928) 'Stare Decisis–Continued' *American Bar Association Journal* 14: 159–62, 159 ('we see that courts are dominantly coerced not by the essays of their predecessors but by a surer thing, by the intuition of fitness of solution to problem, and a renewed confidence in judicial government is engendered').

[44] See Andrew Gold et al (eds) (2020) *Oxford Handbook of New Private Law*, Oxford: Oxford University Press.

it more difficult for our modern legal system to maintain the benefits of determinate rules.

V. CONCLUSION

We have argued in the past, and again here, that general, determinate rules, enforced without exception, serve important functions in law. They support interpersonal coordination and they settle controversy that might otherwise result in disputes. General, determinate rules, however, will sometimes require results that are at odds with the purposes of the rules. When this is the case, or appears to be the case, it is not fully rational for actors to follow the rules or for judges to enforce them. This dilemma is an unavoidable feature of any system of law that aims at settlement.

Rules are not the only method of governance: law makers can provide standards that govern a determinate zone of conduct but provide only indeterminate guidelines for behaviour, leaving actors free to exercise judgement. Standards can provide guidance in areas in which settlement and coordination are not of paramount importance, contexts vary too widely to permit effective rule making, or private norms are more reliable and more adaptable than authoritative rules. Traditionally, courts have also used standards to provide relief from the effects of general, determinate rules in particular cases, though a safety valve of this type is difficult to maintain over time without significant harm to the efficacy of rules.

9

Working with a Body of Rules: On the Nature of Doctrinal Legal Disagreement in Judge-Made Law

JAMES PENNER*

I. INTRODUCTION: TWO OPENING METHODOLOGICAL THEMES

THIS CHAPTER IS part of a larger project on legal reasoning. In order to get our bearings, let me say something about its methodology, which is Wittgensteinian in spirit. As is well known, Wittgenstein's approach (in his later philosophy) to philosophical puzzles was to 'assemble reminders for a purpose', that is, to investigate actual cases in an area of human activity in order to get an overview ('*ubersicht*') of that area of human activity (a 'form of life'), to see what the participants are actually up to.[1] Although it takes a substantial amount of work, if we do that, we should be in a position to dissolve any philosophical puzzles that beset the area. In particular, in doing so we may be able to dislodge inaccurate 'pictures' of that human activity, roughly those unexamined assumptions that underlie philosophical controversies in that area. The approach can also be called Ramsayan, for it takes the following as a guide to this kind of philosophical methodology. Frank Ramsay famously suggested that where there is an ongoing dispute in philosophy

* Thanks to Patrick Emerton, Peter Hacker, Duncan Horne, Grant Lamond, Mark McBride, Jan Mihal, Adam Rigoni, Emily Sherwin, Peter Watts and Fred Wilmot-Smith for helpful comments and discussion. I am also grateful to the National University of Singapore funds provided to me via grant (WBS No R-241-000-127-133) and as Kwa Geok Choo Professor of Property Law. This essay reprises some of the themes of JE Penner (2010) 'An Untheory of the Law of Trusts, or Some Notes Towards Understanding the Structure of Trusts Law Doctrine' *Current Legal Problems* 63: 653–75. Where the two accounts differ, the present statement is to be preferred.

[1] Ludwig Wittgenstein (1958) *Philosophical Foundations*, Oxford: Basil Blackwell Ltd, paras 89, 127; GP Baker and PMS Hacker (1983) *Wittgenstein: Meaning and Understanding*, Oxford: Basil Blackwell Ltd, 295–309.

between two sides, for example as between 'nominalists' and 'realists' regarding our concepts,

> it is a heuristic maxim that the truth lies not in one of the two disputed views but in some third possibility which has not yet been thought of, which we can only discover by rejecting something assumed as obvious by both the disputants.[2]

It will be a main theme of this project that certain philosophical puzzles concerning legal reasoning in the last 50 years or so have arisen because we have been accepting a number of false presuppositions, or pictures, about legal analysis, that is, what lawyers and judges do when they reason about legal rules in actual cases. This chapter touches on some of those presuppositions and pictures, whilst starting on the project of providing an overview of legal analysis that might, with a bit of luck, dislodge them.

The second methodological theme is that I shall be pursuing an analogy throughout my discussion of legal rules and legal analysis, an analogy with natural languages.[3] In particular, I shall suggest that learning legal doctrine is very much akin to learning a second natural language. Consider the following:

- Philosophers distinguish two kinds of knowledge, although the distinction is intuitive and familiar to laypersons as well, the distinction between knowing *that* and knowing *how*.[4] The former is knowledge that is more or less explicit and can be framed in terms of propositions such as 'in chess the queen may move any number of spaces in any direction'. Knowing *how*, by contrast, is having a kind of ability, which is not reducible to knowing this, knowing that and so on.
- The knowing *how* relevant to my project is the ability to apply a *body of rules*. One of the points I shall be making later on is that legal philosophy tends to take the standard case of legal disagreement as disagreement over the application of some particular rule.[5] (Think of Hart's famous example

[2] Frank P Ramsay (1960) *The Foundations of Metaphysics*, Patterson, NJ: Littlefield Adams & Co, 115–16, quoted in Avishai Margalit (2009) 'Wittgenstein's Knight Move: Hacker on Wittgenstein's Influence on Analytic Philosophy' in *Wittgenstein and Analytic Philosophy*, eds Hans-Johann Glock and John Hyman, Oxford: Oxford University Press, 1–25, 22.

[3] See also AWB Simpson (1973) 'The Common Law and Legal Theory' in *Oxford Essays in Jurisprudence*, 2nd Series, ed AWB Simpson, Oxford: Clarendon Press 77–99, 94; JH Baker (2001) *The Law's Two Bodies*, Oxford: Oxford University Press, 65; Thomas D Eisele (1987) 'The Actividy of Being a Lawyer: The Imaginative Pursuit of Implications and Possibilities' *Tennessee Law Review* 54: 345–89, 383.

[4] In my view the best short discussion is PMS Hacker (2013) *The Intellectual Powers: A Study of Human Nature*, Chichester: Wiley Blackwell, 186–90. The distinction was originally set out in these terms by Gilbert Ryle (1949, 2000) *The Concept of Mind*, London: Penguin. For a careful and persuasive defence of the distinction, see David Wiggins, 'Knowing How To and Knowing That' in Glock and Hyman (eds) (n 2) 263–77. For a fairly recent debate between a proponent of the distinction and a proponent of the 'intellectualist' position, *viz* that 'knowing how' can be reduced to 'knowing that', see Jennifer Hornsby and Jason Stanley (2005) 'Semantic Knowledge and Practical Knowledge' *Proceedings of the Aristotelian Society, Supplementary Volumes* 79: 107–45.

[5] Or, similarly, determining which rule or relation between reasons provides the effective resolution of a case. See Horty, Lamond and McBride in chs 7, 6 and 5 of this volume, respectively.

of 'No vehicles in the park'.[6]) I shall argue that the reality is different in typical cases of doctrinal disagreement, in that the disagreement is typically over which of two competing legal analyses is better, legal analyses that draw upon many rules relevant to making legal sense of the particular fact situation in question.

- It is not uncommon to analogise the norms of law to the rules of a game. And in a sense games can explain the knowing how/knowing that distinction. So, for example, the rules of chess, such as the one I mentioned above, can be formulated fairly easily. And given the particular 'confined' activity of game playing, it is easy to learn how to apply these rules in practice. And moreover, the importance of playing with the entire body of rules is revealed. Knowing how to move the individual pieces and what 'check' is, is entirely insufficient for playing the game *well*. That takes lots of practice, and this is so in part because the body of rules provides a player with an infinite array of possible sequences of moves, moves that must also respond to the moves of one's opponent. But again, when rules of a game are considered as apt to explain legal disagreement, this typically concerns focusing on the application or existence in the game of a single rule (think of Dworkin's example[7] of whether there is a rule in chess about distracting one's opponent.)
- I shall argue that a *much* better analogy to legal practice is the learning of, and speaking in, a second natural language. (To avoid getting into controversies regarding the age-specific facility for second-language learning of young persons, assume that we are speaking of learning a second natural language as an adult.) This is so for a number of reasons, as I shall enumerate in a moment. But I must make something clear at the outset: I am not drawing this analogy because of anything to do with the use of language *within* law. Of course law is a discursive, linguistic activity in many respects. We write our statutes and judgments in language, we argue before the courts using language, and so on. But this is irrelevant to the analogy I am suggesting. Rather, the analogy focuses on the vast number of rules, concepts and so on we find in both the law and in natural languages, and on their *internal* complexity, that is, the complexity of the interactions between these various norms within both law and language taken as distinct human activities or forms of life.
- The strength of the law/second natural language analogy is supported by the following considerations:
    1. Learning the law and learning a second natural language involves coming to acquire a mastery of a body of rules. Learning the law is akin to learning a second natural language because of the complexity of

[6] HLA Hart (1994) *The Concept of Law*, 2nd edn, Oxford: Oxford University Press, 128–29.
[7] Ronald Dworkin (1978) *Taking Rights Seriously*, London: Duckworth, 101–05.

the rules in play. I speak French poorly. As any student of French, I had to memorise a fair amount of vocabulary and rules of grammar, but having done that did not mean I could speak French very well, simply because the mastery of a body of language rules is a matter of working with the expressive power of those rules. Getting the 'knowing that' part, whilst necessary, does not get you to the 'knowing how' mastery, which is more or less a matter of sustained practice. The law is very much like this. Mastering the law also involves a lot of memorisation, typically of rules but also of the facts of cases, concepts, organising principles and so on. But the first thing we have to explain to incoming law students is that learning the law is not memorising a rule-book, a book of rules that 'self-apply' in some straightforward way. In large part it is coming to understand *which* of its rules can be employed to resolve any particular legal problem. A good lawyer or judge is able to apply the rules so as to generate a compelling legal analysis of the facts of a case, in the same way that a speaker of a second natural language is able to draw upon the language's vocabulary and syntax to express herself well.

2. In learning both a second natural language and the law, beginners often make clear mistakes. This is obvious to any teacher of either. The disanalogy here with games is obvious. People clearly play to different standards, but learning the rules of chess or tennis is typically easy, and mistakes about what the rules require are sorted out early and easily. This is not the case with second natural languages. It is not uncommon for non-native speakers to make errors throughout their lives, or to use awkward constructions (particularly in writing), which is one reason why they can so easily be recognised as non-native speakers. And the same is very much true about the law. Lawyers and judges make mistakes, err in law, *all the time*, otherwise we would not need courts of appeal.
3. People differ considerably, indeed very considerably, in their second language or legal aptitude. This just seems to me to be obvious, so I shall say no more on that point. But there is another pedagogical insight, which is that whilst some kinds of error are typical, and perhaps in that sense systematic, much error is unpredictable. I have been teaching law for almost 30 years, and one of its interests is seeing the *new* mistakes that students make in trying to analyse a legal problem that I never anticipated.
4. Both law and languages are 'open' or 'unrestricted' in scope. Both are, in this sense, general purpose bodies of rules that can in principle apply to anything. Anything can, in principle, be the subject of linguistic discussion. And anything can, in principle, be the subject of legal regulation. This obviously is not so of the rules of games.
5. Both law and language are multifarious, divisible into what Wittgenstein called 'language games' in the case of natural languages. What

Wittgenstein meant by that is that language is a motley, entering into many kinds of activities: following a recipe, writing poetry, teaching physics and so on, and since 'meaning lies in use', our language will be sensitive to the contexts in which we use it. By analogy we can talk of 'law games'. The law figures in our lives in many different ways for many different purposes, from pursuing an action in damages for conversion, to entering into contracts, to instituting and paying taxes, and on and on. And as with language, the laws relating to these different activities will likewise be sensitive to their contexts of application. Given the vast expanse of legal doctrine, it follows that all lawyers have a restricted sphere of genuine competence, typically to one or two areas of practice. This has distinct consequences, the most obvious being that very few judges are likely to be very good in dealing with all the cases that come before them, at least outside of specialised courts such as the commercial division of the Queen's Bench in England. The same is true, of course, *mutatis mutandis*, of the legal academy. In short, in all of the courts, the profession and the academy, standardly, any person will have a more or less limited legal expertise, and no one is a master of all of the law.

6. We often speak of learning to 'think like a lawyer'. This is akin to learning to 'think like a French speaker'. Regarding the latter, you come to stop 'translating' everything from English. Regarding the former, you have to get into the *artificial* moral reasoning of the law, which is not about translating your considered moral positions, for example about who should pay for accidents, whether property in land is just and so on, into your legal analysis. I shall say more about the connection between moral and legal reasoning in section V.B.
7. In saying all this, I am not denying that there are not significant differences between the acquisition, possession and exercise of linguistic as opposed to legal skills. To take one, for example, language A can be translated into language B, whereas I think it is only metaphorical to say that the common law of contract can be translated into the civil law of contract, when, for example, a comparative lawyer finds a 'functional' equivalence between the two systems.

I shall return to both of these methodological considerations in section VI, but I think that is enough methodology to be getting on with for now.

II. A FIRST GLANCE AT THE PICTURE TO BE DISLODGED

In 1897, Oliver Wendell Holmes provided us with the following, now famous, passage:

> The danger of which I speak is … the notion that a given system, ours, for instance, can be worked out like mathematics from some general axioms of conduct. This is

the natural error of the schools, but it is not confined to them. *I once heard a very eminent judge say that he never let a decision go until he was absolutely sure that it was right.* So judicial dissent often is blamed, as if *it meant simply that one side or the other were not doing their sums right, and, if they would take more trouble, agreement inevitably would come.*

This mode of thinking is entirely natural. The training of lawyers is a training in logic. The processes of analogy, discrimination, and deduction are those in which they are most at home. The language of judicial decision is mainly the language of logic. And the logical method and form flatter the longing for certainty and for repose which is in every human mind. But certainty generally is illusion, and repose is not the destiny of man. Behind the logical form lies a judgment as to the relative worth and importance of competing legislative grounds, often an inarticulate and unconscious judgment, it is true, and yet the very root and nerve of the whole proceeding. You can give any conclusion a logical form. You always can imply a condition in a contract. But why do you imply it? It is because of some belief as to the practice of the community or of a class, or because of some opinion as to policy, or, in short, because of some attitude of yours upon a matter not capable of exact quantitative measurement, and therefore not capable of founding exact logical conclusions. Such matters really are battlegrounds where the means do not exist for determinations that shall be good for all time, and where the decision can do no more than embody the preference of a given body in a given time and place. We do not realize how large a part of our law is open to reconsideration upon a slight change in the habit of the public mind. No concrete proposition is self-evident, no matter how ready we may be to accept it …[8]

That something lies 'behind' legal rules (akin to thinking something lies beneath or behind the everyday explanations of the norms of natural language as they are given by speakers[9]) that judges claim to refer to to render their decisions, seems to me to be something of a shared conviction these days, at least amongst legal philosophers. Not that they all share what is behind. Very roughly, we might say that Holmes and the American Legal Realists thought 'policy considerations', or extra-legal notions of justice and fairness lay behind. For Dworkinians it is a sort of moral-political philosophical orientation. Critical Legal Scholars find ideological convictions. Modern-day Kantians and Hegelians pay close attention to legal doctrine, and hope to persuade us it reveals basic principles of right concerning our interpersonal relations – relations, however, that judges themselves never refer to. If this is right, I shall be defending a minority position. I want to endorse the spirit of the italicised parts of Holmes's admonition. In order to set this endorsement up, I shall look at a case, and its reception. The case is *Target Holdings v Redferns*.[10]

[8] Oliver Wendell Holmes (1897) 'The Path of the Law' *Harvard Law Review* 10: 457–78, 465–66 (emphasis added).

[9] eg, some interpretations of 'truth-conditional semantics'. See GP Baker and PMS Hacker (1984) *Language, Sense and Nonsense*, Oxford: Basil Blackwell, 121–242.

[10] *Target Holdings v Redferns* [1996] AC 421.

III. A SAMPLE LEGAL ANALYSIS: *TARGET HOLDINGS V REDFERNS*

I fear the reader may find the following analysis rather tedious, even recalling a certain kind of nightmare from law school. But that is partly one of the lessons to be (re)-learned here. In particular, I have set out the facts pretty fully, more fully than a concise summary for those familiar with the case, even those set out in the case's headnote.[11] The facts of *Target* are somewhat complex, but the case concerned a very common form of trust. Target Holdings was a mortgage lender advancing money to its client to purchase land, and, as is typical in such transactions, it transferred the £1.5 million loan moneys to the solicitor whose job it was to complete the purchase of the land and obtain a mortgage over it in Target's favour to secure repayment of the loan.

Four companies were involved in the sale of a property in Birmingham, England:

- Mirage Properties Ltd, 'Mirage', who owned the property
- Panther Ltd, 'Panther'
- Kohli & Co Ltd, 'Kohli'
- Crowngate Developments Ltd, 'Crowngate'.

Panther, Kohli and Crowngate were clearly associated companies, and a Mr Kohli was arguably, perhaps with associates of his, in control of all three. The later dealings with the money also suggest that Mirage was not simply an arm's-length vendor of the property, and its controller(s) may have known about and been involved in the whole business.

In June of 1989 Crowngate applied to Target for a mortgage loan of £1.7 million to purchase the property, the sale price being £2 million; £1.5 million of the loan money was to be used for the purchase of the property, the remainder for other purposes of Crowngate. Unbeknownst to Target, the title to the property was going to be flipped in a series of sub-sales. The arrangement was as follows:

- There was a contract of sale, Mirage to Panther, for £775,000.
- There was a contract of sub-sale, Panther to Kohli, for £1.25 million.
- There was a contract of sub-sale, Kohli to Crowngate, for £2 million.

It was not clear on the facts how the sub-sales were dated, or whether the sub-sales were meant to give bogus grounds for a valuer to show a rising property market, but in any case Target was not told these facts. I should add that this arrangement was not necessarily fraudulent. The various sub-sales might simply

[11] I have attached the statement of facts in the headnote in an appendix. The point of doing so is that I think it shows that relying only on its summary would be inadequate to understanding the various analyses that followed, which is a useful reminder of our telling our students to read the actual case.

have been a way of distributing the purchase moneys amongst associated companies for legitimate business purposes. In this case, however, the fact that none of this was disclosed to Target makes the transactions prima facie suspicious, a point I shall return to.

We now come to Target's instructions to Redferns. As stated by Lord-Browne Wilkinson:

> On 28 June 1989 Target transferred £1,525,000 to Redferns without giving any express instructions to Redferns as to its release. It is common ground that Redferns had implied authority to pay the money to or *to the order of* Crowngate when the property had been conveyed to Crowngate and Crowngate had executed charges in Target's favour.[12]

Then the following transactions ensued:

- 29 June 1989: Redferns transferred £1.25 million to Panther.
- 30 June 1989: Panther distributed £773k to Mirage and £300k to others.
- 3 July 1989: Redferns transferred £240k to Kohli.
- 4 July 1989: Redferns falsely informed Target that the purchase in the name of Crowngate was completed and that Target's first mortgage for £1.7 million was obtained.
- 6 July to 31 July: The transfers of title through the sub-sales were completed, and Crowngate was registered as owner; Target's first mortgage for £1.7 million was obtained.

One point that was not taken, as far as I can see, by any of the counsel involved, and one that only occurred to me when I was reading the case carefully again, was that it was arguable, on the facts, that given the close associations between the companies and parties involved, the series of payments *were* proper, in that they *were* 'to the order' of Crowngate. If that was so, the breach of trust did not lie in paying away the moneys to 'strangers', that is, persons not entitled to receive the funds, as Lord Browne-Wilkinson found,[13] but only in paying away the moneys *early*, that is, without first getting the transfer of title to Crowngate and the charge securing Target's loan.[14]

If this point is well taken then the facts in *Target* are essentially on all fours with the hypothetical example with which Lord Brown-Wilkinson began his substantial analysis in the case:

> For example, say an advance is made by a lender to an honest borrower in reliance on an entirely honest and accurate valuation. The sum to be advanced is paid into the client account of the lender's solicitors. Due to an honest and non-negligent

[12] *Target* (n 10) 429A–B (emphasis added).

[13] ibid, 429H, 431C, 436G–H.

[14] This is indeed the way Lord Toulson set out the facts of target in *AIB Group (UK) Plc v Mark Redler & Co Solicitors* [2014] UKSC 58, [21]; [2015] AC 1503, 1519B–C.

> error (eg an unforeseeable failure in the solicitors' computer) the moneys in the client account are transferred by the solicitors to the borrower one day before the mortgage is executed. That is a breach of trust. Then the property market collapses and when the lender realises his security by sale he recovers only half the sum advanced. As I understand the Court of Appeal decision, the solicitors would bear the loss flowing from the collapse in the market value: subject to the court's discretionary power to relieve a trustee from liability under section 61 of the Trustee Act 1925, the solicitors would be bound to repay the total amount wrongly paid out of the client account in breach of trust receiving credit only for the sum received on the sale of the security.
>
> To my mind in the case of an unimpeachable transaction this would be an unjust and surprising conclusion.[15]

It is not clear to me that whether a breach of trust involves paying a *proper* recipient at the *wrong time*, as opposed to paying a stranger, someone who is not entitled to receive trust funds at all, makes a prima facie difference to the correct analysis. Both are payments of trust moneys away in breach of trust. But obviously, the latter sort of breach would be more difficult to correct or iron out, whereas the former is much more easily seen as a kind of 'technical' breach, as indeed Lord Browne-Wilkinson seemed to regard it. Indeed, on this analysis, the breach is essentially 'self-correcting' so long as any condition for a proper payment is later met. If this is correct then Redferns's strongest point might have not entered into the court's analysis.

When Crowngate defaulted on the mortgage payments (the company went into insolvent liquidation about two years after the purchase), Target was only able to realise £500,000 on the sale of the land, so it lost £1 million in round figures. Target sued the solicitor's firm for the loss. It claimed that because the solicitor breached the trust by paying the money to a stranger, and upon that breach immediately came under a liability to repay £1.5 million, the solicitor had no defence to a claim for summary judgment for £1.5 million less the £500,000 Target got from the sale. Now, although it seemed pretty evident that a fraud of some kind lay in the background, because the case came to the court by way of an application for summary judgment, the issue of fraud was not before the court,[16] and it had to be assumed that the solicitor had simply made a non-fraudulent error in paying away the money to the third party.[17]

Lord Browne-Wilkinson began his judgment by saying that the case raised a novel point.[18] At the time, I think that was right, in the sense that the trust lawyers I spoke to about it agreed that there did not seem to be clear authority dealing with similar facts, nor was the correct legal analysis obvious.

[15] *Target* (n 10) 432C–E.

[16] Then under RSC Ord 14, r 1(2)(b). Many thanks to Fred Wilmot-Smith for locating the rule for me.

[17] At first instance the judge held that it was a triable issue whether Target would have proceeded with the transaction had it been given all the facts about the sub-sale arrangements, and this finding was not overturned in the courts above.

[18] *Target* (n 10) 428B.

Lord Browne-Wilkinson, in a kind of 'fusionist' spirit, took the view that the principles for awarding 'equitable compensation' and common law damages were essentially seeking to achieve the same end, that is, to put the plaintiff in the position he would have been in but for the defendant's breach of duty. Implicitly, Lord Browne-Wilkinson adopted what might be called the 'compensatory principle', a principle by which a plaintiff should only be awarded money compensation for *consequential* loss. This is not, however, the only principle upon which money awards are made either at common law or in equity.[19] Very briefly, what have come to be called 'substitutive' awards are made both at common law and equity. As for the common law, the standard case is that of a sale of goods. Traditionally, where a seller delivers defective goods to a buyer, the buyer is entitled to damages reflecting the difference in value between the goods contracted for and the defective goods delivered. The buyer need not prove any consequential losses that flowed from this to succeed in his claim, nor does the seller's showing that the buyer suffered no consequential loss defeat the buyer's claim.[20] A similar award is made in equity where a trustee wrongfully pays away trust money (eg to make an unauthorised investment). The trustee will be ordered to put the fund in the position it would have been in had he not breached his duty. As with the sale of goods damages award, this is essentially a valuation exercise, not one in which the beneficiaries have to prove a consequential loss. Indeed, it is not clear that the idea of consequential loss even makes sense in the standard case where a trustee must account in this way for his administration of the trust.

Before applying the 'compensatory' reasoning to the facts, Lord Browne-Wilkinson made one further point that. He sought to distinguish the kind of trust in this case, a 'commercial' trust, from a traditional family trust, in which he seemed to accept that monetary awards against trustees were 'substitutive', as just explained. He said:

> The depositing of money with the solicitor is but one aspect of the arrangements between the parties, such arrangements being for the most part contractual. Thus, the circumstances under which the solicitor can part with money from the client account are regulated by the instructions given by the client: *they are not part of the trusts on which the property is held.*[21]

I think this is quite right, but it would have been helpful here, I think, if Lord Browne-Wilkinson had elaborated on this point, because what he is saying here is that the solicitor is not just a trustee but also an *agent*, and in this case the agents (the members of the law firm) breached their principal's instructions.

[19] For excellent discussions, see Robert Stevens (2009) 'Damages and the Right to Performance: A Golden Victory or Not?' in *Exploring Contract Law*, eds Jason W Neyers, Richard Bronaugh and Stephen GA Patel, Oxford: Hart Publishing, 171–98; and Peter Watts (2016) 'Agents' Disbursal of Funds in Breach of Instructions' *Lloyd's Maritime and Commercial Law Quarterly* 118–34.

[20] *Slayter v Hoyle* [1920] 2 KB 11.

[21] *Target* (n 10) 436B (emphasis added).

One would therefore have expected the court, having drawn our attention to this, to have discussed whatever principles of agency law applied to make sense of the facts. But agency principles were never discussed.

Applying the principles of liability for consequential loss, Lord Browne-Wilkinson assessed whether Target's loss could properly be regarded as the consequence of the solicitor's breach of trust. That is, he invoked principles of causation and remoteness to say that, on a but-for basis, the loss was not a consequence of the solicitor's breach but rather was a loss arising because of Target's initial decision to lend £1.5 million on a property worth only half that at the time of sale; the cause of that loss was either that Target had been fraudulently induced by its borrower to make the loan on a property of insufficient value, or a decline in the property market. Since the Court could not adjudicate the fraud claim, the loss could only be attributed to the decline in the property market, for which the solicitor was, of course, not liable.

What I now want to do is look at the subsequent discussion of the Court's reasoning. Shortly after the case was decided, Lord Millett, writing extra-judicially, said:

> The solicitor held the plaintiff's money in trust for the plaintiff but with its authority to lay it out in exchange for an executed mortgage and the documents of title. He paid it away without obtaining these documents. This was an unauthorised application of trust money which entitled the plaintiff to falsify the account. The disbursement must be disallowed and the solicitor treated as accountable as if the money were still in his client account and available to be laid out in the manner directed. It was later so laid out. The plaintiff cannot object to the acquisition of the mortgage or the disbursement by which it was obtained; it was an authorised application of what must be treated as trust money. To put the point another way; the trustee's obligation to restore the trust property is not an obligation to restore it in the very form in which he disbursed it, but an obligation to restore it in any form authorised by the trust.[22]

In my view this criticism is sound, because it showed that Lord Browne-Wilkinson did not need to depart from traditional trust accounting principles in order to resolve the case. As far as I know Lord Millett was the first person to think up this alternative solution (certainly the first person to publish it).

Of course the discussion did not end there. James Edelman[23] disputed Lord Millett's analysis.[24] Edelman argued that a trustee cannot himself 'cure' his own breach if it involved paying away the money in breach of his instructions – unless his cure is adopted by the beneficiary or the right to return of the money is waived,

[22] PJ Millett (1998) 'Equity's Place in the Law of Commerce' *Law Quarterly Review* 114: 214–27, 227.

[23] Now a justice of the High Court of Australia.

[24] James Edelman (2010) 'Money Awards of the Cost of Performance' *Journal of Equity* 4: 122–39; James Edelman (2017) 'An English Misturning with Equitable Compensation' in *Equitable Compensation and Disgorgement of Profit*, eds Simone Degeling and Jason N Varuhas, Oxford: Hart Publishing, 91–109.

he remains liable. This too is a valid point, raising the issue of whether a trustee or agent loses his authority upon committing a breach. Lord Millett, perhaps thinking along the lines of one argument put to the court in *Target* by Jonathan Sumption QC, that 'The analysis of the Court of Appeal would appear to leave no room for the trustee voluntarily to make good the loss after the breach', did not explore in his analysis whether there are cases where a trustee cannot rectify a breach on his own. In reply to this point, Matthew Conaglen has argued[25] that a trustee's trusteeship does not end just because he has committed a breach of trust, and that in this case the trustee remained authorised to proceed to get in the mortgage. Edelman reasoned to the result in the case this way: he argued that Target accepted the charge over the property and held it for two and a half years, and that this amounted to an election to waive the right to bring a claim for the money wrongly paid away. I am doubtful about this analysis. Target only found out the facts very late in the day, and in my view both beneficiaries vis-à-vis their trustees and principals vis-à-vis their agents must be in full possession of the relevant facts before any adoption or ratification can take place.

Finally, we turn to the application of agency principles. Commenting upon Conaglen's argument, Peter Watts said:

> It must be a question of construction whether there is scope for an agent who has deviated from instructions to cure the breach. Particularly where there is an ongoing mandate, even a serious breach may not bring the agent's authority, and any associated agency contract, to an end unless the principal takes steps to cancel the agency. Where the agent has no reason to believe that the principal would not want the transaction completed, an inference of residual authority must be strong.[26]

IV. SOME PLATITUDES ABOUT LEGAL ANALYSIS

In light of the preceding discussion of *Target*, here I shall simply state some platitudes about judicial reasoning, or about legal doctrinal analysis more broadly, to try to get an overview of this practice:

1. This sort of back and forth between lawyers, judges and commentators is very typical and entirely familiar in the case of legal analysis, or 'black letter' law, a term I do not use pejoratively.
2. This critical back and forth is easily described. All the commentators claimed that the House of Lords got the law wrong, that is, applied a faulty legal analysis. In particular, these comments can be said to show either that a wrong principle, rule or other norm of the law was applied, or that the analysis failed to consider a relevant legal norm.[27]

[25] Matthew Conaglen (2010) 'Explaining Target Holdings v Referns' *Journal of Equity* 4: 288–94.
[26] Watts (n 19) 121.
[27] In English law, such a failure renders an authority unsafe, under what is called the '*per incuriam*' doctrine.

3. Points of legal analysis very typically are tested with the use of hypothetical fact situations. Lord Browne-Wilkinson's judgment begins with one, and this is deeply reflected in the study of law, moot courts and so on. It is beyond the scope of this chapter to offer an even modestly theoretical description of casuistic or case-based reasoning, but its presence in legal analysis is undeniable.[28]
4. These commentators are concerned to advance their counter-analyses even though they generally agreed with the result. It is sometimes said by legal theorists that judicial decisions are important merely for the result of the case – that the result of a case has binding force, not the reasoning the judge employed to get to the result.[29] Clearly none of the parties to this exchange think that, nor do any other lawyers I know.
5. These criticisms imply, and sometimes state, that there is a single right legal analysis, even if it takes much time and mental effort to get to. At the same time, there is no very clear distinction between a right legal analysis and the 'better view', as we say, the better legal analysis. Call coming to regard an analysis as the better one akin to coming to reflective equilibrium if you want, but I think it is closer to the truth that at some point our legal imagination runs out. Even when the 'better' analysis is alighted upon, that may not be the end of the story. We may find the analysis, upon further consideration, to be flawed in some way, and hope that a later discussion, in court or out, will reveal this.
6. The criticisms at play here are in some sense *demonstrative* of the error in legal analysis made by Lord Browne-Wilkinson and later commentators. What I mean by that is that a relevant criticism of some legal analysis, if it is sound, cannot just be ignored. This points to what might be called a 'metanorm' of legal analysis. In this case, no informed expert in trusts law – judge, practising lawyer or academic lawyer – could just ignore what Lord Millett or Edelman or Watts had said, which is not to say that a later court has a legal obligation to discuss it in detail. Relatedly, we understand that judgment is required to execute a legal analysis, and that even the best trusts lawyers and judges can be shown to make *mistakes*, 'get their sums wrong' as Holmes would put it. Also, by *demonstrative*, I mean to point out that lawyers with expertise in the area very generally see that a mistake, once explained, is a mistake. Disagreement ends at that point. This does

[28] The practice is ancient. See Baker (n 3) 10. One important point to be made here, which I must leave to further work, is that the obligatory reference to precedent in itself has nothing to do with the principle of *stare decisis*.

[29] Simmonds and Dworkin, for example; they argue that what justifies a particular decision is its falling within a theory or conception of justice that justifies the particular area of law, not whatever reasons a judge himself gave for it (though those reasons should be accorded some 'respect'). See Nigel E Simmonds (1984) *The Decline of Juridical Reason*, Manchester: Manchester University Press, 117–18; Dworkin (n 7) 113, 115, 118–19; Ronald Dworkin (1986) *Law's Empire*, London: Fontana, 247–48.

not mean that disagreements may not arise, but that what the correct legal analysis of the problem is will be agreed upon. And this is not to say that a good legal analysis will be determinative of a decision, for there may be lines of authority that, soundly followed, reveal a conflict when applied to the instant case. When that happens we are in the territory of 'hard cases', of which conflicting authority is but one example.[30]

7. On the hard/easy case distinction: this can obviously be drawn in different ways, and in one respect *Target* could be called an easy case, but in another not. It was easy in the sense that a sound legal analysis of the facts proved possible, so easy in the sense that it did not raise large issues of principle or policy. But it was not easy at all in the sense that arriving at the right analysis was easy. In many cases, as in this one, the necessary legal analysis is difficult and time-consuming. I admire Lord Browne-Wilkinson and all of the other players in this dispute. It is not as if the norms of law immediately leap to mind just upon a survey of the facts. Of course some do, which is why we can roughly fit fact situations into the relevant areas of doctrine. But this case shows clearly that not all the relevant legal considerations do. Great lawyers 'see' more at once in this way than do lesser lawyers.
8. Legal analysis *always* requires the consideration of a *number of legal rules*, never just a single rule. This is true of applying individual provisions of a statute as well, for not only can rules of language, of grammar and vocabulary be involved, but statutes are always interpreted in light of canons of interpretation and legal concepts (for example the concepts of the background common law) not defined by the statute itself.
9. The back and forth discussion of legal analyses also shows that there is no very clear distinction between applying the law and modifying it.[31] In cases not covered by clear precedents, we sometimes say the law is being 'developed', which captures the idea nicely, I think. This also reflects the imagination or creativity necessary for doctrinal legal analysis. This, I suggest, is akin to the imagination and creativity required to express oneself well in language. But in doing this, in neither case are these actors making up new rules as they go along, or at least not typically. In the legal case the commentators we have considered do not think they are inventing legal rules or concepts in proposing their analyses, but 'seeing them aright', noticing their appropriateness as standards in the instant case. In some cases the legal development is very clearly closer to modifying the law than applying it, when a court is, for instance, asked to extend a legal concept, for example 'bill of lading', which historically had to be a paper document, to 'electronic bills of lading'.

[30] For a survey of different kinds of 'hard case', see James Penner (2002) 'Legal Reasoning' in *Introduction to Jurisprudence and Legal Theory: Commentary and Materials*, eds James Penner, David Schiff and Richard Nobles, London: Butterworths, 649–717, 663–67.

[31] A point emphasised by Raz: see Joseph Raz (2009) *The Authority of the Law*, 2nd edn, Oxford: Oxford University Press, 206–09.

10. Judges and lawyers always write for an audience, and in the case of legal analysis that is pretty much exclusively for the 'caste of experts', as Simpson puts it.[32] In particular, without meaning to endorse the American Legal Realist project,[33] lawyers and judges are very much in the business of predicting how others would reason to decide a case – no judge wants his judgment to be successfully appealed because he erred in law. At the same time, a judge providing a legal analysis is not in the business of 'public justification' in Rawls's sense.[34] Anyone clever and willing enough to spend the time and money can join the caste of lawyers, but their audience in terms of applying legal norms is themselves, not the public, any more than doctors or scientists are in the business of public justification. Of course, like doctors, lawyers interact with and advise non-practitioners, the public if you will. And they both need to have what might be called a good 'bedside manner' to do this part of their jobs well, and this includes providing lay-accessible explanations of medicine or the law. But their opinions and so on are clearly not to be judged by any lay standard, and in particular not by any standard that requires formulations that amount to a 'public justification', whatever that is understood to be. Or rather, any such public justification regarding legal doctrine or medical doctrine could only ever be accomplished very indirectly, in terms of assessments of the institutions that maintain these practices, that keep these practices in more or less good working order. Up until fairly recently, say the turn of the twentieth century, it could reasonably be argued that many aspects of legal and medical practice and their sustaining institutions could hardly be justified in this way at all,[35] which is not to say that we do not still face many challenges ourselves.

V. A FEW TENTATIVE THEORETICAL CONSIDERATIONS

A. Hershovitz on Wittgenstein and Legal Rules

Scott Hershovitz argues that relying on Wittgenstein's later writings on rule following gets us nowhere in trying to make sense of legal reasoning. He writes '[Here I shall] focus on the feature of Wittgenstein's view which will be most important for us – the *unreflective nature* of rule-following.'[36]

[32] Simpson (n 3) 80.

[33] For a like thought see Baker (n 3) 1–2.

[34] John Rawls (2005) *Political Liberalism*, New York: Columbia University Press, 212–54.

[35] Though for different reasons. See also Filipe Jimenez (2021) 'Contracts, Markets & Justice' *University of Toronto Law Journal* 71: 144–63, 154–57, on the public justification of contract law.

[36] Scott Hershovitz (2002) 'Wittgenstein on Rules: The Phantom Menace' *Oxford Journal of Legal Studies* 22: 619–40, 628 (original emphasis).

To explain the unreflective nature of rule following, Hershovitz points out three related things. First, we can follow a rule without interpreting it.[37] This is the sense in which Wittgenstein has said that we follow rules 'blindly'.[38] If I have mastered a rule, I know what it requires me to do when I have an occasion to apply it. Of course, this does not mean that we may not face circumstances where we may not know whether a rule applies, or are uncertain about which rule to apply.[39] But that cannot be the general case or otherwise rules would not be able to guide us at all.

Second, we can learn rules because we can be *trained* to apply them, and this is so because of the kind of creatures we are. As Hershovitz says, 'it is a fortunate fact about human beings that we tend to make the same generalisations from training; that we are trainable to follow rules'.[40]

Third, following on from this training conception of the acquisition of rules, Hershovitz states, 'Following rules is a social practice, a custom.'[41]

I am in basic agreement with Hershovitz about all of this, in particular his first and second points, that is about the cognitive basis of our ability to see things as the same ('make the same generalisations'). However, three things point to possible differences in our views. Hershovitz explains our ability to go on in the same way in terms of our susceptibility to training. Whilst we do have this ability to respond to training, it is our ability to see things as the same that makes this training possible, and seeing this allows us to see that 'training' here does not require repeated instruction in any rigorous sense. For example, it seems quite clear that young children acquire the grammatical norms and vocabulary of their first natural language without a great deal of explicit training, although errors are typically corrected. Having the ability to pick up on similarities, they are also adept at learning by noticing and following the behaviour of their conspecifics. Since Wittgenstein was centrally concerned with the rule-following aspects of linguistic behaviour, it is right to point this out.[42]

Second, Hershovitz seems to think that for Wittgenstein, following rules 'is a social practice, a custom'. This seems misjudged, although Wittgenstein's remarks can be read to lead to two particular misconceptions. One is that a rule must actually be practised for it to be a rule, to be understood as a standard for behaviour. The best way of explaining a rule to someone might be to 'practise' it in the sense of showing them some examples of its application, and making them apply the rule to cases is one of the best ways of testing whether they have grasped the rule; but practising a rule is not strictly speaking necessary for having understood it. For example, many statutory rules are perfectly

[37] ibid, 628.
[38] ibid, 629–30; Wittgenstein (n 1) para 219.
[39] Text to n 45.
[40] Hershovitz (n 36) 629.
[41] ibid, 628.
[42] Of course the concept of 'training' is itself very multifarious, as the history of legal education itself shows.

well understood by those who read statutes, even if it turns out that the rule is never actually applied. The second misconception in understanding what Wittgenstein says about 'custom' is that rules only exist when there is a body of people applying them. This is obviously false. Whichever of Leibniz or Newton first developed the calculus, one of them was the first and only person who was able to follow the rules of calculus to generate the results of that mathematical operation. He was following the rules of calculus despite being the only person who had mastered the rules he himself had invented.

Finally, whilst Hershovitz is also right to emphasise the idea that following some rules 'blindly' captures the idea that we do not follow rules for a reason in the sense of applying some formula or interpretation of a rule, or justifying a rule as we apply it, the idea that Wittgenstein's insights only apply to 'unreflective' applications of a rule is misleading if not simply mistaken, as I shall now explain.

Discussing Fuller's well-known example of applying the 'No vehicles in the park' rule to the jeep to be mounted on a plinth as a statue,[43] Hershovitz writes:

> The case of the jeep on a plinth is a classic hard case in law. What makes it hard is that the jeep is obviously and non-controversially a vehicle if anything is. Judges might eventually construct a legal fiction that jeeps on platforms, or vehicles as part of monuments, are not vehicles, but this will be just that, a fiction (or more generously, a technical use of 'vehicle'), and it will probably be controversial as well. What makes the case hard is that though the jeep is in the extension of the prohibited class of items, some believe that the law does not really prohibit it. … The upshot of this is that even though the application of the key descriptive term in a law (the term on which the case seems to turn, so to speak) may be an easy case of rule-following in the Wittgensteinian sense, the application of the law itself can still be a hard case in the legal sense. The distinctions come apart.
>
> … Wittgenstein's remarks on rules do not provide deeper insight into the legal [hard/easy case] distinction. To the extent that they tell us something about clear cases of rule-following, they do not by any immediate implication tell us anything about clear cases in law. To think so is to confuse two different types of clarity.[44]

Hershovitz is right to think that Wittgenstein's rule-following considerations provide no resources for resolving the kind of legal hard case presented by the jeep on a plinth, but I would submit he is wrong to think they do not clarify what is going on here. What is at issue is *what rule* the statute is laying down, expressed as 'No vehicles in the park'. Determining that may be called statutory construction or interpretation, but as Hershovitz says later on, this sort of interpretation is not what Wittgenstein means by 'interpretation' when he discusses interpretation of rules. But that in itself is useful to know because of the indeterminate use of 'interpretation' in legal discourse. And Wittgenstein's

[43] Lon L Fuller (1958) 'Positivism and Fidelity to Law: A Reply to Professor Hart' *Harvard Law Review* 71: 630–72.

[44] Hershovitz (n 36) 632, 633.

'interpretation' does occur in law, as Hershovitz himself points out, so the disambiguation of the term does real work. What disagreement there is here between Hershovitz and me seems to be about how frequently Wittgensteinian interpretation occurs in the law, that is, judges providing different formulations or expressions of a legal rule. I think this happens all the time, especially where the common law is concerned,[45] whereas Hershovitz seems to think this only happens 'on occasion'.

But Hershovitz's real objection to the idea that Wittgenstein's remarks on rule following illuminate the law is that law often, and typically, involves a 'reflective' application of rules:

> [Wittgenstein's remarks] tell us almost nothing about legal rules. Law is a reflective activity; one of our most reflective. We offer justifications and reasons for the way we apply legal rules, and we are willing to entertain doubts about whether or not we are applying them correctly. People come to blows over the right way to go on. And when doubts are raised, we almost always respond with reasons why one understanding of what the law requires is preferable to another. This is not to say that the application of legal rules is on all occasions reflective; perhaps it is often not. But Wittgenstein's remarks are not directed at reflective instances of rule-following, and many applications of legal rules, especially by judges in courts, are carried out reflectively.[46]

I think these thoughts reveal a dangerous and misleading ambiguity. Legal disagreement, as we have seen, is typically about which rules of the system properly apply – it is not about 'doubts' about how any particular rule applies if it is determined to be applicable. No one doubts that making that kind of determination is a reflective activity. But that 'reflection' does not transfer onto the very application of the legal rule itself, once the rule to be applied has been fixed upon. In that important sense, legal rules are just as much rules as are the rules of grammar. Hershovitz's claim here is all the more surprising since later in the article, Hershovitz himself recognised that the law is a *system* of rules:

> Law, we might say, is not an assemblage of individual rules unrelated to each other. Laws are part of a system of rules. Though we might ask what does *this rule* require, and consider a rule individually, this is not what judges are supposed to do in adjudication. Adjudication is about determining what *the law* requires, not just a particular law.[47]

I think that this is absolutely right, but then Hershovitz immediately goes on to more or less to reprise the view that I have just criticised:

> To this end, any law must be considered as part of a system of laws, and this requires forming an interpretation of what role it plays in the system. Context can change meaning, and a law located in the context of a legal system may have a different

[45] Text to n 50.
[46] Hershovitz (n 36) 636.
[47] ibid, 639 (original emphasis).

meaning that we might attach to it individually. Interpretation is required to discover this.[48]

Whereas the non-Wittgensteinian status of legal rules in the prior passage turned on the 'reflective' nature of their application, here the idea seems to be that, unlike in the case of Wittgensteinian rules, legal rules depend upon interpretation for their application. Worse, a legal rule's meaning or application seems to vary according to context. I would deny the truth of both claims. For reasons given, legal 'interpretation' here can only mean something like statutory or case law interpretation in the sense of determining what the rule actually is, or providing an 'interpretation' of a rule in order to express what the rule actually is. It does not mean determining a fresh rule upon each instance of its application, for such a 'rule' would be no rule at all, legal or otherwise.

Although this discussion of Wittgenstein's rule-following considerations has been relatively brief, we can see that it immediately yields two rather interesting results for our understanding of legal analysis. First, of particular relevance to the common law, it is clear that no pattern of judgments in past judicial decisions 'logically' requires us to say that those decisions embody any one particular rule. Our understanding that a particular rule underlies a series of cases depends upon our seeing those cases in the same way. If, for example, different judges or lawyers find two different rules that explain a line of cases, and we can 'see' the force or plausibility of both as candidate rules underlying the decisions, then we are faced with a genuine choice between rules, or a genuine uncertainty as to which rule led to that series of decisions. But by the same token, a lawyer or judge cannot just propose any rule to explain the cases, proposing rules akin to the rule of 'addition' that would require 68 + 57 = 5.[49] While we cannot 'logically' rule out any preposterous rule, we are perfectly capable of judging rules of this kind to be 'non-starters'. And so we can see how Wittgenstein's analysis both makes sense of, and restricts, the scope of rule scepticism in law. The thoroughgoing rule sceptic is not ruled out of order by any logical pattern in past cases; but by the same token, he cannot assume that in any legal case he can make what he wants of the past decisions. Our going-on-in-the-same-way sense or judgment allows us perfectly well to find that in many cases only one candidate rule plausibly underlies past decisions. In order to claim that a line of cases is uncertain, someone must do the work of proposing two or more candidate rules that really do plausibly account for the decisions. Scepticism must be earned, case by case.

Second, our attention to the distinction between rule formulations or interpretations of rules, and the rules themselves, helps explain why the common law typically frowns upon treating particular statements in a case as 'canonical'

[48] ibid, 639.

[49] To borrow Kripke's famous example: Saul Kripke (1982) *Wittgenstein on Rules and Private Language*, Oxford: Blackwell, 8.

rule statements, and why statutory interpretation is often a locus of legal argument. Rules lie in the behaviour they require, not in the way we might express them. When we read a case, we see judges trying to express what they mean with many different formulations; they try to put the point in different ways, so as not to give the impression that any one formulation is to be treated as a sacred statement. They thus wisely realise that the goal is for the reader of the judgment to 'get' the rule, not to memorise some form of words, for no form of words uniquely captures the rule. In a later case, in a different context, the rule might better be formulated differently. Statutes present a constant problem in this respect. The point here is not to claim that rules cannot be expressed in language. The point is just that because a rule and its formulation are different things, the same formulation may be compatible with different rules.

B. Law and Morality

In the case of our ability to use rules, or a body of rules, there seems to be interesting differences in their intentionality (with a 't'), what they are about or represent, from one domain to another. In particular, certain bodies of rules are autonomous in the sense that they do not 'answer' to empirical reality. Consider this from Hacker:

> [The grammar of a language] is autonomous in so far as it is not answerable to reality for truth or correctness. It can also be said to be arbitrary or akin to arbitrary. The arbitrariness of grammar is an aspect of its autonomy.[50]

This can be contrasted with the rules governing, say, cookery.[51] These rules relate to the goal of producing tasty and nutritious food, a result which can be described independently of the means, or the techniques, by which it is produced. These rules can be contrasted with the rules of a game, such as chess.[52] There is no 'goal' of amusement that can be specified independently of following the rules of, that is playing, chess. So the rules of chess cannot be 'right or wrong' in the sense that rules of cookery can be – if your recipes and techniques in the kitchen are poor then you will produce insipid or ill-tasting dishes.

But rules of grammar are *not* 'arbitrary' in another sense of that word:

> The claim that [grammar] is arbitrary does not mean that it is capricious, unimportant, or a matter of individual whim. Nor does it mean that we cannot ever give *reasons* why such-and-such grammatical rules are useful, or that there cannot be reasons why, for rather specialised purposes, we choose to adopt new grammatical

[50] PMS Hacker (1989) *Insight and Illusion: Themes in the Philosophy of Wittgenstein*, rev edn, Bristol: Thoemmes Press, 192, references omitted.

[51] ibid, 192.

[52] ibid.

> structures. Relativity physics employs the expressions 'space' and 'time' differently from the ways in which ordinary speakers do and also from the ways Newtonian physics does. They are used in accord with different grammatical rules and determine different *concepts*. Reasons can be given for this …, not in terms of truth or correctness ('space really is Riemannian' is as absurd as 'A kilometre really is 1000 metres') but in terms of predictive and explanatory fruitfulness of the theories expressed in that grammar. The grammar, however, is not a theory about anything – it determines what makes sense and asserts nothing about the facts.[53]

The question these considerations raise for us is how we are to conceive the rules of law, say the rules of trusts law doctrine. Are they like rules of cooking, instrumental means to achieve some external goal, or are they more like grammatical rules, like the rules of a natural language? Notice that simply framing some sort of external goal, like 'amusement' in the case of chess, does not decide the case in favour of the instrumental, cooking interpretation. I take it that Hacker would accept that one might frame any of our rules or bodies of rules in terms of very abstract desiderata that they might, in some sense, 'satisfy', such as the goal of 'communication' as a way of giving some explanation of the goal of all the particular rule-constituted language games in the repertoire. But I also take it that Hacker would regard pushing the grammatical rules of natural languages into the 'cooking rules' camp as decidedly misconceived.

Let me finish with a few considerations that, to my mind, suggest that the rules of the law of trusts have at least some considerable affinity both with rules of grammar or the rules of games, but also with the instrumental rules of cooking. We can begin with their affinity to the latter.

As has been pointed out many times, the more concrete concepts of the law, such as property, contract, damage, negligence and so on, have clear affinity with their non-legal uses from which they arose. As Baker says:

> On the one hand, there are those general propositions of law, good sense, and basic morality, and those usages in relation to everyday dealings, which guide and control the conduct of lay people in their different walks of life; and on the other there is the detailed, scholarly professional learning which is not shared by the public at large. The former might be categorized as fact rather than law. Usage and custom are treated by the law as fact rather than opinion, and the general assumptions of society are facts. This is historically as well as legally sound. Judges did not invent contracts, or trusts, or bonds, or even (I suspect) contingent remainders, before they were used in real life. No more have our present generation of judges invented credit cards or electronic bills of lading.[54]

I will put to one side the interesting question of which parts of the judge-made law reflect more or less lay notions of justice, and which reflect more technical

[53] ibid, 193 (original emphasis).
[54] Baker (n 3) 59.

legal ideas (eg contingent remainders) engineered, as it were, by practitioners and put into use long before any legal disputes brought them before a court. But surely a great deal of our legal understanding of a concept like property very much reflects the morally-charged commonsense concept.[55] To this extent legal rules are like rules of cooking. We can, though perhaps vaguely and unsatisfactorily, independently specify the moral considerations that the court must answer to in rendering a sound decision. This humble truth is the foundation stone for 'instrumentalists' about the law like the late John Gardner and myself.[56] On this conception, morality is incurably vague and indeterminate in many cases, and one of the chief functions of the law is to resolve these uncertainties so as to resolve disputes in as fair a way as possible, as well as giving concrete directives that aim to avoid disputes in the first place. On this conception, the law formalises and regiments our commonsense moral reasoning, akin to the way symbolic logic formalises and regiments our commonsense inferential reasoning. But in the same way that '∧' does not mean the same as 'and',[57] 'property' in law does not express the same concept as 'property' does in ordinary language, though they are of course more or less closely related.

But it seems to me that it is much more dubious to claim that the law reflects any very clear lay concepts of 'justice' or 'equality' or 'efficiency'. These very abstract values, like the value of amusement vis-à-vis chess, do not do any work I can see in explaining any person's mastery of the rules of legal doctrine. I can learn the rules of chess even if I do not find the game amusing at all, and I should say the same *mutatis mutandis* about the law, say, of trusts, that is, without considering whether it aligns with any notions I have of equality or justice, to the extent I even operate with such abstract concepts in my personal moral life, which I almost never do as a matter of fact.

In any case, rules of law are like rules of grammar in the relative independence of their concepts from their ordinary language counterparts. *Target* provides a clear example. The concepts of account, compensation, ratification and so on are regimentations engineered to resolve the issues that arise when a trustee breaches his obligations, and to that extent commonsense morality is more or less insulated from their applications. At the same time we see that Lord Browne-Wilkinson thinks that a legal analysis that gives rise to an 'unjust and surprising conclusion'[58] must have something wrong with it.

[55] I have elsewhere tried to show that the layman's concept of property has ill-deserved the abuse it has received at the hands of legal scholars. See JE Penner (2020) *Property Rights: A Re-Examination*, Oxford: Oxford University Press, 39–40.

[56] For discussion see James Penner (2021) 'Justifying Private Law: "Reasons Fundamentalist" Instrumentalism and the Kantian Account' in *Justifying Private Rights*, eds Simone Degeling, Michael Crawford and Nicholas Tiverios, Oxford: Hart Publishing, 45–62.

[57] One example is the fact that '∧' is order indifferent, whereas 'and' is frequently not. Consider the difference in meaning between 'He died and was buried' and 'He was buried and died'. For discussion see Baker and Hacker (n 9) 171–74, 178–79.

[58] *Target* (n 10) 432E.

VI. CONCLUSION: LAW AND JUDGMENT – REJECTING THE HOLMESIAN PICTURE

This chapter is only a start at rejecting the Holmesian picture of legal reasoning. All I have really sought to do here is reveal something we already know about doctrinal legal reasoning and the kinds of disagreements to which it gives rise. Save for attempts to formalise the judicial technique of distinguishing cases, which has received extensive theoretical attention,[59] this garden-variety practice has seemed to me to be mostly ignored or mischaracterised by theorists. For reasons I shall pursue in further work, I think it has more theoretical interest than has heretofore been recognised. But this must all be framed by the frank recognition that doctrinal legal reasoning is not all that judges do. Arguably, in some areas of law doctrine is rarely controlling of judicial decision making. An obvious example would be US constitutional litigation concerning the Bill of Rights, where the US Supreme Court regularly fractures on political lines. That phenomenon and other like cases deserve theoretical attention too, but my project here has been to explore something else.

APPENDIX – SUMMARY OF THE FACTS TAKEN FROM THE HEADNOTE OF *TARGET*[60]

A finance company instructed a firm of solicitors to act for it in the provision of a loan as mortgagee on commercial property. The solicitors were also instructed by the proposed mortgagor who had informed the finance company that the property had been valued by a firm of surveyors at £2 million. Unknown to the finance company, the proposed mortgagor was in fact paying only £775,000 for the property. The finance company gave the solicitors a total of £1,525,000 to be held on a bare trust and transferred to the mortgagor once the property had been purchased and charged to the finance company. In breach of trust and before the prospective mortgagor had purchased the property, the solicitors paid away a total of £1,490,000 without having received any charge on the property. The solicitors untruthfully informed the finance company that the purchase and charges had been completed. Almost a month later, the property was charged to the finance company, which subsequently contracted to sell it for £500,000. The finance company brought an action against the solicitors alleging, inter alia, breach of trust and claiming restitution of the entire sum. On the finance company's application for summary judgment, Warner J gave the solicitors leave to defend, conditional on bringing £1 million into court and, subject to the finance company's providing a bank guarantee, paying it over to it as an interim payment. On the solicitors' appeal and on the finance company's cross-appeal,

[59] See the essays in chs 7, 6 and 5 of this collection by Horty, Lamond and McBride respectively.
[60] *Target* (n 10) 421D-G.

the Court of Appeal dismissed the appeal but (by a majority) allowed the cross-appeal, holding that in the circumstances the solicitors were liable to replace all the moneys paid away in breach of trust, subject only to the finance company's giving credit for any moneys recoverable on the realisation by it of its security, and judgment was given for the finance company.

Part III

Doctrine and Practice

10

Thinking Like a Lawyer: An Introduction to Common Law Method

SUNDRAM PETER SOOSAY

ACADEMIC CHARACTERISATIONS OF legal reasoning typically present this activity as requiring little more than rigorous analysis of words and concepts. To 'think like a lawyer' is, under this view, no different from thinking like an academic philosopher or scholar. In this chapter, a radically different characterisation of the process is offered, one that understands the work involved to be much more practical in nature, a form of concrete professional activity not so unlike the methods or practices employed by doctors and engineers. To achieve the reorientation envisioned, attention will be drawn to several aspects of common law practice, among them the doctrine of precedent, and a number of doctrinal curiosities. The chapter will show that such practices arise in answer to the central concern of the professional method employed, which is the improvement of normative structure through the articulation and modification of organic norms.

I. INTRODUCTION

To what extent do law schools offer a meaningful training in law? Readers familiar with the work of anti-formalist thinkers like Oliver Wendell Holmes Jr, Karl Llewellyn and Lon Fuller will know that the earliest days of the law school were troubled by doubts as to the appropriateness and efficacy of legal education in its modern form.[1] Though rarely expressed in so stark a manner, doubts

[1] See Oliver Wendell Holmes Jr (1897) 'The Path of the Law' *Harvard Law Review* 10: 457–78; Karl N Llewellyn (1935) 'On What is Wrong with So-Called Legal Education' *Columbia Law Review* 35: 651–78; Lon L Fuller (1948) 'What the Law Schools Can Contribute to the Making of Lawyers' *Journal of Legal Education* 1: 189–204.

of this kind remain with us today.[2] Such doubts arise, more than anything else, from the fact that law schools in their present form generally eschew the vocational approach preferred by other professional schools in favour of a method of instruction almost exclusively centred upon the analysis and criticism of legal doctrine. What is most notable about this approach to legal education is that it does away with need for anything resembling a distinctive understanding of law as a practical enterprise. This is achieved by taking for granted that law is borne by rules that are themselves conceived of as mere bearers of information. If this is true, a person interested in creating or interpreting law requires little in the way of special knowledge or ability beyond the ordinary person's capacity for language use and logical analysis. This should give us pause. Though it is frequently said that the aim of legal education is to teach students to 'think like lawyers', what is taught is really nothing of the sort. To a cynical eye, legal education can resemble little more than the use of legal material as fodder for simple exercises in analysis and rhetoric.

In this chapter, we will take 'thinking like a lawyer' a good deal more seriously and understand the activities of common lawyers in much the same way we habitually think of comparable activities undertaken by doctors, engineers and architects. Under this view, creating and interpreting law requires technical abilities only lawyers possess, abilities the legal profession has developed over generations, and which an individual lawyer can acquire only through years of a specialised form of training that is predominantly practical in character. What judges and lawyers employ is not a process of reasoning that is primarily logical and analytical; it is, rather, a collection of methods, techniques and practical devices, all contrived specifically to aid lawyers in securing the unique purposes of the enterprise in the face of practical constraints and difficulties that are themselves unalterable. In common law practice, the ultimate end sought is autonomous order.[3] In any given instance, this will require the legal practitioner to remedy defects in the organic normative organisation of a particular human relationship or social setting. Legal practice is constituted by the employment of special methods and techniques to achieve this end, methods and techniques that derive their curious form from the natural constraints and difficulties that lawyers face in carrying out their work. This chapter will provide a brief account of some of what this entails.[4]

[2] Doubts of this nature were expressed in 2013 by Lord Sumption, former Justice of the UK Supreme Court, first in an interview with *Counsel Magazine* (www.counselmagazine.co.uk/articles/interview-lord-sumption), and subsequently in a debate with Cambridge academic Graham Virgo (www.youtube.com/watch?v=uMR1NIEifWM).

[3] The phrase 'autonomous order' is derived from the work of Lon Fuller. See Lon L Fuller (1966) *Law In Quest of Itself*, Boston, MA: Beacon Press, 99–140.

[4] This essay is presented here in abbreviated form. The complete essay contains a third section on the moral dimension of the common law. This third section focuses, particularly, on the ubiquity of reasonableness as a consideration within common law reasoning.

II. WORKING WITH CASES

A. Curating Sites of Social Interaction

We will begin with precedent, and with the peculiar emphasis placed within common law reasoning on facts and fact-situations. When we think of rules, we typically imagine that we can apprehend these rules in isolation, wholly separate from the factual situations in which they are applied. This understanding of the matter is central to our naive conception of rules, and consequently, to the way we think of law and legal reasoning. Norms, however, remain always bound to specific factual circumstances in a way that contrasts sharply with this view. Norms are a property of factual situations, inseparable from the way we perceive and function within our surroundings.[5] To engage with norms, judges must engage directly with the relevant life- or fact-situations themselves, and must continue to do so as experience brings to light fresh complications and difficulties within these life- or fact-situations.[6] This remains true even after the norm in question is given articulate expression in the form of a rule. Even when this has been accomplished, the normative content of the rule remains bound to the specific factual situation the articulate rule now regulates. As our understanding of the situation changes, the norm, and consequently the rule, changes with it.

Working with norms is therefore quite unlike the process we imagine when we assume legal processes invariably concern the use of formal rules. Indeed, the activity of common law judges and lawyers only derivatively concerns the interpretation and application of rules. It is more centrally dedicated, rather, to the ongoing maintenance and development of the normative aspect of the

[5] All references made to 'norms' throughout this chapter refer to organic norms of the kind traditionally studied by sociologists and anthropologists. These are the informal, often inarticulate regularities in human behaviour that arise from the way human beings come to understand their surroundings, and in particular their own behaviour and the behaviour of others. The word 'norm' is sometimes used more broadly, particularly within analytic philosophy, where it is associated with the activity of ordering in human life in a more general sense. When used in this way, the word encompasses artificial means of ordering, including formal rules, commands and orders. For an example, see Joseph Raz (1999) *Practical Reason and Norms*, Oxford: Oxford University Press. All references to norms and the activities associated with them in this chapter refer to norms in the former, narrower sense. The choice of the word 'norm' was inspired, particularly, by Karl Llewellyn, who wrote of 'normative generalization' and 'incipient norms', for instance, with this use of the word in mind. See Karl N Llewellyn (1940) 'The Normative, the Legal, and the Law-Jobs: The Problem of Juristic Method' *Yale Law Journal* 49: 1355–1400.

[6] The phrase 'fact-situation' is derived from Karl N Llewellyn (1960) *The Common Law Tradition*, Boston, MA: Little Brown and Company. The understanding of common law reasoning presented in this chapter is drawn in large part from Llewellyn's *Common Law Tradition*, his 'Law-Jobs' article ((1940) n 5), and Lon L Fuller (1969) 'Human Interaction and the Law' *American Journal of Jurisprudence* 14: 1–36. The ideas presented in this chapter, drawn as they are from the anti-formalist literature, are incompatible with formalist theories of law, including the tradition of positivism associated with HLA Hart and Jeremy Bentham.

social fabric that binds members of the community together and provides the basis for their shared social life. Common law practice is best understood, under this view, as a process that aims at the curation of the actual sites of social interaction that legal subjects inhabit. Common law judges do this by engaging with the shared reciprocal expectations members of the community use to navigate their social world, reasoning through these expectations and changing them in the manner most conducive to autonomous order. Judges conduct this repair activity amid the spontaneous life of the community, acting to reconcile the conflicting interests that come to light by adapting the existing social fabric in such a way as to accommodate the various pressures in a harmonious relation.

By way of illustration, consider a dispute between two parties, between a seller of goods or services and a buyer who has purchased these goods or services. When a dispute of this nature is brought before a common law judge, what is sought is not merely an equitable resolution to the specific dispute between the parties, nor the appropriate application of a formal rule. What is sought, rather, is clarification of the normative organisation of a generic social relationship, one involving buyers and sellers more generally, as this relationship is understood by the community at large. Under this view, the transaction between the parties is viewed as a site of recurring social interaction that possesses, within itself, guidance as to its own optimal ordering. The judge will proceed, then, by attempting to realise this inherent potential for order, identifying for participants the reciprocal expectations that must obtain within the setting in question for it to operate autonomously. The result will be applicable in all future interactions between sellers and buyers on the particular issue under dispute.[7]

Though at times exotic in appearance, the solution sought in every case is simply a norm of conduct of the sort found in every social setting. The following are examples of norms articulated by common law judges:

- If a product is reasonably expected to be dangerous if negligently made and the product is known to be used by those other than the original purchaser in the normal course of business, a duty of care exists.[8]
- If a person brings, or accumulates, on his land, anything which, if it should escape, may cause damage to his neighbour, he does so at his peril. If it does escape, and cause damage, he is responsible, however careful he may have been, and whatever precautions he may have taken to prevent the damage.[9]

[7] See Llewellyn (1960) (n 6) 122: 'Every fact-pattern of common life, so far as the legal order can take it in, carries within itself its appropriate, natural rules, its right law. This is a natural law which is real, not imaginary; it is not a creature of mere reason, but rests on the solid foundation of what reason can recognise in the nature of man and of the life conditions of the time and place; it is thus not eternal nor changeless nor everywhere the same, but is indwelling in the very circumstances of life. The highest task of law-giving consists in uncovering and implementing this immanent law.' The passage is not Llewellyn's own but taken from Levin Goldschmidt. It is nevertheless fundamental to Llewellyn's thought, and, accordingly, to the view of common law practice presented in this chapter.

[8] *MacPherson v Buick Motor Co*, 217 NY 382, 111 NE 1050 (1916).

[9] *Rylands v Fletcher* [1868] UKHL 1.

- Consequential damages for breach of contract can be recovered only if, at the time the contract was made, the breaching party had reason to foresee that consequential damages would be the probable result of breach.[10]
- Where clauses incorporated into a contract contain a particularly onerous or unusual condition, the party seeking to enforce that condition must show that it had been brought fairly and reasonably to the attention of the other party.[11]
- Performance of a pre-existing duty is not legally sufficient consideration for a new contract.[12]

Though we might be inclined to think of the above as 'rules', in fact the examples are not really rules at all, if by 'rule' we have in mind a directive issued by a political superior to an inferior.[13] Each is instead better understood as presenting us with a provisional statement of normative organisation. This is a statement articulating a form or pattern perceived within recurring social conduct that, when explicitly acknowledged or intuited, has the effect of drawing actual behaviour into conformity with that same form or pattern. Statements of this kind are not handed down from above, the work of a great law-giver, but are instead shaped carefully in workman-like manner from raw material already present in the existing social reality of the community. In each case, the relevant interaction already exists in the world but is defective and prone to conflict. Common law judges are asked to evaluate the problem and determine a form for the interaction that is in keeping with the interests, expectations and tolerances of members of the community. This, in essence, is the work that common law judges are asked to do.

B. Rules as Symbols or Mnemonic Devices

In light of the preceding, the academic preoccupation with legal doctrine, and with linguistic and logical clarity within this doctrine, is misguided. As is to be expected given the emphasis placed on practical problem solving, common law judges and lawyers are, for the most part, little concerned with providing clear, definitive statements of the law in force. This is because the result sought within common law practice is not conceptual clarity of the sort that can be captured readily in the crisp legal rules envisioned by the likes of Jeremy Bentham and

[10] *Hadley & Anor v Baxendale & Ors* [1854] EWHC Exch J70, (1854) 9 Ex Ch 341, (1854) 9 ExCh 341, 156 ER 145.

[11] *Interfoto Picture Library Limited v Stiletto Visual Programmes Limited* [1987] EWCA Civ 6.

[12] *Stilk v Myrick* [1809] EWHC KB J58, (1809) 170 ER 1168.

[13] That law is by its very nature a statist phenomenon is fundamental to the positivist conception of law. Austin expressed this explicitly, but the presupposition is implicit in all positivist theories of law. See, eg, Lecture I in John Austin (1832) *The Province of Jurisprudence Determined*, London: John Murray.

Herbert Hart.[14] Rather, what is sought is practical and moral transparency in the site of interaction itself, organisation in the social world that can be grasped effortlessly in action and accepted without question by participants immersed in just those situations. Against this background, the formal or doctrinal dimension of the law must be understood as an institutional resource cultivated to provide support to the more demanding practical undertaking central to the enterprise.

This is plainly the case where the law in its written form is found in recorded decisions. Here it is perfectly obvious that the decisions do not themselves embody the law in any simple way; instead, they provide necessary practical support to an inductive process undertaken by judges and lawyers. A system of precedent is not required where disputes are addressed in isolation, where what is sought is an equitable resolution to the immediate dispute and nothing more. Nor is it needed where decision turns solely on the content of a formal rule. Common law adjudication is not exclusively concerned with the immediate dispute, however, nor with the application of a rule. It is instead oriented towards a more deep-rooted problem found within the normative organisation of the setting, activity or relationship in question. As any one dispute will, on its own, furnish only a partial view of the underlying problem, the matter must be addressed iteratively, with the court returning to the problem repeatedly as new variations of the dispute arise, each one revealing as yet unanswered questions or the unintended consequences of earlier interventions. Each time the problem is revisited in this way, the court will evaluate the problem in light of previous interventions, learn whatever it can and modify its solution.

Throughout this process of iterative development, the historical record kept of the decisions is indispensable if the law is to move in the direction of the desired solution. Careful maintenance of this record ensures that judges always have available to them an interrogation of each problem, along with a record of the reasoned interventions of their predecessors. This historical record enhances each judge's ability to solve the problem before the court, and at the same time ensures that attempts made by the various judges over time all cohere and build one upon the other in a rational way. The discipline provided by the historical record is not of the straightforward kind imagined by those who accept the naive conception of rules, however, as judges are throughout primarily concerned with the fitness of their solution to the problem before them. Each judge is required to exercise his or her judgement throughout as to what constitutes an optimal normative solution to the problem before the court. This judgement is pragmatic in character and is therefore both open and inherently fallible. Judges will disagree, but if due regard is given to precedent, clarity will emerge over time.

[14] HLA Hart in particular repeatedly emphasised the importance of using language clearly. For an example, see the opening to HLA Hart (1958) 'Positivism and the Separation of Law and Morals' *Harvard Law Review* 71: 593–629.

By proceeding in this way, by addressing the underlying problem repeatedly and making the necessary adjustments at each step, judges work steadily towards an optimal ordering of the conflicting interests in question. This drawn-out process – a groping towards a sort of transparent order in relations – should, in time, achieve a form of organisation that participants in the setting or activity or relationship find effortlessly satisfying in its normative balance. When this is achieved, the law will have 'worked itself pure'. The phrase is from Lord Mansfield and captures very well the way the common law method is employed to steadily wear away normative irregularities that serve to disfigure and disrupt the interactive flow of communal life.[15] Through the application of the common law method, judges work towards an optimal arrangement that effortlessly reconciles the many conflicting pressures arising from social life, redirecting the relevant human energies into a harmonious pattern.[16]

All of the above is no less true where 'law in the books' takes the form of precisely formulated rules. Even here, the formal or doctrinal dimension of the law exists merely to aid judges and lawyers in a process more centrally concerned with discerning and instantiating organic normative order. Indeed, legal theories that equate law with the linguistic or logical content of rules badly misunderstand the matter. The development of the law is best understood as a process in which judges and lawyers work progressively towards the most transparent articulation of a sought-after normative solution. As we have noted, this can take some time and no small amount of trial and error. The rule-form only becomes viable when some clarity has been achieved as to the final normative solution sought. The appearance of a rule or principle therefore signals that judges and lawyers have travelled some way towards discovering and instantiating this solution. The value of the rule-form is found in the way in which it instantiates and fixes the normative solution judges have established.

This view of the matter is challenging, of course, because it means that formulating a rule is not merely a matter of determining the appropriate outward form of the rule on the basis of logical analysis or the application of a utilitarian calculus. As the essence of the rule is found in the effect the rule has in the world, the rule can be given articulate form only after we are satisfied that the rule we have in mind serves the purpose we have in mind for it. Oliver Wendell Holmes Jr described the process involved very well in an early essay.

[15] The phrase is from Lord Mansfield's judgment in *Omychund v Barker* (1745) 26 ER 15. The relevant passage from the decision reads 'All occasions do not arise at once; … a statute very seldom can take in all cases, therefore the common law, that works itself pure by rules drawn from the fountain of justice, is for this reason superior to an act of parliament.' The phrase became a favourite of Lon Fuller's, cited in several of his works.

[16] Reference to the redirection of human energies is derived from the work of Lon Fuller. See, eg, Lon L Fuller (1958) 'Positivism and Fidelity to Law: A Reply to Professor Hart' *Harvard Law Review* 71: 630–72. Fuller refers to law's providing 'direction posts for the application of human energies': ibid, 632.

According to Holmes, 'It is the merit of the common law that it decides the case first and determines the principle afterwards.'[17] Holmes continues:

> [L]awyers, like other men, frequently see well enough how they ought to decide on a given state of facts without being very clear as to the ratio decidendi. … It is only after a series of determinations on the same subject-matter, that it becomes necessary to 'reconcile the cases,' as it is called, that is, by a true induction to state the principle which has until then been obscurely felt. And this statement is often modified more than once by new decisions before the abstracted general rule takes its final shape. A well settled legal doctrine embodies the work of many minds, and it has been tested in form as well as substance by trained critics whose practical interest is to resist it at every step.[18]

This way of understanding the matter represents a considerable challenge to commonsense thinking, for we generally assume that the form of words used in any particular formulation is the means with which we uncover the formulation's intended meaning. It is this assumption that led the likes of Bentham and Hart to place so much emphasis on clarity in doctrinal formulations. This assumption and emphasis is characteristic of the thinking of academic lawyers more generally. In fact, the comprehension of any given rule entails movement in the opposite direction, from apprehension of the rule's purpose or function to the correct expression and interpretation of the rule's outward form. This is not a simple matter, however. The rule does not function simply by directing legal subjects to carry out a prescribed form of behaviour in the manner of an order or a command. Rather, the rule instantiates a norm that is itself introduced to treat a problem, to resolve conflict that has emerged among social actors with diverse and complex interests, expectations and tolerances.[19] In fashioning this norm, judges and lawyers must identify the full range of normatively-relevant considerations, apportion the appropriate weight to each consideration and arrive at a reconciliation that is acceptable to those who are to be subject to the norm. Until this is achieved, doctrinal expressions will reflect the inquiring and experimental character of the process as a whole, becoming truly definitive only when the problem examined by the court is thoroughly understood and a satisfying solution found. This is the process Holmes describes in the passage above.

All of this is to say that the outward formulation of any given rule must be regarded always as nothing more than a literary presentation of the rule's underlying function or purpose. And while this literary presentation will, if well chosen, aid the judge, lawyer or legal subject in grasping the underlying function or purpose of the rule, ultimately the rule is not truly apprehended until

[17] Oliver Wendell Holmes Jr (1870) 'Codes, and the Arrangement of the Law' *American Law Review* 5: 1–13, 1.

[18] ibid.

[19] This characterisation of what is involved in interpreting a legal provision, that of treating a problem, is derived from Lon Fuller. See Fuller (n 16) 666.

the intended purpose or function of the rule is grasped directly. This understanding of the relationship between the purpose or function of the rule and its outward articulation led Holmes's contemporary and friend Frederick Pollock to describe the maxims of legal doctrine as 'mere symbols', useful to the lawyer as a kind of technical shorthand:

> Except in the simplest cases, lawyers are most careful to make their inductions from particulars to particulars, to beware of general propositions, and to express their opinions in more or less qualified form. Legal maxims afford a good instance of the true character of general propositions in law. They are for the most part mere symbols, which are useful to the lawyer as a kind of technical shorthand, suggesting definite groups of legal facts, but which are only misleading if they are supposed to mean anything else. One often sees legal maxims hopelessly misapplied by people who, not understanding their real value, make them the starting-point of deduction for purposes quite foreign to their true scope.[20]

The scepticism shown towards rules expressed by Holmes and Pollock was later taken up by Realist thinkers like Herman Oliphant and Hessel Yntema. In 'A Return to Stare Decisis', for instance, Herman Oliphant insists that judges respond not to 'vague and shifting rationalizations' but to 'the stimulus of human situations'.[21] Judges, he says, are 'dominantly coerced, not by the essays of their predecessors, but by a surer thing, by an intuition of fitness of solution to problem'.[22] In his article 'The Hornbook Method and the Conflict of Laws', Hessel Yntema provides an account of the interaction between fact and rule along the same lines.[23] In a passage that brings to mind Pollock's reference to 'mere symbols', Yntema describes legal rules as little more than mnemonic devices, each one a 'useful but hollow diagram of what has been':

> It should be obvious that when we have observed a recurrent phenomenon in the decision of cases by the courts, we may appropriately express the classification thus adopted in a rule. But the rule will be only a mnemonic device, a useful but hollow diagram of what has been. It will be intelligible only if we relive again the experience of the classifier and will be safely employed only with the knowledge of its limited purpose and of the scientific deficiencies of the decisions from which it is abstracted.[24]

These thinkers and others all insisted on nothing more than that we not mistake the map for the terrain, that we accord rules their rightful place within a larger process that is more centrally concerned with factual experience. References to symbols, diagrams and mnemonic devices all serve as useful correctives to our

[20] Frederick Pollock (1882) *Jurisprudence and Legal Essays*, London: Macmillan & Co,182.

[21] Herman Oliphant (1928) 'A Return to Stare Decisis' *American Bar Association Journal* 14: 71–76, 107, 159–62: 159.

[22] ibid.

[23] Hessel Yntema (1928) 'The Hornbook Method and the Conflict of Laws' *Yale Law Journal* 37: 468–83.

[24] ibid, 481.

habitual way of thinking in these matters. Where the naive conception of law and legal reasoning reduces law to its formal or doctrinal dimension, in fact this dimension is merely a necessary interface. The purpose of this interface, whether rule or principle or recorded case, is to provide judges, lawyers and legal subjects with the means with which to engage with the true substance of the law in fixed and articulate form.

C. Articulating Normative Structure in the Form of a Rule

What, then, does common law reasoning entail if it is not the simple application of rules? The essence of the process is found in an effort judges and lawyers make to discern the precise dimensions of the normative standard to be applied in the immediate case. Though this normative standard can be articulated in the form of a rule, the standard more naturally takes the form of a generic or standard characterisation of the setting, interaction or relationship under review. When resolving the dispute between the buyer and seller offered as illustration in section II.A, for instance, what is sought is a clarification of the buyer-seller relationship as it is already established within the experience of the community. These expectations may be very well-established and effective. If this is the case, the application of the normative standard in the immediate case will be relatively straightforward. Where standards are clear in this way, disputes are less likely to be brought before the court, certainly not the higher courts.[25] In more interesting cases, however, the immediate dispute brings to light an aspect of the communal understanding of the setting, interaction or relationship in question that is unclear or poorly formed. These are 'trouble cases', disputes that bring to light the inadequacy of the existing scheme of normative organisation underpinning the relevant aspect of communal life.[26]

The trouble afflicting a particular setting, interaction or relationship can take any number of different forms and can be more or less profound. The form of interaction may be relatively novel, for instance. Here, the trouble the court must address arises from the fact that members of the community are still unsure as to the expectations participants are entitled to hold. In other instances, the form of interaction may be relatively well-established and clear in many respects, but there may remain aspects of the interaction that are still subject to uncertainty. The work the court must do here is more subtle, requiring a sharper focus.

[25] These have come to be known as 'easy cases' within legal theory. Under the view submitted here, the difference between easy and hard cases is found in the degree to which the normative organisation of the situation is clear. In 'hard cases', the situation is clearly disordered, and it is obvious that there is work to be done if an optimal form of normative regulation for the situation is to be found. Clarity in the form of language used is a separate matter and does not influence whether a case is easy or hard.

[26] The phrase 'trouble cases' is derived from Karl Llewellyn. See 'Law-Jobs' ((1940) (n 5)) 1375.

For a quick sense of what this work can involve, consider the following dispute, from the 1987 English contract decision, *Interfoto Picture Library Ltd v Stiletto Visual Programmes Ltd*.[27] In that case, the plaintiffs ran a photographic transparency lending library. Following a telephone inquiry by the defendants, the plaintiffs delivered a set of transparencies to the defendants, along with a delivery note containing nine printed conditions. One of these conditions stipulated that all the transparencies could be held for 14 days. After this time, a daily holding fee would be charged for each transparency retained. The defendants, who had not used the plaintiffs' services before, did not read the conditions and returned the transparencies four weeks later. The plaintiffs invoiced the defendants for £3,783.50 and, when the defendants refused to pay, brought an action to recover the sum.

In this dispute, the court was concerned with a fairly specific question, one that had not arisen in the past, or had not arisen in sufficiently serious form to warrant bringing the matter before the court. To answer this question, the court had to carry out two separate tasks. In the first of these, the court was asked to extract a normative question or proposition from the dispute. When reading the published decision, we might think that the question raised by the case is self-evident. Crystallising this question is, however, an important part of the work carried out by the lawyers and judges involved in the case. In this instance, the court took the normative question raised by the case to be whether or not onerous clauses are to be taken to be incorporated into contracts as a matter of course.

The second task the court faced was in settling upon an appropriate answer to the question raised. This answer is presented not merely as the resolution to the particular dispute immediately before the court, but in the form of a general normative proposition bearing something like the following shape:

> When person occupying generic position A interacts with person occupying generic position B, in generic circumstances C, performing acts D and E respectively, normative consequences F follow.

In the *Interfoto* decision, the court decided that onerous clauses were not enforceable as a matter of course but become effective only where reasonable notice of the clause is given to the other party. The normative proposition presented by the court was therefore the following one:

> Where a contracting party seeks to incorporate a particularly onerous or unusual condition into a contract, this party must show that it had brought the clause fairly and reasonably to the attention of the other party if the clause is to be enforceable.[28]

As this example demonstrates, what is most distinctive about common law reasoning is the way it draws upon the common lawyer's ability to see or think

[27] *Interfoto Picture Library Limited v Stiletto Visual Programmes Limited* [1987] EWCA Civ 6.
[28] ibid.

normatively; that is, to recognise within the contingent and variable interactions of human life a potential for structure. This capacity must extend to an ability to distinguish good normative structure from bad normative structure, and an ability to recognise how defective forms of normative structure can be improved and, if possible, made optimal. This is not merely a technical ability but requires that the judge exercise a sympathetic understanding of how human agents experience their movement through the social world. Good structure directs agents into patterns of behaviour that are in keeping with those agents' natural inclinations to act, bringing them into relationships with their neighbours that are agreeable. Well-formed structure feels natural to participants, and for this reason is readily embraced, quickly becoming 'the way' the relevant interactions are carried out.

The essence of common law reasoning is found, then, not in the application of a formal rule to the facts of the immediate dispute in the deductive style, but in the work the common law judge must do to discern optimal normative structure from within the raw material provided by particular disputes. This work is inductive rather than deductive, requiring the judge to determine or clarify the many elements of the situation's normative structure, accord weight or significance to each of these elements and divine the proper configuration to be given to the elements as a group.

In other words, if the 'rule' takes the form

If {A, B, C, D, E}, then F

this rule is not applied to the facts in the deductive manner. Rather, the primary aim of the process of reasoning involved is the working out of the content and organisation of A, B, C, D, E and F. The 'rule' is something like a container into which the various constituent elements are placed and given organised form. As we have seen, this is not something that can be achieved all at once, in a single pass. The rule-form is rather a gestalt that emerges gradually over an extended period, as the reactions of many judges to many related but subtly different factual situations slowly cohere into a social universal that is embraced not only by the judiciary but by the wider community.

D. Making Sense of the Ratio Decidendi, and the Practices of Distinguishing and Overruling

The drawn-out process described in the preceding sections, the careful way judges form normative structure by sifting through and organising particular factual elements, explains many of the characteristic features of common law reasoning. Take, for instance, the mysterious ratio decidendi.[29] Stated simply,

[29] The classic article on the ratio decidendi is Arthur L Goodhart (1930) 'Determining the Ratio Decidendi of a Case' *Yale Law Journal* XL: 161–83. Goodhart wrote his famous article in response

the ratio of any given case is the clarification the court has given to the particular element of the underlying norm brought concretely to light by the dispute before the court. To understand what is involved here, we must keep in mind that judges are not able to articulate the organic norms central to the common law all at once, but must rather work towards definitive statements of these norms over time. This involves a drawn-out process, which sees successive courts considering different constituent elements of the norm in piecemeal fashion as these elements are brought to light by particular disputes. In addressing each dispute in the series, the court concentrates its attention on a particular aspect of the generic normative relation before it. To employ the formulation adopted earlier, if the larger generic normative relation can be summarised in the following way,

> When person occupying generic position A interacts with person occupying generic position B, in generic circumstances C, performing acts D and E respectively, normative consequences F follow,

the ratio of a decision in the series will be found not in the entirety of this statement but in the clarification the court offers as to one or more of the constituent elements that go towards making up the entire formulation. The ratio will clarify the composition of one or more such elements, or the weight to be given one or more of the elements, or the configuration into which the various elements are to be put.

Of course, if the court is to clarify a particular element of the norm, it must have some conception of the norm as a whole. In any given decision, the court may or may not give this conception articulate expression in its judgment. Crucially, however, the binding part of the decision – the ratio – concerns only those parts of the norm that are instantiated concretely in the dispute before the court, where contact is made with the actual social reality of the community. Around this, there will be a great deal of speculation and argumentation concerning the optimal form of normative regulation to be given to the social relation in question. This latter material is an important part of the intellectual life of the court, and is not unlike the speculative conclusions and proposals that scientists include in their published writing alongside the concrete conclusions they derive from their experiments. In both contexts, speculation makes an important contribution to the growth of knowledge over time.

This fact, the way the norm itself becomes clear only after the various constituent elements of the norm have been put before the court in concrete form and have received the court's attention, is why the rule or principle crystallises only after a series of decisions. As we have noted, unlike formal rules, organic norms do not enjoy an existence separate from the concrete factual circumstances they describe. Such a norm cannot meaningfully be formulated in the abstract.

to the article by Oliphant cited earlier (n 21), to make clear that common law judges do not merely respond to facts but actively shape these facts to create generic situations capable of supporting forward-looking normative propositions.

Instead the various elements of the relation must be attended to, one after the other, through a painstaking and thoroughly workman-like process of practical reasoning. The ratio of each decision in a line of such decisions represents the falling into place of a constituent element of the norm. In the latter stages of the process, judges will become more and more confident in offering explicit statements of the norm itself, and decisions will come to be characterised to a greater degree by an effort on their part to 'reconcile the cases', as Holmes put it.[30]

The gradual way in which norms are crystallised by common law judges also explains the distinctive common law practices of distinguishing and overruling. Both practices reflect the uncertain and experimental character of the process, which must advance in small, reversible steps. Distinguishing and overruling provide the means with which judges can refine and, if necessary, significantly revise their understanding of the norm as it emerges over a series of decisions.

Distinguishing is the more common of the two practices. An earlier precedent is distinguished where a latent element within the steadily crystallising norm has come to the attention of the court, an element that escaped notice in the earlier decisions in the series. In acknowledging this latent element, the court sharpens its understanding of the underlying norm. While the effect of this is generally to limit the scope of the norm's applicability, distinguishing does not fundamentally change the court's understanding of the norm itself. The outcome in an earlier decision may nevertheless need to be distinguished, however, as the norm, now accepted in more sharply drawn form, may produce outcomes that, on their face, are not consistent with decisions given in earlier cases.

Clarifying a norm in the sense envisioned here is not at all the same as modifying a rule, which is the view of distinguishing that is often accepted by academic thinkers.[31] On the contrary, the effect of distinguishing is to deepen and sharpen the established formulation of the norm, and by so doing further entrench the norm in the understanding and practice of the community. There is no modification here, in other words, just greater illumination of what is already accepted. Indeed, the technique is only likely to be accepted where this is the case, where the later court can make a convincing case that its efforts leave the law essentially unchanged. It is precisely because judges are not understood to be changing the law that lower courts are empowered to distinguish the decisions of superior courts.

Overruling is less common than distinguishing, and for good reason. In these instances, the later court concludes that the earlier development of the law was mistaken in some fundamental way and a radical change in direction is required. Here, the information revealed by the later case makes clear that earlier courts have placed too much weight on one factual element over others, or have organised the various elements into the wrong configuration. It is not merely that a

[30] Holmes (n 17) 1.

[31] See, for instance, Joseph Raz (1979) 'Law and Value in Adjudication' in *The Authority of Law*, Oxford: Oxford University Press, 180–209.

latent element has been neglected, then, but that the view taken of the factual elements considered by the court and the way these factual elements have been crystallised into a norm require significant revision. The revised norm cannot be reconciled with the earlier decision, however, and so a sharp break with the past must be accepted. When this course is adopted, the later decision is given retrospective effect. Where the law previously took one form, it now takes another.

This is of course a radical course for the court to take, one that is destructive of the clarity and settledness the community requires of its scheme of normative regulation. Courts therefore engage in overruling only when it is absolutely necessary. As the effect of overruling has the effect of rending and resetting the social fabric, courts are most likely to engage in it where the earlier formulation of the norm has been of limited practical effect, or alternatively, where the practical circumstances of the community have changed sufficiently to justify so radical a change in the scheme of normative organisation accepted by the community.

The practices of distinguishing and overruling are useful for our purposes here, for they make clear both the priorities accepted by common law judges and the constraints they face in acting to realise these priorities. On the one hand, the court has an obligation to establish a stable scheme of normative regulation. Frequent and gratuitous change to this scheme is antithetical to the enterprise. At the same time, the court is also required to make that scheme of regulation the best it can be, to ensure that the scheme reflects as closely as possible the interests, expectations and tolerances of the members of the community who are to be subject to that regime.

III. COMMON LAW DOCTRINE

Just as the elaborate common law practices around precedent cannot be explained by accounts that reduce legal life to a simple matter of formulating and administering formal rules, the same is true of common law doctrine, for what we find here is far too elaborate and eccentric to be explained by the simple rule-conception of law. When we understand the centrality of normative regulation to the common law method, however, the complex forms taken by common law doctrine become a good deal easier to understand.

Take, for instance, the preference for objective standards of liability. Though this feature of the common law frequently draws criticism from outsiders, the use that is made of objective standards within the common law is unavoidable, arising directly from the normative form of regulation adopted. As Holmes famously put it, the common law, 'by the very necessity of its nature, is continually transmuting moral standards into external, objective ones'.[32] If Holmes's

[32] Oliver Wendell Holmes Jr (1881) *The Common Law*, Boston, MA: Little Brown and Company, 31.

statement appears mysterious on its face, it merely asserts that the common law method, by its very design, operates to furnish normative solutions to problems of social order.[33] The common law does not resolve disputes in the familiar manner, the backward-looking, particularistic approach to adjudication we are inclined to take for granted. It operates instead by attending to defects found within the schemes of organic normative organisation that serve to structure recurring social activities. As these schemes of organic normative organisation are composed of structural elements that by their nature are external and objective, the products of the common law cannot but take this form.

Over and above objectivity, there is a wide range of constraints inherent in the normative form, which adds to its technical character and complicates the work undertaken by common law judges. Working around these constraints provides much of what is of interest within common law practice, but the strange contortions required also serve to alienate outsiders, exposing judges to criticism from observers who lack insight into the priorities and inner workings of their method. In what remains of this chapter, we will look briefly at a number of illustrative examples, arising from difficulties of the following kinds:

(a) Where there is insufficient factual basis to support a behavioural norm.
(b) Where a behavioural norm of sufficient specificity cannot be formulated and a local supplement is required.
(c) Where moral and policy considerations inhibit the formulation of the behavioural norm and these considerations must be addressed outside the norm, through separate doctrinal means.
(d) Where the sought-after behavioural norm exhibits a forbidding degree of internal complexity, making formulation of the norm a fraught and sometimes futile process.

A. Where there is Insufficient Basis to Support a Behavioural Norm

The formulation of common law doctrine, organised as it is around behavioural norms, can pose challenges where the norms themselves are not already present in the required form within the settled behaviour of the community. In the starkest instances, there is simply no clear factual basis for the norm in question. For an example, we need only think of the way omissions are addressed within the common law. As readers will know, omissions are addressed in a relatively restricted way within common law doctrine. A more relaxed approach to omissions could conceivably be taken within a system of law that operates exclusively in the backward-looking, particularistic manner. A general moral standard

[33] It is submitted that this is the essence of the argument Holmes struggled to convey throughout his writing on the common law. According to Holmes, the common law is 'legislative in its grounds'. See ibid, 29–30.

could be articulated within such a system, one that attaches legal consequences to failures to act that are so offensive to the moral sensibilities of the community as to warrant the imposition of a penalty. With such a law in place, diverse examples of omissions could be considered, with decision in each instance based upon simple moral judgement.[34]

The common law does not function in this way. The common law is concerned not with moral standards but with forward-looking behavioural norms. If there is to be liability under the common law, the behaviour under consideration must arise within well-defined interactions and relationships that are themselves amenable to the sort of normative structuring that is the central concern of the common law. The behaviour in question must already be 'patterned in fact' to some extent.[35] Omissions are problematic because the instances in question are often idiosyncratic, and as such do not regularly appear in the same recognisable form. For this reason, omissions generally do not give rise to legal consequences unless prior actions or a prior relationship has the effect of establishing recognisable forward-looking expectations.[36] Here the omission is found embedded within a larger pattern of behaviour that is itself enough of a recognisable and reliable feature of the life of the community to secure the forward-looking objective of the process. The omission is something like the hole in a doughnut, a well-defined failure to act that receives definition from the pattern of positive behaviour that surrounds it.

It is important to note that the problem here is not 'definitional uncertainty' so much as it is normative indeterminacy, which are two very different things.[37] Within the common law, everything turns on the thoroughly practical question of whether the relevant pattern of behaviour is sufficiently regular to support a forward-looking norm of behaviour. Where this is the case, omissions do give rise to legal responsibility.[38] The problem with imposing penalties for omissions in most instances is that there is simply no way to translate what is involved into forward-looking normative guidance with the required degree

[34] This is the approach taken in the French and German legal systems.

[35] The phrase 'patterned in fact' is derived from the work of Karl Llewellyn. See Llewellyn (1940) (n 5) 1360.

[36] The viability of a general duty to rescue is often discussed in this context. It is notable that the common law and the Civilian approaches diverge in their responses to this issue. In the former, legal subjects are expected to observe communal norms. The fact that a particular act is so callous as to shock the conscience of the community is not itself sufficient to justify the imposition of a legal duty. It is submitted that Holmes offered his 'bad man' to make clear just this distinction between moral and normative adjudication. Provided that he is not violating a clearly-defined behaviour-guiding norm, a 'bad man' can witness a child drowning in a pond, do nothing and not face legal consequences for doing so. See Holmes (n 1) 460–61.

[37] See Andrew Ashworth (2013) *Positive Obligations in Criminal Law*, Oxford: Hart Publishing, 40.

[38] In practice, omissions are recognised across the common law world in a number of distinct forms. In each of these forms, the defendant's omission is embedded within a larger pattern of positive recurring behaviour capable of supporting forward-looking normative expectations. For a discussion of the different categories, see ibid, 42–65.

of determinacy. A general duty to rescue is not viable for this reason. A duty to offer help when one encounters a traffic accident is more promising, as the situation is sufficiently well-defined. The question then becomes, what kind of help? A duty to contact the authorities is sufficiently well-defined to support the imposition of liability for an omission. A duty to 'take all reasonable steps to help' is more problematic. Ultimately, whether or not this last proposal is viable will depend on whether we can take for granted agreement on the part of legal subjects as to what does and does not constitute 'reasonable steps' in the relevant situations. If the court is unable to articulate a clear behavioural standard capable of guiding the autonomous actions of legal subjects in a forward-looking way, the omission in question cannot give rise to liability under the common law.

B. Where a Behavioural Norm of Sufficient Specificity Cannot be Formulated and a Local Supplement is Required

Omissions illustrate well the way common law judges must work with, and in some instances around, the raw material they are given. The normative form requires clear, reliable patterns in outward behaviour. Difficulties arise where these patterns are absent or especially elusive. Where this is the case, judges must employ remedial measures that are variable in both form and efficacy. Causation provides an example. Causation generally emerges as an issue where the court finds that there is need for better calibration of fault or liability within the behavioural norm the court is asked to apply. Where the explicit rendering of the norm includes reference to the causing of harm or damage, the effort the court must make to clarify the question of fault or liability often will take the form of an inquiry into causation. The emphasis placed on causation as a concept is misleading, however, because the true subject of the inquiry is the function or purpose of the legal measure under review. The English judge Lord Hoffmann is a prominent advocate of this view:

> [O]ne cannot give a common sense answer to a question of causation for the purpose of attributing responsibility under some rule without knowing the purpose and scope of the rule. … Before answering questions about causation, it is therefore first necessary to identify the scope of the relevant rule.[39]

Lord Hoffmann elaborated in his non-judicial writing:

> In my view, all this wringing of hands is quite unnecessary. It might be easier if, instead of speaking of proof of 'causation', which makes it look as if we are dealing with one monolithic concept which can be defined … we [should] speak of the 'causal requirements' of a legal rule. This would make it clear that causal requirements are

[39] From his judgment in *Empress Car Company (Abertillery) Ltd v National Rivers Authority* [1998] 2 WLR 350, [1998] UKHL 5, [1999] 2 AC 22, [1998] 1 All ER 481.

> creatures of the law and nothing more. The causal requirements of one rule may be different from those of another.[40]

Though problems of this kind all arise for the same ultimate reason – a lack of clarity as to the requirements of the law – the problems themselves manifest for a number of different and quite specific reasons. In tort, for instance, difficulties sometimes arise where there are multiple causes of the relevant harm. As instances where several causes contribute to a single outcome are rare and idiosyncratic, they are not generally amenable to normative generalisation. There will therefore almost certainly be need for a local supplement to the existing normative standard in these cases. It is an effort to determine the nature of this supplement that occupies the court, as opposed to causation as a general concept.[41]

A different sort of problem sometimes arises, and this is where the legal measure receives its definition directly from the harm or damage itself, rather than from an identifiable pattern of behaviour known reliably to bring about this harm or damage. As the concrete manifestations of the problem take diverse forms, the behavioural norm used to determine fault or liability invariably will be articulated at too high a level of generality or abstraction. There will sometimes be need, then, for more precise calibration of the degree of fault or liability required in particular cases. Prosecutions for manslaughter – an ill-defined result-crime, with an ill-defined fault element – often give rise to this problem.[42]

A third, perhaps more mundane reason for causation to emerge as an issue is where the legal measure in question takes the form of a statutory provision that the court finds is insufficiently clear in its treatment of fault or liability. In these instances, the court engages in searching interpretation of the word 'cause' to ensure that the application of the law meets evident policy objectives, or alternatively, satisfies the moral expectations of legal subjects. Where the aim is to ensure that the provision meets a policy objective, causation will likely be interpreted more liberally.[43] Where the aim is to temper the harshness of the provision, causation will be interpreted in a more restricted way, with the court refining or adding to the causation requirement within the provision.[44] In both variations, the resulting interpretations depart from what would result from a literal reading of the term in preference for a purposive reading.

The fact that what causation entails within one legal measure can be very different from what the notion entails in another, renders futile the cherished academic project of fashioning a single, technically rigorous conception

[40] Lord Hoffmann (2011) 'Causation' in *Perspectives on Causation*, ed Richard Goldberg, Oxford: Hart Publishing, 3–9, 9.

[41] See, eg, *Fairchild v Glenhaven Funeral Services Ltd* [2002] UKHL 22.

[42] For a recent example, see *Ceon Broughton v R* [2020] EWCA Crim 1093.

[43] The *Empress Car Company* decision (n 39) is an example of this first category.

[44] For an example, see *Hughes* [2013] UKSC 56, [2013] 1 WLR 2461.

of causation.[45] The problem is even more profound than this, however. It is not merely that causation is not reducible to a single concept that can be employed in the same form across the law. It is rather that words like 'causing' and 'intending', as these words are used within the law, are not really used as isolated concepts at all.[46] They are instead in each case employed within normative statements which cannot themselves be reduced to atomic elements. Judges proceed, then, not by refining individual concepts in a context-independent way, but rather by working to identify an optimal form of normative organisation for the specific generic situation under review. The context-independent meanings of words like 'causing' and 'intending' contribute relatively little to this.

C. Where the Presence of Moral and Policy Considerations have the Effect of Inhibiting the Formulation of the Behavioural Norm and these Considerations Must be Addressed Outside the Norm, Through Separate Doctrinal Means

For our third example, we turn to the common law defences. The separation of common law doctrine into primary and secondary parts – into criminal offences and defences, for instance – remains an abiding mystery to many academics. This confusion is understandable if we take for granted the backward-looking, particularistic approach to adjudication. Under this approach, all relevant evidence is more naturally considered within a single inquiry, the sole aim of which is to determine the legal responsibility of the defendant. If our aim is for doctrine to perform both a forward- and backward-looking function simultaneously, however, a more complicated approach is required, for the two modes do not always sit easily together. Separation of the material relevant to the respective modes is sometimes necessary if one function is not to undermine the other.

For an illustration of why the separation is necessary, consider self-defence in criminal law. On the one hand, it is a general objective of the criminal law to enforce a prohibition on violence. At the same time, there are exceptional circumstances where the use of violence is tolerated. If we attempt to address both of these concerns simultaneously, however, we send legal subjects a

[45] In *Empress* (n 39), Lord Hoffmann went further: 'Not only may there be different answers to questions about causation when attributing responsibility to different people under different rules … but there may be different answers when attributing responsibility to different people under the same rule.'

[46] In 'Causation' (n 40), Lord Hoffmann had the following to say about the interpretation of legal rules, 'the object of the exercise is to ascertain what should count as causing death, or intending to kill, for the purposes of the rule in question. You are declaring what the rule means, what its proper interpretation should be. This process is exactly the same whether you are deciding what should count as "causing", "intending" or as falling within any other concept employed by the rule.' We will return to intention as a concept later in this chapter.

mixed signal. We convey to individuals the message that violence is sometimes permitted, sometimes not, and leave it to the individual himself or herself to decide in any given instance. The community loses its ability to arrive at clear expectations about the forms of behaviour that are proscribed.

In the traditional common law approach to criminal law, this difficulty is addressed by separating guilt from responsibility. The court first asks whether the defendant has violated a behavioural norm. If this is true, the defendant is found guilty. This sends a clear message: behaviour of this character constitutes violation of a communal norm and as such attracts a penalty. After guilt is established, the court turns to the separate question of responsibility. The court now considers factors that bear upon the individual's responsibility for his or her act. These considerations influence the penalty imposed, with the defences representing a special, codified part of this second inquiry.[47]

That the defences exist to support the greater normative emphasis of the law is, I think, clear enough from their content. Generally, the main or primary part of the law provides forward-looking guidance that is behavioural in character. The defences supplement this guidance by addressing circumstances behind or around the acts in question that bear upon their moral significance. In criminal law, for instance, the defences generally are concerned with circumstances that bear upon the authenticity of the will found to animate the defendant's act.[48] Defences concerned with compulsion, mental impairment and loss of control do not call into question the wrongfulness of the particular acts deemed to be criminal, but instead raise questions as to whether the defendant can be held entirely responsible for his or her decision to so act. The defences codify matters affecting responsibility that arise frequently and therefore can be given a more regimented treatment within the law.

We see this same logic animating many of the defences available within contract law. Contract defences like fraud and duress function in much the same way as the criminal defences described above. The defences allow the court to consider questions relating to the authenticity of the agreement between the parties without taking away from the clarity the law offers as to what amounts to 'contracting behaviour' more generally. Other defences in contract, tort and criminal law address concerns of different kinds while preserving clarity as to

[47] The distinction made here between guilt and responsibility is derived from AL Goodhart (1953) *English Law and Moral Law*, London: Stevens & Sons Limited.

[48] The normative explanation provided here of the defences – that they exist to help judges isolate the central behavioural norm from moral and policy considerations that might obscure it – explains why the distinction between justification and excuses, an analytical distinction beloved by academics, has no application within the common law as it is practised. Whether the successful raising of a defence in a particular case amounts to acceptance of a justification or an excuse is less important than ensuring that the twin objectives of the common law are met, namely, that clarity is achieved in the wider community's normative order and that morally acceptable outcomes are produced in particular cases. When priority is given to these objectives, there is simply no room for concern over whether a particular defence is a justification or an excuse. The distinction serves no practical purpose.

normative guidance in this same way. Defences like diplomatic immunity in criminal law and illegality in contract allow the court to recognise policy considerations without compromising the clarity of the law on the more essential question of normative form. Limiting defences in contract and tort also preserve clarity as to the relevant norms, while at the same time ensuring that special circumstances relevant to damages are given due consideration.

D. Where the Behavioural Norm Exhibits a Forbidding Degree of Internal Complexity, Making Formulation of the Norm a Fraught and Sometimes Futile Process

A further difficulty, distinct from those explored previously, arises from the forbidding complexity required by some of the behavioural norms the court is asked to formulate. The problem here is that the sensitivity required of the norm is so great as to make the task of formulating the norm extraordinarily challenging. In the worst instances, the degree of complexity the norm entails is so great as to make the enterprise impracticable. A behavioural norm that initially appears extremely difficult to pin down may be revealed, after much futile effort, to simply be too difficult to accomplish.

The problem of complexity arises from the peculiar moral logic characteristic of norms. Where norms are at issue, adverse judgement attaches to deviations from expected patterns of behaviour, and it is this fact of deviation from the expected alone that justifies condemnation. The moral logic involved is therefore binary and somewhat crude. The individual is condemned for acting or failing to act in the manner expected, rather than for acting with the explicit intention of bringing about a particular result. This logic is uncontroversial where the matter under consideration has a regulatory cast and the penalty that follows from the violation of the norm is modest. The normative form is for this reason a natural fit in areas of law more directly concerned with the regulation of public behaviour. The tort of negligence and the regulatory part of the criminal law are examples. The moral logic of norms can sit less happily with the more serious criminal offences, however. Here, the adoption of a normative analysis can seem inappropriate in light of the seriousness of the offence and the severity of punishment to follow conviction. If the normative form is to be accepted for use in such circumstances, great care has to be taken to ensure that the behavioural norm administered by the court meets these heightened expectations.

For a sense of the difficulty involved, consider the following scenario: the defendant points a gun at another person's head and pulls the trigger. That legal consequences should follow from such an act is uncontroversial. At issue, however, is the correct analysis. Where a normative analysis is applied, liability arises not from the defendant's intention to bring about the result, but from his or her decision to carry out the act itself. Intention remains relevant, but it here receives a more technical treatment. The court directs its attention to two distinct questions. The first asks whether the act can be equated with a particular outcome so completely as to make the decision to carry out the act morally equivalent to intending the outcome. Where this is true, the decision to carry out the act is tantamount to intending the outcome.[49] A common example of this is where the defendant stabs the victim several times in the chest, causing death. Under the normative analysis, it does not matter whether or not the defendant intended to cause death, it is enough that he or she voluntarily carried out an act objectively known to be fatal. Even if the defendant did not intend specifically to cause death, he or she 'ought to have known' or 'must have known' that death would result from the act. Insofar as intention is relevant, it is always the intention to carry out a particular proscribed act that matters.[50]

This is followed by the second question, which asks whether the individual can be said to have been truly responsible for the act he or she has carried out. For this part of the analysis to be satisfied, the act must have been completely under the individual's control, and he or she must have fully appreciated the significance of the act. What is most important here is not the defendant's intention to cause the outcome but the knowledge he or she has of the relevant circumstances. Instead of asking whether the defendant really intended to cause the outcome, in other words, the court asks: did the defendant possess sufficient knowledge of the circumstances of his or her act to justify conviction under the offence?

If both parts of the analysis above are satisfied, the parts combine to make a complete and entirely comprehensible moral proposition. The defendant will be held responsible for the outcome of his or her action, and in our 'folk' or commonsense rendering of this, we will say that he or she 'intended' the outcome, whether or not he or she actually did intend it. It is this analysis that lies behind the much-maligned common law maxim that presumes individuals to intend the natural and probable consequences of their actions. The maxim articulates a fundamental presupposition of normative, and therefore common law, thinking, which is that outcomes can follow so inevitably from actions as to make the decision to act indistinguishable from a decision to cause the outcome.

Though the approach taken to moral reasoning may appear unduly technical and, indeed, somewhat tortured, it is perfectly defensible, provided the

[49] HLA Hart captured the underlying intuition very well: ' [W]here a foreseen outcome is so immediately and invariably connected with the action done that the suggestion that the action might not have that outcome would by ordinary standards be regarded as absurd, or such as only a mentally abnormal person would seriously entertain: the connexion between action and outcome seems therefore to be not merely contingent but rather to be conceptual.' See HLA Hart (1968) *Punishment and Responsibility*, Oxford: Oxford University Press, 120.

[50] Under the normative approach, 'ought to have known' is acceptable. When intention is subjective, 'must have known' is preferred. The latter is assimilated into the commonsense conception of intention by dubbing it 'oblique intention'. In fact there is no practical difference between the two characterisations. The process by which liability is attributed to the defendant is in both variations an external and objective one. In both, the defendant is held to a communal standard.

requirements set out above are met. The respective parts of the analysis give rise to specific points of difficulty, however. The first part of the analysis, the need to ensure that the act can be equated with the outcome, can lead to a need for exacting calibration of the causal relationship between the act and the outcome. Where this is the case, the sought-after behavioural norm will include explicit reference to the likelihood or objective foreseeability of the outcome, and a good deal of time may well be spent calibrating this part of the norm appropriately.

The second part of the analysis, whether the defendant can truly be held responsible for his or her act, can lead to searching questions of different kinds. As noted, principal among these is a concern for the knowledge the defendant possessed as he or she carried out the act. Questions that arise around knowledge can be further complicated by a need to address the way in which this knowledge is held within actors. While in some instances the knowledge in question can be presumed to be held by all social actors in ordinary circumstances, in more difficult cases the knowledge in question must be held explicitly in mind by the actor as he or she acts. This difference can have implications for the viability of the norm the court hopes to formulate, as we shall see in the murder example below.

As should be obvious, getting the formulation right can be extremely challenging in practice. Unsurprisingly, repeated interventions may be required. It may take some trial and error for judges to calibrate the degree of likelihood appropriately, for instance. Similarly, issues that bear upon the defendant's responsibility for the act may come to light only gradually, and may not show up in readily identifiable form. Even worse, hanging over the court throughout this groping process of development is the very real possibility that the sought-after behavioural norm simply cannot be formulated to the community's satisfaction. This is the worst-case scenario. Common law judges may spend years working to arrive at the appropriate calibration of a hoped-for behavioural norm, only to find that their efforts were misguided and futile from the outset.

Intractable difficulties of just this type lay behind the extended period of controversy surrounding the English court's handling of the offence of murder in the second half of the twentieth century. This controversy arose in answer to the court's attempt to modernise the mental element of murder, an attempt that saw the English judiciary's instinctive inclination to develop the law along normative lines clash with heightened expectations around the appropriateness of punishment. This led to a series of controversial decisions, beginning with the notorious 1961 House of Lords decision in *DPP v Smith*.[51] The decisions address murder in one particular form, and this is where death results from wantonly dangerous acts carried out by individuals who nevertheless acted with no intention to inflict bodily injury or to kill. Though death in such instances is accidental, the court began its inquiry assuming, not unreasonably, that the

[51] *DPP v Smith* [1961] AC 290.

wantonly dangerous character of the defendant's act justifies prosecution for murder in some instances. Arriving at the right normative formulation for murder in this form proved challenging, however.[52]

The enterprise began poorly, with the Law Lords explicitly endorsing the normative approach in *DPP v Smith*. The decision was greeted with universal disapproval, prompting Parliament to intervene and impose a subjective interpretation on intention. The English judges were then left with the thankless task of integrating this subjective interpretation of intention into the offence in a manner that was rational and transparent. The judges eventually gave up, leaving the question of what actually constitutes intention to the 'jury's good sense'.[53]

We will return to subjectivity a little later. For our immediate purposes, it is worth noting that the *Smith* formulation can be criticised without abandoning the normative orientation of the common law. From within this perspective, the murder problem is best understood as an episode in which common law judges strained at the limits of their expertise and ultimately were defeated by the difficulty posed by the problem they were given.

To appreciate this, it helps to understand the problem the judges faced. In *Smith*, the Law Lords articulated murder in behavioural form. The law on the matter is captured, in other words, in a behavioural norm proscribing a specified act. Where the defendant violates the norm by carrying out the proscribed act and death results, this fact alone is sufficient to justify conviction for murder, whatever the intention of the individual. The norm itself was articulated by the Law Lords in the following form:

> For a defendant to be found guilty of murder, he or she needs only to have carried out an unlawful and voluntary act, the natural and probable result of which is grievous bodily harm.[54]

There are two clear weaknesses with this formulation. While it requires that the act the defendant carried out be likely to cause grievous bodily injury, no mention is made of the degree of likelihood that death will follow from the injury. This is clearly unacceptable, and, indeed, the English judges would go on to address the matter later in the series of decisions.[55] The second, perhaps

[52] The decisions in the series were: *DPP v Smith* (ibid); *Hyam v DPP* [1975] AC 55; *R v Moloney* [1985] AC 905 (HL); *R v Hancock and Shankland* [1986] AC 455; *R v Nedrick* [1986] 1 WLR 1025; *R v Woollin* [1999] AC 82.

[53] After a searching effort by the Law Lords in *Hyam v DPP* (n 52), the peculiar facts of *R v Moloney* (n 52) led the court to abandon its attempt to define intention. See Lord Bridge in *Moloney*, ibid, 926, '[t]he golden rule should be that … the judge should avoid any elaboration or paraphrase of what is meant by intent, and leave it to the jury's good sense to decide whether the accused acted with the necessary intent'. See n 46 for Lord Hoffman's related discussion on the concept of 'causing' an outcome.

[54] *Smith* (n 51).

[55] *Nedrick* (n 52).

more notable weakness exhibited by the formulation in *Smith* concerns the knowledge element. Though it is not in the nature of the normative approach to require explicit contemplation of the outcome, the approach does require that the individual possessed sufficient knowledge of the relevant circumstances to appreciate the gravity of his or her act. This issue was a critical one in *Smith*, because it was not at all clear in the trial that the defendant was in a position to appreciate the danger he was creating by acting in the way that he did.

In light of the above, we might say that the true problem with *Smith* was not that the Law Lords opted for an objective standard of liability. It is, rather, that they made a first pass at articulating the offence in normative form and did a poor job. This is not at all uncommon, and ordinarily weaknesses of this kind are addressed in subsequent decisions. The common law needs time to work itself pure. From the brief discussion above, we can even hazard a guess at what the final formulation might have looked like:

> For a defendant to be found guilty of murder, he or she needs only to have carried out an unlawful and voluntary act, the natural and probable result of which, as a matter of virtual or practical certainty, is death, provided that the act was carried out with full knowledge of all relevant circumstances.

It is submitted that this is the sort of formulation the English judges were instinctively working towards. There were two reasons they did not arrive at their destination. The first is the obvious one, and this is the violent opposition the judges' efforts met from academics and other outsiders impatient with the workings of the common law.[56] The second is more interesting: the offence is simply not viable in behavioural form. The reason for this becomes obvious when we look more closely at the knowledge requirement. It is clear, first of all, that the defendant must have a good deal of quite specific knowledge of his or her circumstances if a conviction is to be appropriate. Moreover, unlike the stabbing example provided above, the knowledge required here is not of the sort that can be presumed from common experience. This means that the court must be convinced that a set of specific facts had been held explicitly in mind by the defendant when he or she carried out the act. It is at this point that the enterprise breaks down, because the knowledge requirement now renders the dangerous act form of murder indistinguishable from that of murder in its more intuitive intentional form. Though a conceptual distinction remains, for all practical purposes reckless murder in this form collapses into the primary form of intentional murder.[57]

[56] The hostility the judges faced from their uncomprehending audience prompted an exasperated response from Lord Goff in defence of the judges' efforts. See Lord Goff (1988) 'The Mental Element in the Crime of Murder' *Law Quarterly Review* 104: 30–59.

[57] This has been the experience in the jurisdictions in which criminal law is governed by the Indian Penal Code. Within the Indian Penal Code, the offence of murder originally included a 'dangerous act' limb, found at s 300(d). In applying the offence in this form, courts found, however, that the provision too easily captured instances more appropriately prosecuted as instances of culpable

The murder example – told too briefly here – is useful to us for several reasons. It makes clear, first of all, that there is a limit to the common law method's much-vaunted genius. For all its power, the method exhibits a forbidding technical complexity, one that occasionally will defeat the best efforts of even the most talented and dedicated judges. Moreover, the method requires not only that judges perform at a high level of professional skill, but that they do so continuously. The dynamic character of the law is such as to require ceaseless tending of its elaborate, interconnected machinery. Common law judges invariably fall short, rising to meet what is expected of them only intermittently, with periods of energetic development punctuating more extended periods of passivity and neglect.

The murder problem is also useful for the insight it gives us into how judges respond when the common law method fails them. When this happens, there is only one course open to judges, and this is to revert to the backward-looking, particularistic form of adjudication. As the common law makes no explicit provision for adjudication in this form, however, judges often have no choice but to contrive opaque, partly spurious doctrinal forms that appear, on their face, to be compatible with the common law but that in reality function in the simpler manner. In the murder example, the spurious solution is subjectivity.

Typically, the substitution of a subjective standard of liability for an objective one is thought unproblematic, the two approaches to liability interchangeable within the same system of law. It does not take a great deal of reflection, however, to recognise that subjectivity is not a realistic proposition if taken literally. We cannot peer into a person's mind to determine what he or she intended at the time of his or her act, after all. What the shift from objective to subjective standards truly represents is a retreat from the use of forward-looking normative standards, and a return to a form of adjudication that is solely concerned with resolving historical disputes on their merits. That this more attentive approach should be favoured in serious offences like murder is not hard to understand, but it is not without its costs. The turn to subjectivity represents an abandonment of the rigour and transparency that is the aspiration and often the achievement of the common law method. The backward-looking adjudicatory process we accept in its place is more flexible and sensitive, yes, but it is also opaque and at times irrational. It is for this reason that subjectivity was resisted by the English judges, and was accepted by them only when it was imposed upon them by Parliament.

It is worth bearing the above in mind when considering the academic deprecation of objective standards of liability, particularly within criminal law. While subjectivity is an article of faith for academic thinkers, behavioural standards are in fact overwhelmingly preferred across the common law. This is true even

homicide not amounting to murder. In Burma, the Code was amended in 1910 to absorb the dangerous act limb into the category of intentional murder.

within criminal law. Contrary to the academic understanding of the subject, the greater part of criminal law is regulatory in nature and is therefore a natural fit for the behavioural approach. When we turn to offences exhibiting a more pronounced moral character, we find that even here, a normative, behavioural treatment is generally preferred. Ultimately, it is only result-crimes, and of these, only the most serious result-crimes, that pose problems for the normative approach. In almost all instances, we find that what we require are not subjective standards but better objective ones. This is the view instinctively accepted by common law judges.

For all that regulation in the normative form might appear exotic to us, it is nothing other than a modern instantiation of custom. For this reason, a preference for behavioural standards is not only natural but inevitable wherever the life of the community in question acquires a sufficient degree of complexity and dynamism. In these settings, scope for social conflict enlarges considerably, with variations of the same disputes arising over and over in more or less the same form. As these disputes are brought repeatedly before the court, dissatisfaction increasingly is voiced about inconsistent and opaque verdicts, and it consequently comes to be felt that there is need for a more aggressive regimentation of the process of decision making. At the same time, the recurrence of essentially the same dispute in social life leads social actors to feel more and more that their movement through the world is beset by needless conflict and uncertainty. This gives rise to a natural desire for the afflicted settings, relationships or interactions in the social world to be similarly regimented. Both of these pressures call out for the same remedy: behavioural norms. While the normative approach to regulation may entail a slight loss in the sensitivity of verdicts in court, this is generally accepted as a price worth paying.

IV. CONCLUSION

To conclude this chapter, let us return to the question of what 'thinking like a lawyer' really entails, and whether a programme of education that promises mastery of existing legal doctrine provides meaningful preparation for this work. Throughout this chapter, I have sought to show that legal doctrine is merely an interface, and that the real work undertaken by common lawyers takes the form of a more direct engagement with the world of facts and practical interests. If we were to reduce the failure of modern legal education to its essence, then, we might say that it is found in the way teachers of law present the work of lawyers, not as a peculiar and abstruse form of problem-solving activity, but as a body of settled information for students to absorb. This was Karl Llewellyn's diagnosis of the problem. He recommended a correction. Attention must turn, he thought, from problems already solved, to an exploration of the method of solution. The legal problem must be presented 'as one for solution, as a problem not with its answer at hand but as one to which possible answers are to be worked out in class'. In this way, every case becomes 'a direct exercise in living law'.[58]

From the account presented in this chapter, we can sketch out some of what such an approach might entail. As argued throughout, the essence of the work involved is that of improving the normative organisation of an actual site of social interaction. The central activity within this work is the effort the lawyer or judge must make to identify a suitable behavioural norm, one capable of supporting autonomous and spontaneous activity within the site in question. As we have seen, several interrelated tasks arise in the course of this work. The following is a non-exhaustive list:

1. The particular dispute before the court must be transformed into one concerned with the normative organisation of a generic social situation. The lawyer here must exercise a capacity for abstraction, not of the mathematical or logical sort, but one more naturally applied to human situations and actions. The lawyer asks, 'What is the action- or situation-type at issue here?'[59]
2. The regulatory question within this recurring situation must be identified and given clear definition. Well-formed social situations have a transparent quality. Effects follow causes in a predictable way, leaving participants able to navigate the situation in question with ease and confidence. The regulatory question will therefore concern the normative implications of a particular action within the situation under review, one that does not yield clear, comprehensible implications for participants. What is this question?
3. Once the specific regulatory problem has been identified, a solution to this problem must be found. To achieve this, all considerations relevant to the normative organisation of the situation must be identified. The particular dispute before the court provides the lawyer with his or her starting point. Insight into the nature of normative organisation is required, however, if the relevant considerations are to be disinterred from the factual matter of the dispute.
4. The immediate dispute will provide only partial insight into the regulatory problem. Historical instances will therefore be explored for additional perspective. This will require some sophistication from the lawyer as a reader, for the historical instances will be captured in abbreviated and stylised form in written reports. A talent for a particular kind of research is required.[60]

[58] Karl N Llewellyn (1948) 'The Current Crisis in Legal Education' *Journal of Legal Education* 1: 211–20, 214.

[59] The notion of a 'situation-type' is derived from Llewellyn, though he preferred 'type-situation'. See Llewellyn (1960) (n 6).

[60] This was one of the reasons Lord Sumption recommended the study of history to prospective lawyers. See n 2.

5. Guidance will be sought, not merely from the present and the past, but also from the possible future. An ability to contrive and get the measure of hypothetical cases, all in the imagination of the lawyer, will prove critical here.[61]
6. Arriving at the sought-after form of normative organisation is not always solely a matter of articulating a single behavioural norm. On occasion, the lawyer will have to parse the raw material of the problem, or the process of decision making, into discrete doctrinal or processual structures. The common law defences are an example. This work of legal structure building is perhaps the part of the process most inscrutable to outsiders, and is the aspect of the lawyer's competence most difficult to acquire without actual experience of legal practice.
7. Accompanying the substantive aspects of the lawyer's work, there is also the business of expression. As the fundamental concern of the enterprise, normative organisation, is elusive, skill in writing is invaluable if the products of the process are to be instantiated in a form that does not foster doubt and confusion. Writing well, and clearly, is an important lawyer's skill.
8. The lawyer must not merely write well; he or she must persuade. Lawyers must persuade judges and juries. Judges must persuade other judges. The essence of this work of persuasion is not mastery of pure logic. A lawyer will get nowhere interrogating the logical structure of a concept, or by composing a well-formed syllogism. What is required is the effective articulation of the various tasks described in the steps listed above.
9. In addition to all of the above, lawyers must have a sophisticated understanding of their place within the constitutional order. Judges must have a good sense, for instance, of how far they can go in expanding or narrowing the scope of a statutory provision.
10. Finally, and perhaps most decisive of all, the common lawyer must have a confident grasp of normative order itself. What is it that makes a situation well-ordered? This is not a technical question. It is, rather, a form of wisdom, and as such, the sophistication a particular lawyer possesses will reflect the breadth and depth of the understanding he or she has acquired of human life more generally. The more learned and experienced the lawyer in question is, the better equipped he or she will be to answer this question.[62]

[61] With this process in mind, Fuller depicted the lawyer pulling his or her mind first in one direction, then in another, to understand a 'fabric of thought'. See Fuller (n 16) 667. In engaging in this activity, the lawyer uses his or her imagination to test the workability of the situation as a site of interaction.

[62] This, too, is reflected in Lord Sumption's advice for aspiring lawyers (see n 2). Wisdom as to normative order was also central to Fuller's thought. This led him to propose the study of 'eunomics'. The study of eunomics, as envisioned by Fuller, encompasses 'the science, theory, or study of good order and workable social arrangements'. See Kenneth I Winston (2001) *The Principles of Social Order*, Oxford: Hart Publishing, 28.

If we consider the tasks enumerated above, we can see that much more is required than mere mastery of doctrine. Similarly, a highly cultivated talent for logic or analysis is of relatively little use. What is needed is instead a wide range of quite specific abilities. This collection of abilities, in the particular form they take within legal work, can only really be acquired through actual legal practice. As Lord Sumption put it, the lawyer must 'practice on the public'.[63] An introduction to this work can, however, be given to law school students. If we follow Llewellyn's prescription, students can be given work that will introduce them to the various skills and that will begin to shape their sensibilities in the manner required. In this way, students can begin, at least, to 'think like lawyers'.

[63] Lord Sumption (n 2).

11

How the Ideal Adversary System's Argumentative Structure Threatens Dignity

KATHARINA STEVENS AND NICOLE LOKSTADT

I. INTRODUCTION

THIS CHAPTER PRESENTS an argument against what we think is a dangerous ideal. It is the idealised version of the adversary system (from now on: the adversary ideal) that describes the legal trial as a competition between two parties, with the adjudicator as the passive umpire whose main job it is to determine a winner. Admittedly, it is unlikely that any existing legal system realises this ideal fully, and many systems that classify as adversary systems have moved away from it.[1] Nonetheless, we believe that the adversary ideal warrants examination because it is still traded as an ideal underlying existing adversary systems, and falling short of it is still presented as a problem. For example, Gorod documents and criticises how the US adversary system falls short of the adversary ideal because courts engage in their own fact-finding.[2] Similarly, when Judge Posner researched facts about the effects of a medicine to counteract what he perceived as an unacceptable power imbalance between parties only one of whom could afford an expert witness, his break with judicial passivity was strongly criticised.[3]

[1] See, eg, JA Jolowicz (2008) 'Adversarial and Inquisitorial Models of Civil Procedure' *International and Comparative Law Quarterly* 52(2): 281–95, doi:10.1093/iclq/52.2.281. It has been suggested to us that existing legal systems may come closest to realising the adversary ideal during the trial stage, and that seems plausible.

[2] Brianne J Gorod (2011) 'The Adversarial Myth: Appellate Court Extra-Record Factfinding' *Duke Law Journal* 61(1): 1–79.

[3] *Rowe v Gibson*, 798 F 3d 622 (7th Cir 2015). Posner's decision to break with judicial passivity and enter his own argument about the facts of a case into the trial resulted in a lively discussion about the boundaries of judicial interference. (See, eg, at www.abajournal.com/news/article/posners_internet_research_in_inmates_gerd_suit_leads_to_sparring_in_7th_cir; https://www.americanbar.org/groups/litigation/publications/litigation_journal/2015-16/summer/the_row_over_rowe_what_do_facts_between_record/.)

We will argue that the adversary ideal, when used for the resolution of legal disputes, is *not* an ideal to aspire to and should not be treated as such. This is because the argumentative structure it sets up threatens the dignity of legal subjects.

This argumentative structure requires, at the most abstract level, three main ingredients. First, two parties, each responsible for the development and presentation of arguments for their respective side of a legal dispute and potentially, but not necessarily, represented by a lawyer. Second, an adjudicator who ensures the orderly process of the trial and evaluates the arguments presented, using them to come to a decision. The adjudicator is largely passive: she is not supposed to engage in fact finding, calling witnesses, etc, but should instead rely largely on what is presented to her by the parties. Third, a set of rules and norms that govern the way a party may present their reasons, which are typically highly complex and require skill and special education to master.[4]

It follows that the argumentative structure of the adversary ideal consists of at least three argumentative roles, two advocates for opposing conclusions (the parties) and one adjudicator (the judge or jury). These roles are governed by role-related argumentative norms – for example, norms for the presentation of arguments with respect to the advocates and, for example, norms of argument evaluation for the adjudicator.[5] Because the law, including the role-related norms, is complex, and knowledge about it is hard to acquire, the parties may be represented by legal representation, a lawyer, adding another potential role to the structure. A legal right to such representation exists only for some kinds of cases in some jurisdiction.

In this chapter, we add to the mounting case against the adversary ideal[6] by arguing that the argumentative structure that lies at its core is not dignity-protecting but instead dignity-threatening. In order to avoid overcomplicating

[4] See, eg, Lon L Fuller (1978) 'The Forms and Limits of Adjudication' *Harvard Law Review* 92(2): 353–409, doi:10.2307/1340368; Stephan Landsman (1984) *The Adversary System A Description and Defense*, Washington, DC: American Enterprise Institute for Public Policy Research; David Luban (1988) *Lawyers and Justice: An Ethical Study*, Princeton, NJ: Princeton University Press; David Luban (2009) *Legal Ethics and Human Dignity*, Cambridge: Cambridge University Press; Ellen Sward (1989) 'Values, Ideology and the Evolution of the Adversary System' *Indiana Law Journal* 64(2): 301–55.

[5] It is important to note that the argumentative advocate-role in the argumentative structure set up by the adversary ideal is not the same as the lawyer-role: Having the role of a lawyer includes much more. Having the argumentative role of an advocate requires, for example, finding reasons for a conclusion with respect to some legal case, representing them in arguments, following the argumentative norms valid for the jurisdiction etc. It does not require, however, things like having a law degree or having passed a bar-exam, or even following lawyer-regarding rules and norms outside of trial. However, it makes sense to say that it is *part* of the role of being a lawyer to play the argumentative role of advocate in legal trials.

[6] See, eg, Arthur Isak Applbaum (2000) *Ethics for Adversaries – The Morality of Roles in Public and Professional Life*, Princeton, NJ: Princeton University Press; Roger Cramton (2002) 'Furthering Justice by Improving the Adversary System and Making Lawyers More Accountable' *Fordham Law Review* 70(5): 1599–1614; Luban (1988) (n 4); Luban (2009) (n 4); Sward (n 4).

things, we restrict our discussion to civil cases, but believe that much of what we say is also applicable to criminal cases.

We will approach the subject matter from the point of view of argumentation theory, in addition to legal ethics and lawyerly role morality, where the discussion about the adversary system is usually at home.[7] As such, we will treat the adversary system as a structure for joined argumentative reasoning and the question about its dignity-protecting function as one about the design of this argumentative structure. We ask: Is the basic design that the adversary ideal gives argument during legal trials dignity-protecting or dignity-threatening?

This limits the scope of this chapter considerably: we concentrate on the basic argumentative set-up for civil trials at the core of the abstract *ideal* of the adversary system, and on the way it affects the dignity of legal subjects.[8] We review the argument that the adversary ideal protects dignity by allowing legal subjects to participate in the resolution of their disputes, thereby respecting their standing as autonomous beings who have the right to influence decisions about them through reasons. We show that the way in which the adversary ideal distributes argumentative tasks between the roles of advocates and adjudicators disrupts argumentation's dignity-affirming effect, instead creating a (potentially) humiliating situation for the legal subject. The dignity threat that results is especially obvious when we examine the case of *pro se* litigants in the United States, where the adversary ideal is realised to a greater extent than elsewhere.[9] However, their case is merely a symptom of the underlying problem.

Our argument proceeds as follows. First, we introduce the Dominant Adversarial Model (DAM) of argumentation, as it is known in argumentation theory, and argue that the adversary ideal's argumentative structure is a version

[7] Luban (1988) (n 4), for example, meticulously examines and rejects arguments for the moral and prudential justification of the idealised adversary system. However, he ultimately endorses it in spite of his criticism on the basis of what he calls a 'pragmatic' argument: the method works, it is better than some of its counterparts and not worse than others (like, eg, the inquisitorial method that is employed in civil law jurisdictions like France or Germany), and replacing it with another method would likely create costs too great to bear for relatively small and uncertain gains.

[8] We acknowledge that the (idealised) adversary system has been defended (and is being defended) with arguments other than ones referring to the protection of the legal subject's dignity. Some of these arguments have been criticised by other authors (see, eg the argument that the idealised adversary system is uniquely good at finding truth, criticised in, eg, Ray Finkelstein (2011) 'The Adversarial System and the Search for Truth' *Monash University Law Review* 37(1): 135–44.

[9] A *pro se* litigant is a person who self-represents in court (Jona Goldschmidt (2018) 'How the Effort to Secure a "Civil Gideon" Morphed into a Call for Mandatory Representation for Self-Represented Litigants: A Discussion of Rabeea Assy's Injustice in Person: The Right to Self-Representation' *Jerusalem Review of Legal Studies* 17(1): 1–21, doi:10.1093/jrls/jlx032), without the assistance of a lawyer. She is responsible for presenting her own case inside the courtroom; she is also responsible for defending her case when it is questioned and challenged. However, a *pro se* litigant may have spoken with, or received some form of assistance from, a lawyer in preparation for the presentation of her case. For example, a *pro se* litigant may have taken advantage of 'lawyer-lite' services, such as 'unbundled legal services' (Jeanne Charn (2013) 'Celebrating the "Null" Finding: Evidence-Based Strategies for Improving Access to Legal Services' *The Yale Law Journal* 122(8): 2206–34), ie consulting a lawyer for only certain aspects of the trial. What makes the person *pro se* is that she is *entering* and *participating* in the courtroom without a lawyer.

of the DAM. We discuss the classic pro-DAM argument, and point out the conditions under which this argument is valid and the DAM succeeds. We move on to discussing the dignity-based case *for* the argumentative structure set up by the adversary ideal and point out the role that the classic pro-DAM argument plays in it. We then show that arguments conducted according to the argumentative structure of the adversary ideal cannot be expected to reliably fulfil the DAM's success conditions. Finally, we show that this failing threatens the dignity of *all* legal subjects whose cases are adjudicated under this structure, something that becomes most visible when examining the situation of *pro se* litigants in the United States.

II. THE DOMINANT ADVERSARIAL MODEL OF ARGUMENTATION

A. The DAM Structure at the Core of the Adversary System

We argue that the adversary ideal's argumentative structure is a version of what argumentation theory calls the Dominant Adversarial Model (DAM)[10] for general argumentation, ameliorated to deal with the special circumstances that apply in legal adjudication. It is therefore important to familiarise the reader with the DAM, its structure, the argument for its appropriateness and the conditions under which this argument succeeds to show the DAM's success.

An argumentative structure consists of the complex of norms according to which the participants in an argument interact with each other. Via these argumentative norms, it sets up argumentative roles, each of which assigns goals and tasks to the individual arguers playing them.[11] The DAM is one of several possible basic argumentative structures. It consists of proponent and opponent roles. Each arguer's individual goal is to present the case for the acceptability of their conclusion or favoured decision and the unacceptability of that of their opponent. They pursue this goal by fulfilling the tasks of finding arguments for the conclusion/decision, defending it against objections, and finding objections against both the conclusion and the arguments of their opponent.[12] And, unlike

[10] The name was introduced by Daniel Cohen (2015) 'Missed Opportunities in Argument Evaluation' in *Reflections on Theoretical Issues in Argumentation Theory*, eds FH van Eemeren and B Garssen, Dordrecht: Springer, 121–30. and has since been used consistently in the argumentation theory literature.

[11] We think of argumentative roles in the same way as of other social roles, like, eg teacher and student, employer and employee, etc. We follow, eg, Ralph H Turner (2009) 'Role Taking: Process vs Conformity' in *Human Behavior and Social Processes*, ed A Rose, Boston, MA: Houghton Mifflin, 20–40.; Ralph H Turner (2001) 'Role Theory' in *Handbook of Socialogical Theory*, ed Ralph H Turner, New York: Springer, 233–54. For more on argumentative roles, see Katharina Stevens (2019) 'The Roles We Make Others Take: Thoughts on the Ethics of Arguing' *Topoi* 38: 693–709 doi:10.1007/s11245-019-09659-0.

[12] In an even simpler version of the DAM model, the proponent has only the task of finding arguments for a pre-chosen conclusion and defending it against objections, while the opponent has only

arguers playing advocate roles in the setting of legal trials, proponent and opponent share an additional goal of coming to a common result, associated with the shared task of evaluating the balance of presented reasons at the end of the argument and of determining the winner.

Even though argumentation, in general, is often associated with the for-and-against of the DAM, the model is not without alternatives. Perhaps its most distinct counterpart is *the cooperative model* of argumentation, in which the arguers take deliberator roles whose goal it is to contribute as many reasons relevant to the issue at hand as possible in any direction, and come to a conclusion by evaluating arguments and objections together.[13]

Basic argumentative structures like the DAM and the cooperative model can be expanded upon, for example by outsourcing certain argumentative tasks to other roles. The argumentative structure set up by the adversary ideal, as well as its most famous counterpart, the inquisitorial ideal, are both different kinds of expansions upon a DAM core: the parties in legal cases are each tasked with arguing that a decision should be made in their favour by finding arguments for their conclusion and objections against their opponent's conclusion and arguments.

However, instead of presenting the arguments to each other and sharing the task of final evaluation, they present them to an adjudicator. The adjudicator's job is to evaluate and make an unbiased decision, something that cannot be expected of the parties themselves because of the typically high stakes involved in legal disputes.[14] Further, the complexity of the law often makes it too hard for legal subjects to identify those among their reasons that count as legal reasons, let alone to formulate these reasons appropriately. As such, the additional role of a legal representative for each party, the lawyer, might be added, whose goal is to help the party they represent win the argument. Sometimes, parties have a right to a lawyer but, as the existence of parties who become *pro se* litigants for lack of money shows, not always.

B. The Classic Pro-DAM Argument

In this chapter, we assume that the goal of argumentation is to identify and adequately weigh the reasons applicable to the argument's issue and, on their basis, to come to the conclusion/decision best supported by the available

the task of finding objections against both the conclusion and the proponent's arguments with the goal of showing that the proponent's conclusion is incorrect (see, eg, Frans van Eemeren (2018) *Argumentation Theory: A Pragma-Dialectical Perspective*, vol 33, Cham: Springer.

[13] Douglas Walton (1998) *The New Dialectic – Conversational Contexts of Argument*, Toronto: University of Toronto Press.

[14] The exact set of tasks and argumentative norms that apply to the adjudicator differ in the adversary and the inquisitorial systems – more on this later.

reasons. We will call such a conclusion or decision the *correct result*. The argument for preferring the DAM over other possible basic argumentative structures is well-rehearsed in and outside the legal context: by pitting two motivated arguers against one another, the best arguments for each side will surely be found, while weak arguments will be weeded out through the criticism provided by the respective opponent. At the end of a kind of battle for the survival of the fittest, only arguments successful at presenting reasons at their appropriate strength will be left.[15] This will enable the two arguers to identify the applicable reasons, and on their basis, the correct result.[16] We will call this argument *the survival-of-the-fittest argument* in favour of the DAM.

This argument has been given a psychological basis by Mercier and Sperber's argumentative theory of reasoning,[17] which shows how the DAM structure can help human reasoners balance out the in-born my-side bias.[18] The my-side bias is a cognitive bias that influences our reasoning so that we prefer arguments and evidence in favour of our pre-chosen conclusions over arguments and evidence against them. It affects us more the higher our stakes in the argument are, but takes hold whenever we take ownership of a claim or conclusion. It makes us interpret even mixed or unfavourable evidence in favour of what we already believe (tempting us to commit fallacies) and undervalue or dismiss evidence against what we believe. It gives us the ability to find flaws in objections against our conclusions, but limits our ability to find flaws in our own reasoning. Interestingly, as Mercier and Sperber point out, the effects of the my-side bias are stronger when producing arguments than when evaluating them – meaning that it is easier to *recognise* a good objection against our favoured conclusion when we are presented with it than to come up with one on our own.

According to Mercier and Sperber, the traditional understanding of reasoning fails.[19] According to it, reasoning is a trait developed in human beings because

[15] One of the most famous formulations of this argument comes from Mill in John Stuart Mill (2007) *On Liberty*, New York: Penguin Classics.

[16] For more discussion, see, eg, Katharina Stevens (2016) 'The Virtuous Arguer: One Person, Four Roles' *Topoi* 35(2): 375–83, doi:10.1007/s11245-015-9309-4; and Katharina Stevens and Daniel Cohen (2018) 'The attraction of the ideal has no traction on the real: on adversariality and roles in argument' *Argumentation and Advocacy* 55(1): 1–23, doi:10.1080/10511431.2018.1504584.

[17] Hugo Mercier and Dan Sperber (2011) 'Why do humans reason? Arguments for an argumentative theory' *Behavioral and Brain Sciences* 34(2): 57–74, doi:10.1017/S0140525X10000968; Hugo Mercier and Dan Sperber (2017) *The Enigma of Reason*, Cambridge, MA: Harvard University Press.

[18] To our knowledge, Zarefsky was the first to translate Mercier and Sperber's work into a defence for the DAM in argumentation theory. See David Zarefsky (2012) 'A Challenge and an Opportunity for Argumentation Studies' *Argumentation and Advocacy* 48(3): 175–78, doi:10.1080/00028533.2012.11821763.

[19] Mercier and Sperber (2011) (n 17); Mercier and Sperber (2017) (n 17). We do not here want to commit to agreeing with Mercier and Sperber that the traditional picture fails – we think it is perfectly possible that both the traditional idea that reasoning enhances one's own inferences and Mercier and Sperber's point that reasoning enhances the ability to persuade could be at the root for the development of the ability to reason. We do, however, find their case for the adaptive value of persuasion and its role in the development of reason and the my-side bias convincing.

it provides the ability of enhancing one's *own* inferences. But this cannot explain one of the most conspicuous characteristics of human reasoning, namely, that it is so heavily influenced by the my-side bias. Instead, Mercier and Sperber propose a different view on the adaptive value of reasoning, namely, that it helps us to get others to believe and act as we want them to. Reasoning is selected for in the evolutionary process because it allows humans to be argumentatively persuasive. It gives us the ability to recognise the inferences from premises to our conclusions, and thereby makes it possible to represent them to others.[20] This enhances the likelihood that these others will also make those inferences and will therefore believe the arguer's conclusions. And it is clearly valuable to be able to make others believe what we want them to believe.

Under this theory of reasoning, the my-side bias is a helpful asset that would be selected for rather than a flaw whose existence remains unexplained: it enables us to find evidence in favour of our pre-chosen conclusions quickly, aiding with the goal of convincing others. That it has less impact when evaluating the arguments and objections of others also makes sense. When determining whether to believe the conclusion for which another advocates, it is most useful to do so in an unbiased manner, because that helps to acquire truths cheaply, that is, without having to engage in resource-intense and potentially risky exploration.

Aided by Mercier and Sperber's theory, we can now see the psychological underpinnings of the survival-of-the-fittest argument in favour of the DAM in general argumentation. The goals and tasks that the adversarial proponent/opponent roles give to the individual arguers seem to work well to exploit the advantages and avoid the disadvantages of the my-side bias. The my-side bias helps arguers to find arguments for their own conclusions as required by the advocate roles. At the same time, the DAM structure ensures that arguers are provided with possible objections by their opponents, something that would be hard for them to do themselves given the effects of the my-side bias. The result is that the arguers are motivated to find the best arguments for their side and weed out the bad ones for the other side, just as the classic argument for the DAM claims. This results in the mutual recognition of each other's reasons.[21] In short, the way that the DAM distributes argumentative goals and tasks via its argumentative roles is conducive to argumentation leading to the mutual recognition of reasons and, on this basis, correct results.

[20] Instead of making inferences unconsciously (eg simply smelling chocolate and being prompted to think 'Chocolate!', without becoming aware of the connection), reasoning allows us to become conscious of our inferences (eg, the smell of chocolate enters your nose and, in addition to thinking 'Chocolate!', you also think 'It smells of chocolate, therefore, chocolate must be near.').

[21] See also Hélène Landemore and Hugo Mercier (2012) 'Talking it out with others vs deliberation within and the law of group polarization: Some implications of the argumentative theory of reasoning for deliberative democracy' *Análise Social* XLVII(205): 910–34; Mercier and Sperber (2011) (n 17).

C. The DAM's Success Conditions

Or at least that is the idea. Unfortunately, the survival-of-the-fittest argument for the DAM overlooks the prevalence of two all-too-human characteristics. First, average arguers are often more strongly driven by the wish to win the argument than the wish to come to the correct result. Second, arguers possess a generally disheartening inability to resist using and *falling for* rhetorical tricks, fallacies and unintentional errors in reasoning, and, more importantly for our argument, the degree to which they are afflicted by this varies widely from individual to individual.[22] As we will now show, the survival-of-the-fittest argument for the DAM succeeds only where two conditions regarding these human traits are fulfilled. Where they are not, the DAM is not conducive to arguers' identification of the relevant reasons, weighing them correctly and identifying the correct result.

The first condition is what we call the *equally-competent-arguers condition*. It requires that both arguers must be somewhat competent, and they must be roughly equal in their abilities. By being a competent arguer, we mean that an arguer is minimally well-versed with respect to the issue, capable of formulating her reasons into arguments and somewhat educated with respect to the validity conditions of various kinds of arguments. All this enables her to formulate good arguments and catch her opponent's fallacies – which also and importantly implies that she has to match her opponent's abilities at least approximately so that tricks and deceit will not succeed.[23] In addition, she must be capable of using the rhetorical 'language' necessary to make herself understood in the context in which the argument takes place.[24] To the degree that this condition is

[22] Compare criticism from, eg, Sylvia Burrow (2010) 'Verbal Sparring and Apologetic Points: Politeness in Gendered Argumentation Contexts' *Informal Logic* 30(3): 235–62; Daniel Cohen (1995) 'Argument is war … and war is hell: philosophy, education, and metaphors for argumentation' *Informal Logic* 17(2): 177–88; Sonja Foss and Cindy Griffin (1995) 'Beyond persuasion – a proposal for an invitational rhetoric' *Communication Monographs* 62(1): 2–18, doi:10.1080/03637759509376345; Sally Gearheart (1979) 'The Womanization of Rhetoric' *Women's Studies International Quarterly* 2: 195–201; Michael Gilbert (1994) 'Feminism, Argumentation and Coalescence' *Informal Logic* 16(2): 95–113, doi:https://doi.org/10.22329/il.v16i2.2444; Catherine Hundleby (2013) 'Aggression, Politeness, and Abstract Adversaries' *Informal Logic* 33(2): 238–62, doi:10.22329/il.v33i2.3895; Janice Moulton (2003/1983) 'A paradigm of philosophy: the adversarial method' in *Discovering Reality: Feminist Perspectives on Epistemology, Metaphysics, Methodology, and Philosophy of Science*, eds S Harding and M Hintikka, Dordrecht: Springer, 149–64; Phyllis Rooney (2010) 'Philosophy, Adversarial Argumentation, and Embattled Reason' *Informal Logic* 30(3): 203–34, doi:https://doi.org/10.22329/il.v30i3.3032; Stevens (n 11); Stevens and Cohen (n 16).

[23] This requirement is acknowledged in the jurisprudence literature, eg by Murray Schwartz (1983) 'The Zeal of the Civil Advocate' *American Bar Foundation Research Journal* 8(3): 543–63, doi:10.1111/j.1747-4469.1983.tb00883.x ('effective implementation of the [Adversary] system requires that the professional advocates satisfied two postulates: they must be equally competent, and they must be equally adversary').

[24] See, eg, Iris Marion Young (1996) 'Communication and the Other: Beyond Deliberative Democracy' in *Democracy and Difference: Contesting boundaries of the political*, ed S Benhabib, Princeton, NJ: Princeton University Press, 120–35, who criticises the tendency to confuse rationality in argument with a certain kind of argumentative rhetoric accessible mainly to the educated elites.

not met, the DAM structure fails to create conditions that will lead to the correct result, because it no longer enables the identification of each party's reasons to an equal degree. Rather, the DAM then organises arguments so that they will be won by the party better able to give her reasons effect (or even to make it appear as if there are reasons where there are none) – because she is more clear on what those reasons are, is better able to formulate them into arguments, is more effective in creating and answering objections, and/or is rhetorically more apt. Instead of leading to a balancing-out of the my-side biases of both parties, the DAM enables the more competent party, and *only* her, to do what the my-side bias is evolutionarily selected for: (merely) persuade.

This is not all, however. A second condition is equally important, though maybe less intuitively obviously so. The success of an argument structured according to the DAM depends on the arguers valuing the goal to come to the correct result over the goal to win.[25] We call this the *underlying-cooperation condition*: even though the DAM ascribes adversarial roles to the arguers, its success depends on a certain kind of *cooperation*.[26] Advocates share the final task of determining the outcome of the argument, so the DAM really provides them with *two* distinct goals: to build the strongest possible case for the acceptability of their own preferred result, but also, at the end of the argument, to determine the correct result. The DAM succeeds only if the arguers succeed in this second goal, and this requires them to cooperate. This is especially important when it comes to the final determination of the outcome – here arguers must set their adversariality aside entirely, or no agreement can be reached. However, it also plays an important role throughout the phase of the argument when arguers formulate arguments and objections. Here, arguers need to value coming to the correct result more than winning because this connects the creation of the argument pool with the goal of determining the correct result. In turn, this directs the arguers towards the identification of reasons rather than the creation of (merely) persuasive arguments.

Without an underlying cooperative attitude informing the adversarial behaviour of defending one's own conclusion and attacking that of the other, arguers have no reason to hold back on fallacious but effective strategies. Similarly, they have no reason to interpret their opponent's contribution charitably, directing objections only against arguments that they really find lacking instead of attacking anything that can be made to look like a weak spot. They are also

[25] Even Mercier and Sperber point out that this condition applies. For a detailed discussion, see, eg Stevens and Cohen (n 16).

[26] Compare Scott Aikin (2011) 'A Defense of War and Sport Metaphors in Argument' *Philosophy and Rhetoric* 44(3): 250–72, doi:10.5325/philrhet.44.3.0250. Of course, parties in legal trials cannot be expected to fulfil this condition. This is one reason why an adjudicator is needed – they are the ones with the interest in the truth. We introduce this condition here to show that a cooperative element is important for the success of argument structures based on the DAM. Our strategy is to argue that the judge cannot fully replace the cooperative element in structures set up according to the adversary ideal.

not motivated to admit where their opponent has made a strong argument or pointed out a fatal flaw in theirs, if they believe that this might go unnoticed. Finally, because the lack of an underlying cooperative attitude leaves only the desire to win the argument, arguers will prefer simple, effective arguments over complex ones, even if some important reasons cannot be represented in simple ways. This means that some reasons might not be taken into account at all.[27]

All this influences the argument pool based on which the final determination of a result is made, distorting and impoverishing it. The effects of this are detrimental even when arguers are evenly matched, simply because the mutual all-out-war attitude will likely hinder the full development of complex ideas. But if the equally-competent-arguers condition is also not met, the effects become downright catastrophic, creating an argument pool heavily distorted in favour of the more competent arguer and considerably diminishing the hope that the argument will actually lead to the correct result. Even Mercier and Sperber acknowledge the importance of the underlying-cooperation condition.[28] This makes sense, because the DAM structure can only counteract the negative effects of the my-side bias if arguers are willing to take advantage of their opponent's ability to come up with arguments and objections they themselves would not have thought of.

In summary: if the equally-competent-arguers condition and the underlying-cooperation condition are not both met, the DAM is a model heavily *biased* in favour of arguers who are argumentatively more competent. The survival-of-the-fittest argument fails, because the battle that takes place is not one of the better reasons but one of the sharper wit.

This does not mean that there is no merit to the survival-of-the-fittest argument. The basic DAM model gives arguers some motivation towards fulfilling the underlying-cooperation condition by tasking them with the joined final determination of the argument's result. This is so because the successful fulfilment of the proponent/opponent roles in non-legal argument is tied to the ability to come to an agreement about the correct result in the end. In addition, if the parties take the cooperative aspect of arguing under the DAM to heart, minor differences in argumentative competency can be compensated for through the application of the principle of charity.

Nonetheless, the underlying-cooperation condition and the equally-competent-arguers condition remain unmet often enough that blindly relying on the DAM's effectiveness is ill-advised. Often, they go unfulfilled to some degree, because people typically engage in argument when something is at stake for them, making winning the argument very important to them. Additionally, people often argue with others who are far above or below their argumentative abilities. This is problematic already in everyday argumentation about such

[27] Compare Moulton (n 22).
[28] Mercier and Sperber (2011) (n 17) 65.

banal topics as, for example, who should take out the garbage. However, the problem becomes more serious the more esoteric the topic of the argument, because expertise will be more unevenly distributed and the language in which the topic can be adequately discussed will be more technical and specialised.

To summarise, the survival-of-the-fittest argument for the DAM works only under the ideal conditions of evenly matched arguers with an overriding interest in the correct result, making the DAM an ideal. This, by itself, would not be a problem. Ideals can be very useful. Unfortunately, the DAM can function similar to what Mills calls an 'ideal theory':[29] argumentative structures with a DAM core are used in the real world on the basis of the classic survival-of-the-fittest argument even when the DAM's success conditions are not met, creating a blind-spot for the detrimental effects that the DAM can have.[30]

In the following, we argue that this is exactly what happens to the argumentative structure set up by the adversary ideal: It is justified as dignity-protecting by a line of reasoning that relies heavily on the survival-of-the-fittest argument. Meanwhile, the way in which the adversary system's structure adjusts the DAM makes it very unlikely that the DAM's success conditions are met. To show this, we first examine the dignity argument in favour of the adversary ideal's argumentative structure and show that it relies on the survival-of-the-fittest argument. Then we show the adversary ideal's uneasy relationship to the DAM's success conditions. Finally, we argue that this means that rather than dignity-protecting, the adversary ideal's argumentative structure is dignity-threatening. This, we argue, is a reason to believe that while the DAM is an ideal whose success conditions are only seldom met, the adversary ideal is not worthy to be thought of as an ideal at all.

III. THE DIGNITY ARGUMENT FOR THE ADVERSARY IDEAL'S ARGUMENTATIVE STRUCTURE

In short, the argument for the claim that the adversary ideal contributes to the protection of the parties' dignity is that it acknowledges the parties as autonomous, reasonable beings with the ability and right to contribute reasons to the legal adjudication of their disputes and have those reasons taken into account adequately in the final decision.[31] According to the argument, this happens

[29] Charles Mills (2005) '"Ideal Theory" as Ideology' *Hypatia* 20(3): 165–84, doi:10.1353/hyp.2005.0107.

[30] Katharina Stevens and Daniel Cohen (2020) 'Angelic Devil's Advocates and the Forms of Adversariality' *Topoi* 40: 899–912, *online first*, doi:https://doi.org/10.1007/s11245-020-09726-x.

[31] Fuller argues that the law is built on the assumption that a person 'is, or can become, a responsible agent, capable of understanding and following rules, and answerable for his defaults' (Lon L Fuller (1969) *The Morality of Law*, rev edn, New Haven, CT: Yale University Press). Compare also Alan Donagan (1984) 'Justifying Legal Practice in the Adversary System' in *The Good Lawyer: Lawyers' Roles and Lawyers' Ethics*, ed David Luban, Totowa, NJ: Rowman & Allanheld, 123–48;

because the adversary ideal's argumentative structure allows each party to enter their own legally relevant reasons into the legal dispute, ensuring that these reasons will be taken into account adequately. We will here present what we think is a strong version of the argument that also makes the role played by the survival-of-the-fittest argument apparent.

A. Dignity Requires Argumentative Integration of the Parties

According to scholars like Fuller[32] and Waldron, the rule of law protects the law's subjects from a unique dignity-threat that materializes when legal systems are introduced.[33]

Following Waldron,[34] we can identify human dignity as a status that each person possesses equally – the status of an autonomous, reasonable being endowed with the ability to direct her own life according to her own reasoning, and the right to demand that others respect and accommodate this status.[35] In this way, possessing dignity is the relevant feature that defines all human persons as being equal to one another. However, ordering the affairs of people via the law necessitates the empowerment of legal officials to make, adjudicate and enforce laws. This means creating power imbalances in which some people (the legal officials) can prescribe the behaviour of other people (the law's subjects) and apply these prescriptions to their circumstances. In other words, introducing the law requires placing some people into positions of power over others, in spite of the equally high status they possess in virtue of their dignity.[36] If this

David Luban (2010) 'The Rule of Law and Human Dignity: Re-examining Fuller's Canons' *Hague Journal on the Rule of Law* 2(1): 29–47, doi:10.1017/S1876404510100025; Joseph Raz (1977) 'The Rule of Law and Its Virtue' *Law Quarterly Review* 95: 208–26; Jeremy Waldron (2012) 'How Law Protects Dignity' *Cambridge Law Journal* 71(1): 200–22.

[32] Fuller's (n 31) claim that the rule of law is the 'inner morality of law' has been criticised, eg by Raz (n 31), who denies that Fuller's requirements can ensure that the law does not threaten dignity given that they cannot prevent harsh or unjust laws. We are here following Luban's (n 31) interpretation of Fuller's claim that the rule of law protects dignity by dealing with the dignity threat it creates merely by existing. But even if dignity was not connected to the rule of law, protecting dignity would still be an important value.

[33] Fuller (n 31); Waldron (n 31).

[34] Jeremy Waldron (2012) *Dignity, Rank and Rights*, Oxford: Oxford University Press; Waldron (n 31).

[35] 'Dignity is the status of a person predicated on the fact that she is recognized as having the ability to control and regulate her actions in accordance with her own apprehension of norms and reasons that apply to her; it assumes she is capable of giving and entitled to give an account of herself (and of the way in which she is regulating her actions and organizing her life), an account that others are to pay attention to; and it means finally that she has the wherewithal to demand that her agency and her presence among us as a human being be taken seriously and accommodated in the lives of others, in others' attitudes and actions toward her, and in social life generally.' Waldron (n 31) 71.

[36] In addition, it is important to note that the state, with its coercive power and available resources, is powerful while the legal subject is weak (RJ Kutak (1984) 'The Adversary System and the Practice of Law' in *The Good Lawyer: Lawyers' Roles and Lawyers' Ethics*, ed David Luban, Totowa, NJ: Rowman & Allanheld, 172–87), further exacerbating this difference in power.

power goes unchecked or is used carelessly, the law might prevent legal subjects from retaining autonomous control over their own lives by submitting them to an unpredictable, inconsistent force.[37] For example, legal officials might enact retroactive or secret laws, or perhaps tailor laws specifically to the situation of individual persons, putting them at a disadvantage. Alternatively, the officials might interpret laws so that the adjudicative process yields outcomes in line with their personal beliefs. This would result in a situation in which, from the viewpoint of the individual legal subject, the law becomes unpredictable. The outcome is what Luban describes as the humiliating situation in which legal subjects live in a constant state of 'uncertainty and fearfulness because [their] fate lies in the hands of official whim, which can choose at will to stigmatize conduct as criminal'[38] or, more broadly, contrary to law, thereby undermining the ability to make reasonable plans for their life. It is this potential to insert man-made uncertainty and treacherousness into the lives of legal subjects that makes the law inherently dignity-threatening.[39]

To avoid threatening the dignity of legal subjects in this manner, the law must preserve the legal subjects' ability to effectively engage in the shaping of their lives according to their own reasons. It must provide a sort of reliable rubric that legal subjects can use to plan their actions around the boundaries that the law sets. If the law fulfils this requirement, the subject's dignity is protected, because it allows her autonomous action within the rules that the law sets up.[40] Importantly for the purpose of our discussion, this includes that the law must give legal subjects some predictability should they find themselves involved in a legal dispute.

Legal subjects do not only need to know what the law requires of them in advance, and be informed about it in clear language, etc, as the *formal* rule of law demands.[41] Legal subjects also need to be assured that when they enter the court, decisions about them will be made according to the law as it was promulgated, and not in an unpredictable way, as would happen, for example, should

[37] This act of ignoring a legal subject's dignified status does not need to be intentional for it to be problematic. Fuller (1969) points out that while it is typically assumed that a person is answerable for harms caused by her fists, the same sense of responsibility does not typically extend to her elbows – despite the fact that her elbows tend to cause more harm to those around her (and more frequently). Fuller thus argue that '[a] strong commitment to the principles of legality compels a ruler to answer to himself, not only for his fists, but for his elbows as well'.

[38] Luban (n 31).

[39] Having decisions made for you is inherently disrespectful of your dignity, though this is especially the case when you have no say in the matter.

[40] Fuller (n 31). From this perspective, it may be unsurprising that Fuller argues that '[e]very departure from the principles of the law's inner morality is an affront to man's dignity as a responsible agent': ibid, 162.

[41] For Fuller, a system of law works well when it meets the requirements of generality, publicity, prospectivity, intelligibility, consistency, possibility, stability, and congruency (ibid). These requirements are often considered the formal aspects of the rule of law (Jeremy Waldron (2016) 'The Rule of Law' in *The Stanford Encyclopedia of Philosophy*, ed E Zalta, doi:https://plato.stanford.edu/archives/fall2016/entries/rule-of-law/).

legal officials decide cases according to their own idiosyncratic reasons. Legal subjects need to know that they will see their legal rights enforced, that they will be given the space to demand this and that their demands will be heeded to the degree that they can support them with legal reasons.

In order to ensure this, legal subjects must be *argumentatively integrated* into the decision-making process by (i) being provided with the opportunity to present their reasons by giving arguments and (ii) the design of the decision-making process being such that it is likely that, if they present legally relevant reasons, these reasons will be recognised, acknowledged at their appropriate weight and integrated into the decision-making process in an unbiased manner. This demand for argumentative integration can be seen, for example, in Waldron's formulation of the *procedural* rule of law requirements as he has adapted them from Tashima:[42]

a) a hearing by an impartial and independent tribunal that is required to administer existing legal norms on the basis of the formal presentation of evidence and argument;
b) a right to representation by counsel at such a hearing;
c) a right to be present, to confront and question witnesses, and to make legal argument about the bearing of the evidence and the various legal norms relevant to the case; and
d) a right to hear reasons from the tribunal when it reaches its decision, which are responsive to the evidence and arguments presented before it.[43]

Integrating the parties argumentatively protects their dignity in two different ways. First, it recognises their standing as dignified beings with the right to influence decisions made about their lives by allowing them to enter their legally relevant reasons into the decision-making process. Second, it ensures that the way in which the law will be enforced during the process of adjudication does not become unpredictable in the sense that, at least after the decision is made, the parties can see how the law leads to it, given the applicable legal reasons: if the process of adjudication is designed so that it adequately integrates the legal reasons each party represents, then that creates conditions conducive to the law's being enforced as it was promulgated. This is so because it enables those who are most motivated to identify legal reasons on both sides of the issue to enter them into the decision-making process. And ensuring that the law is enforced as it was

[42] Wallace Tashima (2008) 'The War on Terror and the Rule of Law' *Asian American Law Journal* 15: 245–65.

[43] Waldron (n 41). The *right-to-counsel-requirement* might, at first glance, stand out as not immediately part of the argumentative-integration demand. As will become clear, this requirement is a derived necessity given the demands that the legal system makes on the rhetorical capabilities of those who want to participate in it argumentatively. Where it is not met, the adversary system's dignity threat turns into almost guaranteed humiliation, as we show in our discussion of *pro se* litigants.

promulgated provides legal subjects with the predictability necessary to protect them from the law's dignity threat.[44]

In summary, by requiring that the adjudicative process is designed in acknowledgement of the legal subject's ability to have and communicate legally relevant reasons, the procedural rule of law protects dignity because it ensures that legal subjects are argumentatively integrated into the legal decision-making process. It is important to note, however, that the argumentative-integration demand requires that the legal subject be enabled to *enter her legally relevant reasons* into the decision-making process. This requires more than just letting her speak or present arguments. It also requires that things are set up in a way that ensures, as much as possible, that she will be understood, and that what she communicates will be taken into account. Otherwise, giving her the opportunity to argue is not much more than a farce.

B. From the Need for Argumentative Integration to the DAM

To summarise, protecting the dignity of legal subjects requires integrating them argumentatively when legal decisions are made about them. This enables them to enter their reasons into the decision-making process, to have their 'day in court' as, for example, Fuller puts it.[45] It might seem that this does not immediately necessitate the adoption of an argumentative structure based on the DAM. Theoretically, a cooperative argument in which all parties share the task of finding and formulating arguments in all directions could also fulfil the argumentative integration demand.[46] However, cooperative models require more of the individual arguers than DAM-based models, because they ask them also to offer arguments in favour of conclusions that might be disadvantageous to them. Issues that need to be decided by a court are typically high-stakes, and parties will be strongly attached to their point of view, making this hard. What is required for the protection of dignity is the institutionally guaranteed chance to present arguments for this point of view.[47] DAM-based models, by defining the roles of parties via the task of formulating arguments representing their own reasons, afford this chance without requiring the parties to formulate arguments against their own point of view.

[44] Additionally, it is important that the legal subject is presented with the final decision and the reasons for it, given that the resolution of the case is intended to alter her future actions (Fuller (n 4)).

[45] Fuller (n 31).

[46] And, in fact, in some cases this may be best, for example when the parties have a common interest, as it might be when it comes to decisions about childcare between separated parents, with the common interest being the well-being of the child (compare Rebecca Aviel (2013) 'Why Civil Gideon Won't Fix Family Law' *Yale Law Journal* 122: 2106–24).

[47] Compare Fuller (n 31); Fuller (n 4).

Of course, the argumentative-integration demand also requires that each party's reasons are adequately integrated into the decision. This is realised not just by allowing parties to argue. After all, arguments are not reasons. Bad arguments exist. There are arguments that over- or understate the weight of a reason, or that only purport to represent a reason while really being nothing but empty words. So, to allow parties to give their *reasons* the adequate effect during adjudication, this process has to be designed such that those reasons are recognised and given the appropriate weight. In turn, this requires that arguments that do not really provide any reasons and objections that do not hit their target are recognised and discounted. This is where the survival-of-the-fittest argument enters: by pitting the parties against one another, the DAM ensures that the chaff is separated from the wheat of reasons, creating the conditions under which it is likely that *each* party's reasons are equally well integrated.[48] The DAM gives each party her day in court and, at the same time, sets up the battle for the survival of the fittest necessary to separate the good from the bad arguments, which ensures that each party's reasons are given the adequate weight in the final decision. It is important to note that this gives the classic DAM argument a central place in the dignity-based case for the adversary ideal's argumentative structure: a legal subject's dignity is protected through her argumentative participation in the trial because she is given a meaningful opportunity to enter her legal reasons into the decision-making process. This requires that the argumentative process is conducive to her legally relevant reasons being understood and fairly considered when she attempts to present them through argument. The survival-of-the-fittest argument is the argument necessary to show that the adversary ideal is conducive to this.

C. From the DAM to the Argumentative Structure of the Adversary System

Both the adversary ideal's and the inquisitorial ideal's argumentative structure for trials is based on the DAM, and both expand the DAM by adding an adjudicator role (typically a judge or a jury) and legal representative roles (lawyers). Proponent/opponent roles, which included having to determine the final outcome, turn into advocate roles, which do not contain this task. The main difference between the argumentative structure of the adversary ideal and that of the inquisitorial ideal can be found in the tasks allocated to the role of the adjudicator (which affects the way that the other roles work): the inquisitorial ideal differs from the adversary ideal in that it gives the adjudicator (typically

[48] Compare, eg Gorod (n 2), on the importance of 'rigorous checking' of all entered facts and arguments through adversarial argument, and Gary Goodpaster (1987) 'On the Theory of American Adversary Criminal Trial' *The Journal of Criminal Law and Criminology (1973–)* 78(1): 118–54, doi:10.2307/1143577, on the perceived fairness of the trial.

a judge) a much more active role, tasking her with researching facts, finding evidence, calling witnesses, questioning, etc. This means that the inquisitorial ideal asks the adjudicator to contribute actively and in many ways to the pool of arguments based on which the final decision will be made. To complete the dignity-based argument for the adversary ideal's argumentative structure, we need to show why it gives the adjudicator a passive role that does not include contribution to the argument pool. The reason found in the literature is that the passivity of the adjudicator preserves her impartiality, thereby ensuring that each party is given an equal chance at integrating her legally relevant reasons into an *unbiased* decision-making procedure. This makes for a fair fight for the survival of the fittest, rather than one in which one party or other may gain an unfair advantage.

First, an adjudicator is needed (in both systems). Where an issue has become a legal dispute, the stakes are typically so high that there is little chance that the underlying-cooperation condition is met to a degree that allows the parties to come to a result they can both agree on, let alone the correct result.[49] Therefore, while the basic DAM assigns the determination of the final balance of reasons and the making of a decision to the advocates together, here it needs to be outsourced to an additional role. In a way, then, we can think of the adjudicator as a role integrated into the process (also) in order to provide the cooperative element that cannot be expected from the parties: it is not possible to rely on the parties to value coming to the correct result more than winning, so someone else has to do it. That someone is the adjudicator.

From here, the choice for the adversary system is motivated by the thought that the process of legal adjudication has to be *unbiased* so that the balanced integration of the parties' reasons will not be frustrated. This could happen because the decision maker prefers one party and therefore gets inflicted by the effects of the my-side bias, which leads her to overestimate the goodness of some arguments while underestimating others. According to the argument for the adversary ideal, the adjudicator risks taking sides prematurely if she allows herself to intervene in the process of argumentation or even develop a tentative theory as to how the dispute should be resolved. Even tentatively adopting a side to make or help make an argument might trigger the adjudicator's my-side bias by giving her some minimal commitment to a pre-chosen conclusion. As Fuller put it in a now classic article, 'what starts as a preliminary diagnosis designed to direct the inquiry tends, quickly and imperceptibly, to become a fixed conclusion, all that confirms the diagnosis makes a strong imprint on the mind while all that is counter to it is received with diverted attention'.[50] The result is that

[49] Presumably, given that the matter has been brought to court in the first place indicates that attempts to resolve the issue without the help of a court have already failed or are not possible to begin with.

[50] Fuller (n 4) 383.

the party who is arguing against the adjudicator's tentative conclusion finds her ability to enter her reasons into the final decision diminished, while the party arguing with the adjudicator finds her ability amplified. In turn, this threatens the disadvantaged party's standing as an equal, dignified person, because her reasons are no longer adequately being taken into account. In keeping with the survival-of-the-fittest analogy, the disadvantaged party finds herself fighting against both her opponent and the umpire, making it an unfair fight. Only by staying out of the development of arguments altogether can the adjudicator remain impartial and avoid biasing the argumentative battle, ensuring that the argumentative-integration demand is fulfilled and the dignity of the parties protected. Therefore, the adjudicator may not help with the development of arguments for either side. To preserve the unbiased nature of the adjudicative process, she needs to stay *passive* while arguments are being presented. She can only engage in the evaluation of the dispute and decide which side should win *after* everyone else has had their full say.[51] This completes the dignity-based case for the adversary ideal.

IV. THE ADVERSARY IDEAL, THE DAM'S SUCCESS CONDITIONS AND TROUBLE WITH DIGNITY

The problem is that the process of legal adjudication can become biased in other ways than through the premature attachment of the adjudicator to a conclusion. In this section, we argue that arguments held according to the DAM-based argumentative structure set up by the adversary ideal are likely to become biased. This is because the way that the adversary ideal amends the DAM structure makes it very unlikely that the DAM's success conditions can be met. As a result, legal subjects can no longer rely on the idea that they will enter an impartial process when they become subject to legal adjudication. This means that the procedural rule of law's argumentative integration demand is not reliably met, which threatens the dignity of legal subjects.

A. The Adversary System's Argumentative Structure and the DAM's Success Conditions

Let us give a succinct recapitulation of several points we have argued so far.

First, in the basic DAM, the underlying-cooperation condition and the equally-competent-arguers condition do the work that is necessary to prevent the DAM structure from biasing the argumentative process in favour of the

[51] Fuller (n 4); Landsman (n 4).

more competent arguer. Their fulfilment ensures that the argument will lead to the recognition and adequate integration of all the arguers' reasons instead of advantaging one of them based on argumentative capability.

Second, where an issue has become a legal dispute, stakes are high, making it unlikely that the parties will prioritise the desire to get to the correct result over the desire to win the argument. But if the decision-making process is supposed to protect the parties' dignity, it must be structured so that reasons are reliably identified and integrated into the decision appropriately. Therefore, *some* replacement for fulfilling the underlying cooperation demand must be found. Adding the role of the adjudicator is meant to ensure that arguments will be evaluated with an interest in their actual merit.

Third, the cooperative element that the DAM requires, namely, that arguers value coming to the correct result more than winning the argument, is important for more than just the final determination of the argument's outcome. Where the arguers fulfil the underlying-cooperation condition, this impacts their entire argumentative behaviour. The motivation to find the best arguments aims at convincingly representing strong reasons, not at persuasion no matter the costs. The wish to defeat the opponent's contributions aims at finding actual flaws in her reasoning, not creating a (potentially mere) perception of weakness. The interest to defend the conclusion and arguments against objections is conditional on continued faith in it, so that arguers are willing to admit where an objection succeeds. All this helps create an argument pool based on which the arguers can together identify the correct result. The fact that the basic DAM assigns the joint determination of the argument's final result to the arguers provides some motivation for them to fulfill the underlying-cooperation condition (even though this motivation is often insufficient).

From this, the reader may already be able to work out how our argument is going to proceed: adding the adjudicator to make up for the parties' inability to fulfil the underlying-cooperation condition, but prohibiting her from contributing to the creation of the argument pool, is not sufficient to fulfil this condition. Instead, it de-couples the creation of the argument pool from its final evaluation, removing the bit of motivation towards fulfilling the underlying-cooperation condition that the basic DAM structure provided to the arguers. This impacts the arguers' playing the advocate roles, and thereby hinders the adjudicator in fulfilling her role.

On the one hand, because the advocate roles do not require the parties to keep an eye on determining the correct result themselves, the way they create arguments and deal with their opponent's contributions is different from arguers' playing proponent/opponent roles. Without the goal of attaining the correct result holding them back, there is no reason to shy away from formulating arguments for mere persuasion, even if they are misleading. Similarly, there is no reason to forgo opportunities for creating the perception of weakness for their adversary's arguments, even if those arguments represent good reasons. And certainly, there is no reason to concede where an objection or an argument of their adversary succeeds.[52] This effect is strengthened when, as it is usually the case because the law is too complex for the average legal subject to navigate, the role of a legal representative, the lawyer, is added. The classic DAM defines the proponent/opponent role over the task of presenting the strongest reasons for the acceptability of a conclusion or decision. By contrast, the legal representative role is defined over the service that the legal representative renders to the party: the lawyer is supposed to help the party *win*. As, for example, Luban,[53] Finkelstein[54] and Goodpaster[55] have pointed out, this means that the lawyer role does not encourage any attachment to coming to the correct result. In fact, where the lawyer knows something about her client that may damage her case, it is considered acceptable or even required to hide the truth, as long as this does not involve illegal conduct. Luban[56] argues that it is not part of the role of a lawyer to have any intrinsic interest in who is in the right with respect to the case. Rather, it is the role of the lawyer to pursue winning the case independent of who *should* win it from an epistemic or moral standpoint. The result is that from the lawyer's point of view, it is entirely adequate that she 'reasons backward to what the facts must be, dignifies this fantasy by labeling it her "theory of the case," and then cobbles together whatever evidence can be offered to support this "theory"'.[57]

On the other hand, the adjudicator cannot fully replace the cooperative element that has been lost in the advocate roles. Even if she is impartial, she must decide based on an argument pool that, by the way the argument is structured, has been geared towards being biased in favour of the more competent arguer. As a result, the adjudicator faces considerable hurdles when she attempts a balanced identification of each party's reasons as they are applicable to the case.[58] This is so because the arguments presented to her are crafted strategically to persuade, untamed by concern for the correct result. The problem is compounded if the equally-competent-arguers condition is also not met, which is likely given the degree of expertise legal argumentation requires: the use of a lawyer is all but necessary, and given the way in which the market typically associates the ability to pay with the ability to hire competent lawyers, argumentative competency will vary widely depending on the parties' respective abilities to pay.

We should also remark that while there is an expectation of passivity on the part of the adjudicator, this does not necessarily ensure that she will remain

[52] Compare Moulton (n 22).

[53] Luban (1988) (n 4); Luban (2009) (n 4).

[54] Finkelstein (n 8).

[55] Goodpaster (n 48).

[56] Luban (1988) (n 4).

[57] ibid, 73.

[58] To add to all of this, it is often the case in the adversary system (especially in the United States) that judges are not trained to be judges but instead are often lawyers who have worked their way up to the position or have been voted in. Sande Buhai (2009) 'Access to Justice for Unrepresented Litigants: A Comparative Perspective' *Loyola of Los Angeles Law Review* 42(4): 979–1020; John Dawson (1961) 'The Function of the Judge' in *Talks on American Law*, ed Harold Berman, New York: Vintage Books, 18–29.

impartial. Given that the lawyer role ascribes the goal of *winning*, lawyers can be expected to attempt winning the sympathies of the adjudicator through *ad hominem*, *ad misericordiam* and *ad baculum* fallacies. It might be that the judge's passivity serves less to prevent her from becoming biased than to obscure her bias, preventing the disadvantaged party from responding, excluding whatever arguments the judge enters into the argument pool from 'rigorous adversarial testing'.[59]

In summary, the way in which the adversary ideal amends the DAM's argumentative structure de-couples the creation of the argument pool from the determination of the final result. Arguers taking the advocate roles are not disincentivised, and may even be encouraged to fully exploit their rhetorical and argumentative abilities in order to win the argument, even if this requires the use of fallacies, etc. The adjudicator is hindered in her task to determine the *correct* result by limiting herself to the evaluation of the arguments in the argument pool created by the advocates, and preventing herself from improving this pool (this problem is diminished, but does not vanish if, as in some real adversary systems, the adjudicator can add to the argument pool in some ways but not in others). Should she nonetheless become biased, or quietly enter her own arguments or ideas into the pool, this stays hidden, excluding what she adds from the rigorous testing that the DAM is supposed to ensure.[60] As a result, the argumentative structure that the adversary ideal sets up results in an argumentative process biased in favour of the argumentatively more competent party, or the party with the more competent lawyer. In the (questionably successful) effort to safeguard the impartiality of the adjudicator, the impartiality of the entire argumentative process has been brought into jeopardy.

B. Effects on Dignity

The way the adversary ideal reshapes the DAM biases its argumentative structure in favour of the more competent arguer (usually the more competent lawyer). As other authors have argued, the adversary ideal is therefore not necessarily well adapted to the discovery of the correct result (or the truth, as they put it).[61]

In fact, *googling* 'differences between adversarial and inquisitorial systems', as a student or layperson in search of information might, leads to webpages that promise to explain the differences in simple terms, that represent the adversary ideal and that make claims like:

> The adversary system is designed to allow the parties to control their own case and to give both parties equal opportunity to win the case. In the process, however, the truth might not always come out. The inquisitorial system is designed to get at the truth.[62]

[59] Compare Gorod (n 2).
[60] ibid.
[61] Finkelstein (n 8); Goodpaster (n 48); Luban (1988) (n 4).

This indicates that the idea that the adversary ideal offers a fair fight but might not lead to the truth has entered common knowledge. Additionally, the claim that the adversary ideal is designed to allow parties to make their own case and give them equal opportunity to win echoes the survival-of-the-fittest argument and its connection to the argumentative-integrity demand.[63] The idea seems to be that the likelihood of attaining the truth is sacrificed to give the parties more input and control, something associated with respecting their dignity.

We said previously that the procedural rule of law's argumentative-integration demand protects the legal subject's dignity by assuring her that if she finds herself in a legal dispute, she will be given adequate opportunity to enter the legal reasons that speak in her favour into the decision-making process. This protects her dignity twice over. First, it respects her in her standing as a reasonable being by recognising her right to take part in decision making that concerns her by entering her reasons. Second, it serves to secure the predictable, stable character of the law, which enables the legal subject to realise her standing as a dignified individual who has the ability and right to plan and influence her life according to her own reasons.

But it is mistaken to think that structuring legal argumentation such that the protection of the legal subjects' dignity is ensured is independent of structuring it so that it is conducive to coming to the correct result. It might seem this way, because the battle for the survival of the fittest remains, even if it has transformed from one of reasons to one of argumentative competence. The survival-of-the-fittest argument still *seems* to work. But it should be obvious now that this is an illusion. Relying on this argument creates a blind-spot for the fact that biasing the argumentative structure in favour of the more argumentatively competent advocate actually threatens dignity. It makes the outcome of trial *un*predictable rather than predictable in the sense that the rule of law requires – namely, that it will be determined by the content of previously promulgated laws and the relevant legal reasons. Just as if officials made unpredictable decisions based on idiosyncratic views, a system that hands the win to the more competent advocate is unpredictable from the legal subject's point of view. Whether she will win no longer depends on whether her actions are in accordance with the law as promulgated and whether she has (legal) reason on her side. Instead, the case is decided to an unacceptably high degree based on whether she (or her representation) is argumentatively more capable than the other advocate. The dignity

[62] See at www.brainscape.com/flashcards/comparison-of-adversary-and-inquisitorial-6149774/packs/8553619, accessed 7 July 2020.

[63] It also echoes the North American trend of do-it-yourself (DIY) (Beth Henschen (2018) 'Judging in a Mismatch: The Ethical Challenges of Pro Se Litigation' *Public Integrity* 20(1): 34–46, doi:10.1080/10999922.2016.1272438; Stephan Landsman (2012) 'Pro Se Litigation' *Annual Review of Law and Social Science* 8(1): 231–53, doi:10.1146/annurev-lawsocsci-102811-173911). If someone can learn almost any skill, without requiring professional training, then the notion that the legal system, and the arguments one makes within it, can also be learnt through self-study and effort does not seem too far-fetched.

protection that her argumentative integration affords her depends on an argumentative structure *actually* designed to make it likely that her legally relevant reasons will be adequately integrated.

We should add that the fact that parties must typically rely completely on their legal representatives, the lawyers, because the law is too complex for the layperson to navigate, only compounds the problem. Obviously, it does so because where lawyers sell their services on a market, more money buys better representation – which means that from the perspective of the legal subject, the survival-of-the-fittest argument is transformed again, this time from one of wits to one of wealth.[64] But it also means that legal subjects, knowing that they need a good lawyer, may not be able to determine whether the lawyer they are hiring is going to be able to represent their reasons adequately.[65] The legal subjects might never really understand what is happening during the legal dispute. In this case, the dignity-affirming function of the argumentative-integration demand on the basis of its respecting the legal subject's right to participate in decisions concerning herself also disappears.[66]

As a result, the argumentative structure that the adversary ideal gives to the adjudicative process at trial *threatens* the dignity of legal subjects instead of protecting them. Legal subjects might not be in a constant state of 'uncertainty and fearfulness because [their] fate lies in the hands of official whim, which can choose at will to stigmatize conduct as criminal';[67] instead, the legal subjects are in that same state of uncertainty because their fate now lies in their unpredictable ability to secure the assistance of lawyers, whose argumentative capacity they can only guess at, and who have an unjustifiably large role in determining their trial's outcome.

V. THE HUMILIATION OF *PRO SE* LITIGANTS

To show how serious this problem is, we can turn to the situation of indigent *pro se* litigants in the United States. Their inability to hire a lawyer means that they not only face a dignity *threat*, but also are subjected to humiliating experiences as a matter of course.

[64] A cynic might remark that this makes the process predictable once more – if you are poorer than your opponent, you are going to lose your case. However, this is not the predictability that the rule of law demands.

[65] In this way, the legal subject needs to rely on two things that are now beyond her control: that the legal process will work appropriately according to the relevant laws, but also that the people certified to represent her will know how best to navigate this system.

[66] When the ability of the lawyer (and in turn, one's ability to pay for that lawyer) is a major determining factor in the legal subject's ability to succeed with her case, the basis for her equal treatment before the law changes. It is no longer her dignified status that assures her equal treatment, but rather the contingent fact (if this is the case) that she has as much money as the other litigant.

[67] Luban (n 31) 41.

Indigent *pro se* litigants are parties who cannot afford a lawyer and therefore try to participate in the adjudication of their cases without one, arguing their cases themselves. At first sight, it might seem that being able to choose self-representation is a form of further empowerment, the ability to fully realise the dignity-asserting right to participate in decisions concerning one's own life. But, as Steinberg points out, it would be a gross misconception to think that *pro se* litigants are parties who freely chose to self-represent.[68] Most often, *pro se* litigants are parties unable to afford a lawyer, and they routinely find themselves facing represented parties.[69] In the United States, for example, landlord-tenant disputes see up to 90 per cent unrepresented tenant parties fighting against up to 90 per cent represented landlords, and similarly high numbers apply to family law, including custody cases.[70]

The degree to which the US adversary system, which remains somewhat close to the adversary ideal in civil courts that typically see these kinds of cases,[71] has replaced the battle of reasons advocated by the classic pro-DAM argument with a battle of argumentative capabilities becomes obvious when considering the difficulties *pro se* litigants face: *pro se* litigants win their cases up to ten times less often than their represented counterparts. They lose because they make procedural errors, like failing to present evidence in the correct way, or failing to file the necessary motions to move the case forward.[72] In addition, they may be unable to make their side of the story heard because they are unable to emulate the rhetorical style required at court.[73] In other words, *pro se* litigants lose cases because they are poor, making it impossible for them to buy

[68] Jessica Steinberg (2015) 'Demand side reform in the poor people's court' *Connecticut Law Review* 47(3): 741–805. Often, the decisions made in cases involving *pro se* litigants can have a significant impact on their lives, even if the monetary amounts dealt with are small. Thus, while it may seem that a *pro se* litigant has chosen to forgo the help of a lawyer, she may actually be forced into the role because of what she stands to lose if she does not try. John Greacen (2014) 'Self-Represented Litigants, The Courts, and the Legal Profession: Myths and Realities' *Family Court Review* 52(4): 662–69, doi:10.1111/fcre.12118; Deborah Rhode (2003) 'Equal justice under law: connecting principle to practice' *Washington University Journal of Law and Policy* 12: 47–62; Rebecca Sandefur (2016) 'What We Need to Know About the Legal Needs of the Public' *South Carolina Law Review* 67(2), 443–59. See also Scott Cummings and Deborah Rhode (2010) 'Managing Pro Bono: Doing Well by Doing Better' *Fordham Law Review* 78(5): 2357–2442; Deborah Rhode, Kevin Eaton and Anna Porto (2018) 'Access to Justice Through Limited Legal Assistance' *Northwestern University Journal of Human Rights* 16(1): 1–21; Deborah Rhode (2004) *Access to Justice*, New York: Oxford University Press.

[69] Greacen (n 68); Jessica Steinberg (2016) 'Adversary Breakdown and Judicial Role Confusion in "Small Case" Civil Justice' *Brigham Young University Law Review* 2016(3): 900–69.

[70] Steinberg (n 68); Jessica Steinberg (2018) 'A Theory of Civil Problem-Solving Courts' *New York University Law Review* 93(6): 1580–1632.

[71] Steinberg (n 69).

[72] According to Steinberg (ibid, 899), in the United States, there are over 140 things a *pro se* litigant can do wrong while she prepares, presents and attempts to complete the process of going through the court system.

[73] Barbara Bezdek (1992) 'Silence in the court: participation and subordination of poor tenants' voices in legal process' *Hofstra Law Review* 20(3): 533–608.

argumentative competency, and because the adversary system has set up argumentation as a battle of argumentative competency more than as a battle of reasons. As Steinberg notes,[74] US judges are often not provided with clear rules on whether, how and when to assist *pro se* litigants in small, civil cases, which leads to a kind of role confusion that can mean that the only *competent* arguers entering reasons into the argument pool from which the judge will make a decision are the lawyers representing their opponents (unlike in some inquisitorial systems, like Germany's, where judges have a duty to bring it to the party's attention when they are about to make a legal error).[75]

As a result, *pro se* litigants in the United States do not just face a dignity threat, they are also routinely humiliated when they enter the process of adjudication: for them, the argumentative-integration demand remains unfulfilled because the argumentative structure they are asked to operate in makes it virtually impossible for them to enter their legally relevant reasons into the decision-making process. The law, therefore, is not predictable for them (eg laws concerning the relationship between tenants and landlords will not be enforced as promulgated because unrepresented tenants make procedural errors that keep them from winning their cases independent of merit), neither is their standing as reasonable beings affirmed by allowing them to present their reasons in court (their inability to formulate these reasons in the 'correct' way, eg by filing evidence correctly, leaves them unable to use their voice).

It is important to realise that the routine humiliation that the adversary ideal's argumentative structure causes *pro se* litigants, also serves to reinforce the argument that all legal subjects face a dignity threat from the adversary ideal's argumentative structure: as no one is safe from finding themselves too poor to hire a lawyer one day, everyone is a potential victim of the dignity-denying way in which the argumentative structure of the adversary ideal organises adjudication.[76]

VI. CONCLUSION

The purpose of this chapter was to add to the mounting case against the adversary ideal by showing that the basic argumentative structure it gives to legal

[74] Steinberg (n 69).

[75] Robert Emerson (2015) 'Judges as guardian angels: the German practice of hints and feedback' *Vanderbilt Journal of Transnational Law* 48(3): 709–54. Ironically, it seems that judges may experience additional personal bias against *pro se* litigants because they dislike the way *pro se* litigants speak (Bezdek (n 73); Jessica Phillips (2016) 'Not All Pro Se Litigants Are Created Equally: Examining the Need for New Pro Se Litigant Classifications Through the Lens of the Sovereign Citizen Movement' *Georgetown Journal of Legal Ethics* 29(4): 1221–35).

[76] It should here be noted that one does not need to fall below a certain poverty line in order to find one's self unable to afford necessary legal services (Steinberg (n 69)). Legal services, in a free market, can be exorbitantly high and difficult to afford even for, say, middle-class persons, which makes the situation for indigent people all the more dire.

adjudication is not dignity-protecting but poses a dignity threat. We do not claim that we have thereby shown that real adversary systems, which only realise the ideal to some degree, should be abandoned. Nor have we shown that other systems, like the inquisitorial system, are necessarily better. We do think, however, that the dignity-threatening nature of the adversary ideal's argumentative set-up is an important reason that speaks against treating it as an ideal. It is also a reason to examine real adversary systems closely, to ensure that they do not realise the adversary ideal's dignity threat.

12

Lesser Evils, Mere Permissions and Justifying Reasons in Law

ROB MULLINS*

DURING THE 2010–11 Queensland floods, the Brisbane River's waters rose so high that they lifted many jetties off their pilings. A friend of mine who owned a jetty told me that a concerned neighbour had, without asking his permission, tethered his jetty to a large tree. When the flood waters receded, my friend recovered his jetty with minimal cost. In order to tether the jetty to the tree, the neighbour had to trespass across my friend's property, as well as the property of several others, as he waded through rising flood waters. I think we can say, as a matter of both criminal law and apparent common sense, that the neighbour's trespass was justified, and therefore permissible.[1] The neighbour's reasons to render aid outweighed any reasons he had not to trespass on others' land.[2] On the other hand, I am reluctant to say

* Thanks to Mark McBride, James Penner and Adam Rigoni for thoughtful comments on a draft of this chapter. An earlier draft, more narrowly focused on justifications in private law, was presented to audiences at the Australian Centre for Private Law in 2017 and the Australasian Association for Legal Philosophy in 2018. I am grateful to both audiences for their comments and criticism on both occasions. Particular thanks are due to Kit Barker and Iain Field. This chapter is dedicated to the memory of John Gardner, who first encouraged me to work on the relation between justification and permission. I wish he were still around to show me my errors.

[1] In private law, the situation is murkier. In some jurisdictions, the neighbour's conduct would be treated as a case of private necessity, which confers an 'incomplete privilege'; *Vincent v Lake Erie Transportation* 109 Minn 456, 124 NW 221 (Minn 1910). The neighbour would still be liable for damage to property caused during their trespass; Restatement (Second) of Torts §197 (1965). James Goudkamp argues that interventions to save the property of third parties should be treated as cases of public necessity in English law, and therefore should attract no liability; James Goudkamp (2013) *Tort Law Defences*, Oxford: Hart Publishing, 116.

[2] The example of trespass unfortunately raises a complication that I will not revisit in this chapter: what is the source of my reason not to trespass? I can trespass on someone's property without harming their interests in any way. Harmless trespass appears to be one instance of what David Owens calls a 'bare wrong'; David Owens (2012) *Shaping the Normative Landscape*, Oxford: Oxford University Press, 164. According to Owens, the bare wrong arises from a violation of a 'normative interest' that the owner has in controlling use of their own property, rather than from any damage to a human interest. For our purposes, it is enough to suppose that we do have a reason not to trespass, and that this reason usually functions to require us not to do so.

that the neighbour was required to help my friend as he did. His intervention was time-consuming and potentially dangerous, and he could just as easily have helped one of the many flood victims in some other way.[3] In spite of the apparent strength of his reason to intervene and save my friend's jetty, it would have been equally permissible for him not to do so.

This chapter is concerned with cases such as these, where we are justified in performing an otherwise prohibited action but do not perform it. The case is one example of what criminal lawyers often call 'lesser-evils' defences. Trespassing across several neighbours' land in order to secure the jetty was a lesser evil than the trespass itself. In criminal law, 'lesser-evil' defences are often regarded as justification defences *par excellence*, and even as a conceptual paradigm for justification defences generally.[4] But I will not base my arguments in this chapter on the assumption that all justification defences involve a choice of lesser evils.[5] What interests me is the curious nexus that these cases illustrate between justifying reasons and the conclusion that conduct is either permitted or required. So-called reason-based or 'reasons-first' accounts hold that our normative conclusions – our conclusions about what we are required to do and what is permissible – are explained by our practical reasons.[6] As I note in section II, it is difficult to offer a reason-based account of lesser-evils justifications that does not collapse the distinction between the required and the permissible with respect to justified conduct.[7] Some justifying reasons generate mere permissions, rather than requirements. I will consider several prominent attempts to account for the distinction. I conclude by suggesting that none of these attempts is adequate without the further concession that some reasons lack deontic or requiring force.

[3] I do not mean to suggest that my reluctance to say that the neighbour was required to help my friend as he did will be universally shared. I return to this issue in section III.A.

[4] The 'lesser evils' doctrine is used as the paradigmatic case of general justification in § 3.02 of the Model Penal Code (1985). For useful discussion see Larry Alexander (2005) 'Lesser Evils: A Closer Look at the Paradigmatic Justification' *Law and Philosophy* 24: 611–43.

[5] For an argument against this view, see Mitchell N Berman (2005) 'Lesser Evils and Justification: A Less Close Look' *Law and Philosophy* 24: 681–709.

[6] Versions of the reason-based view are espoused by, eg, TM Scanlon (1998) *What We Owe to Each Other*, Cambridge, MA: Harvard University Press; TM Scanlon (2014) *Being Realistic About Reasons*, Oxford: Oxford University Press; Joseph Raz (1999) *Practical Reason and Norms*, 2nd edn, Oxford: Oxford University Press; Jonathan Dancy (2004) *Ethics Without Principles*, Oxford: Oxford University Press; Mark Schroeder (2007) *Slaves of the Passions* Oxford: Oxford University Press; Derek Parfit (2011) *On What Matters*, vol 1, Oxford: Oxford University Press.

[7] For the purposes of discussion I will treat 'ought' and 'must' statements as synonymous – I will use the generic 'requirements' to refer to both, and treat requirements as the dual of permissions: if ϕ is required then it is not permissible that not ϕ. I do this to avoid difficulties introduced by the distinction between strong necessity operators, like 'must' and 'have to', and weak necessity operators like 'ought' and 'should'. Though 'ought' is often used by practical philosophers to express the notion of requirement, 'must' or 'have to' may be more apt for this purpose; Paul Portner (2009) *Modality*, Oxford: Oxford University Press, 79–81; Alex Silk (2015) 'What Normative Terms Mean and Why It Matters for Ethical Theory' in *Oxford Studies in Normative Ethics*, vol 5, ed Mark Timmons, Oxford: Oxford University Press, 296-319, 298–303; Justin Snedegar (2016) 'Reasons, Oughts, and Requirements' in *Oxford Studies in Metaethics*, vol 11, ed Russ Shafer-Landau, Oxford: Oxford University Press, 155–81, 158–62.

Justifications are an important point of interaction between law and practical reason. When law creates justification defences, it makes a concession about the limitations of general legal rules for the guidance of conduct. It creates a discretionary space in which it permits its subjects to be guided by reasons for non-conformity with a legal prohibition.[8] Justificatory reasoning may not, strictly speaking, be legal reasoning.[9] It is certainly not unique to law. Nonetheless, it is a form of practical reasoning that is often incorporated in law and given clear legal effects. One source of disagreement amongst theorists of the criminal law is whether justified conduct is merely permissible, creating a 'licence' or 'privilege', or whether the presence of a complete justification renders conduct 'warranted', 'objectively right' or 'correct'.[10] (This tension is particularly clear in commentary and criticism of George Fletcher's work.[11]) The accounts of justifying reasons that I will explore all seek to resolve the apparent conflict between these two positions. I will argue that it is coherent to insist that justified conduct is both warranted and merely permissible. I begin with a survey of the general problem that I wish to address.

I. LESSER EVILS AND JUSTIFICATORY REASONS

All action calls for rational justification. One of the fundamental roles played by practical reasons is to justify conduct – to render it intelligible from the standpoint of practical rationality. It does not seem to be controversial that reasons can play this role.[12] If I decide to go swimming in my lunch hour, I can cite, as

[8] As John Gardner puts it, justification defences seem to create 'a gap in the mandatory force of a mandatory norm'; John Gardner (2007) 'Fletcher on Offences and Defences' in *Offences and Defences: Selected Essays in the Philosophy of Criminal Law*, Oxford: Oxford University Press, 141–54, 148.

[9] Fletcher traces the incorporation of lesser evils defences in law to two distinct jurisprudential trends. Within German jurisprudence, it took the form of 'recognition of transcendental norms in the legal system', while in Anglo-American law it arose from utilitarian legislative concerns; George Fletcher (1978) *Rethinking Criminal Law*, Boston, MA: Little, Brown & Co, 775ff.

[10] For the former language see, eg, ibid 562–66 (referring to 'licenses' and 'privileges'); Eric Colvin (1990) 'Exculpatory Defences in Criminal Law' *Oxford Journal of Legal Studies* 10: 381–407, 392 ('contextual permission'). For the latter see, eg, Kent Greenawalt (1984) 'The Perplexing Borders of Justification and Excuse' *Columbia Law Review* 84: 1897–1927, 1903 ('warranted'); Fletcher (n 9) 761–62 ('objectively right'); Paul H Robinson (1975) 'A Theory of Justification: Societal Harm as a Prerequisite for Criminal Liability' *UCLA Law Review* 23: 266–92, 274 ('correct'); George P Fletcher (1979) 'Should Intolerable Prison Conditions Generate a Justification or an Excuse for Escape?' *UCLA Law Review* 26: 1355–69 (equating justified conduct with 'right' conduct).

[11] For useful discussion of this tension in Fletcher's work, see esp Joshua Dressler (1984) 'New Thoughts About the Concept of Justification in the Criminal Law: A Critique of Fletcher's Thinking and Rethinking' *UCLA Law Review* 32: 61–99, 69–76, 81–91; see also Douglas N Husak (1989) 'Justifications and the Criminal Liability of Accessories' *The Journal of Criminal Law & Criminology* 80: 491–520.

[12] Cf John Gardner (2007) 'Justifications and Reasons' in *Offences and Defences: Selected Essays in the Philosophy of Criminal Law*, Oxford: Oxford University Press, 91–120; Joseph Raz (2011) *From Normativity to Responsibility*, Oxford: Oxford University Press, 18–19; Joshua Gert (2016)

my justification for doing so, my reason to enjoy the warm weather or my reason to get some much-needed exercise. In legal settings, however, it is typically only prohibited conduct that calls for justification. Justifications are invoked defensively, in order to explain why normally prohibited conduct is in fact legally permissible.

The notion of justification plays an important role in theoretical accounts of defences in criminal law, where it underlies the basic distinction between justification defences and excuses.[13] (More recently, the role of justifications in other areas of law – torts especially – has begun to attract attention.[14]) On one view, the existence of a legal justification creates an exception to the general prohibition. The late John Gardner identified this approach with the 'closure view', according to which justified conduct is not in breach of a legal duty and therefore not a legal wrong.[15] According to the closure view, justified conduct falls within an exception to the general legal rule, and therefore does not comprise a wrong (at least in the eyes of the law). I am sympathetic to the closure view, at least as an account of legal rules, which are capable of being specified either in advance or over time through the acknowledgement of exceptional cases. Nonetheless, it is worth noting that there is a difficulty with this approach that is, broadly speaking, interpretive. While some legal rules do specify the absence of justification as a requirement for wrongdoing, in other cases there is a separate norm providing for a defence where conduct is justified. This distinction seems to carry procedural implications. In the former case, the absence of justification must be established by the plaintiff or prosecution. For instance, the negligence standard in tort law explicitly prohibits only unreasonable or unjustified conduct. A defendant is not in breach of the primary norm unless their conduct is unjustified. As a result, the absence of justification must be proved by the plaintiff. On the other hand, many criminal rules do not require the prosecution to establish the absence of relevant legal justification, at least not as a matter of course. The presence of a justification must be raised by the defendant. According to critics of the closure view, these procedural distinctions reflect underlying notions of moral responsibility. The wrongness of the defendant's conduct is sufficient reason to call them to account for their actions. Justification

'The Distinction Between Justifying and Requiring: Nothing to Fear' in *Weighing Reasons*, Oxford: Oxford University Press, 157–72, 160.

[13] The literature on the question is now too vast to cite exhaustively, but see, eg, Robinson (n 10); Fletcher (n 9) ss 10.1–10.2; Greenawalt (n 10); George Fletcher (1996) 'The Nature of Justification' in *Action and Value in Criminal Law*, eds Stephen Schute, John Gardner and Jeremy Horder, Oxford: Clarendon, 175–86; Gardner (n 12).

[14] See, eg, Goudkamp (n 1) ch 4.

[15] John Gardner (2007) 'In Defence of Defences' in *Offences and Defences: Selected Essays in the Philosophy of Criminal Law*, Oxford: Oxford University Press, 77–78. Cf Fletcher on the 'unity thesis' in Fletcher (1996) (n 13). Gardner offers Hart as an exponent of the closure view; HLA Hart (2008) *Punishment and Responsibility: Essays in the Philosophy of Law*, Oxford: Oxford University Press, 13.

does not negate the wrongdoing; it merely renders it permissible, all things considered.[16]

In any case, the merits of the closure view are orthogonal to the main problem I will be discussing here. From the perspective of reason-based accounts, the content of the legal rule – whether it contains an explicit exception for the justified conduct – is a secondary issue. As Joseph Raz notes, rules are 'expressions of compromises, of judgements about the outcome of conflicts'.[17] Even where a legal rule creates an explicit exception for justified conduct, that exception reflects a judgement about the outcome of an underlying conflict of reasons. In the case of lesser-evils justifications, it reflects a legal judgement that the reason not to engage in certain conduct is defeated by my reason to pursue the lesser evil.[18] Even where a reason is defeated by another reason of greater weight or stringency, it still functions as a reason.[19] The residue generated by non-conformity with the defeated reason becomes a basis for regret, and, at least in some cases, a reason to repair the harm caused by the justified action.[20]

I will focus on the apparent asymmetry of reasons that underlies a choice of lesser evils. The asymmetry in question appears to track the distinction between 'reasons for' and 'reasons against' an action, or 'pros' and 'cons'.[21] It is not so much a matter of the content of the reasons in question as their differing normative force. Choices of lesser evil arise in the context of a conflict between reasons that have requiring or 'mandatory' force and justificatory reasons.[22] Criminal prohibitions purport to give us reason not to do something, but, more fundamentally, they give us reason to rule out otherwise worthwhile options. My reason not to trespass is not simply a reason not to trespass, it is a reason that, ordinarily, rules out pursuit of otherwise good options that involve

[16] Versions of this argument are made in Gardner (n 15) 77–82; RA Duff (2007) *Answering for Crime*, Oxford: Hart Publishing; but see Luís Duarte D'Almeida (2015) *Allowing for Exceptions: A Theory of Defences and Defeasibility in Law*, Oxford: Oxford University Press, ch 8.

[17] Raz (n 6) 187.

[18] Strictly speaking, the reason need not be defeated. As I discuss in section III.B, it is enough that some other inconsistent reason be of equal or incomparable strength. For the time being it is enough to note that the rhetoric of 'lesser evils' suggests that our reason to pursue the lesser evil is stronger than the reason to engage in prohibited conduct.

[19] There is an analogue of the closure view in the realm of reasons, which is the view that reasons, once completely specified, do not conflict; Joseph Raz (1999) *Engaging Reason: On the Theory of Value and Action*, Oxford: Oxford University Press, 136; cf Raz (n 6) 40–46. I do not consider this view further here. I do not think it is widely held.

[20] In private law, this residue provides the rationale for an ongoing duty to repair the initial wrong. This explains why in some cases even justified conduct can attract liability; John Gardner (2011) 'What Is Tort Law For? Part 1. The Place of Corrective Justice' *Law and Philosophy* 30: 1, 41–42; Raz (1999) (n 19) 189–92. So-called 'moral residue' arguments feature prominently in the argument that defeated reasons still function as reasons; for recent discussion see Peter BM Vranas (2018) '"Ought" Implies "Can" but Does Not Imply "Must": An Asymmetry Between Becoming Infeasible and Becoming Overridden' *Philosophical Review* 127: 487–514.

[21] Gardner (n 12) 95. See also Patricia Greenspan (2007) 'Practical Reasons and Moral "Ought"' in *Oxford Studies in Metaethics*, vol 2, ed Russ Shafer-Landau, Oxford: Oxford University Press, 172–94 (on the asymmetry between 'positive' and 'negative' reasons).

[22] On reasons and mandatory norms see Raz (n 6) ch 2. Cf Victor Tadros on 'prohibition reasons'; Victor Tadros (2007) *Criminal Responsibility*, Oxford: Oxford University Press, 272.

trespass. Ordinarily, it is not permissible for me to trespass across a neighbour's land to repair his jetty.

Unlike the reasons associated with the prohibition, however, justifying reasons are often associated with a kind of optionality. There are some cases where the lesser evil justification involves a conflict of duties: conformity with the duty of higher priority is judged to be a lesser evil than conformity with the other duty.[23] But cases of lesser evil need not involve a conflict of duties. My friend's neighbour did not have to expose himself to potential danger to rescue the jetty – I think he could have done something else with his time without behaving impermissibly. This sort of optionality arises in cases like my friend's neighbour, in which the justified conduct appears to be supererogatory – in the sense that it is commendable or highly morally desirable but not required – as well as in cases where the greater evil we seek to avoid is adverse to our own interests.[24] The defendant in *Cross v State*, who protected his property by slaughtering wild game, was presumably not *required* to do so, even supposing the slaughter of game was the lesser evil than allowing damage to his property.[25] The sailors in *United States v Ashton* were not duty bound to mutiny – they would have been permitted to sacrifice their own interests for the good of the mission, and to try their luck with an unseaworthy ship.[26] I can be justified in speeding a seriously unwell friend to the hospital without being required to do so – my reason to speed only needs to be sufficient to render my speeding permissible in the circumstances.[27] In this regard, the law reflects an aspect of commonsense morality, which allows that a choice of lesser evils is at least sometimes morally permissible, rather than required. These cases of mere permission create a problem for reason-based accounts of justification.

II. THE PROBLEM OF MERE PERMISSION

Justifications and permissions are intimately related.[28] The existence of a valid and complete justification permits me to engage in conduct that in other circumstances would be prohibited.[29] The relationship entailment between

[23] Cf *Perka v the Queen* [1984] 2 SCR 232, 274 (Wilson J); *In Re A (Children) (Conjoined Twins: Surgical Separation)* [2001] Fam 147, 202 (Ward LJ), 236 (Brooke LJ), 254 (Walker LJ).

[24] For useful discussion of the structure of these 'agent-favouring' permissions, see Thomas Hurka (2012) 'Permissions to Do Less Than the Best: A Moving Band' *Oxford Studies in Normative Ethics*, vol 2, ed Mark Timmons, Oxford: Oxford University Press, 1–27.

[25] *Cross v State*, 370 P2d 371 (1962).

[26] *United States v Ashton*, 24 F Cas 873 (No 14,470) (CCD Mass 1834).

[27] Though see the Scottish High Court's decision in *Moss v Howdle* 1997 JC 123, criticised by Victor Tadros (n 22) 271.

[28] Cf Husak (n 11) 500–01 (acts are' justified if and only if they are permissible'). I will only defend the left-right direction of the biconditional.

[29] On partial justifications, see esp Douglas N Husak (1998) 'Partial Defenses' *Canadian Journal of Law & Jurisprudence* 11: 167–92. The idea of partial justification deserves more philosophical

justificatory reasons and permissions can be easily stated. I act with justification if I act on a 'good', 'sufficient' or undefeated reason.[30] It is always permissible to act on an undefeated reason, at least on the assumption that whenever we face inconsistent undefeated reasons, we are permitted to follow any one of the inconsistent reasons for action.[31] Thus I am justified in doing something just in case I am permitted to do that same thing. But, on the other hand, there appears to be an equally tight relationship between justifications and requirements. It is plausible to think that we are required to conform with our strongest reasons.[32] According to John Gardner, 'it is a basic principle of practical rationality' that 'one should always act for *some* undefeated reason'.[33] If I choose a lesser evil, then I am acting on reasons that are stronger than my inconsistent reasons not to engage in the prohibited conduct. (For instance, the neighbour's reasons to secure my friend's jetty were stronger than his reasons not to trespass.) But in the absence of other, inconsistent reasons, it follows that I am required, and not merely permitted, to act on my justifying reasons. This is the problem that I wish to address in the remainder of this chapter. I will call it the problem of mere permission.

It is useful to set out the problem in a slightly more formal way, albeit with considerable oversimplification.[34] (I think the oversimplification is harmless for our purposes.) I will treat reasons as propositional. A reasoning context will be characterised in terms of a set of reasons applicable to an agent in a given context. The notation $R(\phi)$ will indicate that in a given context there is some subset

attention than it has received. Gardner suggests that partial justifications arise where one has at least some reason for engaging in the prohibited conduct; Gardner (n 12) 95.

[30] The conception of justifications as undefeated reasons is particularly clear in John Gardner's work. See John Gardner and Timothy Macklem (2002) 'Reasons' in *The Oxford Handbook of Jurisprudence and the Philosophy of Law*, eds J Coleman and S Shapiro, Oxford: Oxford University Press, 440–75; Gardner (n 12); John Gardner (2010) 'Justification Under Authority' Canadian Journal of Law and Jurisprudence 23: 71–98, 81. See also Tadros (n 22) 121–24, 267–73.

[31] I ignore the possibility of so-called 'tragic' moral dilemmas, in which an agent is forced to make a choice between two impermissible options; cf Bernard Williams (1973) 'Ethical Consistency' in *Problems of the Self: Philosophical Papers 1956–1972*, Cambridge: Cambridge University Press, 166–86; Ruth Barcan Marcus (1980) 'Moral Dilemmas and Consistency' *Journal of Philosophy* 77: 121–36; John Gardner (2005) 'Wrongs and Faults' in *Appraising Strict Liability*, ed Andrew Simester, Oxford: Oxford University Press, 51–80; John Horty (2012) *Reasons as Defaults*, Oxford: Oxford University Press, ch 4.

[32] I find it difficult to identify proponents of this account of requirement with any certainty. Some philosophers explicitly defend the view that we ought to act on our strongest reasons, but it is unclear whether they take the word 'ought' to express requirement, or whether they use it in a weaker sense; see, eg, Schroeder (n 6) 130–31; but compare Douglas W Portmore (2019) *Opting for the Best: Oughts and Options*, New York: Oxford University Press, 185–86; and Snedegar (n 7) 158–62. Gert compiles a list of philosophers who, he argues, have endorsed the thesis: Joshua Gert (2004) *Brute Rationality: Normativity and Human Action*, Cambridge: Cambridge University Press, 19, fn 3.

[33] Gardner (n 12) 100 (original emphasis).

[34] In Robert Mullins (2021) 'Formalizing Reasons, Oughts, and Requirements' *Ergo* 7: 568–99, I set out the problem of distinguishing between permissions and requirements within the framework of a simple version of Horty's default theory; see Horty (n 31).

of these applicable reasons supporting the proposition ϕ. In a given reasoning context, there may be subsets of reasons that are inconsistent with each other. Two sets of reasons $R(\phi)$ and $R'(\psi)$ are inconsistent just in case the set of propositions supported by both sets is inconsistent. We will also suppose that, in a given reasoning context, there is an ordering of 'weight' or strength over subsets of reasons that holds when one subset of reasons is stronger than the other.[35] To allow for the possibility of sets of reasons of equal or incomparable strength, the order is partial: in a given reasoning context there may be sets of reasons such that neither set is stronger than the other.[36] We begin with a definition of a set of 'good' or undefeated reasons in a given reasoning context:

> **Undefeated Reasons:** In a reasoning context, a subset of reasons $R(\phi)$ is defeated just in case there is some other subset of reasons $R'(\psi)$ such that (i) $R(\phi)$ and $R'(\psi)$ are inconsistent, and (ii) $R'\psi$ is stronger than $R(\phi)$. A subset of reasons that is not defeated is undefeated.

The idea underlying this account is that if a subset of reasons is inconsistent with some other, stronger, subset of reasons, it is no longer eligible for rational choice. It is no longer permissible to act on the defeated subset of reasons. As a corollary, it is always permissible to act on an undefeated subset of reasons:

> **Undefeated Reasons Entail Permissions:** In a reasoning context, if there is some subset of undefeated reasons supporting the proposition ϕ, $R(\phi)$, then it is permissible that ϕ.

We then complement this thesis about the relation between undefeated reasons and permissions with a seemingly attractive thesis about the relations between our strongest reasons and requirements:

> **Strongest Reasons Entail Requirements:** In a reasoning context, it is required that ϕ if there is some subset of reasons supporting the proposition that ϕ, $R(\phi)$, such that for any subset of reasons $R'(\psi)$ that is inconsistent with $R(\phi)$, $R(\phi)$ is stronger than $R'\psi$.

This account partly formalises the idea that we are required to act on our strongest reasons. It is easy to see that our strongest reasons will be undefeated reasons. If a subset of reasons is stronger than all other inconsistent subsets of reasons, there will be no subset that defeats it. It will also follow that the other incompatible subsets are defeated by the strongest set. It will be impermissible to conform with the weaker subsets of reasons, and we will therefore be required to conform with the remaining subset of undefeated reasons. Thus the theses that **Undefeated Reasons Entail Permissions** and that **Strongest Reasons Entail Requirements** are compatible with the intuitively appealing idea that requirement entails permission.

[35] Largely for simplicity, I am following Mark Schroeder in treating the relation of weight or strength as holding between sets of reasons, and not between individual reasons; Mark Schroeder (2007) *Slaves of the Passions*, Oxford: Oxford University Press, 123–45.

[36] More formally, the strength relation over subsets of reasons is transitive, non-reflexive and asymmetric.

If your strongest reasons support the proposition that ϕ, then you will have a set of undefeated reasons supporting ϕ, and it will be permissible that ϕ.

The problem of mere permission arises in cases where it appears as though our strongest reasons do not require conformity. Suppose that an agent is faced with two inconsistent subsets of reasons: a subset of reasons supporting the proposition that they not engage in prohibited conduct, denoted $R_1(\neg P)$, and a subset of reasons supporting the proposition that they pursue the lesser evil, which we denote $R_2(LE)$, where the two subsets of reasons are inconsistent. If the proposition supported by the latter reasons, $R_2(LE)$ is indeed a 'lesser evil' than the prohibited conduct, then $R_2(LE)$ is stronger than $R_1(\neg P)$. This means that the set $R_1(\neg P)$ is defeated, and the set $R_2(LE)$ is undefeated. I am therefore permitted to pursue the lesser evil. But it also follows, since I am required to act on reasons stronger than any other inconsistent reason, that I am required to act on $R_2(LE)$. Thus lesser-evils justifications entail requirements, rather than mere permissions. It is true that pursuit of the lesser evil is permitted, but seemingly only in virtue of the fact that it is required, and requirement entails permission. The distinction between justified conduct that is required and justified conduct that is merely permissible has been lost.

III. NON-REVISIONARY RESPONSES

I will ultimately suggest that we should abandon the thesis that our strongest reasons entail requirements. The thesis that Gardner identifies as a 'basic principle of rationality' is in need of revision. Some undefeated reasons for action justify conduct without requiring it. Before considering this possibility, however, I want to critique several non-revisionary solutions to the problem. These responses are non-revisionary in the sense that they do not entail the abandonment of either the thesis that undefeated reasons entail permissions or the thesis that strongest reasons entail requirements. I think these solutions are inadequate. If we want to solve the problem of mere permissions, we need to abandon the thesis that our strongest reasons entail requirements. Some of these alternatives are worthy of greater discussion than I will be able to give them. (I feel that the role of incomparability in some cases of mere permission is particularly important.) Nonetheless, I will set out some reasons for regarding these responses as insufficient.

A. Rejecting Mere Permissions

The most straightforward answer to the problem is to assert that in order to qualify as a legal justification, conduct must be morally required. The function of the lesser-evils defence is to permit the law's subject to deliberate free from the rational interference of a legal prohibition. Thus, though we are not legally required to pursue the lesser evil, we are morally or rationally required to do so. A proponent of this approach might argue that, when we avail ourselves of a lesser-evils justification, we are like the disinterested bystander who attempts an easy rescue in the absence of a legal duty: we act as we are morally or rationally required to act, although the law will not enforce our moral requirement. At various points in his work, George Fletcher appears to take something like this view. Though he concedes that justifications create a legal permission, Fletcher argues that legal 'justification renders conduct right'.[37] He further rejects the view that legally 'justified conduct is not necessarily right, but merely tolerable or permissible'.[38] Fletcher's approach is most easy to reconcile with philosophical frameworks – such as those in the Kantian and utilitarian traditions – that deny that justified conduct could ever be merely permissible. Some Kantians, for example, will insist that the neighbour was fulfilling an imperfect duty of beneficence. My friend's neighbour conformed with a non-enforceable or 'non-juridical' duty – his actions are meritorious in the sense that he did 'more in the way of duty than he can be constrained by law to do', but that does not make his action *merely* permissible.[39] The existence of mere permissions in law reflects conceptual limits on the law's ability to enforce imperfect duties of virtue (like the duty of beneficence), not the absence of these duties. Consequentialists may likewise argue that we have a general moral requirement to promote the overall good, and that this requirement is baldly inconsistent with the thesis that it can be merely permissible to act on our strongest reasons.[40] If either of these approaches is correct then there is no need for us to address the problem of mere permission.

Nonetheless, approaches that deny the possibility of mere permissions face their own explanatory burdens. They run counter to a commitment to the existence of agent-centred options that appears to be deeply embedded in commonsense morality.[41] Within commonsense morality, justified conduct includes conduct that is morally merely permissible rather than required. We are permitted – but not required – to pursue our projects and interests at the expense of what would be optimific. We are also permitted – but not required – to sacrifice our own interests for the interests of others, even where doing so does not promote the overall good or ensure conformity with impartial duty.[42] In various guises, these forms of commonsense permission have puzzled philosophers working across different traditions in moral theory. Sidgwick noted that 'Common Sense

[37] Fletcher (1979) (n 10) 1358. See also George P Fletcher (1985) 'The Right and the Reasonable' *Harvard Law Review* 98: 949–82, 977–80.

[38] Fletcher (1979) (n 10) 1359.

[39] Immanuel Kant (1996) *The Metaphysics of Morals*, ed Mary J Gregor, Cambridge: Cambridge University Press, s 6:226 (citation refers to volume and page number in the Akademie edition).

[40] See, eg, Shelly Kagan (1994) 'Defending Options' *Ethics* 104: 333–51.

[41] Henry Sidgwick (1877) *The Methods of Ethics*, London: Macmillan, 431–39.

[42] Michael Slote refers to these as agent-centred permissions; Michael Slote (1985) *Common-Sense Morality and Consequentialism*, London: Routledge & Kegan Paul, ch 1.

praises (though it does not prescribe as obligatory), a suppression of egoism beyond what Utilitarianism approves'.[43] Bernard Williams famously deployed similar agent-centred considerations in his critique of Kantian and utilitarian traditions in moral philosophy.[44] The problem of accommodating these agent-centred permissions is one that continues to occupy philosophers across a variety of traditions in moral theory.[45]

A full defence of mere permissions is beyond the scope of this chapter. Instead I will take their existence as an aspect of commonsense morality at face value. If we do concede that there are moral justifications that create mere permissions then Fletcher is wrong to seek to rule them out with the simple conceptual stipulation the justified conduct is 'right' conduct. Theoretical accounts of the function of justifications in law ought to cohere with our understanding of ordinary practical reasoning. Justificatory reasoning in law may not exactly replicate moral justificatory reasoning, but it is surely safe to observe that there is some sort of structural equivalence between the two.[46] Our understanding of justifications in law can only be enriched through study of justificatory reasoning as a form of practical reasoning. Different systems of law will choose to institutionalise justificatory reasons in different ways.[47] Before we consider the way in which particular legal systems do or should incorporate justificatory reasoning in law, it is useful to pay attention to the salient rational distinction between requirements and mere permissions.

While Fletcher suggests justified conduct is morally or rationally required, other criminal law theorists are happy to accept the possibility of 'weaker' standards of justification, whereby a defendant is able to argue that their behaviour, though otherwise prohibited, was permissible in the circumstances.[48] On these accounts, defences that permit but do not require a defendant to act out of self-interest, such as self-defence against a culpable attacker, are properly considered to be justification defences.[49] Anthony Duff further suggests

[43] Sidgwick (n 41) 431. See also WD Ross (1939) *Foundations of Ethics*, Oxford: Oxford University Press, 73–75, 273–74.

[44] See esp Bernard Williams (1981) 'Persons, Character and Morality' in *Moral Luck: Philosophical Papers 1973–1980*, Cambridge: Cambridge University Press, 1–19.

[45] See, eg, Slote (n 42); Shelly Kagan (1989) *The Limits of Morality*, Oxford: Oxford University Press; Shelly Kagan (1994) 'Defending Options' *Ethics* 104: 333–51; Samuel Scheffler (1994) *The Rejection of Consequentialism: A Philosophical Investigation of the Considerations Underlying Rival Moral Conceptions*, Oxford: Oxford University Press; Douglas W Portmore (2011) *Commonsense Consequentialism: Wherein Morality Meets Rationality*, New York: Oxford University Press; Hurka (n 24).

[46] These structural equivalencies are explored in Mitchell Berman (2003) 'Justification and Excuse, Law and Morality' *Duke Law Journal* 53: 1.

[47] Cf John Gardner (2007) 'Reply to Critics' in *Offences and Defences*, Oxford: Oxford University Press, 239–84, 256; Antony Duff (2003) 'Rethinking Justifications' *Tulsa Law Review* 39: 829–50, 831–32.

[48] See, eg, Suzanne Uniacke (1994) *Permissible Killing: The Self-Defence Justification of Homicide*, Cambridge: Cambridge University Press, 14.

[49] Duff (n 16) 276. Cf Claire Finkelstein (1995) 'Self-Defense as a Rational Excuse' *University of Pittsburgh Law Review* 57: 621–49; Larry Alexander (1998) 'A Unified Excuse of Preemptive Self-Protection' *Notre Dame Law Review* 74: 1475–1505, 1495–96.

that the distinction between requirements and mere permissions is important to resolving a problem that has divided theorists of the criminal law: whether justification defences should apply in cases where the motive for justified conduct was malicious or improper.[50] So it may well be that the proper understanding of mere permissions has important ramifications for our doctrinal understanding of defences in criminal law.

B. Reasons of Incomparable Strength

We could appeal to incomparability, or imprecise comparability, in the strength of reasons to resolve the problem. According to the account of the relation between reasons and requirements I offered in section II, we are required to ϕ if we have a set of undefeated reasons to ϕ and that set of reasons is stronger than any incompatible set of reasons. The account allows for the possibility that where we have inconsistent sets of reasons of equal or incomparable strength, we are required to choose between them but permitted to choose either one.[51] Suppose that the defendant in *Cross v State* had reasons to protect his property against damage by protected game animals and reasons not to kill the protected game that were either incomparable or imprecisely comparable, so that neither was stronger than the other. Since both sets of reasons are undefeated, it is permissible for the defendant to choose to conform with either set. In circumstances where they face a choice between preserving their property and killing the game, the defendant is permitted to choose between either course of action.[52] But, since his reason not to kill the protected game is not stronger than his reason to protect his property, he is not required to protect his property. The optionality of the conduct in question can thus be said to be a result of the law's tolerance of these sorts of choices between evils that resist complete comparison. (We could also argue, seemingly implausibly, that our reasons to avoid either evil have equal strength.[53]) Where neither evil is the lesser evil, the subject is required to make a choice between evils, and the law permits them to make their choice.

This explanation is at odds with law's presentation of these cases as involving *lesser* and *greater* evils, but this should not stop us from regarding

[50] Duff (n 47) 849–50. There is a voluminous literature on this problem, which is often described as involving cases where a defendant performs 'the right deed for the wrong reason'; George P Fletcher (1975) 'The Right Deed for the Wrong Reason: A Reply to Mr Robinson' UCLA Law Review 23: 293–321.

[51] This corresponds to what is known as the 'disjunctive' account of deontic conflict; see Horty (n 31).

[52] As in *Cross v State* (n 25); Larry Alexander offers the case as an example of a choice between incommensurable options in Alexander (n 4) 614.

[53] For a recent proposal allowing for reasons that have equal strength, see Douglas W Portmore (2013) 'Perform Your Best Option' *Journal of Philosophy* 110: 436–59.

it as plausible.[54] Law could well be wrong about the moral basis of its own doctrines. It seems to me to be particularly plausible to think that in some cases it is permissible to choose between two evils because neither evil is lesser than the other.[55] The problem with an appeal to ties or incomparability is that it accommodates only a narrow range of cases. There are cases where it is merely permissible to choose an evil, even when our reason to choose it is clearly stronger than its alternatives. I think that cases of heroic self-sacrifice offer the most compelling example. I am permitted, but not required, to imperil my own life by breaking into my neighbour's property to defuse a bomb. A proponent of incomparability as a source of optionality must argue that my reasons not to trespass, including my reasons of self-interest, are not fully comparable with my reasons to defuse the bomb.[56] This does not seem to me to be the correct explanation of the source of the optionality. In fact I think that in these cases my reason to defuse the bomb is clearly stronger than either my reasons not to trespass – it has superior moral weight or priority – but that nonetheless I am merely permitted, and not required, to imperil myself. The commonsense understanding of cases of supererogation (including heroic self-sacrifice) is that they create a state of affairs that is better than the alternative, but which we are nonetheless not required to bring about. The argument that such cases actually involve a choice between incomparable evils is at odds with this conventional understanding. This does not make the argument wrong, of course, but it does suggest there is value in exploring other plausible explanations.

C. Rationally Required, Morally Permitted

Many cases in which justifications generate mere permissions involve a choice by an agent as to whether to favour or sacrifice their own interests. The defendant in *Cross v State*, for instance, had an apparent choice between sacrificing their own interest in property and acting to defend it. Some philosophers argue that mere permissions of this sort arise where we have most moral reason to act in a way that we do not have most reason to act, all things considered. Our strongest moral reasons for action are not our strongest 'non-moral' reasons for action, so a choice between them is morally permissible. Naive attempts to formulate an account along these lines will imply that acting on our strongest

[54] In this regard, for example, § 3.02(1)(b) of the Model Penal Code requires that the harm or evil avoided be strictly 'greater' than the alternative harm or evil.

[55] 'Symmetric' moral dilemmas offer particularly plausible examples; see Walter Sinnott-Armstrong (1985) 'Moral Dilemmas and Incomparability' *American Philosophical Quarterly* 22: 321–29, 324–25. The importance of these symmetric cases was first noted by Ruth Barcan Marcus (n 31).

[56] For arguments to this effect, asserting that reasons of self-interest are not fully comparable with moral or altruistic reasons, see, eg, Parfit (n 6) 137–41; Raz (n 19) 243.

moral reasons in these cases is irrational.[57] In recent work, Douglas Portmore develops a sophisticated version of this approach, which allows him to avoid this and other implausible commitments.[58] But any argument along these lines, including Portmore's, needs to offer a convincing account of the distinction between moral and non-moral reasons. It is notoriously hard to make a rigid distinction between morality and self-interest. This makes appeal to non-moral reasons in order to explain mere permissions unattractive.[59] It is also plausible to think that, at least in some cases, we have moral reasons to promote our own interests, even where we are not morally required to promote them. Suppose, for example, that the neighbour who rescued the jetty had self-interested reasons to do so, because if the jetty had lifted from its pilings it would have travelled downstream and damaged his property. He had at least two reasons to rescue the jetty: a reason to protect my friend's property and a reason to protect his own. It seems implausible in this context to say that his reason to preserve his own property is not a moral reason.[60] Surely the destruction of property is something we have moral reason to avoid, even when the property in question is our own.

Moreover, it is plausible to think that mere permissions arise in contexts other than those that involve a trade-off between self-interested reasons and moral reasons. Consider a standard trolley problem, in which an operator chooses between diverting a trolley towards a single person or allowing it to continue and kill five people. In the absence of any significant relationship between the operator and the track-workers, it seems plausible to say that the operator is permitted to divert the trolley, but that they are not required to do so.[61] Neither the reason to divert the trolley nor the reason not to divert the trolley is properly characterised as a reason of self-interest. The problem of mere permission seems to arise in a broader category of cases, and requires a broader form of explanation.

Rather than appealing to any of the three above-mentioned strategies to accommodate mere permissions, I think we need some way of accommodating the idea that some undefeated reasons do not support requirements. We ought to concede that in some cases it is permissible not to act on our strongest reasons.

[57] This was Shelly Kagan's objection to a version of the same response offered by Michael Slote; Shelly Kagan (1991) 'Replies to My Critics' *Philosophy and Phenomenological Research* 51: 919–28, 927–28.

[58] Portmore (n 45) ch 7; Portmore (n 53).

[59] For further criticism of Portmore's account along these lines, see Joshua Gert (2014) 'Perform a Justified Option' *Utilitas* 26: 206–17; Seth Lazar (2019) 'Accommodating Options' *Pacific Philosophical Quarterly* 100: 233–55.

[60] See further Lazar (n 59) 237–43.

[61] Cf Judith Jarvis Thomson (1985) 'The Trolley Problem' *Yale Law Journal* 94: 1395–1415, 1395–96; Alexander (n 4) 615.

IV. PROTECTED REASONS, EXCLUSIONARY PERMISSIONS AND CANCELLING PERMISSIONS

In Joseph Raz's work, the asymmetric conflict between requirements and justifications is embodied in the well-known idea of a protected reason.[62] Prohibitions are mandatory norms, which are understood as protected reasons – a 'first-order' reason not to engage in the prohibited activity, and a 'higher-order' exclusionary reason not to act on otherwise good reasons that are inconsistent with the prohibition.[63] The requirement not to trespass, for instance, comprises both a reason not to trespass and a reason to exclude otherwise good reasons to trespass. The apparatus of protected reasons offers an elegant explanation of how the reasons associated with requirements come to rule out otherwise attractive options that are available to me. On a sunny day I might be tempted to sit by the river on a neighbour's jetty. The requirement not to trespass gives me good reason to exclude this option, at least not without my neighbour's permission.

Protected reasons offer a very attractive account of the distinction between those reasons that appear to have requiring normative force and those reasons that do not. But in order to accommodate mere permissions, the idea that justifications involve conflict between an ordinary reason to perform the prohibited act and a protected reason to conform with the prohibition needs to be supplemented, at the very least, with an account of how the ordinary reason can come to defeat the protected reason without, itself, generating a requirement. How is it that a reason to trespass in order to rescue property can both (i) fail to be excluded by my protected reason not to trespass and (ii) defeat the reason not to trespass, without itself generating a requirement? I am aware of two attempts to accommodate mere permissions within a framework of practical reasoning that involves protected reasons. The first is Joseph Raz's appeal to exclusionary permissions, which he uses to explain supererogation and other phenomena.[64] The second is John Gardner's idea of a 'cancelling' permission, which he invokes specifically to explain the rational character of justification defences.

A. Exclusionary Permissions

Mere permissions might be explained by appealing to Raz's notion of an 'exclusionary permission', which is a permission to exclude an otherwise good or

[62] Raz (n 6).

[63] ibid, 49–84.

[64] Joseph Raz (1975) 'Permissions and Supererogation' *American Philosophical Quarterly* 12: 161–68; Raz, *Practical Reason and Norms* (n 6) 89–96.

undefeated reason.[65] Exclusionary permissions can permit us not to act on our strongest reasons for action.[66] Cases of supererogation, for instance, arise where on a complete 'balance of reasons' we would be required to perform the supererogatory act, but where we are given permission not to act on those reasons.[67] In the context of lesser-evils justifications, mere permissions could be said to arise where law confers permission to exclude reasons for conformity with the prohibition. We are permitted, but not required, to exclude our reasons to conform.

There are technical difficulties with the idea of exclusionary permissions that need not concern us here.[68] In the context of lesser-evils justifications, an appeal to exclusionary permission is problematic. It fits poorly with our understanding of the rationale and function of justifications in law. The very idea of justification involves a weighing of conflicting reasons, rather than a reason not to act on conflicting reasons.[69] The prohibition continues to exert some form of rational weight or force, but the law affords some recognition that we have a stronger reason for acting that justifies our conduct. The defendant who invokes a lesser-evils justification argues that he acts on a good or undefeated reason that is stronger than his competing reasons, not merely that he was permitted to exclude competing reasons for action. Although the reason associated with the prohibition is defeated, it continues to play a role in practical deliberation. As Joshua Gert notes, the model of exclusionary permission cannot accommodate this – permission to exclude another reason means that the reason is assigned either a 'full role' or 'no role' in rational deliberation, depending on whether the permission is exercised or not.[70] Exclusionary permissions cannot accommodate the sense in which justifications are the result of a conflict of practical reasons, in which a requiring reason is matched or defeated by a competing justifying reason.

B. Cancelling Permissions

John Gardner developed a nuanced reason-based account of justification in criminal law in terms of what he called 'cancelling permissions'.[71] Gardner follows Raz in appealing to second-order 'exclusionary' reasons to accommodate the asymmetric conflict between requirements and justifications. According to Gardner, cancelling permissions 'do not cancel the reasons not to perform the

[65] Raz (n 64); Raz (n 6) 89–96.
[66] Raz (n 6) 89.
[67] ibid, 94.
[68] I discuss some technical difficulties in Mullins (n 34); see also Gert (n 32) 107–09.
[69] Cf Tadros (n 22) 270–73.
[70] Gert (n 32) 108.
[71] See especially Gardner, 'Justifications and Reasons' (n 12) 106–07; Gardner (n 8) 148–49.

criminalised action, but merely cancel the second-order protective reasons not to act for certain countervailing reasons'.[72] The justifying reason is not excluded, but rather is regarded as an 'acceptable' or 'permitted' reason for engaging in the otherwise prohibited conduct.[73] The norm associated with the prohibition is not cancelled, since it still exerts its 'ordinary rational pull as a reason not to commit the offence'.[74] Gardner's account is intended to explain justifications as exceptions to the authority of legal norms, but it can be adapted to any case in which a justifying reason is able to defeat a requirement. In the context of legal prohibitions, cancellation of the second-order exclusionary reasons is a matter of positive law's recognising limits to the scope of the prohibition. Outside of law, these limits to the scope of the protective reason could well emerge as the result of reasons holism: a valid justification could cancel or disable the exclusionary reason associated with the prohibition.[75]

Gardner's account of cancelling permissions allows for the possibility that it will remain permissible to conform with the reason not to engage in the prohibited conduct. I think he is right to think that, in the case of justified failure to conform with a prohibition, the reason to conform with the prohibition continues to make the option rationally intelligible. It accommodates mere permissions as cases of conflict between two ordinary, non-protected reasons. Where a valid justification is present, the reason not to engage in prohibited conduct loses its requiring force but not its justificatory force. Gardner's approach is also able to overcome the problem that faced Raz's account, since he is able to explain how the reason to conform with the prohibition continues to play a role in rational deliberation.

Unfortunately Gardner's exposition of cancelling permissions is brief, and he offers no clarity on the interaction between the strength of the justifying reason and the strength of the otherwise protected reason. Supposing, as we have, that the justifying reason is stronger than the reason not to engage in the prohibited conduct, how is it that the stronger justifying reason can fail to generate a requirement? Gardner suggests that in at least some cases, these ordinary reasons are incomparable, so that 'one acts on undefeated reasons whichever way one acts'.[76] But, as I have noted, incomparability between reasons does not seem to be a necessary condition for a mere permission.

Though the distinction between ordinary reasons and protected reasons offers a plausible starting point for addressing the asymmetric practical conflict between justifications and requirements, the distinction cannot accommodate mere permissions without the further stipulation that some of our strongest reasons do not entail requirements.

[72] Gardner (n 12) 107.
[73] ibid.
[74] Gardner (n 8) 148.
[75] Cf Dancy (n 6) ch 3.
[76] Gardner (n 12) 101, fn 21.

V. PURELY JUSTIFICATORY REASONS

I think that the most plausible solution to the problem of mere permissions invokes what Gert calls 'purely justificatory' reasons for action, and contrasts these with the class of reasons that support requirements.[77] There are reasons that, in spite of their strength, do not support requirements. In the context of a choice between evils, strong justifying reasons can support the conclusion that we are justified, and therefore permitted, to act without supporting the conclusion that we are required to do so. Acceptance of the possibility of purely justificatory reasons allows for a straightforward resolution of the problem of mere permissions. Mere permissions arise when a subset of purely justifying reasons defeats (or matches in strength) other incompatible subsets of reasons that arise in a given reasoning context.

It seems uncontroversial, at least amongst those theorists who assign a fundamental role to reasons in generating normative conclusions, that reasons can perform both a justifying and a requiring function.[78] The motivation for the distinction between purely justificatory reasons and reasons that also support requirements lies partly in the rational asymmetry between reasons for and reasons against that we noted at the beginning of this chapter. The asymmetry in question arises because there are reasons for pursuing certain options that do not seem to play a requiring role – they support the conclusion that certain choices are rationally intelligible and permissible, but they do not support the conclusion that the support of other inconsistent options is forbidden or impermissible. We can explain this asymmetry by invoking the existence of purely justificatory reasons.

Recognition of the possibility of purely justificatory reasons raises a number of technical complications concerning their interaction with reasons that support requirements. (Gert's presentation of the view, which attributes different 'degrees' of requiring and justifying strength to reasons, is particularly complicated, since it seems to allow for cross-scalar comparison.[79]) I will avoid sketching a complete framework here.[80] The rudiments of the approach involve an abandonment of the idea that the strongest reasons in a given reasoning context support requirements. According to the **Strongest Reasons Entail Requirements** thesis I considered in section II, I am required to act on a set of reasons that is stronger than any other set of inconsistent reasons. As we saw, this account generates implausible conclusions in cases where our strongest reasons appear to entail mere permissions rather than requirements. Postulating

[77] Gert (n 32); Greenspan (n 21).

[78] See, eg, Gert (n 12) 158; Raz (n 12) 18–19; Scanlon (2014) (n 6) 107–08.

[79] Cf Joshua Gert (2007) 'Normative Strength and the Balance of Reasons' *Philosophical Review* 116: 533–62.

[80] In 'Formalizing Reasons, Oughts, and Requirements' (n 34), I attempt to sketch a workable version of such a model.

the existence of purely justificatory reasons resolves the problem by allowing for the possibility that some of our strongest reasons do not support requirements. I will refer to reasons that generate requirements as 'deontic' reasons, in order to distinguish them from purely justificatory reasons.[81] These reasons are 'deontic' in the strict sense, since they support obligations or requirements, but they can also perform a justificatory role. Both deontic reasons and purely justificatory reasons can be invoked in the justification of conduct, but where purely justificatory reasons never support requirements, our strongest deontic reasons do.[82] More formally, we will now define a reasoning context in terms of both a set of purely justificatory reasons and a set of deontic reasons applicable to an agent. We will stipulate that the 'stronger than' relation can obtain between subsets of deontic reasons and subsets of purely justificatory reasons. We then retain our earlier definition of **Undefeated Reasons**, noting that the reference to a subset of reasons in the definition can now be taken to refer to either a subset of deontic reasons, or a subset of purely justificatory reasons. The approach therefore accommodates the fact that purely justificatory reasons and deontic reasons can be comparable in strength: a subset of purely justificatory reasons may be stronger than an inconsistent subset of deontic reasons, and thus defeat them. Likewise, a stronger subset of deontic reasons will defeat an inconsistent subset of justificatory reasons. We then replace our early account of the relationship between reasons and requirements with the following:

> **Strongest Deontic Reasons Entail Requirements:** In a reasoning context, it is required that ϕ if there is some subset of deontic reasons supporting the proposition that ϕ, $R(\phi)$, such that for any subset of reasons $R'(\psi)$ that is inconsistent with $R(\phi)$, $R(\phi)$ is stronger than $R'(\psi)$.

In a practical conflict between a set of reasons not to engage in prohibited conduct $R_1(\neg P)$, and a stronger and inconsistent set of reasons to pursue the lesser evil, $R_2(LE)$, the conflict will generate a mere permission where the reasons to pursue the lesser evil are purely justificatory reasons. $R_1(\neg P)$ is defeated by $R_2(LE)$, since the two subsets are inconsistent, but, if the strongest subset of reasons $R_2(LE)$ is purely justificatory, it does not support the conclusion that pursuit of the lesser evil is required and that compliance with the prohibition is impermissible. In spite of their strength, purely justificatory reasons do not make it impermissible to pursue an inconsistent option. If our reasons to pursue the lesser evil, $R_2(LE)$ are purely justificatory, then acting on the weaker subset of reasons to conform with the prohibition, $R_1(\neg P)$ will not

[81] The language of deontic and non-deontic reasons is taken from Margaret Olivia Little (2013) 'In Defence of Non-Deontic Reasons' in *Thinking About Reasons: Themes from the Philosophy of Jonathan Dancy*, eds David Bakhurst, Margaret Olivia Little and Brad Hooker, Oxford: Oxford University Press, 112–36; R Jay Wallace (2013) 'The Deontic Structure of Morality' ibid, 137–65.

[82] In other words, all reasons are justificatory reasons, but purely justificatory reasons are not deontic reasons.

be impermissible or wrong. It is still permissible to conform with the defeated set of reasons, $R_1(\neg P)$. This approach also allows us to retain the thesis that **Undefeated Reasons Entail Permissions**, as the conflict between $R_1(\neg P)$ and $R_2(LE)$ demonstrates. If any subset of reasons (either purely justificatory or deontic) is strong enough to be undefeated, then it will always be permissible to conform with those reasons.

As I noted previously, deontic reasons still occupy a justificatory role within this framework. If one set of deontic reasons is not weaker than any other inconsistent subset of reasons, it will be permissible to act on them. What sets them apart from purely justificatory reasons is that they also act to preclude the pursuit of other rational options. Consider, for example, a reasoning context based on the situation in *Cross v State* involving a choice between two inconsistent subsets of reasons, $R_1(PP)$ and $R_2(\neg KG)$, representing the defendant's reasons to protect his property by killing the protected game and his reason not to kill the protected game, where the evils in question are incomparable and thus neither subset of reasons is stronger than the other. Neither set of reasons will defeat the other. Even supposing that $R_1(PP)$ and $R_2(\neg KG)$ are both subsets of deontic reasons, choice of either evil will still be justified and permissible. The defendant acts with justification if he acts on either set of reasons.

By stipulating the existence of purely justificatory reasons, this approach abandons the ordinary view of the relationship between reasons and requirements. The entailment between justifications and permissions is retained: it is always permissible to act on a subset of undefeated reasons, whatever the character of the reasons in question. And yet in the absence of a subset of undefeated deontic reasons, it is permissible to act on any set of reasons, even a defeated one. In acting on a defeated subset of reasons I may expose myself to some sort of criticism or negative appraisal, but I do not necessarily act impermissibly. Purely justificatory reasons do not operate negatively – they do not rule out other options by rendering them rationally unintelligible or impermissible. The special function of deontic reasons is to exclude or preempt otherwise intelligible options. Deontic reasons are needed to capture the sense in which a certain subset of rational considerations function as *sui generis* constraints on our practical deliberation – constraints that seem to rule out otherwise rational options and mandate the pursuit of others.[83]

I think that this proposal can be interpreted in a manner that is compatible with the Razian distinction between reasons and protected reasons.[84] Raz's proposal that mandatory norms be interpreted as protected reasons is an attempt to offer a reductive explanation of the negative character of deontic reasons: deontic reasons are ordinary reasons that rule out

[83] Cf R Jay Wallace (2019) *The Moral Nexus*, Princeton, NJ: Princeton University Press, 26.
[84] See especially Raz (n 6) 94.

otherwise good options by excluding them from their role as reasons for action.[85] In order to reconcile Raz's account with the framework offered here, we only need to add the further stipulation that ordinary non-protected reasons do not support requirements. In other words, non-protected reasons are purely justificatory reasons. Whatever other practical functions they might serve, non-protected reasons do not support the conclusion that inconsistent conduct is impermissible.[86] Raz himself notes that the 'primary function of reasons' is to 'make certain responses eligible, appropriate' and that only sometimes do the facts make 'one response non-optional' or the 'required response'.[87] The thesis that non-protected reasons are purely justificatory reasons provides us with an explanation of reasons' primary function in supporting the rational intelligibility of options. If we augment Raz's framework with the stipulation that non-protected reasons do not support requirements, we have the resources to explain mere permissions. The explanation follows Gardner's suggestion that justifications arise in the context of cancelling permissions, in which the force of the protective reason that would ordinarily exclude reasons for non-conformity is cancelled. The resulting conflict between non-protected, first-order reasons does not generate any requirement. We are permitted to act on any of our first-order reasons, even when one subset of reasons is stronger than another set of inconsistent subset of reasons.

VI. CONCLUSION

The problem of mere permissions as I have defined it is a problem about the relationship between the strength of reasons and their normative consequences. It is a problem about practical reasoning, and not a problem that arises solely in the context of institutionalised, legal reasoning. Studying the problem in the context of the lesser-evils justification in law is nonetheless instructive. Most fundamentally, mere permissions demonstrate the limits of naive utilitarian or consequentialist analysis of legal justifications. The language of 'lesser evils' is sometimes taken to suggest a utilitarian calculus of social harm and benefit, whereby justifications arise just in case we are morally and rationally required to pursue the lesser social evil at the expense of breaching a prohibition.[88] As others have recognised, focus on the rational structure of justifications makes this interpretation of lesser-evils defences difficult to maintain.[89]

There is another respect in which resolving the problem of mere permissions, along with my proposed solution, is informative in the context of legal

[85] Wallace ((n 83) 133–34) expresses doubts about Raz's reductive project in this regard.
[86] Cf Gert (n 12) 169–71.
[87] Raz (n 12) 5; cf Raz (1999) (n 19) 99–105.
[88] For an interpretation along these lines, see Robinson (n 10).
[89] Alexander (n 4) 615–16; Husak (n 11) 498–99.

justification. As I noted at the beginning of this chapter, some theorists of the criminal law contrast the view that justified behaviour is correct or commendable with the view that justified behaviour is merely permissible. As a result, they argue that we should allow that the category of justification defences include conduct that is merely 'tolerated' (for example, killing an innocent aggressor in self-defence).[90] If we wish to insist that justified conduct involves acting on our strongest reasons, then we can admit that justified conduct is merely permissible without conceding that justified conduct is simply tolerated. Conduct can be correct or warranted, in the sense that it conforms with our strongest available reasons, without being required. We need not abandon the view that justified conduct involves acting on the strongest reasons in order to accommodate mere permissions. On the other hand, if we wish to argue that justified conduct need only be permissible, we can also take mere permissions to illustrate the rational intelligibility of acting on a set of weaker reasons. There are cases where failure to conform with our strongest reasons is permissible, even if not commendable or desirable. I take no view here as to which of these approaches is the correct one. Criminal theorists have long suspected that focus on labels like 'justification' and 'excuse' have the potential to occlude other salient rational distinctions in the discussion of defences.[91] Perhaps it is helpful to distinguish two senses in which an act can be justified. In the first sense, we are justified when we act on our strongest reasons. In the second sense, we are justified when we act on a set of reasons that, while not necessarily our strongest, remain eligible for rational choice.

[90] See, eg, Robinson (n 10) 284; Dressler (n 11) 84–85.
[91] See especially Greenawalt (n 10); Duff (n 16) 264–67; Colvin (n 10).

13

First Among Equals: Abduction in Legal Argument from a Logocratic Point of View

SCOTT BREWER

I. INTRODUCTION: WHAT IS A LEGAL ARGUMENT?

WHAT IS A legal argument? More specifically, what are the criteria of identity that specify what constitutes a single legal argument? When a legal arguer offers what seem to be several broadly related arguments, how exactly does one distinguish them into their component parts? Although the argumental phenomena that concern me and the explanations I will offer are not limited to the domain of legal argument, they occur prevalently there. Judges and litigants typically make several arguments that seem clearly to be orchestrated to achieve a single goal, arguing either to establish a litigative position (as do parties' attorneys) or to resolve a contest of litigants' arguments (the task of the judge of that competition).

To illustrate and explain my topic more fully, I quote a judicial opinion that is well-known in American Contract Law pedagogy. The opinion is *Dougherty v Salt*,[1] written by Benjamin Cardozo, one of the acknowledged masters of American common law for the highest court in the State of New York. In full, the opinion reads as follows:

> The plaintiff, a boy of eight years, received from his aunt, the defendant's testatrix, a promissory note for $3,000, payable at her death or before. Use was made of a printed form, which contains the words 'value received.' How the note came to be given was explained by the boy's guardian, who was a witness for his ward. The aunt was visiting her nephew.
>
> 'When she saw Charley coming in, she said, "Isn't he a nice boy?" I answered her, Yes; that he is getting along very nice, and getting along nice in school; and

[1] *Dougherty v Salt*, 125 NE 94 (NY 1919) (Cardozo, J).

> I showed where he had progressed in school, having good reports, and so forth, and she told me that she was going to take care of that child; that she loved him very much. I said, "I know you do, Tillie, but your taking care of the child will be done probably like your brother and sister done, take it out in talk." She said, "I don't intend to take it out in talk; I would like to take care of him now." I said, "Well, that is up to you." She said, "Why can't I make out a note to him?" I said, "You can, if you wish to." She said, "Would that be right?" And I said, "I do not know, but I guess it would; I do not know why it would not." And she said, "Well, will you make out a note for me?" I said, "Yes, if you wish me to," and she said, "Well, I wish you would."'

A blank was then produced, filled out, and signed. The aunt handed the note to her nephew, with these words:

> 'You have always done for me, and I have signed this note for you. Now, do not lose it. Some day it will be valuable.'

The trial judge submitted to the jury the question whether there was any consideration for the promised payment. Afterwards, he set aside the verdict in favor of the plaintiff, and dismissed the complaint. The Appellate Division, by a divided court, reversed the judgment of dismissal, and reinstated the verdict on the ground that the note was sufficient evidence of consideration.

We reach a different conclusion. The inference of consideration to be drawn from the form of the note has been so overcome and rebutted as to leave no question for a jury. This is not a case where witnesses, summoned by the defendant and friendly to the defendant's cause, supply the testimony in disproof of value. Strickland v Henry, 175 NY 372, 67 NE 611. This is a case where the testimony in disproof of value comes from the plaintiff's own witness, speaking at the plaintiff's instance. The transaction thus revealed admits of one interpretation, and one only. The note was the voluntary and unenforcible promise of an executory gift. Harris v Clark, 3 NY 93, 51 Am Dec 352; Holmes v Roper, 141 NY 64, 66, 36 NE 180. This child of eight was not a creditor, nor dealt with as one. The aunt was not paying a debt. She was conferring a bounty. Fink v Cox, 18 Johns 145, 9 Am Dec 191. The promise was neither offered nor accepted with any other purpose. 'Nothing is consideration that is not regarded as such by both parties.' Philpot v Gruninger, 14 Wall 570, 577 [20 L Ed 743]; Fire Ins Ass'n v Wickham, 141 US 564, 579, 12 Sup Ct 84, 35 L Ed 860; Wisconsin & M Ry Co v Powers, 191 US 379, 386, 24 Sup Ct 107, 48 L Ed 229; De Cicco v Schweizer, 221 NY 431, 438, 117 NE 807, LRA 1918E, 1004, Ann Cas 1918C, 816. A note so given is not made for 'value received,' however its maker may have labeled it. The formula of the printed blank becomes, in the light of the conceded facts, a mere erroneous conclusion, which cannot overcome the inconsistent conclusion of the law. Blanshan v Russell, 32 App Div 103, 52 NY Supp 963, affirmed on opinion below 161 NY 629, 55 NE 1093; Kramer v Kramer, 181 NY 477, 74 NE 474; Bruyn v Russell, 52 Hun, 17, 4 NY Supp 784. The plaintiff through his own witness, has explained the genesis of the promise, and consideration has been disproved. Neg Instr Law, § 54 (Consol Laws, c 38).

We hold, therefore, that the verdict of the jury was contrary to law, and that the trial judge was right in setting it aside. He went too far, however, in dismissing the complaint. He might have dismissed it if he had reserved his ruling on the defendant's motion for a nonsuit or for the direction of a verdict. Code Civ Proc §§ 1185, 1187. Instead of reserving his ruling, he denied the motion absolutely. Upon the return of the verdict, he should have granted a new trial.

A new trial was also necessary because of error in rejecting evidence. The defendant attempted to prove that the signature to the note was forged. The court refused to hear the evidence, because forgery had not been pleaded as a defense. The answer did deny the execution of the note. The evidence of forgery was admissible under the denial. Schwarz v Oppold, 74 NY 307; Farmers' L & T Co v Siefke, 144 NY 354, 39 NE 358.

The judgment of the Appellate Division should be reversed, and the judgment of the Trial Term modified by granting a new trial, and, as modified, affirmed, with costs in all courts to abide the event.

Hiscock, CJ, and Chase, Collin, Hogan, Crane, and Andrews, JJ, concur.

Judgment accordingly.[2]

Abstracting from several details to which we will return, before us is a dispute about whether an aunt made a legally enforceable promise to her nephew to give him $3,000.[3] In his opinion for New York Court of Appeals (which is the highest court in the State of New York), Judge Cardozo concluded that Tillie did not make a legally enforceable promise. How did he arrive at that conclusion? Did he offer *an* argument whose conclusion it was? Several arguments? If there are several arguments, how are they related? Are there several arguments for the same conclusion? Several partial arguments that add up to one conclusion? Are arguments analysable into elements that can be added in this way? Cardozo concluded that although the trial judge was correct to overrule the jury's verdict in favour of plaintiff Charley, the trial judge was mistaken in dismissing the complaint outright and mistakenly refused to grant a new trial to determine whether, as the defendant claimed (directly or indirectly), the note allegedly given by Tillie to Charley was forged. Is this argument about the mistaken dismissal and the need for a new trial the same argument as the argument about the promise from Tillie to Charley? Different? If different, how are they related? In general, how does one determine whether an arguer is offering one argument with several conclusions, or several arguments for one conclusion, or several arguments for several conclusions? What are the identity criteria of *an* argument?

[2] ibid.

[3] Cardozo's opinion also reveals additional procedural details and complexity. The action for breach of contract initiated at the trial court was on behalf of Charles Napoleon Dougherty ('Charley'), an 8-year-old boy, by Susan M Teves, who was Charley's guardian. The action was against Emma L Salt, who was the executrix of the last will and testament of Helena M Dougherty, Charley's aunt (and also the testatrix for Salt), who had died by the time of the action for breach of Contract. In effect, the boy's Contract claim was that his aunt made him a legally enforceable promise to give him $3,000 in the circumstances that Cardozo offers in the opinion quoted above.

The answer I will offer is an *abduction*, that is, an argument whose premise is some phenomenon to be explained and whose conclusion is an explanation of that phenomenon. The phenomena that concern me in this abduction are the *practices of argument*, both legal argument specifically and argument more generally. Fractal-like, abduction ramifies. The explanation of the identity criteria of argument is supplied by an abduction. That abduction itself also provides an explanation of the nature of abduction – creating an abduction of abduction, or a meta-abduction.[4] This meta-abduction is, like all arguments, a tool, which I have come to call the *Logocratic Method*. The Logocratic Method is a philosophical system for explaining and evaluating arguments, their formal structures and their principal uses in contexts of argument, including, but not limited to, varying contexts of legal argument. (A fair – and aspirational! – analogue is Charles Sanders Peirce's semiotic system, which is a philosophical system for explaining and evaluating signs, their types and their uses.)

Why are the questions about the identity criteria of argument and the Logocratic explanatory (abductive) answer to those questions important? One reason among others is this: arguments, like language (the medium in which arguments exist), are tools used by arguers for many different purposes. Tools, in turn, are used for (literally) instrumental purposes, to achieve specific tasks. There are features of a hammer, for example, that make it a good hammer, and there are features of instruments other than those originally designed as hammers that might make them good *as* hammers.[5] How is the efficacy of the tool of argument to be measured? Put another way, if a specific argument is regarded as a tool, how well does it serve its purpose as a tool – how good is it *as* an argument? Obviously, a single arguer can have many distinct purposes for a given argument, and different arguers can have different purposes for different arguments. There are, accordingly, different ways to assess the efficacy of arguments. One of the central goals that legal arguers have for their arguments is to *justify* the legal judgments that are those arguments' conclusions. This goal is reflected in conceptions of the *rule of law*, an action or judgment *according to law*.[6] A moment's reflection shows that, in order to assess the efficacy of the tool of legal argument as a tool of justification, one must be able to identify instances in which that tool is operating. One cannot know how good a tool is at its intended purpose without being able to tell *what* the tool is, *when* it is being used and *how* it is being used.

[4] 'My colleague, Leon Lipson, once described a certain species of legal writing as "Anything you can do, I can do meta." What follows is a pure instantiation of his category.' Arthur Allen Leff (1979) 'Unspeakable Ethics, Unnatural Law' *Duke Law Journal*: 1229–49, 1230, fn 2. Perhaps needless to say (but still said), this often applies to philosophical writing, as it does in this chapter.

[5] I anticipate a point developed further in discussion below, see n 34 and accompanying text.

[6] I have long urged this point. See, eg, Scott Brewer (2000) 'On the Possibility of Necessity in Legal Argument: A Dilemma for Holmes and Dewey' *John Marshall Law Review* 34: 9–47, 46–47.

To anticipate, the Logocratic abduction I present and rely on offers answers to these *what*, *when*, and *how* questions about legal arguments:

1. The criteria of identity of *any* argument, including legal arguments (such as in *Dougherty*) are supplied by *interpretive abduction*, which is an inference to the explanation of the meaning of a text.
2. According to the best explanation *of* abduction (meta-abduction[7]), all abductions are rendered from a *point of view*, and all *legal abductions* are rendered from a *legal point of view*.
3. The fundamental form of legal argument is *legal abduction*.
4. All legal abductions include *within them* (in a relation of logical subsumption[8]) both *interpretive abduction* and *rule-based deduction* (Cardozo relies on both within his legal abduction in *Dougherty*). Very often, especially in Anglo-American legal-argument practice, legal abductions also involve induction and analogical argument (but Cardozo does not rely on either of these in *Dougherty*).
5. Best explained, Cardozo's legal abduction in *Dougherty* consists of two legal abductions each of which contains both interpretive abductions (of the legal rules Cardozo judges to be applicable to the case) and rule-based deductions (under those rules). This makes for a total, within the relatively short judicial opinion, of two overall legal abductions, within each of which is an interpretive abduction and a deduction, thus a total of six arguments.

Explaining and defending these claims – and along the way trying to indicate that the complexity of the Logocratic meta-abduction, applied to *Dougherty* is warranted – are my central overarching goals. To be sure, this is a complex explanation in answer to the question: *What is a legal argument?* We should not sacrifice explanatory power to oversimplification, and my closing remarks suggest the fruitility (fruitful utility) of a more general exploration of coherence and resonance among theories of argument and many of the multiple-disciplinary studies of complexity itself.

II. OUTLINE OF THE (META) ARGUMENT

I proceed as follows. Like the land of those who had the Gauls to oppose Caesar, this chapter presents arguments about the nature of argument, meta-arguments, in three main parts. First, I present the elements of the Logocratic theory of argument that in turn explains the nature of abduction – including interpretive abduction, which is central to the explanation of the identity criteria of argument, and legal abduction, which is central to the explanation of cases like *Dougherty*. Second, using a close application of Logocratic theory, I use *Dougherty* to explain and

[7] See Leff (n 4).

[8] In set-theoretic terms, logical subsumption is the *proper-subset* relation of sets. Set A *properly subsumes* Set B if and only if every element of Set A is an element of Set B, but the converse does not hold.

to illustrate how legal abduction serves as the core of legal argument both for the Logocratic account of the identity criteria of legal argument specifically and arguments in general. Finally, I conclude with a summary of the complex argumental path taken and a very brief suggestion for further research in light of the analysis I have offered.

III. ELEMENTS OF THE LOGOCRATIC POINT OF VIEW

In this section, I sketch those parts of the Logocratic Method (hereinafter also 'LM') that I draw on for my answers to the central questions of the chapter: *What is a legal argument?* and, more generally, *What is* an *argument?*, answers I shall illustrate by my analysis of *Dougherty*.

Before framing the theory explicitly as the 'Logocratic Method',[9] I developed explanations of different types of arguments that anticipated the Logocratic approach, including an explanation of interpretive arguments[10] (which I later came to refer to as 'interpretive abduction'[11]), analogical arguments,[12] and arguments relied on by non-experts facing a practical reasoning task (judges and juries in litigation are examples of practical reasoners who face this task) in consulting and deferring epistemically to experts to aid them in their practical-reasoning decisions.[13] I have also identified and articulated a distinct domain of

[9] I first used that term in Scott Brewer (2007) 'Satisfaction and Posner's Morin Opinion: Aliquando Bonus Dormitat Posnerus?' *Harvard Law Review* 120: 1123–36, but did not develop the first full articulation of the method until Scott Brewer (2011) 'Logocratic Method and the Analysis of Arguments in Evidence' *Law, Probability & Risk* 10: 175–202.

[10] In Scott Brewer (1988) 'Figuring the Law: Holism and Tropological Inference in Legal Interpretation' *Yale Law Journal* 97: 823–43, I modelled interpretation as a two-place relation between a text being interpreted (*interpretandum*) and a distinct text that offers the interpretation, where the relation is *states the meaning of*. The model also explained interpretation as the application of a set of inference rules leading from the *interpretandum* to the *interpretans*. Although I did not at the time style this process as 'abduction', the model coheres strongly and well with my later framing of interpretation as 'interpretive abduction': see sources cited in n 11.

[11] See Scott Brewer (2020) 'Interactive Virtue and Vice in Systems of Arguments: A Logocratic Analysis' *Artificial Intelligence & Law* 28: 151–79; Scott Brewer (forthcoming) 'Logic and the Life of the Law (Professor): A Logocratic Lesson from Hohfeld' in *Wesley Hohfeld A Century Later: Edited Work, Select Personal Papers, and Original Commentaries*, eds Shyamkrishna Balganesh, Ted Sichelman and Henry E Smith; Jack Weinstein, Norman Abrams, Scott Brewer and Daniel Medwed (2017) *Evidence*, 10th edn, St Paul, MN: Foundation Press. Other theorists of abduction have also explained interpretation as a type of abduction. See, eg, Atocha Aliseda (2008) *Abductive Reasoning: Logical Investigations into Discovery and Explanation*, Netherlands: Springer, 43–44 ('In linguistics, abduction has been proposed as a process for natural language interpretation, where our "observations" are the utterances that we hear (or read). More precisely, interpreting a sentence in discourse is viewed as providing a best explanation of why the sentence would be true.'); Dov M Gabbay and John Woods (2005) *The Reach of Abduction: Insight and Trial*, 1st edn, Amsterdam: Elsevier Science, ch 9, 'Interpretation Abduction'.

[12] See Scott Brewer (1996) 'Exemplary Reasoning: Semantics, Pragmatics, and the Rational Force of Legal Argument by Analogy' *Harvard Law Review* 109: 923–1028.

[13] See Scott Brewer (1998) 'Scientific Expert Testimony and Intellectual Due Process' *Yale Law Journal* 107: 1535–1681.

Jurisprudence, the 'Jurisprudence of Logical Form', whose subject matter is the jurisprudential significance of the question of how one might fairly interpret the logical form of legal arguments.[14]

Most of these explanations[15] assert and rely on two principal explanatory propositions that comprise what I have called the Logocratic 'interactive virtue' theory of argument.[16] It is this aspect of Logocratic theory that provides the identity criteria of arguments and that allows me to answer the questions that I posed (in section I) about Cardozo's opinion in *Dougherty v Salt*. Two theses are at the core of this interactive virtue theory:

(a) There are precisely four argument forms, deduction, induction, abduction and analogy, which are logically distinct, none of which is reducible to any other.[17]
(b) Both the *identity* criteria and the distinct *evaluative* criteria for each individual argument form are best explained such that some forms include other forms in the multi-step inferential process from premises to conclusion.

In accord with proposition (b), I have argued that: analogical argument is a multi-step inferential process that involves both abduction (*analogical abduction*) and either induction or deduction;[18] induction always involves abduction;[19] and, like analogical argument, abduction always involves either induction or deduction. I have never argued that deduction always involves some other mode of inference, but even concluding that deduction does *not* necessarily involve any other logical form may presuppose a non-nominalist semantics.[20]

A. The Evidential Conception of Logic

The Logocratic Method endorses an *evidential conception of logic*, according to which *logic is the study of the evidential relation between the premises*

[14] See Scott Brewer (2000) 'Traversing Holmes' Path Toward a Jurisprudence of Logical Form' in *The Path of the Law and Its Influence: The Legacy of Oliver Wendell Holmes, Jr*, ed Steven J Burton, Cambridge: Cambridge University Press, 94–132.

[15] Unlike other cited sources, Brewer (n 10) did not discuss argument forms generally, though, as noted, it did model interpretation as a type of argument in a 'Logocratic-friendly' way, providing details to fill out what has become the Logocratic model of *interpretive abduction*. See also discussion in section V of this chapter.

[16] See Brewer (2020) (n 11).

[17] Contrast assimilative accounts that, for example, explain induction as a type of abduction, as in Gilbert H Harman (1965) 'The Inference to the Best Explanation' *The Philosophical Review* 74: 88–95, 88 ('all warranted inferences which may be described as instances of enumerative induction must also be described as instances of the inference to the best explanation'; the former are a 'special case' of the latter), or that explain analogy as a type of induction, as in Heather Walters and Kristen Stout (2019) *Understanding Argument in a Post-Truth World*, San Diego, CA: Cognella, 116–17 (treating 'Argument by Analogy' as a 'Type of Induction').

[18] See Brewer (n 12).

[19] Weinstein, Abrams, Brewer and Medwed (n 11) ch 2, esp 128–29 and fn 8.

[20] I have in mind here the kind of considerations that Friedrich Nietzsche adduces in 'On Truth and Lying in a Non-moral Sense': 'Let us consider in particular how concepts are formed; each word

and conclusions of arguments.[21] This conception explains that at the root of all references to 'evidence', including visual evidence, testimonial evidence and physical evidence, is the basic idea that evidence is *propositional*. The key reason for conceiving evidence in this way is to capture the role that evidence plays in reasoning to conclusions about matters that are (purportedly) justified on the basis of evidence. When evidence enters the process of reasoning, it is *propositional* and *argumental* (that is, it plays an inferential role in arguments, as defined in section III.C). When judges and lawyers claim that some object (eg a knife with fingerprints) or an action or event (eg a person's running away when police come to his house) is evidence for some proposition (the person whose fingerprints were on the knife committed the stabbing; the person who ran from the police was guilty of the crime whose culprit the police were seeking), those judges and lawyers are actually 'propositionalising' the object or action or event. That is, they are claiming that the *fact* that the defendant's fingerprints can be found on the knife that was at the scene of the crime serves as evidence for the hypothesis that the defendant committed the stabbing. And facts are expressed as propositions.

immediately becomes a concept, not by virtue of the fact that it is intended to serve as a memory (say) of the unique, utterly individualized, primary experience to which it owes its existence, but because at the same time it must fit countless other, more or less similar cases, ie cases which, strictly speaking, are never equivalent, and thus nothing other than nonequivalent cases. Every concept comes into being by making equivalent that which is nonequivalent. Just as it is certain that no leaf is ever exactly the same as any other leaf, it is equally certain that the concept "leaf" is formed by dropping these individual differences arbitrarily, by forgetting those features which differentiate one thing from another, so that the concept then gives rise to the notion that something other than leaves exists in nature, something which would be "leaf", a primal form, say, from which all leaves were woven, drawn, delineated, dyed, curled, painted – but by a clumsy pair of hands, so that no single example turned out to be a faithful, correct, and reliable copy of the primal form. We call a man honest; we ask, "Why did he act so honestly today?" Our answer is usually: "Because of his honesty." Honesty! – yet again, this means that the leaf is the cause of the leaves. We have no knowledge of an essential quality which might be called honesty, but we do know of numerous individualized and hence nonequivalent actions which we equate with each other by omitting what is unlike, and which we now designate as honest actions; finally we formulate from them a *qualitas occulta* with the name "honesty".' Friedrich Nietzsche (1873) 'On Truth and Lying in a Non-Moral Sense' in *The Birth of Tragedy and Other Writings*, eds Raymond Guess and Ronald Speirs, Cambridge: Cambridge University Press (1999), 145 (citation omitted). These kinds of considerations suggest that one's ontology does or should contain only individuals whose grouping under concepts is affected only by what we might call *analogical grouping*, groupings in which distinct individuals are regarded as sufficiently similar to warrant including under one conceptual name, eg, in Nietzsche's examples, *leaf* and *honest*. Israel Scheffler offers this kind of rigorous ontology in Israel Scheffler (1979) *Beyond the Letter: A Philosophical Inquiry into Ambiguity, Vagueness, and Metaphor*, Boston, MA: Routledge & Kegan Paul. John Wisdom also considers whether deduction always presupposes 'case by case' reasoning that is, according to my Logocratic account, paradigmatic of analogical argument. See John Wisdom (1991) *Proof and Explanation: The Virginia Letters* 49, Lanham, MD: University Press of America ('The deductive proof of C from P is no more than a case-by-case proof of C.').

[21] Here I extend Brian Skyrms (2000) *Choice and Chance: An Introduction to Inductive Logic*, 4th edn, Australia: Thomson Learning, 15: 'Logic is the study of the strength of the evidential link between the premises and conclusions of arguments.'

B. The Asserted-Support Conception of Argument and Definition of 'Argument' as Dyadic Relation

The basic subject matter of Logocratic theory is arguments, where *argument* is defined as *a set of premises, E, that is or could be offered to provide support for a set of conclusions, H*. Put in formal terms, an argument is a *dyadic relation* between two types of sets of propositions. One set is called *premises*, the other set is called *conclusions*, and the relation is identified by this phrase: *is or could be offered to provide support for.*

This definition reflects LM's reliance on an *asserted-support conception of argument*, according to which the identity criteria of argument are whether a given set of premises is or could be offered to support a given set of conclusions.[22] This is a permissive standard, since in principle any set of premises could be offered (by someone or other) to support any set of conclusions. The work of *evaluating* the support that a given set of premises provides for a given set of conclusions is conducted at a later stage of Logocratic analysis, using a framework of 'virtues' (see section III.E).

C. Argument, Evidence and Mode of Logical Inference

Building on this evidential conception of logic, Logocratic theory conceives of an argument's premises as providing evidence for its conclusions and defines an argument's *mode of logical inference* as *the evidential relation between the argument's premises and its conclusion.* Logocratic theory says that, by definition, the set of premises, *E*, provides *evidence* for and is claimed, or can be taken to claim, to provide support for the set of conclusions, *H*.

[22] This is in contrast to an *actual-support* conception of argument, which would build into the identity criteria of an argument a requirement that the support be good or adequate. Asserted-support conceptions of argument are perhaps most common, and surely seem most explanatorily fruitful. See, eg, Trudy Govier (2014) *A Practical Study of Argument*, Boston, MA: Cengage Learning, 1 ('An argument is a set of claims in which one or more of them – the premises – *are put forward* so as to offer reasons for another claim, the conclusion.') (emphasis added); Skyrms (n 21) 13 ('An argument is a list of statements, one of which *is designated* as the conclusion and the rest of which are designated as premises.') (emphasis added). The Logocratic conception slightly broadens the scope of these versions of asserted-support conceptions to include the modality that the premise 'could be' offered to support. LM also completes the explanatory circle of concepts of evidence and argument (evidence is a type of argument, and argument is a type of evidence), and accordingly endorses an asserted-support conception of evidence as well as an asserted-support conception of argument. *Actual-support* conceptions of evidence are easier to find than are actual-support conceptions of argument but are explanatorily inferior to asserted-support conceptions of evidence. Actual-support conceptions of *evidence* disusefully conflate the concepts of *evidence* and *good evidence*, while actual-support conceptions of *argument* disusefully conflate the concepts of *argument* and *good argument*. LM also uses the concept of the *virtues* of arguments to provide an analysis of two of the most important ways in which arguments and evidence can be 'good'. See section III.E.

The Logocratic Method fashions and endorses a conception of *evidence as argument*, according to which evidence is any factual proposition (including but not limited to factual propositions regarding some action, event, object, mental state or proposition) that a person does or could assert as the basis for inferring a proposition about some action, event, object, mental state or proposition (including, in principle, the same thing – that is, something can in principle be evidence for itself). Without loss of explanatory power, other conceptions of evidence in law, philosophy and everyday life can be recast in terms of evidence as argument. For many conceptions of evidence, this recasting will actually enhance explanatory power.

The conceptual relation between evidence and argument is central to LM's explanation of the four distinct modes of logical inference. What differs among the four modes is well described, perhaps even best described, as a distinction in the *types of evidential support* that the premises of the different modes of inference provide for their conclusions. Terminologically, this account provides us with a way to express these distinctive types of argumental-evidential support as follows: the set of premises of a deductive argument provides *deductive* evidence for the set of propositions in its conclusion; the set of premises of an inductive argument provides *inductive evidence* for the set of propositions in its conclusion; the set of premises of an analogical argument provides *analogical evidence* for the set of propositions in its conclusion; and the set of premises of an abductive argument provides *abductive evidence* for the set of propositions in its conclusion.

D. The Centrality of the Enthymeme and its Fair Formal Representation

The Logocratic Method articulates a conception of the *enthymeme* that is central to Logocratic explanation of the identity criteria of arguments and their interaction. On the Logocratic conception, an enthymeme is any rule (*rule-enthymeme*) or argument (*argument-enthymeme*) whose logical form is not explicit in its original mode of presentation – in the domain of legal argument, for example: a judicial opinion, a lawyer's brief, a regulation or a statute.[23] This is a deliberated extension and modification of the classical conception of the enthymeme, often (mis)attributed to Aristotle, of the enthymeme as a syllogism in which one of the three steps is not expressly stated.[24]

[23] I first articulated the extended concept of the enthymeme in Brewer (n 12) 984.

[24] There are, to my mind, cogent arguments that the strong tendency among logic textbooks to explicate the enthymeme as a syllogism with a missing or 'suppressed' step is historically misguided in its reliance on Aristotle's conception of the enthymeme in *The Rhetoric*. See Brewer (n 12) 984, fn 184; and Myles Burnyeat (1994) 'Enthymeme: Aristotle on the Logic of Persuasion' in *Aristotle's 'Rhetoric': Philosophical Essays*, eds David J Furley and Alexander Nehamas, Princeton, NJ: Princeton University Press, 3–56, 3.

To illustrate these basic ideas, consider a 'Common Law Family' in which Mom is an authorised law-promulgator and interpreter and Jane is subject to Mom's laws. Suppose Mom says to Jane:

(1) 'On a weeknight, you can watch TV only when you've done all your homework, and you haven't tonight. No TV!'

Is there a *rule* in what Mom has said? Has she offered an *argument* based on that rule? Recall (section III.B) that an *argument* is a set of propositions some of which, premises, are or could be offered to support members of another set of propositions, namely, conclusions. If (1) is an argument, what is the set of premises and what is the set of conclusions? (Note that a set may have only one member.) This is an *interpretive* decision. If one does explain Mom's behaviour as a speech act of *argument*, what is its mode of logical inference? That is, is it *fairly represented, as a matter of interpretation*, as a deductive, or as an inductive, or as an abductive, or as an analogical argument? And if, as a matter of interpretation, one decides that it has one of these modes of inference, does it have those distinctive characteristics (distinctive of deduction, or of induction, or of abduction, or of analogy) that make it a good argument of its kind? For example, if one interprets (1) as a deductive argument, does it have the *characteristic virtue* (see section III.E.ii.b) of a deductive argument, namely, validity?[25]

Note that if one takes Mom's utterance in (1) to be an argument, it is an *argument-enthymeme*, that is, its mode of logical inference (its status as a deduction, or an induction, or an abduction, or an analogical argument) is not explicit in the mode of presentation of the utterance. We may give a fair formal representation of the argument-enthymeme, that is 'argufy' it,[26] by identifying ε_1 and ε_2 as the set of premises containing two elements, and h as the unit set comprising the conclusion:

ε_1 For all weeknights, if Jane has permission to watch TV then Jane has done all of her homework.

ε_2 On this weeknight, Jane has not done all of her homework.

h On this weeknight, it is not the case that Jane has permission to watch TV.

This argument, as interpreted and represented above, is both deductive and valid.[27] Note that the first premise is a *rule* for the circumstances under which Jane may watch TV, so this 'argufication' of the argument-enthymeme contains

[25] An argument is *valid* when in any possible set of circumstances in which all its premises are true, the conclusion is also true.

[26] In Logocratic terms, to give a fair formal representation of an argument-enthymeme is to *argufy* it, and to give a fair formal representation of a rule-enthymeme is to *rulify* it.

[27] Construed thus, her argument-enthymeme becomes an instantiation (here using the grammar of propositional logic, without the further complexities of either predicate or deontic logics) of *modus tollens*, the pattern of argument that corresponds to the tautologous conditional proposition $(P \supset Q) \wedge {\sim}Q) \supset {\sim}P$. For discussion of using non-deontic logical grammars to represent

a 'rulification' of a rule-enthymeme, namely, Mom's utterance 'On a weeknight, you may watch TV only when you've done all your homework.'

i. Enthymemicity and the Surface Structure-Deep Structure Distinction

The basic idea of the Logocratic conception of the enthymeme is familiar to theorists of argument, as well as to philosophers of language and linguistics who rely on a distinction of 'deep structure' from 'surface structure' of language.[28] Consider, for example, this statement in *Dougherty*, in which Cardozo states the main rule of consideration on which he relies (quoting and citing a US Supreme Court opinion and citing additional sources as well):

(1) '"Nothing is consideration that is not regarded as such by both parties."'[29]

This is a rule-enthymeme. By the definition offered above, it is a rule whose logical form is not explicit in its original mode of presentation – that mode being, in this case, the text of Cardozo's opinion for the Court. All rules have the deep logical structure of conditional, that is, an 'if … then' structure.[30]

natural-language concepts of permission, requirement and prohibition, see Brewer (forthcoming) (n 11) section 5.45, fn 64.

[28] See Alexandro Lenci and Gabriel Sandu (2009) 'Logic and Linguistics in the Twentieth Century' in *The Development of Modern Logic*, ed Leila Haaparanta, New York: Oxford University Press, 775–847, 810: 'The idea that the logical form of sentences differs from their surface structure is a leitmotif in twentieth-century logic and analytic philosophy.' A classic example of this distinction, outside of and preceding structuralist linguistics, is Russell's analysis of definite descriptions in Bertrand Russell (1905) 'On Denoting' *Mind* 14: 479–93. See n 30.

[29] See *Dougherty* (n 1) 95 (citing *Philpot v Gruninger*, 81 US 570, 577; *Fire Ins Ass'n v Wickham*, 141 US 564, 579 (1891); *Wisconsin & M Ry Co v Powers*, 191 US 379, 386, (1903); *De Cicco v Schweizer*, 221 NY 431, 438 (1917)).

[30] Going further, according to Logocratic theory, not just rules but all norms have the *deep structure* logical form of conditionals and are explained by the concept of the enthymeme. Norms that are hypothetical imperatives are obviously both rules and have a conditional form. One can model both norms of practical reasoning and norms of theoretical reasoning in this way. How does one handle norms that may not seem to have a conditional structure, like those in the Old Testamentary Ten Commandments ('Thou shalt not steal', etc), or those in HLA Hart's 'primary rules of obligation' ('Don't murder')? For these, Logocratic theory deploys the distinction of surface structure from deep structure to explain that a norm may have a surface structure, indicated by grammar (such as the person, number, tense, mood and voice of a verb) and a deep structure, which is (or should be) its fair formal representation in a chosen logical grammar, such as, for deductive representations, the grammar of propositional or predicate, or modal or deontic logic. Applying the Logocratic model to Russell's well-known example, the surface grammar of the sentence *The present king of France is bald* is an indicative, and the fair formal representation of its deep structure, where 'P' is the unary predicate *the present king of France* and 'B' is the unary predicate *is bald* is: $(\exists x)\ (Px\ \&\ (y)\ (Py \supset y = x)\ \&\ Bx))$. Similarly, in Logocratic terms, the command (a type of norm) 'Don't steal' is a rule-enthymeme whose surface grammatical structure is an imperative and whose deep logical structure, that is, whose *fair formal representation*, is a type of deontic conditional, **If** *you are doing what you ought* [or, *If you are doing what you must*] **then** *you will not steal*. In Leibniz's terms – Leibniz being one of the founders of formal deontic logic, *If you are doing as a good man would do, then you will not steal*. See Leibniz's 1671 letter to Arnauld, quoted and discussed in Alberto Artosi and Giovanni Sartor (2018) 'Leibniz as Jurist' in *The Oxford Handbook of Leibniz*, ed Maria Rosa Antognazza, Oxford: Oxford University Press ('That is permissible (*licitum*) which is possible for a

But many rules articulated in ordinary language have a surface structure that is not conditional. The rule for consideration that Cardozo asserts does not have an explicit conditional structure. Its surface structure has the grammatical form of an indicative, 'Nothing is X that is not Y'. But *fairly formally represented*, its structure is the conditional that, in the grammar of predicate logic, is:

> (1') *If* something is consideration *then* it is regarded as consideration by both parties.[31]

E. The Explanatory Role of Virtue

Logocratic theory relies extensively on a conception of virtue, harking back to Aristotle's conception but also departing from it in significant ways.

i. (Non-Moral) Virtue as Functional Excellence

In Logocratic theory, the term *virtue* means *functional excellence*. The basic framework used here is found in Aristotle's conception of arete (Greek, ἀρετή), translated as *virtue* or *excellence*. If some object x is an F, then the virtue of x as an F is that characteristic of x that makes x a good F. Put concisely: an object x's virtue reflects its good performance of the function of Fs. For example, consider an object (x) that is a hammer (F). The virtues of a hammer are those features

good man. That is duty (*debitum*) which is necessary for a good man.'). Similarly, Hohfeld, another deontic pioneer, relied on a surface structure-deep structure distinction in his analysis of lawyers' and judges' talk of 'rights' (surface structure) in terms of Hohfeldian 'correlative' and 'opposite' relations, which, to my present point, are (as properly understood) articulated as conditionals, such as *person A has a claim right against person B if and only if person B has a duty to person A*. For comparison of Hohfeldian and Logocratic analysis of legal arguments, see Brewer (n 11). According to Cardozo's argument in *Dougherty*, for example, one might say that the boy did not have a 'right' to payment from the aunt. This would be a surface structure-level claim, and the Hohfeldian deep structure claim is that the boy did not have a claim right against the aunt. An additional nice complexity is that Hohfeld presented his original articulation of the deep logical structure of rights not in formal language but in the natural language of English, so that his articulation of the deep structure is itself enthymematic, receiving many, sometimes competing, formal interpretations from later deontic logicians following and developing Hohfeld's ideas. See discussion Brewer (n 11).

[31] Where the unary predicate C is *is consideration* and the unary predicate *R* is *is regarded as consideration by both parties*, in symbolic terms one may represent the deep logical structure of (1) as:

> (1'') $(x)\ (Cx \supset Rx)$.

At the deep structure level, this is logically equivalent to:

> (1''') $\sim (\exists x)(Cx\ \&\ {\sim}Rx)$.

> [There does not exist anything that is consideration and is not regarded as consideration by both parties.]

The expression (1''') is not conditional, but I rely on the claim that anything that is logically equivalent to a conditional at the level of deep structure is fairly formally representable, 'deeply', as a conditional.

that make it a good hammer, such as having a 'face' (the part of the hammer that strikes the types of objects the hammer is intended to strike) of appropriate diameter, or having the hammer head be made of appropriate material. We say 'appropriate', because, for example, as one can see on quick reflection, the virtue of a claw hammer used to strike ¾ inch diameter steel nails differs from that of a rubber mallet used to force plasterboard into place without damaging it. (Yet other types of hammers are distinguished by their use as *philosophical* tools.[32])

Many and varied kinds of things can be 'bearers' of virtue, that is, can properly be said to be virtuous (or not). Among this vast array of possibly virtuous (or non-virtuous) items are: implements, such as knives, hammers and spoons; institutions, such as schools, universities, legal institutions, and doctrines that comprise the 'rule of law';[33] professionals, such as lawyers, doctors, judges and professors; and *arguments*, which are the central focus of LM. An explanatory theory (such as LM) can also have virtue in this sense, *explanatory virtues*, and LM aspires to exhibit those virtues in its explanation of the nature of argument.

ii. Two Types of Argumental Virtue: Mode-Independent and Mode-Dependent

The Logocratic Method focuses on two distinct types of virtue an argument can possess. It distinguishes them by reference to two distinct *functions* that arguments perform for arguers, which serve as the measure of an argument's virtue. Here one might just as well speak of the *purposes* or *goals* that arguers have for arguments.

As noted, the *virtue* of an argument is its functional excellence; the *vice* of an argument is its lack of functional excellence. The virtues (and vices) of arguments are tied to the function and purpose of argument as a tool. The virtue of an argument is its strength as measured by the function (goal, purpose) the arguer has for it. Arguers seek to do different kinds of things with arguments, and Logocratic theory focuses on two of these goal-purpose-functions for argument that are prevalently used by and of special interest to arguers.[34]

[32] See, eg, Friedrich Nietzsche (1889) *Götzen-Dämmerung oder Wie man mit dem Hammer philosophiert*, Leipzig: CG Naumann.

[33] See Joseph Raz (2009) *The Authority of Law: Essays on Law and Morality*, New York: Oxford University Press, 210–28.

[34] In his classic and lovely treatise by that title, Georg Henrik von Wright explores and explains the 'varieties of goodness', including virtue as a type of goodness. See Georg H von Wright (1963) *The Varieties of Goodness*, New York: Humanities Press. The Logocratic analysis of the 'goodness' of arguments, is, in von Wright's terms, an overlap of the 'instrumental goodness' of the argument-tool itself ('Instrumental goodness is mainly attributed to implements, instruments, and tools-such as knives, watches, cars, etc', ibid, 19), and the 'technical' goodness of the user of that tool, that is, the arguer ('The goodness called technical relates to ability or skill. Somebody, we say, is *good at* (doing) this or that.', ibid).

a. Mode-Independent Argumental Virtues

There are two analytically distinct mode-independent argumental virtues, but they stand in a subsumption relation. Such a relation can also be found in the logical relation of general-specific or a proper subset to its superset as, for example, the relation between the set of cats and the set of animals, or the relation of the set of regular polygons to the set of all polygons. The mode-independent argumental virtues are: *dialectical-rhetorical virtue* and *internal-inferential virtue*.[35]

1. Dialectical-Rhetorical Virtue

As measured by its goal (see section III.E.i), the dialectical-rhetorical virtue of an argument lies in its capacity to persuade the authorised referee of a given argument contest to accept an argument that the arguer-contestant submits to

[35] Explaining inferential-internal virtue as a type of dialectical-rhetorical virtue is an important change in Logocratic theory, which has previously regarded these types of virtue as analytically distinct. I cannot here discuss the reasons for the change in much detail, but the point is important (for, among other things, explaining the role of arguments in a so-called 'post-truth' world). The basic argument is as follows. Even the identification of the degree of evidential support that the premises of a given argument (more precisely, a given argument-enthymeme) provide for its conclusion is always in principle a matter of exercising *contestable* judgement from a putatively expert point of view. The evaluation of the degree of evidential support of any given argument is determined by some (putatively) expert referee of the argument or arguments in question. Hilary Putnam's emphasis on the social dimension of epistemic expertise well illustrates this important point. See Hilary Putnam (1975) *Mind, Language and Reality: Philosophical Papers*, vol 2, New York: Cambridge University Press, 215–71. Putnam argues that in linguistic communities there is a 'division of linguistic labor' between epistemic experts and epistemic non-experts in the use of natural-kind terms like *gold*, *beech* and *elm*, such that, when non-experts use these terms, they manage to refer, for example, to real gold, or to distinguish beech from elm trees, even though they do not have the epistemic expertise that would be required to make these distinctions accurately. The experts, by contrast, do have the sort of knowledge that is relevant to the accurate identification of the referents of *gold*, *beech*, *elm* and other natural-kind terms, and the rest of the community defers to them epistemically in their use of the terms. That is to say, the non-experts use natural-kind terms *to mean, in effect, whatever the experts mean by them*. Putnam's basic idea here seems correct, and importantly for my point here, extends to non-natural-kind terms, even though, one must emphasise, expertise itself – who has it, who should have it, over what domains – is deeply politically contested. See, eg, Thomas M Nichols (2017) *The Death of Expertise: The Campaign against Established Knowledge and Why It Matters*, New York: Oxford University Press. Though this issue has received a good deal of attention in recent years because of its salient role in political conflicts around the world, it seems obvious that the contestation of proper expertise is not a new cultural phenomenon. It was, for example, a central plank of Paul Feyerabend's various epistemic manifestos, culminating in his 'Dadaist' epistemology. See, eg, Paul Feyerabend (1978) *Science in a Free Society*, New York: Schocken Books, 120–21. But the fact of that contestation actually reinforces the explanatory power of Putnam's idea that communities operate with a kind of allocation of power according to some such idea, with different communities vying over who is or should be deferred to. Because of the contests of expertise, actual and potential, Putnam is right regarding the politics of argument. Thus, even establishing what counts as a valid deductive argument – for example, and more generally, establishing for any argument the degree of evidential support that the argument's premises provide for its conclusion – is a matter of persuading a dialectical-rhetorical referee, operating explicitly (as in litigation or jury panels for mathematical prizes) or implicitly.

the referee as the basis for deciding in favour of that contestant.[36] Both the existence and the measurement of this virtue depend on there being:

(a) a *contest* of arguments in some *forum* of argument;
(b) at least two *argument-contestants*, although they need not be distinct persons. The criteria for a contestant are an actual arguer or hypothetical arguer[37]

[36] LM insists on the importance of the distinction between a dialectical-rhetorical referee's *accepting an argument*, on the one hand, and *accepting the conclusion of an argument*, on the other. For an argument from premise set Φ to conclusion set θ (that is, the argument is *Φ therefore θ*), this is the difference between a referee's (intentionally) accepting θ *on the basis of* Φ and simply coming to accept θ but not necessarily for the reasons in Φ. The distinction is, for example, central to Cass Sunstein's idea of 'incompletely theorized agreement'. See Cass R Sunstein (1996) *Legal Reasoning and Political Conflict*, New York: Oxford University Press, 35–61. It is important to note that it can sometimes be much easier to determine which *arguer* wins a dialectical-rhetorical competition than it is to determine which, *if* any, of the arguer's *arguments* was responsible for the victory. Consider a thought experiment in which Arguer *A* is competing against Arguer *B* in front of dialectical-rhetorical referee *R*. *A* offers three distinct arguments for conclusion θ (each of the Φ_i is a distinct set of premises offered for the same conclusion):

Φ_1 therefore θ
Φ_2 therefore θ
Φ_3 therefore θ

and *B* offers one counterargument to each of those arguments, and *R* declares *A* to be the winner *but without stating reasons* for the declaration. In such a case we would know that arguer *A* was the winner of the dialectical-rhetorical competition, but we would not know which of the *arguments* that *A* offered for θ was the basis for the referee's decision. And in this case, we could not confidently say which of the arguments that *A* offered was the winner. Indeed, there might be reasons for a dialectical-rhetorical referee to declare *A* the winner that are wholly apart from *any* argument for θ that *A* offers, such as a bribe from *A* to the referee. We may call such a circumstance *dialectical-rhetorical-virtue opacity*. There are circumstances like this in American litigation before juries, who are dialectical-rhetorical referees (acting along with trial judges, who guide and constrain them in some ways) and who are often not required to offer reasons for their votes in favour of one or the other litigant. (Use of special verdicts can mitigate this opacity to some extent but is not a widely used procedural mechanism in American law.) Competitive elections also involve candidates who make several arguments for the conclusion (among many other conclusions) that the candidate should be elected, and when one candidate wins it can be difficult to know which of the candidate's *arguments* was responsible for a voter's vote or the voters' votes. Here, as in the case of bribing a judge, a voter might vote for a candidate partly, mostly or wholly apart from the arguments the candidate offers for his election, such as the race, gender or ethnicity of the candidate. In general, the private intentions and reasons for which a referee declares an argument to be a winner of a dialectical-rhetorical contest can be hidden, either from others or (if one believes Nietzsche and Freud, who followed Nietzsche's steps in this regard) from the referee himself. It is possible, that is, for the arguer in *bad faith* (knowingly offer a reason for declaring victory other than the real motivating reason) or *ignorant faith* (unknowingly doing so) to declare a winner of a dialectical-rhetorical argument contest. There are well-developed strains of Legal Realism and Critical Legal Studies that maintain that a great many legal arguments offered by judges are in this sense offered in bad or in ignorant faith. The LM provides an effective way to measure which *arguer* wins a contest under rules that are known, but cannot always discern which *argument* has won. Even so, sometimes a careful analysis (Logocratic and Logocratic-like) of a referee's overtly declared argument for a judgement so withers under scrutiny as to raise serious doubts about the referee's good faith. Such, for example, would be the result of Logocratic analysis of *Bush v Gore*, 531 US 98 (2000) – as it was the result of many other Logocratic-friendly analyses, see, eg, Bruce Ackerman (ed) (2002) *Bush v Gore: The Question of Legitimacy*, New Haven, CT: Yale University Press.

[37] Wayne Booth explores a phenomenon similar to that of the hypothetical arguer in his concept of the 'implied author'. See Wayne Booth (1983) *The Rhetoric of Fiction*, 2nd ed, Chicago, IL:

who is *advancing* the argument (*advancing* an argument is the speech-act of offering the premises of the argument as support for its conclusion). On this view, argumental contests are ubiquitous in the practices of both reaching judgements for oneself and articulating judgements to others. Such contests not only take place, for example, in the litigative domains familiar to jurists, but also extend to every domain of argument, including the domain of internal argument comprised of a single person's deliberatively assessing pros and cons of possible theoretical or practical judgements;[38]

(c) some *referee*, that is, a person or persons who is (are) authorised to apply rules of argument so as to declare the winner of the contest.

2. Internal-Inferential Virtue

On the Logocratic evidential conception of logic, internal-inferential virtue is explained as the *degree of evidential support* that an argument's premises provide for its conclusion(s). The greater the degree of internal-inferential support, the greater the degree of internal-inferential virtue. 'Degrees' in this sense can be explicated in at least three different ways, all pointing to the same argumental phenomenon. Degrees can be explicated in *modal* terms, where one says that if the argument's premises are true, it is not possible for the conclusion to be false. Degrees can be explicated in *epistemic* (or perhaps *psychological*) terms, where one says that if the argument's premises are true, it is not conceivable that the conclusion is false. And degrees can be explicated in *probabilistic* terms, more specifically, in terms of *conditional probability*, where one measures the degree of likelihood that the conclusion is true conditioned on the (assumed) truth of the premises.[39]

The concept of internal-inferential virtue also provides an analysis of *defeasible* arguments. Defeasible arguments are arguments in which it is possible to reduce the level of the internal-inferential support (virtue) that premise set S_1 provides for conclusion set C by adding members of an additional set, S_2 to the premises of S_1, so that the degree of support that $S_1 \cup S_2$ provides for C is lower than the degree of support that S_1 alone provides for C. For defeasible

University of Chicago Press, 73: 'Our sense of the implied author includes not only the extractable meanings but also the moral and emotional content of each bit of action and suffering of all of the characters. It includes, in short, the intuitive apprehension of a completed artistic whole; the chief value to which this implied author is committed, regardless of what party.'

[38] Two well-known examples in the domain of philosophical argumentation are Descartes' *Meditations* and Wittgenstein's *Philosophical Investigations*, works in which a single author (person) presents multiple arguers debating one another. And, of course, philosophical texts written as dialogues, as in works by Plato, Berkeley and Hume, are also examples of a debate enacted 'within' the mind of the dialogue's author.

[39] Walter Sinnott-Armstrong uses the model of conditional probability in his explication of the 'strength' of inductive generalisations in Walter Sinnott-Armstrong (2018) *Think Again: How to Reason and Argue*, Oxford: Oxford University Press (discussion 'How Strong Are You'). If I recall correctly, in conversation with me, Walter also suggested that the model of conditional probability could serve to explain the strength of arguments (in Logocratic terms) in all modes of inference, not only induction. Anyway, the model is quite usefully generalisable in this way.

arguments, there is in principle a spectrum of probabilities from 0 to something short of 100, perhaps approaching 100 asymptotically. For indefeasible arguments, the premises provide the maximal degree of support – and are thus maximally internally-inferentially virtuous – for the conclusion(s). Logocratic theory is in accord with other theories of argument in explaining that the premises of valid deductive arguments provide *indefeasible* or *incorrigible* evidential support for their conclusion; this kind of evidential support is also the condition of the entailment of the conclusion by the premises.

Logocratic theory explains the possible degrees of internal-inferential virtue thus: All valid deductions are *maximally internally-inferentially* virtuous (their premises provide incorrigible or indefeasible internal-inferential support for their conclusions) and all inductions, no matter how high the degree of internal-inferential support their premises provide for their conclusions, are *less-than-maximally internally-inferentially* virtuous (their premises provide corrigible or defeasible internal-inferential support for their conclusions). These conclusions it shares with many, perhaps most or all, other theories of argument. Unusually among theories of argument, however, Logocratic theory explains that some analogical arguments and some abductive arguments, are *maximally* internally-inferentially virtuous, while some analogical arguments and some abductive arguments are less-than-maximally internally-inferentially virtuous.[40]

b. Mode-Dependent Argumental Virtues ('Characteristic Virtues')

As defined in section III.A, an argument's mode of logical inference is the evidential relation between the set of the argument's premises and the set of the argument's conclusions. Recall also that there are four fundamental, irreducible modes of logical inference. They are distinguished from one another by the relation that obtains between the premises of the argument and its conclusion when the argument yields the most warranted inference from premises to conclusion that it is logically capable of yielding, or, to put the same point in another way, when it has the highest possible degree of internal-inferential virtue (see section III.E.ii.a.2) that an argument of its form can have.

The Logocratic Method describes this feature of arguments as *characteristic virtue*. Thus, the characteristic virtue of a deductive argument is validity, the property in which the premises provide incorrigible or indefeasible evidence (again, see section III.E.ii.a.2) for the conclusion. Put another way, the characteristic virtue of a type of argument (deductive, inductive, analogical or abductive) is that property or set of properties of that type of argument that makes it the best exemplar of that type. All four modes of logical inference are found in

[40] I offer the arguments regarding analogical arguments in Brewer (n 12) and Scott Brewer (2018) 'Indefeasible Analogical Argument' in *Analogy and Exemplary Reasoning in Legal Discourse*, eds Hendrik Kaptein and Bastiaan van der Velden, Amsterdam: Amsterdam University Press, 33–48. Regarding this point about induction, see discussion in section V.B.

legal argument and in arguments in every domain of argument. A clear understanding of the mode-specific virtues of an argument, that is, the characteristic virtues of a deductive, inductive, analogical or abductive argument, is essential to the LM as a type of philosophical abduction (specifically, explanation of the nature of argument) and to its application to assess the strengths or weaknesses (virtues or vices) of particular arguments.

It is easiest to state the characteristic, mode-dependent virtue of deduction. In a valid deductive argument, it is logically impossible that the premises should all be true while the conclusion is false. That is, the truth of the premises of a valid deductive argument provides incorrigible and indefeasible evidence for the truth of its conclusion. (See discussion in section III.E.ii.a.2.) Validity is the characteristic virtue of a deductive argument. Some arguments are deductive but lack this virtue – they are invalid – and in that way, they are vicious. Explanation (abduction) of the characteristic virtues of the other three modes, namely, induction, abduction and analogy, requires a detailed look at the structures of those arguments, which is beyond the scope of this chapter. However, I will say something about the characteristic virtues of abduction in the course of presenting the Logocratic analysis of *Dougherty*.

IV. ABDUCTION FROM A LOGOCRATIC POINT OF VIEW ('META-ABDUCTION')

A. Abduction: Goals, Purposes and Truth

The Logocratic Method offers a distinctive explanation (abduction, thus, 'meta-abduction') of abduction as a mode of logical inference.[41] The basic idea is that abduction is an inference to an explanation. Like all arguments, by definition, it is a set of propositions, called *premises*, that are or could be offered as warrant for a distinct[42] set of propositions, called *conclusions*. Theorists of argument

[41] See discussions of the Logocratic 'meta-abduction' (abduction of abduction) in Brewer (2020) (n 11) section 2.6.5; Brewer (forthcoming) (n 11) sections 5.7 through 5.11 Scott Brewer (2017a) 'Agonophobia (Fear of Contest) In the Theory of Argument?: The Case of Gary Lawson's Evidence of the Law' *Boston University Law Review* 97: 2303–19, 2316; Scott Brewer (2017b) 'Evident Virtue' in *Evidence, Cases and Materials*, 10th edn, eds Weinstein, Abrams, Brewer and Medwed, St Paul, MN: Foundation Press, 205–11; Scott Brewer (2013) 'An Essay by S Brewer: Law, Logic, and Leibniz. A Contemporary Perspective' in *Leibniz: Logico-Philosophical Puzzles in the Law*, eds Alberto Artosi, Bernardo Pieri and Giovanni Sartor, New York: Springer, 199–226, 205, 213, fn 24; Brewer (2018) (n 40) 34, fn 2 and 47; Brewer (2011) (n 9) 178. I offered precursor, 'proto-Logocratic,' explanations of abduction in, most importantly, Brewer (n 12) 978–83, sections IIC, V, IX Brewer (n 13) 1658–69, section VIE; and Brewer (n 14) 109–17.

[42] Note that in a single argument the same proposition could occur in both the set of premises and in the set of conclusions. The argument *P, therefore P*, is both deductively valid and paradigmatically both *question-begging* and *circular*. An argument is *question-begging* just when one of its conclusion-propositions Φ_i appears also as one of its premise-propositions. An argument is *circular* just when one of its premise-propositions Φ_i is offered as warrant for a conclusion-proposition θ_I and θ_i is offered as warrant for a Φ_i. An example of explanatory circularity that is particularly apt for my concerns in this chapter is from Molière's *Le Malade imaginaire*, in which a 'learned' doctor,

disagree about the proper use of the names for this type of inference. Most often it is referred to as either *abduction* or *inference to the best explanation*, and these are in turn often treated as synonyms. Charles Sanders Peirce, who perhaps most influentially called attention to this as a mode of logical inference, used different labels for it, including *abduction, retroduction* and *hypothesis*, and his own explanation of its structure varied significantly over his career.

The Logocratic Method's explanation of abduction shares with most accounts of this logical form its structure as an argument that contains three types of premises offered as support for one type of conclusion, namely, an inference to an explanation (an *explanans*) of an *articulated phenomenon* to be explained, an *explanandum*, which appears as the first premise of the argument, often in the form of one complex proposition comprised of a conjunction of component propositions. One of the ongoing debates in the literature on this logical form is whether what Peirce referred to as *abduction* is actually the same inferential process, as Gilbert Harman seems to believe it is, as what Harman christened *inference to the best explanation*.[43] There is good textual evidence that Peirce thought of abduction as only one step – roughly, the discovery step – of the full inference to the best explanation to which Harman referred.[44] The Logocratic Method has in its explication of this logical form consistently regarded abduction and inference to the best explanation as synonymous. Without overlooking Peirce's changing explanations of this form, LM accepts Harman's basic conception of the process:

> In making this inference one infers, from the fact that a certain hypothesis would explain the evidence, to the truth of that hypothesis. In general, there will be several hypotheses which might explain the evidence, so one must be able to reject all such alternative hypotheses before one is warranted in making the inference. Thus one infers, from the premise that a given hypothesis would provide a 'better' explanation for the evidence than would any other hypothesis, to the conclusion that the given hypothesis is true.[45]

The Logocratic Method differs substantially from many conceptions and discussions of this logical form in four principal ways.

in a mélange of Italian, French and Latin, offers a causal explanation (a causal abduction) according to which a potion causes sleep because it contains a 'dormitive principle' (*Vertus dormitiva*) that is, a sleep-producing principle ('Mihi a docto doctore/ Demandatur causam et rationem quare/ Opium facit dormire./ A quoi respondeo,/ Quia est in eo/ *Vertus dormitiva*/ Cujus est natura/ Sensus assoupire.'). There are interesting issues, beyond my scope here, of whether valid deductive arguments are always problematically circular in some way, as are the Humean (possibly Pyrrhonian) arguments about whether inductive inference also rest on problematically circular reasoning.

[43] See Gilbert H Harman (1965) 'The Inference to the Best Explanation' *The Philosophical Review* 74: 88–95, 88–89: '"The inference to the best explanation" corresponds approximately to what others have called "abduction" "the method of hypothesis" "hypothetic inference" "the method of elimination" "eliminative induction" and "theoretical inference". I prefer my own terminology because I believe that it avoids most of the misleading suggestions of the alternative terminologies.'

[44] The debate is presented in detail in William HB Mcauliffe (2015) 'How Did Abduction Get Confused with Inference to the Best Explanation?' *Transactions of the Charles S Peirce Society* 51: 300–19. See also Susan Haack (2014) 'Credulity and Circumspection: Epistemological Character and the Ethics of Belief' *Proceedings of the American Catholic Philosophical Association* 88: 27–47.

[45] Harman (n 43) 89.

First, taking the form to be, as Harman conceives it, an inference to an explanation that is 'best' among several possibly competing explanations of a given *explanandum*, the Logocratic (and proto-Logocratic) theory of abduction has always maintained that it is a condition of adequacy on any account of this logical form that it provide an accompanying account of what it is to *explain*. The Logocratic Method has developed and defended such an explanation – meta-explanation (explanation of explanation, or, equally from the Logocratic point of view, a meta-abduction, abduction of abduction).

Second, in an explanation (abduction) of this logical form and its related abduction of explanation that is rooted in pragmatics,[46] LM emphasises the context-dependency of abduction as a type of speech-act (namely, the speech-act of *arguing to an explanation*).

Third, one structural feature of this context-dependency is the interests and purposes an arguer has for offering an explanation, and of course those interests and purposes vary from arguer to arguer.

Fourth, *which* of the possible alternative explanations an arguer actively considers is also a function of the arguer's interests and purposes. Harman's assertion that '[i]n making this inference one infers, from the fact that a certain hypothesis would explain the evidence, to the truth of that hypothesis'[47] under-describes the reasoning process. There must be some kind of filter on the process of selecting those alternative hypotheses that are worthy of consideration – selecting, one might say, the worthy contestants of the contest for the 'bestness' of a particular explanation.[48]

A simple example comes from an exercise I have used for years in introducing audiences to the Logocratic abduction of abduction. I ask the audience to imagine that one is walking along and gets a sudden sharp pain in one's heel. I solicit answers from them to the question 'What might it be?' The answers I have received over many audiences around the world tend strongly to converge around such answers as 'a pebble in your shoe' (or some other sharp object either inside or penetrating the shoe) and 'plantar fasciitis' (or some other description of a medical condition of which an audience member happens to know). None of them suggests that it might be an invisible creature from Mars stabbing

[46] See Brewer (n 12) sections V, VI, and VIII.

[47] Harman (n 43) 89.

[48] Peirce correctly observes that 'Proposals for hypotheses inundate us in an overwhelming flood, while the process of verification to which each one must be subjected before it can count as at all an item, even of likely knowledge, is so very costly in time, energy, and money – and consequently in ideas which might have been had for that time, energy, and money, that Economy would override every other consideration even if there were any other serious considerations. In fact there are no others.' CS Peirce (1931–35) *Collected Papers of Charles Sanders Peirce*, eds C Hartshorne and P Weiss, Cambridge, MA: Harvard University Press, para 5.602. WM Brown, an astute Peirce interpreter, explains Peirce's point thus, 'As a matter of social policy, or of individual practice and personal commitment, one ought not to bother entertaining a hypothesis if the "money, time, thought, and energy" which are likely to be needed to test it, exceed that needed by any other competing hypotheses.' WM Brown (1983) 'The Economy of Peirce's Abduction' *Transactions of the Charles S Peirce Society* 19: 397–411, 401.

the walker though the shoe with a laser spear. Now, *if* it were true, the Martian spear-creature hypothesis would explain the pain, but no abductive reasoner in my audience poses anything like it. Instead, within the economy of their interests and purposes, they filter the possible explanations to those that are *sufficiently plausible for their argumental purposes*, here, the purpose of abducing an explanation for the (hypothetical) pain in the heel.

The Logocratic Method explicates this step of abduction-cum-inference to the best explanation as a norm that abductive arguers follow that directs them to consider only those alternative hypotheses that are *serviceably plausible* given their interests and purposes. This is a slight but improving and clarifying sharpening of the concept of 'plausibility' that has been central to prior Logocratic accounts of abduction.[49] It connects *the interest-and-purpose relativity of explanations* on which LM relies to the process of abduction. It also provides a criterion, surely crucial to any adequate conception of abduction, of the criteria of 'bestness', namely, best according to the abductive arguer's interests and purposes. And it also makes clear that, from a Logocratic point of view, arguments in general (including but not limited to abductive arguments) are explained not as *truth-conducive* but instead as *interest-and-purpose-advancing*. It focuses on and seeks to explain not what *is* true but rather what is *asserted to be true by means of the tools of argument*.

The Logocratic Method does not purport to offer a theory of *truth*, instead focusing, as noticed, on *truth claims* that are made and purportedly justified by argument. Nevertheless, its focus on truth claims might be mistaken for a type of idealism. It is not. It seems neither plausible nor correct to say, as some relativists, constructivists, irrealists, idealists and Pragmatists do, that descriptions of the world and phenomena in it *make* the world or its phenomena. What seems true in the claims of Irrealists & Co should be carefully separated from what seems false. What seems true is that we (humans) seem to have no access to what is true about the world apart from descriptions of the world that are asserted and defended by means of arguments – principally (*prima inter pares* among the four modes of logical inference), abductive arguments. Postulate that there is objective reality, or God, or what have you. There are always competing arguments (both actual and hypothetical) about what are the features and objects of that reality, or what are the commands of that God.

But – and here is what seems false in the position of Irrealists & Co – the argument-dependence of claims to truth (including objective truth, God's truth, gods' truths, etc) should not be mistaken for the argument-dependence of the referents of those arguments. As even the Ur-Irrealist Nelson Goodman puts this point (though not consistently across his *oeuvre*), 'A version saying that there is a star up there is not itself bright or far off, and the star is not made up of letters.'[50]

[49] See sources cited in n 41.

[50] Nelson Goodman (1984) *Of Mind and Other Matters*, Cambridge, MA: Harvard University Press, 41. Israel Scheffler, one of Goodman's most careful and sympathetic students and colleagues,

One ought not to do as do those 'philosophers [who] sometimes mistake features of discourse for features of the subject of discourse', for '[w]e seldom conclude that the world consists of words just because a true description of it does'. We also should not 'conclude that the world is made by us just because a true description of it is'.[51] It is intellectually courageous[52] to accept that we do not have the godlike power to make the world as we would like it to be and must instead find ways to play within what seem to be our limits.[53] 'In any science … the requisite objectivity forbids wishful thinking'.[54]

B. Abduction as Reasoning from a Point of View

As I have asserted, a successful meta-abduction – inference to the best explanation of inference to the best explanation – must have or rely on some cogent conception of the speech-act of explanation. Reasoners offer explanations that take different forms, such as: *why* something is what it is; or *how* something is what it is; or *how something came to be what it is* (its genealogy); or *what* something is.

According to the Logocratic account of abduction (presented in additional detail in section V), explanations are always offered from and according to the criteria of a *point of view*. One might be said literally to have a point of *view*, that is, to occupy some position in space that gives one a particular visual vantage, as in a 'bird's-eye view'. Expertise provides another type of point of view, as when an expert witness tells a jury or judge what the facts are from the point of view of a biologist, a chemist, a ballistician, a psychiatrist and so on. One might also identify an institutional or social point of view, the point of

has long argued, convincingly, that Goodman is inconsistent on this point. See, eg, Israel Scheffler (2009) *Worlds of Truth: A Philosophy of Knowledge*, Malden: Wiley-Blackwell, ch 3 and other sources cited there.

[51] Scheffler (n 50) 61 (quoting and citing Israel Scheffler (1996) 'Reply to Goodman' in *Starmaking: Realism, Anti-Realism, and Irrealism*, ed Peter J McCormick, Cambridge, MA: The MIT Press, 173 (quoting Nelson Goodman (1972) *Problems and Projects*, Indianapolis, IN: Bobbs-Merrill, 24).

[52] One of the most important aspects of the virtue I have in mind here is what Raymond Guess describes as the 'prized Nietzschean trait', *Tatsachen-Sinn*. See Raymond Guess (2005) 'Thucydides, Nietzsche, and Williams' in *Outside Ethics*, Princeton, NJ: Princeton University Press, 219–33, 220 (citations omitted): 'Nietzsche found Thucydides more illuminating about human life than Plato … Socrates, however, dragged moralizing into science, and Plato followed in his wake. Such moralizing, Nietzsche thought, was a result of weakness, of a deep-seated inability to bear looking the facts of the world in the face; it crippled Plato intellectually and prevented him from ever developing that most highly prized of Nietzschean traits: "*Tatsachen-Sinn*," a "sense for the facts," that steely realism that is so abundantly evident on every page of Thucydides.'

[53] For the conception of 'play' I have in mind, see Ian Bogost (2016) *Play Anything: The Pleasure of Limits, the Uses of Boredom, and the Secret of Games*, New York: Basic Books, x, '[T]o play [is] [t]o take something-anything on its own terms, to treat it as if its existence were reasonable …. Play, generalized, is the operation of structures constrained by limitations. Play is not an alternative to work, nor a salve for misery. Play is a way of operating a constrained system in a gratifying way.'

[54] Nelson Goodman (1968) *Languages of Art: An Approach to a Theory of Symbols*, Indianapolis, IN: Bobbs-Merrill, 251. Nevertheless, emotion is an inevitable part of the cognitive architecture of abduction. See the discussion in n 59.

view of a particular type of actor in an institutional or other social setting – the points of view, for example, of a legislator, a judge, a lawyer, a citizen, a president, a 'bad man', a parent, a child, a professor, a student.

One might also identify an 'enterprise' conception of point of view, and indeed the enterprise conception is the common thread that runs through all the notions of point of view mentioned above, both the more ordinary and the more reflectively philosophical. This point of view might even be understood as the point of view of an enterprise, an enterprise in which particular methods of analysis are chosen both to produce factual judgements and to serve specified cognitive goals. Examples of such enterprises include: systems of legal reasoning (the 'legal point of view'); systems of moral reasoning (on a cognitivist account of morality, at least, this yields the 'moral point of view'); philosophical reasoning (the 'philosophical point of view'); systems of reasoning in support of business objectives (the 'business point of view'); the 'military point of view'; the 'economic point of view'; 'the religious point of view'; 'the political point of view'; and so on for many other enterprises.

An abductive reasoner does, and must, rely on some point of view in order to *justify some explanatory claim*, a claim about either what one ought to believe (a theoretical claim) or how one ought to act (a practical claim).[55] Note that simply identifying the general point of view of an enterprise does not by itself answer the following question: What are the specific cognitive aims of the enterprise for abductive reasoners who recognise themselves as pursuing the same generic enterprise, but who often disagree about what are the proper specific aims of the enterprise? Such disagreements are a principal source (but not the only source) of the difference among theories within an enterprise. It is, for example, a source of disagreement regarding the legal point of view among legal theorists who march under banners such as 'Legal Positivism', 'Natural Law', 'Legal Realism' and 'Critical Legal Studies'. (There are also competing 'Contract-Law points of view', as I shall discuss later.[56])

Borrowing from Larry Laudan's model of scientific explanation, LM explains the enterprise conception of a point of view as a reason-giving enterprise (one that operates in what Sellars calls the 'space of reasons' as distinct from the 'space of causes'[57]) that produces three types of justificatory claims:

(a) factual judgements;
(b) the distinctive methods that the enterprise uses to generate those factual judgements (methodological rules);
(c) the distinctive axiological goals that the methods are chosen to advance and serve.

[55] Like many conceptions of Pragmatism, LM does not see a sharp separation between so-called theoretical and practical reasoning, endorsing instead the view that believing is best explained as a type of action. See n 63 and accompanying text.

[56] See nn 112 and 113 and accompanying text.

[57] See Wilfrid Sellars (1963) *Science, Perception, and Reality*, New York: Humanities Press, 169: '[I]n characterizing an episode or a state as that of knowing, we are not giving an empirical

These three elements yield a definition of *point of view* as that idea operates in the Logocratic Method:

> The *point of view* of enterprise *E* consists of the factual judgements, produced by the methodological rules, that are adopted to serve the axiological goals of *E*.

These justificatory components of a point of view operate in a *coherent* pattern of mutual support and not in a linear and foundationalist structure of justification from, say, (c) to (b) to (a).[58] To serve this justificatory function, the point of view is assumed to be a reliable method of achieving the (explicit or implicit) axiological goals of some reason-giving enterprise, an enterprise that uses the tool – sometimes, a weapon-tool – of argument.[59]

Although the Logocratic meta-abduction follows the same basic structure found in many other meta-abductions (see the discussion in section IV.C), one of the most distinctive aspects of the Logocratic account is the contention that abductive reasoners seek to use explanations as tools to serve their chosen cognitive aims-axiological goals, which, in turn, guide their choice of methods, which, in turn, produce the explanatory judgements that are the conclusions of their

description of that episode or state; we are placing it in the logical space of reasons, of justifying and being able to justify what one says.' See also John McDowell (2018) 'Sellars and the Space of Reasons' *Claves de Pensamiento Contemporaneo* 21: 1–22.

[58] In his model of scientific explanation, Laudan refers to this as a 'reticulated' structure of justification. See Larry Laudan (1984) *Science and Values: The Aims of Science and Their Role in Scientific Debate*, Berkeley, CA: University of California Press, 50–66; ibid, 63 ('No longer should we regard any one of these levels as privileged or primary or more fundamental than the others. Axiology, methodology, and factual claims are inevitably intertwined in relations of mutual dependency. The pecking order implicit in the hierarchical approach must give way to a kind of leveling principle that emphasizes the patterns of mutual dependence between these various levels.').

[59] LM recognises both 'reason' and 'emotion' as among the axiological goals that operate to guide abductions, abducing the existence and operation of *cognitive affects* among those aims. A kindred account is the discussion of 'Emotion and Cognition' in Scheffler (n 51) ch 6. See also Goodman (n 54) 251: '[I]n any science, while the requisite objectivity forbids wishful thinking, prejudicial reading of evidence, rejection of unwanted results, avoidance of ominous lines of inquiry, it does not forbid use of feeling in exploration and discovery, the impetus of inspiration and curiosity, or the cues given by excitement over intriguing problems and promising hypotheses.' Similarly, Peirce offers an abduction of *emotion as abduction*: 'Now, when our nervous system is excited in a complicated way, there being a relation between the elements of the excitation, the result is a single harmonious disturbance which I call an emotion. Thus, the various sounds made by the instruments of an orchestra strike upon the ear, and the result is a peculiar musical emotion, quite distinct from the sounds themselves. *This emotion is essentially the same thing as an hypothetic inference, and every hypothetic inference involves the formation of such an emotion.*' Charles Sanders Peirce (1931–58) *Collected Works*, Cambridge, MA: Harvard University Press, para 2.643 (emphasis added). Cognitive affects functioning as axiological goals are powerful elements of the divisive moral, political, legal and cultural abductions that drive members of politically contesting groups around the world and through history. These cognitively-affective abductions provide a crucial part of the explanation of political and cultural phenomena that currently afflict the world, such as the sometimes violent contentions over 'post-truth', 'fake news' and alleged political conspiracies, not to mention millennially deadly religious strife. See, among many sources, Amy Chua (2018) *Political Tribes: Group Instinct and the Fate of Nations*, New York: Penguin Press; Spencer Critchley (2020) *Patriots of Two Nations: Why Trump Was Inevitable and What Happens Next*, Independently Published; Thomas E Patterson (2019) *How America Lost Its Mind: The Assault on Reason That's Crippling Our Democracy*, Norman, OK: University of Oklahoma Press.

abductive arguments. Sometimes, but by no means always, do these aims include producing a factual *claim* that is true. In a nutshell, there are many instances in which an abductive arguer seeks to produce an argument for a conclusion that will be accepted by the dialectical-rhetorical referee of an abductive argument (see section III.E.ii.a.1) but whose conclusion the abductive reasoner does not himself accept or to whose truth or likely truth he is indifferent.[60] Important examples include settings of abductive argument in which the abductive reasoner offers an argument with a goal or cognitive aim other than truth-telling, such as garnering votes (LM models the dialectical-rhetorical referee of elections as the electorates to whom abductive arguments are made by the candidates regarding, for example, why the candidate or his policies are the best among those of the electoral contestants) or winning a litigative contest (LM models the dialectical-rhetorical referee of litigation as the judge or the judge along with a jury in a division of legal decision-making authority guided by rules).[61]

The cognitive aims-axiological goals of an abductive reasoner guide her decision about both *plausibly serviceable explanations* and the *most serviceable among the set of serviceably plausible explanations*. Stephen Toulmin trenchantly explains that arguments in general have an implicitly dialectical structure, that is, they exist in *competition* with other arguments, either explicitly or implicitly.[62] Put in Logocratic terms, Toulmin's insight is that all arguments, in whatever setting (law, politics, mathematics, philosophy, *la vie quotidienne*) are parts of a *contest of arguments* before some dialectical-rhetorical referee. Sometimes that

[60] In such circumstances: (i) the reasoner violates Grice's maxim of 'quality', namely, that one ought in conversation (including argumental conversation) not to say that which one knows to be false or for which one lacks adequate evidence. See HP Grice (1975) 'Logic and Conversation' in *Syntax and Semantics 3: Speech Acts*, eds Jerry L Morgan, Peter Cole and Paul Grice, New York: Academic Press, 41–58; (ii) the abductive reasoner engages in what Harry Frankfurt calls 'bullshit', namely, a speech act in which the utterer is indifferent to the truth or falsity of an utterance (including an argumental utterance). See Harry Frankfurt (2005) *On Bullshit*, Princeton, NY: Princeton University Press.

[61] In an account of abduction that has both many similarities and some very substantial differences (including, unlike the Logocratic Method, *not* regarding all abductions as inferences to explanations), Gabbay and Woods come close to recognising the abductive phenomenon that Logocratic theory identifies in their discussion of 'Non-Plausibilistic Abduction'. See Gabbay and Woods (n 11) ch 5; ibid, 115 ('A … distinction … of great salience to abductive logic … is that between abductions that advance prepositionally plausible hypotheses and those that advance prepositionally implausible hypotheses.'). LM's explanation of the role of plausibility obviously differs somewhat. In Logocratic terms, it may suit the explanatory goals of an abductive reasoner to offer (endorse) an explanation that some members of the intended audience might regard, at least prima facie, as implausible. In such a case, on the Logocratic model of abduction these explanations would be *plausibly serviceable* for that reasoner.

[62] See Stephen E Toulmin (2003) *The Uses of Argument*, New York: Cambridge University Press, 7–8: 'There is one special virtue in the parallel between logic and jurisprudence: it helps to keep in the centre of the picture the critical function of the reason. … A sound argument, a well-grounded or firmly-backed claim, is one which will stand up to criticism, one for which a case can be presented coming up to the standard required if it is to deserve a favourable verdict. How many legal terms find a natural extension here! One may even be tempted to say that our extra-legal claims have to be justified, not before Her Majesty's Judges, but before the Court of Reason.'

referee, who declares the winner of the competition, is external to the arguer (as with juries and judges and electorates and professional colleagues in a self-identified discipline), and sometimes that referee is the arguer herself (as in deliberating about a course of action, including the *action* of accepting a proposition as true[63]). Enthusiastically motivated by this understanding of the pragmatics of arguments, LM recognises that one of the most important aspects of the *serviceability* of arguments in abduction is *anticipating arguments that compete with those that the arguer might prefer to be the winner of competition.* This is why Toulmin's insight so appropriately draws on the comparison of argument in general to legal argument in particular, where elementary legal pedagogy in a contestatory litigative system (such as the Anglo-American 'adversarial' system) teaches that a lawyer favouring one side of a litigation (his client) is well-advised to anticipate and counter a competitor's arguments that the judge or the judge and jury, acting as dialectical-rhetorical referees, might find persuasive.

C. The Abstract Structure of Abduction

A good many expositions of abduction, which follow Harman's reconstrual of abduction as *inference to the best explanation* (in contrast to one of Peirce's conceptions of the abduction involving only the inference process concerned in generating possible plausible explanations), present abduction as a four-step argument to one explanation that is superior to all other plausible explanations. An example is this presentation from two leading theorists of abduction:

> We take abduction to be a distinctive kind of inference that follows this pattern pretty nearly:
>
> *D* is a collection of data (facts, observations, givens).
> *H* explains *D* (would, if true, explain *D*).
> No other hypothesis can explain *D* as well as *H* does.
> Therefore, *H* is probably true.[64]

With some very important differences (including one addition) to be discussed presently (pages 309–10), the Logocratic exposition of abduction has also long endorsed this pattern of abduction as a four-step inference from the statement of some phenomenon to be explained to the conclusion stating the best

[63] Writing in a Pragmatist tradition, Israel Scheffler puts the point well and concisely: '[A] … pervasive parallel unites the realms of cognition and action. Cognition is a kind of action, and justifiability applies to the one as it does to the other.' Scheffler (n 50) 119.

[64] John R Josephson and Susan G Josephson (1994) *Abductive Inference: Computation, Philosophy, Technology*, New York: Cambridge University Press, 5 (in turn attributing this model to William Lycan).

explanation of that phenomenon.[65] The Logocratic version of the model, at this level of abstraction and with symbolic abbreviations,[66] is as follows:

Premise ε_1 — Θ [some phenomenon to be explained, the *explanandum*]

Premise(s) ε_{2n-m} — For each candidate Φ_i, '$\Phi_i \surd \rightarrow \Theta$' is true.

['$\Phi_i \surd \rightarrow \Theta$' is the *plausibly serviceable explanation conditional*, read as 'if explanans Φ_i were true or otherwise warranted, it would provide a *plausibly serviceable explanation* of Θ.']

Premises ε_3 and ε_4 — For candidate Φ_n, '$\Phi_n \surd\surd \rightarrow \Theta$' is true.

['$\Phi_n \surd\surd \rightarrow \Theta$' is the *most serviceable explanation conditional*, that is, the one member of the set of proposed explanations that, in the abductive reasoner's judgement, is the *most serviceable among the set of plausibly serviceable explanations*. This step is constituted by the disconfirmation of all of those plausibly serviceable explanations identified in the articulation of Premise(s) ε_{2n-m} until one, Φ_n is 'left standing' to be endorsed as *the most* serviceable explanation. The Logocratic explanation of abduction, like the accounts that regard abduction as inference to a single best explanation among those that are plausible, regards all abductions as instances of what some philosophers refer to as *contrastive inferences*.[67]]

Conclusion h — Φ_n

[Φ_n is the explanation identified in step ε_3 that is settled on as *the* explanation, the *explanans* of the explanandum.]

Two points about these two types of conditional are important for the Logocratic explanation of the identity criteria of argument. First, neither type

[65] See sources cited in n 41.

[66] One finds in the literature a variety of formalisations of abduction. See, eg, Gabbay and Wood (n 11); Aliseda (n 11).

[67] Possible explanatory coherence between the literatures of contrastive inference, on the one hand, and formal and informal logic, on the other, is interesting and worth more discussion than is within the scope of this chapter. Walter Sinnott-Armstrong provides a clear and cogent overview of (in Logocratic terms) the abductive utility of contrastive explanations in several domains of philosophical inquiry. See Walter Sinnott-Armstrong (2008) 'A Contrastivist Manifesto' *Social Epistemology* 22: 257–70 (2008). See also Anjan Chakravartty (2010) 'Perspectivism, Inconsistent Models, and Contrastive Explanation' *Studies in History and Philosophy of Science* 41: 405–12.

of conditional is fairly formally represented as a *material* conditional.[68] Instead, in Logocratic theory, the meaning of these conditionals is given by the role of generating an explanation from a specified point of view (see section IV.B). The explanatory conditionals in abduction, on the Logocratic account (as in some other accounts of abduction), are subjunctive conditionals to the effect '*If this were* the explanation, *then that would explain* …'.[69]

Second, while the model of abduction as a four-step inference, which many prior statements of the Logocratic account of abduction share with many other accounts,[70] is not incorrect, it is importantly incomplete – incomplete, indeed, in a way that numerous examples of legal abduction, including *Dougherty*, make quite clear. The four-step model does not make explicit the fact that there is a structure reasoning process *within* the final three steps of an abduction, that is, in the transition from those premises coming after the first premise, which state the phenomenon to be explained, leading to the conclusion. As I will illustrate below with *Dougherty*, a more fully explicit model of abduction represents it not in four steps but in five steps (in this articulation of the fuller model, I embolden the step that supplements the model offered above):

Step 1: Premise ε_1	Θ
	[statement of the *explanandum*]
Step 2: Premise(s) $\varepsilon_{2n-(n-1)}$	For each candidate Φ_i, '$\Phi_i \surd \rightarrow \Theta$' is true.
	[statement of 1-(n-1) plausibly serviceable explanation conditionals, *If Φ_i were true or otherwise warranted, then Φ_i would serviceably plausibly explain θ*]

[68] The material conditional symbolized by '⊃' (or, often instead by '→') is the truth-functional relation such that, for any two propositions Φ and θ, $\Phi \supset \theta$ is true if and only if θ is true or Φ is false, that is, for the arguments (in the sense of inputs to a truth-function) <T,T>, <F,T>,<F,F>. This standard interpretation of the material conditional makes the conditional proposition true whenever the antecedent is false, which yields the so-called 'paradox of material implication' (eg, both propositions, *If the Nazis won World War II then everyone would be happy* and *If the Nazis won World War II then everyone would be unhappy* are true on the material implication construal of the conditional). Despite these paradoxes, there is a deep utility to using material implication to represent conditionals in natural language, including legal language, instead of, for example, causal conditionals (*If it rains the sidewalk gets wet*), strict conditionals (*If Sam is a bachelor then Sam is an unmarried adult male*) and stochastic conditionals (*If there are six dinner places set then six people are expected for dinner*). A nice discussion of that utility is Raymond Bradley and Norman Swartz (1979) *Possible Worlds: An Introduction to Logic and its Philosophy*, Oxford: Blackwell, 266–67. Nelson Goodman's original identification and articulation of what John Rawls (borrowing from Goodman) later called *reflective equilibrium* concerned the justification of rules of inference. Goodman's profound insight applies to the choice to interpret natural language conditionals as material implications. See Nelson Goodman (1983) *Fact, Fiction, and Forecast*, 4th edn, Cambridge, MA: Harvard University Press, 62 (original emphasis): 'The point is that rules and particular inferences alike are justified by being brought into agreement with each other. *A rule is amended if it yields an inference we are unwilling to accept; an inference is rejected if it violates a rule we are unwilling to amend.*'

[69] See, eg, the discussion of 'Subjunctive explanationism' in Gabbay and Wood (n 11).

[70] See n 64 and accompanying text.

Step 3: Premise(s) $\varepsilon_{3n-(n-1)}$ **Each candidate Φ_i in $\Phi_1 \ldots \Phi_{(n-1)}$ is *disconfirmed.***

[statement that each Φ_i of $\Phi_1 \ldots \Phi_{n-1}$ of the plausibly serviceable explanation conditionals is false or otherwise not warranted *as* the explanation of the *explanandum*]

Step 4: Premise ε_3 For candidate Φ_n, 'Φ_n $\surd\surd \rightarrow \Theta$' is true.

[statement that Φ_n of the plausibly serviceable explanation conditionals is *the most serviceable* explanation of the *explanandum* among those that are considered]

Step 5: Conclusion h Φ_n

[assertion of Φ_n as *the* explanation offered by the argument]

Note that there is an *internal structure* involved in moving from Steps 2 to 5. Using the grammar of propositional logic, where each proposition Ψ_i stating a plausibly serviceable explanation conditional is $\Psi_1, \Psi_2, \Psi_3 \ldots \Psi_{n-1}, \Psi_n$, we may model that internal structure as:

$\Psi_1 \vee \Psi_2 \vee \Psi_3 \vee \ldots \Psi_{n-1} \vee \Psi_n$

$\sim \Psi_1$

$\sim \Psi_2$

$\sim \Psi_3$

.

.

.

$\sim \Psi_{n-1}$

$\therefore$

Ψ_n

Table 13.1 (page 311) sets out a tabular version of this inference pattern, which reveals the internal structure of the steps that comprise the second, third and fourth steps of an abductive argument. It is done in that table for an abduction that considers a total of five plausibly serviceable explanations. The number of plausibly serviceable explanations obviously will vary from context to context; sometimes there is only one, which then by default serves as *the most* plausibly serviceable explanation. The table models a process in which the reasoner considers five explanations in total, rejects four and concludes that one is the most serviceable.

Table 13.1 The Logocratic 5-Step Model of Abduction

Step of abduction	**Proposition type and number**	**Description**	**Abstract expression of proposition**
Step 1 Statement of the *explanandum*	Premise ε_1	**Explanandum: Statement of conjunction of material facts**	θ
Step 2 A set of five premises comprise Step 2. Each premise in this set asserts that the explanation mentioned in the premise would serviceably plausibly explain the *explanandum*	Premise $\varepsilon_{2\text{-}1}$	**Serviceably plausible explanation conditional #1**	$\Phi_1 \surd \rightarrow \Theta$
	Premise $\varepsilon_{2\text{-}2}$	**Serviceably plausible explanation conditional #2**	$\Phi_2 \surd \rightarrow \Theta$
	Premise $\varepsilon_{2\text{-}3}$	**Serviceably plausible explanation conditional #3**	$\Phi_3 \surd \rightarrow \Theta$
	Premise $\varepsilon_{2\text{-}4}$	**Serviceably plausible explanation conditional #4**	$\Phi_4 \surd \rightarrow \Theta$
	Premise $\varepsilon_{2\text{-}5}$	**Serviceably plausible explanation conditional #5**	$\Phi_5 \surd \rightarrow \Theta$
Step 3 Assertion that each of these, despite its capacity serviceably to explain the *explanandum*, is disconfirmed as the most serviceable explanation	Premise $\varepsilon_{3\text{-}1}$	**Disconfirmation of serviceably plausible explanation conditional #1**	$\sim \Phi_1$
	Premise $\varepsilon_{3\text{-}2}$	**Disconfirmation of serviceably plausible explanation conditional #2**	$\sim \Phi_2$
	Premise $\varepsilon_{3\text{-}3}$	**Disconfirmation of serviceably plausible explanation conditional #3**	$\sim \Phi_3$
	Premise $\varepsilon_{3\text{-}4}$	**Disconfirmation of serviceably plausible explanation conditional #4**	$\sim \Phi_4$
Step 4 Asserted confirmation of the one *most* serviceably plausible explanation – compare hypothetical syllogism (see page 310 and n 72)	Premise ε_4	**Confirmation of serviceably plausible explanation conditional #5**	$\Phi_5 \surd\surd \rightarrow \Theta$
Step 5 Conclusion, assertion that the most serviceably plausible explanation is the actual explanation of the explanandum	Conclusion h	**Assertion of serviceably plausible explanation conditional #5 as *the most serviceably plausible explanation***	Φ_5

It is worth pausing a moment to discuss why the LM presents this as a five-step model, when other models present it as a four-step model.[71] The short answer is that the five-step model explains a greater variety of abductions, because there is behavioural variety among abductive reasoners. In some abductions, a reasoner will offer additional reasons to support the explanation that is chosen as most serviceable, and do so as a step separate from arguing for the rejection of the alternative he considers. In these abductions, the argument-enthymeme is fairly formally represented with a distinct set of premises for Steps 4 and 5. In other abductions, a reasoner will not offer additional reasons to support the explanation that is chosen as most serviceable and instead will rely on the disconfirmation of each rival explanation *as* support for the ultimately chosen explanation. This model has a structure similar to that of the deductive *disjunctive syllogism* – although, importantly, it is not to be understood as inherently deductive in form.[72] In these abductions, there is effectively no difference between Steps 4 and 5, but it seems best even so to regard abduction as a five-step inference process in which Step 4 offers no additional reasons for endorsing the explanation.

I have just asserted that, for abductive argument-enthymemes in which Steps 4 and 5 are explicitly distinct, the pattern is similar to that of the deductive disjunctive syllogism. The Logocratic Method also maintains, however, that this abductive pattern is *not* to be understood as inherently deductive in form. There are several reasons for this interpretive decision. One is that such a construal would attribute question-begging arguments to abductive reasoners in a way that seems inconsistent with a compelling principle of interpretive charity.[73]

[71] See, eg, the model offered by Josephson and Josephson (n 64) and accompanying text.

[72] For discussion of the form of the deductive hypothetical syllogism, see Bangs Tapscott (1976) *Elementary Applied Symbolic Logic*, Englewood Cliffs, NJ: Prentice-Hall, 384. Tapscott refers to various names in the logic literature for the inference

p v q
~p
∴ q

– namely, *cancellation disjunctive syllogism*, *modus tollendo ponens*, *V-elimination*, *elimination of alternate*, *denying one alternant*. I offer reasons for not construing abduction as a version of hypothetical syllogism, see n 73 below and accompanying text.

[73] Note that, interpreted as a deductive inference,

p v q
~p
q
∴ q

– although deductively valid, would also be paradigmatically question-begging. A properly charitable interpretation of abductions in natural language should avoid it. (See section V.A for a discussion of the Logocratic version of the principle of interpretive charity.) The domain of argument theory here is what I have called 'structural enthymemicity'. See Brewer (n 12) 985: 'The theorist of informal (including legal) argument must reconstruct enthymematic arguments in order to explain, from a theoretical point of view, what logical form they have in general – deductive, inductive, analogical (exemplary), or abductive. That is, what is not perspicuous in the manner of presentation of an informal argument, and what therefore calls for theoretical explication, is its logical type (inductive,

Another is that, according to Logocratic theory, two kinds of inference operate *within* abduction (and this point is central to my main thesis in this chapter): one kind is evaluable as a deductive inference, as is the true disjunctive syllogism; the other is evaluable as an inductive inference, that is, as defeasible *modus tollens*. This is a crucial aspect of Logocratic theory, and one that sharply separates its meta-abduction (its explanation of the nature of abduction). On the Logocratic account of abduction, in some contexts, such as abduction in mathematics and logic, the premises of abductive arguments provide *indefeasible evidence* (see section III.A) for their conclusions.[74] In other contexts, such as empirical abductions, the premises of abductive arguments provide *defeasible evidence* for their conclusions. I return to this important point later,[75] and it is vital for understanding the Logocratic analysis of the identity criteria of arguments, as illustrated by the Logocratic analysis of legal abduction in *Dougherty*, to which I now (re)turn.

V. INTERPRETIVE ABDUCTION FROM A LOGOCRATIC POINT OF VIEW

A. The Structure of Interpretive Abduction

The Logocratic model of abduction presented in section IV.B illustrated how explanations have a three-part structure, operating in the space of reasons, which produces three types of justificatory claims:

(a) factual judgements;
(b) the distinctive methods that the enterprise uses to generate those factual judgements (methodological rules);
(c) the distinctive axiological goals that the methods are chosen to advance and serve.

From a Logocratic point of view, interpretation is a type of abduction, which for obvious reasons is called *interpretive abduction*. Much more can fruitfully be said about this form of abduction than I can say within the scope of this chapter. Even so, I can here sketch the basic elements and note that *interpretive* abduction is not only an essential part of *legal* abduction but also figures pervasively in the everyday production and consumption of spoken and written language.

On this view, interpretation is a dyadic (that is, two-place) relation between a text being interpreted (an *interpretandum*) and a text doing the interpretation

deductive, etc). We may call this type of nonperspicuity "structural enthymemicity."' My point here is that we should not construe the abductive structural enthymeme as containing a question-begging deductive inference.

[74] See, eg, G Polya (1954) *Mathematics and Plausible Reasoning*, vol I: *Induction and Analogy in Mathematics*, Princeton, NJ: Princeton University Press; G Polya (1968) *Mathematics and Plausible Reasoning*, vol II: *Patterns of Plausible Inference*, Princeton, NJ: Princeton University Press. Polya does not refer to abduction using that term, but, according to the Logocratic explication of abduction, he is clearly presenting examples of abduction in mathematics.

[75] See section VI.B.ii.b and n 104.

(an *interpretans*). The predicate for the relation is the dyadic relation *is the meaning of*. To take a simple example, if the *interpretandum* is

(1) Juliet is the sun

as it occurs in Shakespeare's play, we might offer (2) as the *interpretans*

(2) Juliet radiates Romeo's life

– where our justificatory claim in offering (2) *as the interpretation* of (1) is that (2) *is the meaning of* (1). In the Logocratic model of explanation, the *interpretandum* is the *explanandum*, and the *interpretans* is the *explanans*.[76]

On this Logocratic model of interpretive abduction:

- The *factual judgements* interpreters make are their statements (to others or to themselves) of the meaning of texts being interpreted – that is, the *interpretantia* (*explananda*) that are the conclusions of their interpretive abductions.
- The *distinctive methods* that interpreters use to generate those factual judgements are many and varied among interpreters and contexts of interpretation. What are judged to be appropriate methods of interpretation for the interpretation of *Finnegan's Wake* may be judged inappropriate for interpreting directions to the bus stop. The example above resorts to interpreting (1) metaphorically. By contrast, a method of literal interpretation would read (1) as a literal assertion that Juliet is the astronomical entity that warms (or threatens to overwarm) planet Earth.[77]
- Like interpreters' distinctive methods, the distinctive *axiological goals* interpreters choose to advance and serve are many and varied among interpreters and contexts of interpretation. In some domains of interpretation, including the domain of legal interpretation, there are ongoing debates about *which* methods of interpretation (for example, literal interpretation *versus* interpretation in accord with the intent of the author) are appropriate for interpretation in that domain.[78]

Vital to the *fair formal representation* (it should be clear by now, see section III.D and page 291, that this is a process of interpretive abduction) of both rule-enthymemes and argument-enthymemes is commitment to the axiological goal of a *principle of charity* – a reasoning procedure that seeks to recover the *intent of the arguer as charitably (but not profligately) construed*.[79]

[76] I here 'Logocratise' the proto-Logocratic modelling of interpretation as 'tropological inference' in Brewer (n 10). See also the discussion of other theories that model interpretation as abduction mentioned in n 11.

[77] Compare one's inclination to interpret Camus' Caligula literally when he asserts, 'I want to possess the moon.' See Brewer (n 10) 832 and fn 37.

[78] The tropological theory I advance in *Figuring the Law* refers to the different methods of interpretation as *interpretive norms*. See Brewer (n 10) 827–36. I also discuss some of the jurisprudential controversies about (in Logocratic terms) what are the proper methods of interpretation for judges to use in making their legal abductions. See ibid, 838–40.

[79] As I have argued, 'The injunction to interpret charitably is an interpretive norm. Following Robert Nozick's trenchant critique of prevalent versions of the principle of charity among analytic

B. The Identity Criteria of Arguments

One of the most distinctive aspects of Logocratic theory is its articulation and defence of two principal explanatory propositions that comprise the Logocratic *interactive virtue* theory of argument:[80]

(a) There are precisely four modes of inference (deduction, induction, abduction and analogy) that are logically distinct, with none reducible to any other.
(b) Both the *identity* criteria and the distinct *evaluative* criteria for each individual argument form are best explained such that some forms include other forms in the multi-step inferential process from premises to conclusion.

It may seem that the dynamic interactive explanation of the identity criteria of arguments is problematically circular. In the example of the Logocratic analysis of *Dougherty*, for example, how can it be that there are four distinct arguments, two legal abductions and two deductions *within* the legal abductions, and yet it also be the case, as LM maintains, that there are precisely four argument forms (deduction, induction, abduction and analogy) that are logically distinct? Additional questions about the ontology of arguments are also raised by LM's endorsement of propositions (a) and (b) above, including questions about whether any of the four distinct modes of inference *supervenes* on any other, provides a *ground* for any other or is *ontologically dependent* on any other.[81] Exploration and application of these concepts to the ontology of argument may indeed be useful. I shall not pursue these questions here, however, merely asserting that the answer I do provide can provide a compelling explanation of the ontology of argument that is wholly consistent with explanations framed in such terms as *supervenience* and *grounding*, and *ontological dependence*.

Logocratic theory, particularly its analysis of the argument-enthymeme and its fair formal representation (an instance of interpretive abduction), provides this answer: the *identity* criteria and the distinct *evaluative* criteria for each individual argument (the distinct characteristic virtues of arguments – recall

philosophers of language, we should understand the content of this interpretive norm as follows: On the Logocratic view, a rule-enthymeme or argument-enthymeme ought to be interpreted *to make as intelligible as possible the fact that in that context that person (or persons) promulgating the rule or making the argument promulgated it or made it*. This accords well with Logocratic theory's deep reliance on pragmatics as a core part of its approach to the interpretation of rules and arguments. Unlike variants of the principle of charity that direct an interpreter to maximize agreement of the author of the text with the interpreter, or to maximize the rationality of the author, this principle seeks to reconstruct the enthymeme as reconstructed by a fair construction of the interpreter's intent. The "maximize agreement" (or "maximize rationality") norm would, for example, seem always to counsel that one find another way to interpret an argument-enthymeme if it seemed prima-facie that it might be offering a deductively invalid argument. But some arguers do offer argument-enthymemes that are accurately represented as invalid, and a principle of fair formal representation should not hide that [possibility].' Brewer (2020) (n 11) 158 (citing Robert Nozick (1993) *The Nature of Rationality*, Princeton, NJ: Princeton University Press, 151–59).

[80] See Brewer (2020) (n 11).

[81] For useful explication of these distinctions in current discussions of metaphysics, see Benjamin Schnieder, Miguel Hoeltje and Alex Steinberg (eds) (2013) *Varieties of Dependence, Ontological Dependence, Grounding, Supervenience, Response-Dependence*, Munich: Philosophia.

section III.E.ii.b) are a function of both the interpretation of argument-enthymemes and the choice of which evaluative criteria to use on the set of sentences that comprise an enthymeme.

The familiar 'Socrates syllogism' provides a clear example of this point. An argument that occurs as a token in a natural language very often has the property of what we may call *enthymeme ambiguity*. Indeed it may be, for reasons I cannot canvas here, that all arguments, not only in natural language but also in the formal argument domains of mathematics and logic) have that property. An example of such ambiguity is the proposition (appearing in written discourse as a sentence or in spoken discourse as an utterance):

(1) Socrates is a man, so he'll die.

Proposition (1) presents four interpretive questions for the Logocratic analyst:

(i) Is (1) an argument-enthymeme?
(ii) If so, what are its premises, and what are its conclusions?
(iii) And if so, what is the mode of logical inference (also referred to as the logical form) of the argument?
(iv) And if so, does the argument have the characteristic virtues of its form, that is, does it have the properties that enable the premises of an argument of its type to provide the greatest degree of evidential support for its conclusion of which an argument of that type is capable? (The easiest example is deduction: for an argument-enthymeme that has been represented as deduction, the question is whether the argument has the characteristic virtue of validity.)

One can easily imagine two contexts in which an arguer utters a token of (1). In one context, the arguer might intend, and expect his hearer to recognise his intention, that (a) the interpreter of the argument will supply a premise that is not explicitly stated but is intended to be assumed by the interpreter, namely, some synonym of

(2) All living men will die.

and that (b) this proposition has the force of a true universal generalisation, which, taken together with *Socrates is a living man* [Note that there is already some *interpretation* – interpretive abduction – involved in extracting what is a basically a *rule* from utterance (1); I represent that rule as (2).], is capable of yielding a valid inference to the conclusion expressible as some synonym of the proposition *Socrates will die* by means of the inference rule of universal instantiation. On this interpretation, the answer to the interpretive questions listed above are, respectively:

(i) Is (1) an argument-enthymeme?: Yes
(ii) If so, what are its premises, and what are its conclusions?: Premises: *All living men will die* and *Socrates is a living man*; Conclusion: *Socrates will die*.

(iii) And if so, what is the mode of logical inference (or, the logical form) of the argument?: Deduction
(iv) And if so, does the argument have the characteristic virtues of its form: Yes, it is valid.

In a different context, the arguer might intend, and expect his hearer to recognise his intention, that (a) the interpreter of (1) will supply a premise not explicitly stated but intended to be assumed by the interpreter, namely,

(2') [Probably] All living men will die.

and that (b) this proposition *does not have* the force of a true universal generalisation but instead is an *inductive specification*, that is, an inductive generalisation applied to a particular case in what is sometimes referred to as *defeasible modus ponens*.[82] According to this interpretation of (1) the answers to the interpretive questions listed above are, respectively:

(i) Is (1) an argument-enthymeme?: Yes
(ii) If so, what are its premises, and what are its conclusions?: Premises: *[Probably] All living men will die.* and *Socrates is a living man*; Conclusion: *[Probably] Socrates will die.*
(iii) And if so, what is the mode of logical inference (or, the logical form) of the argument?: Induction (specifically, inductive specification).
(iv) And if so, does the argument have the characteristic virtues of its form: Yes, it meets the criteria of a strong inductive inference.[83]

This example supports two important conclusions. First, one must always *interpret* an argument-enthymeme into an 'argufied' argument, that is, an argument that is (or at least, aspires to be) a fair formal representation of the argument-enthymeme in order to determine which mode of inference might provide a fair formal representation of the argument. Second, often the same argument-enthymeme is capable of being fairly formally represented (that is, interpreted), as distinct modes of inference. In the example above, the argument-enthymeme *Socrates is a man, so he'll die.* could, depending on contextual considerations, be fairly formally represented as either a deductive or an inductive argument. This is the property possessed by argument-enthymemes that we may call *argument-enthymeme underdetermination*. It is the fact of argument-enthymeme underdetermination that shows that there is no circularity in the Logocratic

[82] See, eg, Henry Prakken (2006) 'Artificial Intelligence & Law, Logic and Argument Schemes' in *Arguing on the Toulmin Model: New Essays in Argument Analysis and Evaluation*, eds David Hitchcock and Bart Verheij, Dordrecht: Springer Netherlands, 231–45 ('the *defeasible modus ponens rule* … is formalised by many systems of nonmonotonic logic … *P./If P then usually Q./Therefore (presumably), Q.*').

[83] See, eg, the criteria for strong (in Logocratic terms, *virtuous*) inductive inference that Trudy Govier offers as "Guidelines for Evaluating Inductive Generalizations" in Govier (n 22) 265.

dynamic interactive theory of the identity criteria of arguments.[84] We may call this view an *interpretive theory of argument identity*.

VI. LEGAL ABDUCTION IN *DOUGHERTY V SALT* FROM A LOGOCRATIC POINT OF VIEW

A. Doctrinal Background Relevant for Understanding Legal Abduction in *Dougherty v Salt*

For those not familiar with the doctrines of US Contract Law, a bit of doctrinal background is useful for understanding my arguments in this section. A 'contract', as understood in American legal practice, is a legally enforceable promise.[85] The whole of Contracts analyses (in Logocratic terms to be explained below, such analyses are *legal abductions* in the domain of Contract Law) can be modelled as a set of legal norms designed to distinguish those promises that are not legally enforceable from those that are.[86] This was the issue for one of Cardozo's two principal arguments in *Dougherty*, the conclusion of which was that Aunt Tillie did *not* make a legally enforceable promise to nephew Charley.

There are two basic methods of forming a contract and several legal norms that guide this formation. In one method (and related set of norms), one party, the *offeror*, makes an *offer* to another party, the *offeree*, and the offeree *accepts* the offer, in circumstances in which each party has *consideration* from the other. *Consideration* is present between offerors and offerees when the parties are trading either a promise for a performance (this is a *unilateral contract*) or a promise for a promise (this is a *bilateral contract*).[87] American Contract Law relies on a

[84] Brian Skyrms also strongly endorses this same underlying account of the interpretive and evaluative nature of the identity criteria of arguments. See Skyrms (n 21) 22 (emphasis added): 'Some books appear to suggest that there are two different types of arguments, deductive and inductive, and that deductive logic is concerned with deductive arguments and inductive logic with inductive arguments ... Nothing, however, is further from the truth, for, as we have seen, all inductively strong arguments are deductively invalid ... *Deductive and inductive logic are not distinguished by the different types of arguments with which they deal, but by the different standards against which they evaluate arguments.*'

[85] *Restatement (Second) of Contracts* § 1. 'Contract Defined: A contract is a promise or a set of promises for the breach of which the law gives a remedy, or the performance of which the law in some way recognizes as a duty.'

[86] I present additional detailed Logocratic analysis of the formation of Contracts under American law in Scott Brewer (2017) 'Using Propositional Deductive Logic as an Aid to Teaching American Contract Law: The Logocratic Approach; in *Law and Logic: Contemporary Issues*, eds Dieter Krimphove and Gabriel M Lentner, Berlin: Duncker & Humblot, 97–124.

[87] Consider the two types of actions (both are speech-acts, and specifically, performative utterances of promising) between two contracting parties, *A* and *B*. Abstractly, we can depict the two actions as follows:

(i) offer and acceptance of a *bilateral* contract

A says to B: *If you promise to do Act X, I promise to do Act Y*. This is an *offer* for a *bilateral contract*, defined as *a promise in exchange for a promise*. When *B* makes the return promise

rule for contractual obligation according to which, if there is offer and there is acceptance and there is consideration then there is a legally enforceable promise (ie a contract), *unless* the inference from antecedent to consequent is blocked by a 'defeator doctrine', such as fraud, duress, mutual mistake, unconscionability, etc. (As we shall see, one of Judge Cardozo's arguments in *Dougherty* concerned the possibility that there was fraud, a defeator doctrine, in the writing of the alleged promissory note from Tillie to Charley.) Another method (and related set of norms) of forming a contract is through some variety of *promissory estoppel*, roughly, a circumstance in which even when a promise has not been part of a trade, the court deems it too unfair or unjust not to enforce it.[88] Consideration, not promissory estoppel, is the main doctrinal concept operating in *Dougherty*.

B. Summary of Cardozo's Two Legal Abductions in *Dougherty*

In Logocratic terms, Judge Cardozo, like every judge called on to resolve a litigative dispute, faced the task of producing an *explanation from a legal point of view* (see section IV.B). The facts and procedure of *Dougherty* presented, as Cardozo saw it, *two* distinct phenomena that required explanation, so

('I promise to do Act X'), B *accepts* the offer and the contract is said to be *formed*. As of that moment, both A's promise and B's promises are legally enforceable, that is, they have a contract. And in this case the *consideration* to A is B's *promise*, and the consideration to B is A's *promise*. In *Restatement (Second) of Contracts* § 1 (n 85), this is the circumstance of a contract's being constituted by 'a set of promises for the breach of which the law gives a remedy'.

(i) offer and acceptance of a *unilateral* contract
A says to B: *If you do Act X, I promise to do Act* Y. This is an *offer* for a *unilateral contract*, defined as a promise in exchange for a performance. Under traditional rules, when B *completes the performance* that A seeks, the contract is said to be *formed*. The *consideration* to A is B's *performance* and the consideration to B is A's *promise*. In *Restatement (Second) of Contracts* § 1 (n 85), this is the circumstance of a contract's being constituted not by a 'set of promises' but instead by virtue of *a* promise exchanged for a performance.

[88] The paradigmatic rule for this in American Contract Law is *Restatement (Second) of Contracts* § 90, which states, in relevant part, 'A promise which the promisor should reasonably expect to induce action or forbearance on the part of the promisee or a third person and which does induce such action or forbearance is binding if injustice can be avoided only by enforcement of the promise. The remedy granted for breach may be limited as justice requires.' This doctrine was not nearly as well-known or established at the time of *Dougherty* as it is now, and even now Contract jurists debate how ready judges are to use it as a reason for legally enforcing promises that is an alternative to consideration. Less than a decade after *Dougherty*, Cardozo himself gave the doctrine a strong if somewhat covert endorsement in his influential opinion in *Allegheny College v National Chautauqua Bank of Jamestown*, 159 NE 173 (NY 1927). See ibid, 175: '[T]here has grown up of recent days a doctrine that a substitute for consideration or an exception to its ordinary requirements can be found in what is styled "a promissory estoppel." … Whether the exception has made its way in this state to such an extent as to permit us to say that the general law of consideration has been modified accordingly, we do not now attempt to say.'

that, on the best interpretation of the *Dougherty* argument-enthymemes (see section I) there are two discernibly distinct, albeit closely related, legal abductive arguments.

i. Cardozo's First Legal Abduction Conclusion: No Contractual Consideration

a. Doctrinal Summary (from a Logocratic Point of View)

One of the two legal abductions that Cardozo offers in *Dougherty* seeks to explain the phenomenon (the *explanandum*, that is, the first premise in the first Step of an abduction, see section IV.C) that Cardozo states as the material facts of the interaction among Aunt Tillie, Charley and Charley's legal guardian (who gave Tillie what turned out to be legal advice that Cardozo ultimately rejects). The central question for this legal abduction, as it seemed to Judge Cardozo, was whether authoritative rules of contract, as properly interpreted, indicated that there was an enforceable promise between Aunt Tillie and her nephew, Charley. (See the discussion of the doctrinal background for *Dougherty* in section VI.A.) Five distinct explanations of the transaction, each corresponding, in the Logocratic fair formal representation, to one plausibly serviceable explanation conditional, seemed serviceable to Judge Cardozo. Four of these were worth considering because (as Toulmin might explain Cardozo's argument[89]), in Cardozo's estimation, other referees of the contest might accept them, and Cardozo thought it important to argue against those other abductions of the transaction. Thus, he discussed them, only to reject them in favour of the one that he concluded was *the* best one among the five serviceable explanations he considered.

b. Abstract Representation

Using the schema presented in section IV.C, in the first legal abduction that he offers (the one in which he assesses, from a legal point of view, whether there is consideration for Aunt Tillie's promise to Charley), Cardozo considers a total of five plausibly serviceable explanations of which he rejects four and endorses one. The first legal abduction in *Dougherty* may be fairly formally represented as shown in Table 13.2.

[89] See Toulmin (n 62) and accompanying text.

Table 13.2 Logocratic Representation of the First Legal Abduction in *Dougherty*

Step of abduction	Proposition type and number	Abstract expression of proposition	Description and Enthymematic Text	Comments
Step 1 Statement of the *explanandum*	Premise ε_1	θ	**Explanandum: Statement of conjunction of material facts** Enthymematic text: 'The plaintiff, a boy of eight years, received from his aunt, the defendant's testatrix, a promissory note for $3,000, payable at her death or before. Use was made of a printed form, which contains the words "value received." How the note came to be given was explained by the boy's guardian, who was a witness for his ward. The aunt was visiting her nephew. … "When she saw Charley coming in, she said, 'Isn't he a nice boy?' I answered her, Yes; that he is getting along very nice, and getting along nice in school; and I showed where he had progressed in school, having good reports, and so forth, and she told me that she was going to take care of that child; that she loved him very much. I said, 'I know you do, Tillie, but your taking care of the child will be done probably like your brother and sister done, take it out in talk.' She said, 'I don't intend to take it out in talk; I would like to take care of him now.' I said, 'Well, that is up to you.' She said, 'Why can't I make out a note to him?'	• To use the common law doctrinal term, this is Cardozo's statement of *material* facts of the case, that is, those facts that have significance given them from applicable substantive, evidentiary and procedural laws

(continued)

Table 13.2 *(Continued)*

Step of abduction	Proposition type and number	Abstract expression of proposition	Description and Enthymematic Text	Comments
Step 1 (cont.)	Premise ε_{-1}	θ	I said, 'You can, if you wish to.' She said, 'Would that be right?' And I said, 'I do not know, but I guess it would; I do not know why it would not.' And she said, 'Well, will you make out a note for me?' I said, 'Yes, if you wish me to,' and she said, 'Well, I wish you would.'… A blank was then produced, filled out, and signed. The aunt handed the note to her nephew, with these words: 'You have always done for me, and I have signed this note for you. Now, do not lose it. Some day it will be valuable"'.	
Step 2 A set of five premises comprises Step 2.	Premise $\varepsilon_{2\text{-}1}$	$\Phi_1 \surd \rightarrow \Theta$	<u>**Serviceably plausible explanation conditional #1**</u> This child of 8 was either a creditor or being dealt with as a creditor. <u>Enthymematic text:</u> 'This child of eight was not a creditor, nor dealt with as one.' *Dougherty*, 125 NE at 95.	**Argumentative economy reflected in this fair formal representation of Cardozo's legal abduction:** • For reasons of argumentative economy, Cardozo, like a great many legal abductive reasoners, simultaneously expresses what he considers to be a plausibly serviceable explanation (serviceable enough to be worth mentioning, if only to reject it, see discussion in section IV.B). I list it twice, in both Step 2 (assertion) and Step 3 (rejection)

Step 2 (cont.) Each premise in this set asserts that each explanation mentioned in the premise would serviceably plausibly explain the *explanandum*	Premise $\varepsilon_{2\text{-}2}$	$\Phi_2 \surd \rightarrow \Theta$	**<u>Serviceably plausible explanation conditional #2</u>** The aunt was paying a debt. <u>Enthymematic text:</u> 'The aunt was not paying a debt.' *Dougherty*, 125 NE at 95.	(continued from previous page) because the assertion of it as worth considering and then rejecting it even so are analytically distinct parts of Cardozo's legal abduction, as fairly formally represented.
	Premise $\varepsilon_{2\text{-}3}$	$\Phi_3 \surd \rightarrow \Theta$	**<u>Serviceably plausible explanation conditional #3</u>** There was both consideration for the promise and offer and acceptance because the parties intended to trade either a promise for a promise or a promise for a performance.[1] <u>Enthymematic text:</u> 'She [the aunt] was conferring a bounty. … The promise was neither offered nor accepted with any other purpose. "Nothing is consideration that is not regarded as such by both parties."' *Dougherty*, 125 NE at 95 (citation omitted).	
	Premise $\varepsilon_{2\text{-}4}$	$\Phi_4 \surd \rightarrow \Theta$	**<u>Serviceably plausible explanation conditional #4</u>** The signed note stating 'value received' sufficed for consideration. <u>Enthymematic text:</u> 'A note so given is not made for "value received," however its maker	

(continued)

[1] See n 87 and accompanying text, discussion of bilateral and unilateral contracts.

Table 13.2 *(Continued)*

Step of abduction	Proposition type and number	Abstract expression of proposition	Description and Enthymematic Text	Comments
Step 2 (cont.)	Premise $\varepsilon_{2\text{-}4}$ (cont.)	$\Phi_4 \surd \rightarrow \Theta$	may have labeled it. The formula of the printed blank becomes, in the light of the conceded facts, a mere erroneous conclusion, which cannot overcome the inconsistent conclusion of the law.' *Dougherty*, 125 NE at 95.	
	Premise $\varepsilon_{2\text{-}5}$	$\Phi_5 \surd \rightarrow \Theta$	**Serviceably plausible explanation conditional #5** The aunt's promise in the promissory note was a promise for a gift, not a legally enforceable promise. Enthymematic text: [Same as for Premise $\varepsilon_{2\text{-}3}$ above.]	
Step 3 Assertion that each of these, despite capacity serviceably plausibly to explain the *explanandum*, is disconfirmed as the most serviceable explanation	Premise $\varepsilon_{3\text{-}1}$	$\sim \Phi_1$	**Disconfirmation of serviceably plausible explanation conditional #1** Enthymematic text: 'This child of eight was not a creditor, nor dealt with as one.' *Dougherty*, 125 NE at 95.	• Again (see the Comments to Step 2), the reason for which several of the disconfirmation texts in Step 3 appear also in Step 2 is Cardozo's (not atypical) argumentative economy; like a great many legal abductive reasoners, Cardozo simultaneously expresses what he considers to be a serviceably plausible explanation (serviceable enough to be worth mentioning, if

Step 3 (cont.)	Premise $\varepsilon_{3\text{-}2}$	$\sim \Phi_2$	**Disconfirmation of serviceably plausible explanation conditional #2** Enthymematic text: 'The aunt was not paying a debt.' *Dougherty*, 125 NE at 95.	only to reject it, see discussion in text above at p 26). I list it twice, in both Step 2 (assertion) and Step 3 (rejection) because the assertion of it as worth considering and then rejecting it even so are analytically distinct parts of Cardozo's legal abduction, as fairly formally represented. • A central part of the Logocratic analysis of *dynamic interactive virtue* of arguments explains that *this step of the abduction relies on the deductive application of a rule.* See discussion in section VI.B.ii.b.
	Premise $\varepsilon_{3\text{-}3}$	$\sim \Phi_3$	**Disconfirmation of serviceably plausible explanation conditional #3** Enthymematic text: ' She [the aunt] was conferring a bounty. … The promise was neither offered nor accepted with any other purpose.' *Dougherty*, 125 NE at 95.	
	Premise $\varepsilon_{3\text{-}4}$	$\sim \Phi_4$	**Disconfirmation of serviceably plausible explanation conditional #4** Enthymematic text: 'A note so given is not made for "value received," however its maker may have labeled it. The formula of the printed blank becomes, in the light of the conceded facts, a mere erroneous conclusion, which cannot overcome the inconsistent conclusion of the law.' *Dougherty*, 125 NE at 95.	

(continued)

Table 13.2 *(Continued)*

Step of abduction	Proposition type and number	Abstract expression of proposition	Description and Enthymematic Text	Comments
Step 4 Asserted confirmation of the one most serviceably plausible explanation – compare hypothetical syllogism	Premise ε_4	$\Phi_5 \surd\surd \rightarrow \Theta$	**Confirmation of serviceably plausible explanation conditional #5** Enthymematic text: 'The transaction thus revealed admits of one interpretation, and one only. The note was the voluntary and unenforcible promise of an executory gift.' *Dougherty*, 125 NE at 95.	• Cardozo does not offer additional separate reasons to support this conclusion over and above asserting the conclusion in the process of rejecting the alternative explanations he considers, so in this case (but, as explained in the text above, not in all abductions), the text comprising Step 4 does not differ from the text comprising Step 5.
Step 5 Conclusion, assertion that the most serviceably plausible explanation is the actual explanation of the *explanandum*	Conclusion h	Φ_5	**Assertion of serviceably plausible explanation conditional #5 as *the most serviceably plausible explanation*** Enthymematic text: [Same as for Step 4].	

ii. Cardozo's Second Legal Abduction Conclusion: Trial Judge Error in Disposition of Case

The second, analytically distinct but obviously closely related phenomenon that Cardozo seeks to explain from a legal point of view concerns the trial judge's disposition of the case. As does Cardozo, the trial judge offered two legal abductions. According to one, the jury was wrong to conclude that there was consideration in the promise from the aunt to her nephew. Cardozo agrees with and endorses this legal abduction (as discussed in the previous section). According to the second of the trial court's two legal abductions, the proper overall disposition of the case was to dismiss it. Cardozo disagrees with this second legal abduction,[90] and his argument explaining his disagreement is what I now model in this section.

a. Doctrinal Summary (from a Logocratic Point of View)

Cardozo's second legal abduction is occasioned by applicable New York State rules of evidence and procedure. What called for explanation from a legal point of view in this argument was whether the trial judge's disposition of the case was proper under the applicable rules of procedure. In Logocratic terms, the jury, as *dialectical-rhetorical referee* of the litigative contest of legal abductions between plaintiff and defendant (see section III.E.ii.a.1), accepted the conclusion of the plaintiff's legal abductive argument that Aunt Tillie's promise was legally enforceable. In turn, the trial judge, in granting the defendant's motion to set aside the jury's verdict, offered a legal abduction of the litigative question of whether Aunt Tillie had made a legally enforceable promise. This legal abduction was in a *dialectical-rhetorical contest* with that of the jury. Under applicable New York State rules of procedure[91] (as, in turn, authorised by the New York State Constitution), the trial judge was empowered to declare himself the winner of this contest, a ruling that would stand unless and until a duly authorised appellate court overturned it. In his second legal abduction in *Dougherty*, Cardozo argued that the trial judge's decision to set aside the verdict was correct under applicable rules of Contract (these rules were the subject of his first legal abduction) and procedure, but that the decision to dismiss the case was incorrect. His conclusion also explained the mistake, as he saw it, of the actions of the intermediate appellate court, which reversed the trial court's judgment notwithstanding the verdict and reinstated the jury's conclusion that the Aunt's promise was indeed legally enforceable.

b. Abstract Representation

Cardozo's second legal abduction assesses whether, from a legal point of view, the trial judge's actions in setting aside the jury verdict and then dismissing the plaintiff's complaint were correct. Using the schema presented in section IV.C, this legal abduction may be fairly formally represented as shown in Table 13.3.

[90] In Logocratic terms, Cardozo, speaking for a unanimous New York Court of Appeals, offered a legal abduction that was in a *dialectical-rhetorical contest* (see section III.E.ii.a.1) with the legal abduction of the trial judge.

[91] See the text of these State rules of procedure (rule-enthymemes, in Logocratic terms) in n 100.

Table 13.3 Logocratic Representation of the Second Legal Abduction in *Dougherty*

Step of abduction	Proposition type and number	Abstract expression of proposition	Description and Enthymematic Text	Comments
Step 1 Statement of the *explanandum*	Premise ε_1	θ	**Explanandum: Statement of the trial court's and intermediate appellate court's disposition of the case after jury trial** Enthymematic text: 'The trial judge submitted to the jury the question whether there was any consideration for the promised payment. Afterwards, he set aside the verdict in favor of the plaintiff, and dismissed the complaint. The Appellate Division, by a divided court, reversed the judgment of dismissal, and reinstated the verdict on the ground that the note was sufficient evidence of consideration.' *Dougherty*, 125 NE at 95.	• This is Cardozo's statement of procedural facts, that is, the disposition of the case by the two prior courts
Step 2 A set of two premises comprises Step 2. Each premise in this set asserts that each explanation mentioned in the premise would serviceably explain the explanandum.	Premise $\varepsilon_{2\text{-}1}$	$\Phi_1 \surd \rightarrow \Theta$	**Serviceably plausible explanation conditional #1** The trial judge correctly granted the motion for judgment notwithstanding the verdict (ie, correctly set aside the jury finding that the aunt's promise was enforceable and the appellate court was wrong to overturn the trial judge's ruling).	• Interpreted in context (as with all interpretation, including interpretation of argument-enthymemes), Cardozo mentions *by implicature*[1] the possibility that the trial judge's disposition was correct.

[1] See the classic discussion of 'conversational implicature' in Grice (n 60). See also my use of Grice to explicate the (proto)Logocratic abduction of analogy in Brewer (n 12) 990–1003.

Step 2 (cont.)	Premise $\varepsilon_{2\text{-}1}$	$\Phi_1 \surd \rightarrow \Theta$	<u>Enthymematic text:</u> 'The trial judge submitted to the jury the question whether there was any consideration for the promised payment. Afterwards, he set aside the verdict in favor of the plaintiff, and dismissed the complaint. The Appellate Division, by a divided court, reversed the judgment of dismissal, and reinstated the verdict on the ground that the note was sufficient evidence of consideration.' *Dougherty*, 125 NE at 95.	• As we interpret Cardozo's argument using principles of implicature, we conclude that his assessment, in his legal abduction, of the possibility that the trial judge ruled *correctly* amounts as well – in economy of expression – to considering the possibility that the trial and appellate courts ruled *incorrectly*.
	Premise $\varepsilon_{2\text{-}2}$	$\Phi_2 \surd \rightarrow \Theta$	**<u>Serviceably plausible explanation conditional #2</u>** The trial judge correctly dismissed the complaint and the appellate court was wrong to overturn the trial judge's ruling. <u>Enthymematic text:</u> [Same as for Serviceably plausible explanation conditional #1.]	

(continued)

Table 13.3 *(Continued)*

<table>
<tr><th>Step of abduction</th><th>Proposition type and number</th><th>Abstract expression of proposition</th><th>Description and Enthymematic Text</th><th>Comments</th></tr>
<tr><td rowspan="2">Step 3 & Step 4
Simultaneous assertion of the correctness of explanation and incorrectness of its counterpart negation. Cardozo judges that each of these, despite its capacity serviceably plausibly to explain the explanandum, is disconfirmed as the most serviceable explanation.</td><td>Premise $\varepsilon_{3\text{-}1}$</td><td>$\sim \Phi_1$</td><td>Confirmation of plausibly serviceable explanation conditional #1 and simultaneous disconfirmation of its contrastive counterpart negation
Enthymematic text: ‘The inference of consideration to be drawn from the form of the note has been so overcome and rebutted as to leave no question for a jury … The transaction thus revealed admits of one interpretation, and one only … We hold, therefore, that the verdict of the jury was contrary to law, and that the trial judge was right in setting it aside.’ Dougherty, 125 NE at 95.</td><td rowspan="2">• In the expressive economy of his legal abduction, Cardozo simultaneously rejects the possible explanation that the trial judge was incorrect to set aside the jury verdict, asserts that the judge was correct to do so and, relatedly, asserts also that the appellate court was incorrect to overrule the trial judge.
• Thus, although the enthymematic text is compressed, the fair formal representation of Cardozo’s rejection of one explanation (Step 3) and endorsement of its contrastive counterpart explanation (Step 4) are analytically distinguishable and distinct.
• A central part of the Logocratic analysis of dynamic interactive virtue of arguments explains that this step of the abduction relies on the deductive application of a rule. See discussion below.</td></tr>
<tr><td>Premise $\varepsilon_{3\text{-}2}$</td><td>$\sim \Phi_2$</td><td>Confirmation of plausibly serviceable explanation conditional #2 and simultaneous disconfirmation of its contrastive counterpart negation
Enthymematic text: ‘[The trial judge] went too far, however, in dismissing the complaint. He might have dismissed it if he had reserved his ruling on the defendant’s motion for a nonsuit or for the direction</td></tr>
</table>

Step 3 & Step 4 (cont.) Simultaneous assertion of the correctness of explanation and incorrectness of its counterpart negation that each of these, despite capacity serviceably plausibly to explain the explanandum, is disconfirmed as the most serviceable explanation.	Premise $\varepsilon_{3\text{-}2}$	$\sim \Phi_2$	of a verdict. Code Civ Proc §§ 1185, 1187. Instead of reserving his ruling, he denied the motion absolutely. Upon the return of the verdict, he should have granted a new trial. A new trial was also necessary because of error in rejecting evidence. The defendant attempted to prove that the signature to the note was forged. The court refused to hear the evidence, because forgery had not been pleaded as a defense. The answer did deny the execution of the note. The evidence of forgery was admissible under the denial. Schwarz v Oppold, 74 NY 307; Farmers' L & T Co v Siefke, 144 NY 354, 39 NE 358. The judgment of the Appellate Division should be reversed, and the judgment of the Trial Term modified by granting a new trial, and, as modified, affirmed, with costs in all courts to abide the event.' *Dougherty*, 125 NE at 95.	

We may now address the questions I have previously posed regarding how many arguments there are in Cardozo's opinion in *Dougherty v Salt* and how are they related. There are two legal abductions, obviously related, but distinct, for each of which five distinct legal arguers offered competing arguments. The pattern of legal-abductive contest lines up in this way:

- plaintiff's legal abductions competed with defendant's
- trial judge's legal abductions competed with jury's
- appellate court's legal abductions competed with trial judge's
- Court of Appeals' (per Cardozo) legal abductions *agreed* with *one* of the trial judge's legal abductions and *competed* with the trial judge on the other legal abduction.

We may also represent this pattern of contesting legal abductions as shown in Table 13.4, using Logocratic concepts already explained (see especially section III.E.ii.a.1).

Table 13.4 Pattern of contesting legal abductions in *Dougherty*

Dialectical-rhetorical referee	**Question posed for legal abduction (the *explanandum*): Legal abduction 1 ('LA1'): Was there consideration for Aunt Tillie's promise of money to Charley and was her promise was legally enforceable?**	**Question posed for legal abduction (the *explanandum*): Legal abduction 2 ('LA2'): What is the proper disposition of the case, in light of the best answer to LA1?**
plaintiff[1]	Yes	Trial court should enforce Aunt's (estate's) promise to pay Charley, appellate court(s) should affirm
defendant	No	Trial court should dismiss the complaint, appellate court(s) should affirm

(continued)

[1] It is worth commenting on the inclusion of plaintiff and defendant as dialectical-rhetorical referees here, amplifying the discussion in section III.E.ii.a.1. Although it is the trial judge, the jury, the appellate court and the Court of Appeals who have state-sanctioned power to decide which legal abductions win the contests of plaintiff and defendant, *each arguer* is also a dialectical-rhetorical referee in his or her deliberation and judgment about which argument to endorse. This is a general point about the vital Logocratic idea of the dialectical-rhetorical competition of arguments. It is not that some argument audiences are dialectical-rhetorical referees while others are not. Instead, every argument audience – *including* the arguer who advances an argument – is a referee. What differs is *how much and what kind of institutional political power* a given audience for an argument has in the settings in which the argument is advanced.

Table 13.4 *(Continued)*

Dialectical-rhetorical referee	**Question posed for legal abduction (the *explanandum*): Legal abduction 1 ('LA1'): Was there consideration for Aunt Tillie's promise of money to Charley and was her promise was legally enforceable?**	**Question posed for legal abduction (the *explanandum*): Legal abduction 2 ('LA2'): What is the proper disposition of the case, in light of the best answer to LA1?**
jury	Yes	Court should enforce Aunt's (estate's) promise to pay Charley
trial judge	No	Trial court should grant defendant's motion to set aside the jury verdict, appellate court(s) should affirm
appellate court (majority of split opinion)	Yes	Trial court judgment setting aside the jury verdict should be reversed, appellate court(s) should affirm
Court of Appeals (per Cardozo unanimously opinion for court)	No	Trial court should set aside the verdict but *not* dismiss the complaint, and instead should grant a new trial (to assess defendant's claim of fraud)

Within each of Cardozo's two *legal* abductions in *Dougherty*, when fairly formally represented, one can discern the operation of two additional argument forms, both related to Cardozo's application of (what he takes to be) applicable legal rules. One is an *interpretive abduction* and one is a *deduction*. The conclusions of these arguments in turn serve as premises in the abduction. Modelling one of the two interpretive-abduction-and-deduction-within-the-legal abductions that Cardozo's opinion exhibits (when fairly formally represented)is sufficient for my purposes here.

Recall that the first legal abduction (LA1 in Table 13.4) concerns whether Aunt Tillie's promise, rendered in the promissory note stating 'value received' and listing an amount to be paid to Charley ($3,000, payable at or before her death), had 'consideration'.[92] On the facts of the case, if the aunt's promise was enforceable, it would be on the basis of consideration – the exchange of a promise for a promise or of a promise for a performance.[93] From a (deductive) logical

[92] American Contract Law relies on a rule for contractual obligation according to which a transaction, in which there is offer, acceptance and consideration, is to be explained as a legally enforceable promise, ie a contract, unless the inference is blocked by a 'defeator doctrine', such as fraud, duress, mutual mistake, unconscionability, etc. See Brewer (n 86).

[93] See n 87 for illustration of these two types of consideration.

point of view, consideration in this case is a necessary condition of the aunt's contractual liability to her nephew. In the course of his legal abduction on the question of consideration (LA1), Cardozo relies on this argument-enthymeme:

> The aunt was not paying a debt. She was conferring a bounty. Fink v Cox, 18 Johns 145, 9 Am Dec 191. The promise was neither offered nor accepted with any other purpose. 'Nothing is consideration that is not regarded as such by both parties.'[94]

Cardozo's argument is fairly formally represented as follows:

ε_1 Nothing is consideration that is not regarded as consideration by both parties. [Equivalently: All consideration *is* regarded as consideration by both parties. Abstractly: All X is Y.]

ε_2 Parties who intend to give [the donor] and receive [the recipient] a gift do not intend consideration. [Abstractly: If something is W then it is not-Y.]

ε_3 Aunt Tillie and Charley intend for her to give Charley a gift. [Abstractly: This case involves W.]

h There was no consideration. [Abstractly: This case involves not-X.]

In the grammar of first-order predicate logic, the fully abstract version of the argument is an instance of *modus tollens*, which is a valid deductive inference, that is, an inference in which whenever all the premises are true, the conclusion must also be true:

ε_1 All X is Y.

ε_2 If something is W then it is not-Y.

ε_3 This case involves W.

h This case involves not-X.

Note here that Cardozo's deductive argument *itself relies on an interpretive abduction*, namely, his own representation of the logical elements of the rule of consideration. *Every legal analyst's use of rule-based deduction within legal abduction* relies on interpretive abduction in this way, whether or not the analyst dwells explicitly on that abduction. In *Dougherty*, Cardozo neither offered nor made explicit his interpretive abduction, and instead quoted the consideration rule he endorsed and relied on from the US Supreme Court's opinion *Philpot v Gruninger*.[95] But under fair assumptions of interpretive charity, he offered a deductive argument[96] whose first premise, which I have represented as a form of *All X is Y*, necessarily relies on his own interpretation of the logic of the

[94] See *Dougherty* (n 1) 95.
[95] See *Dougherty* (n 1) 95 (citing *Philpot v Gruninger*, 81 US 570 (1871)).
[96] An important issue in the Jurisprudence of Logical Form (see Brewer (n 14) and accompanying text) is whether some, if not all, legal arguments are best fairly formally represented as deductions.

consideration rule that he applies to yield his legal abduction regarding the question of consideration.

A deductive inference with this same basic structure also serves Cardozo's first legal abduction in which he rejects, as noted in section VI.B.i.b, the possible explanations of the aunt's promise as paying a debt or making an enforceable promise simply by saying 'value received' (as if this was a performative utterance, making the assertion true just by virtue of making the assertion). Another occurrence of deduction, whose conclusion then serves as a premise in Cardozo's abduction, comes in his abduction of the issue of whether the trial court made the proper disposition of the case after the jury verdict. The conclusion of Cardozo's abduction on this point (see Table 13.3 and Table 13.4) is that the trial judge was mistaken. This legal abduction relies, in turn, on a deductive application of two rules of New York State procedure that Cardozo cites.[97]

The Logocratic explanation of Cardozo's legal abduction in *Dougherty* is but one instance of a general point that has long been part of Logocratic (and proto-Logocratic) theory, which I have referred to as the *dynamic interaction* of arguments. In the proto-Logocratic model of practical reasoning, in which practical reasoners take account of expert testimony, I have argued that an argument modelled as a practical syllogism, which is a legal abduction, will interact with expert empirical abductions offered by expert witnesses.[98] And as noted in section I, LM explains that each of the four modes of inference – deduction,

Some Legal Realist theorists seem to deny this, in contrast to other theorists, including me. I have offered detailed reasons for concluding that deduction does operate in legal argument in Brewer (n 12) 989–1003.

[97] One is New York Code of Civil Procedure § 1185, which states, in relevant part (bracketed numbers added):

> Where, [1] upon the trial of an issue by jury, the case presents only questions of law, [2] the judge may direct the jury to render a verdict subject to the opinion of the court. [3] Notwithstanding that such a verdict has been rendered, [4] the judge holding the trial term may, at the same time, set aside the verdict, and direct judgment to be entered for either party, with like effect and like manner, as if such a direction had been given at trial.

The other is New York Code of Civil Procedure § 1187. Both of these are, in Logocratic terms, *rule-enthymemes* (see section III.D). Just to illustrate briefly the 'Method' in the Logocratic Method, one may fairly formally represent this using the grammar of propositional deductive logic. I refer to the bracketed number [1] that I have added in the quoted text above in this fair formal representation, which represents the enthymematic statutory text as two rules:

> Rule 1: *If* [1] upon the trial of an issue by jury, the case presents only questions of law, *then* [2] the judge may direct the jury to render a verdict subject to the opinion of the court.
>
> Rule 2: [3][4] [*If* the judge holding the trial term is acting within his authorised powers,] *then* the judge holding the trial term may, at the same time, set aside the verdict, and direct judgment to be entered for either party, with like effect and like manner, as if such a direction had been given at trial.

This fair formal representation proceeds in accord with the Logocratic view that all norms, including deontic norms, have a 'deep structure' of conditionals even when the 'surface structure' grammar is not conditional. I have represented that deep structure in the representation of rule elements labelled '[3]' and '[4]' as the deontic antecedent '[If the judge holding the trial term is acting within his authorised powers]'. Recall the discussion of this point in n 30.

[98] See Brewer (n 13).

induction, analogy and abduction – is logically distinct, that is, each is not reducible to (an instance of) any of the others.

But, unusually among theories of argument, LM also explains, indeed emphasises, the dynamic interactive nature of several of the four modes of inference.[99] On this explanation, analogical argument always involves both abduction and either induction or deduction,[100] induction always involves abduction, and abduction, in turn, always involves either deduction or induction. Offering a much-needed correction of a widespread misunderstanding of the nature of abduction, Logocratic theory explains that there are many abductions whose premises provide *indefeasible argumental evidence* (see section III.E.ii.a.2) for their conclusions.[101] According to the Logocratic-friendly Jurisprudence of Logical Form that I endorse, legal abductions, which are rule-based (even when vague rules must first be interpreted – very often through reasoning by analogy[102]), rely on deductive application of rules. In this way, legal abductions are like abductions used in mathematics and logic.[103]

This explanation of the role of rule-based deductive reasoning coheres strongly with the Logocratic explanation of abduction. Recall that, on the Logocratic explanation (abduction), abduction is explanation from a *point of view*, and a point of view consists of the distinctive *methods* of an enterprise that generate the kinds of *factual judgements* of the sort that the enterprise generates, whose methods are in turn chosen to serve particular the *axiological aims* of that enterprise.[104] The practices of legal abduction, namely, offering explanations from a legal point of view (as Cardozo does in *Dougherty*), involve the distinct *methods* that are familiar to lawyers, judges and students who learn to 'think like a lawyer'. Those methods include: (i) reasoning under applicable rules, which involves deduction; (ii) reasoning about the empirical world in ways necessary to apply legal rules whose concepts have empirical content, which means using the inputs of empirical (including expert) inductions;[105] (iii) reasoning about judgements of similarity and difference (reasoning by analogy) – which is especially prominent in Anglo-American 'common law' reasoning in which judges are overtly empowered to make judgements about the scope of meaning of potentially authoritative precedents;[106] and (iv) interpretive reasoning, judging the meanings of cases, statutes, regulations and constitutions.[107]

[99] See Brewer (2020) (n 11).

[100] See Brewer (n 12) 968–78; Brewer (2018) (n 40).

[101] Thus, for example, consider this *explanandum*: How is it possible for two chess pawns of the same 'team' (colour, side) to be in the same column as the result of legal play, that is, play permitted under the rules? On the Logocratic model of abduction (meta-abduction) presented above (see section IV), there are, as far as I know, only two serviceably plausible explanations of this explanandum: that one pawn moved diagonally to capture an opposing piece, or did so using the *en passant* option. This is an abduction – induction has nothing to do with it, despite the many theories that conflate abduction and induction in one way or another.

[102] See Brewer (n 12) 978–83.

[103] See the discussion in n 74 and accompanying text.

[104] Recall the discussion of 'point of view' in section IV.B.

[105] See Brewer (n 13).

[106] See Brewer (n 12).

[107] Recall the discussion in nn 10 and 11 and accompanying text.

Additionally, as a matter of what one might explain as philosophical-anthropological investigation,[108] judges in American Contract Law tend to sort into two 'tribes' with regard to the axiological goals that they use legal methods to serve. Detailed examination of those aims is beyond the scope of this chapter, but I can sketch them. Fairly tracking the literature of American Contract jurisprudence, I label one set of rationales 'Classical' and the competing set of rationales 'Romantic'.[109] According to the explanatory scheme I have developed, the judge who endorses *Classical* axiological goals in his Contract-Law legal abductions relies on a strong presumption that the parties should be given very wide latitude to arrange their contractual deals themselves, without modification by judges; presumes against using the tools of Contract-Law legal abduction to redress inequalities between the parties to a contract (such as inequalities in bargaining power, information and resources); and similarly presumes against reallocating the risk that a more-or-less literal interpretation of the transaction has imposed on the parties. The judge who endorses *Romantic* axiological goals in his Contract-Law legal abductions, by contrast, gives much narrower latitude to the parties to arrange their contractual deals themselves, without modification by judges; is quite ready to use the tools of contract legal abduction to redress inequalities between the parties to a contract; and quite ready to reallocate the risk that a more or less literal interpretation of the transaction has imposed on the parties, including by resorting to non-literal interpretations of the terms of the transaction. Cardozo himself is one of the pioneers of the Romantic values of Contract Law, although he does not rely on them in his legal abduction in *Dougherty*.[110]

C. So, How Many Arguments in *Dougherty*, and How Are They Related?

At the end of a winding road, based on the abductions and meta-abductions offered, my bottom-line answer to the question I posed early in this chapter

[108] As I understand and deploy this concept, philosophical anthropology is the investigation of the conceptual relations and commitments of the contingent methods of reasoning of cognitive agents. See, eg, the discussion of von Savigny in Brewer (n 6) 41–46.

[109] To offer just one example, the casebook I have used for many years of teaching Contracts, *Problems in Contract Law*, by Knapp, Crystal, Prince, uses the concept of 'Classical' throughout to label what I refer to as the set of Classical rationales. See also the detailed explication of these norms in Jay M Feinman (2004) *Un-Making Law: the Conservative Campaign to Roll Back the Common Law*, Boston, Beacon Press; and Duncan Kennedy (2006) *The Rise and Fall of Classical Legal Thought*, Washington, DC: Beard Books. Common among writers who use 'Classical' in their explanations of law (Contract Law as well as other domains of law) is the use of 'post-classical' as the conceptual antonym. I use 'Romantic' to label this set of Contracts rationales, partly under the influence of the superb essay by James Whitman (1987) 'Commercial Law and the American Volk: A Note on Llewellyn's German Sources for the Uniform Commercial Code' *Yale Law Journal* 97: 156–75, arguing that '[Karl] Llewellyn's conception for the [Uniform Commercial] Code, … his love for the "law merchant" and his peculiar ambitions for a political transformation of the United States all had common roots in little-known corners of German Romantic and post-Romantic legal thought'.

[110] Within a decade of *Dougherty*, he took a paradigmatically and very influentially Romantic approach in his legal abduction in *Allegheny Coll v Nat'l Chautauqua Cnty Bank of Jamestown*, 159 NE 173 (1927).

about how many arguments there are in *Dougherty* is this: there are two legal abductions, one concerning contractual liability, the other concerning the proper disposition of the case. Each of those legal abductions relies, as is typical of legal abductions, on a deductive application of rules – rules for consideration and two procedural rules. And the deductive arguments rely in turn on interpretive abductions – one for each of the deductive arguments – in their fair formal representation of the legal rules on which the deductive argument relies. This makes for a total of six arguments: two *overarching* arguments (the legal abductions) *within* each of which is one deductive argument within each of which, in turn, in one interpretive abduction (recall the discussion on page 334).

VII. CONCLUSION AND DIRECTIONS FOR FURTHER RESEARCH

In this chapter, I have offered a detailed analysis of a well-known American Contracts case to illustrate the Logocratic answer to what seems to be a simple question: *What is a Legal Argument?* I have tried to show that the best answer to this simple question is complex, thereby mirroring the complexity of arguments themselves and the specific complexities of legal arguments. Arguments are composed of propositions, and the assembly of a given set of propositions into *an* argument is always an interpretive decision. That same interpretive decision in turn guides one's evaluation of the argument. *All* arguments have one or another of the four modes of inference – deduction, induction, abduction and analogy – but *no* set of propositions has any *inherent* logical form. What logical form it has is always a function of an *interpretive* decision about how to evaluate the support that the premises of the argument provide for its conclusion. In general, there is no entity without identity, in the familiar Quinequip.[111] On the best explanation of the phenomena of argument, there is no argument, no logical form of argument and no evaluation of argument, without interpretation. To be *an argument* is to be taken as such.

This Logocratic explanation of the identity criteria of arguments made perspicuous the complexity of what might have seemed like Cardozo's short, simple argument in *Dougherty v Salt*, revealing a structure of six arguments, two of which are legal abductions, each of which in turn contains a deductive argument and an interpretive abduction. Many other legal arguments have a good deal more complexity than does *Dougherty*.

Two lines of further research arise from this kind of analysis. First, one may profitably continue to develop explicit criteria for the adequacy of interpretations of (in Logocratic terms) argument-enthymemes into their fair formal representations. Second, it seems likely that the rich multi-disciplinary

[111] Willard Van Orman Quine (1981) *Theories and Things*, Cambridge, MA: Harvard University Press, 102.

bodies of research into complexity – including, to name a few, biology,[112] physics,[113] social science,[114] law[115] and philosophy[116] – could also yield additional insights into the nature of arguments that broaden and deepen the Logocratic analysis of the dynamic interactive virtue of arguments. What is complex in its nature can be made simple to a suitably trained Logocratic understanding.

[112] See the richly provocative and evocative discussion in Lawrence B Slobodkin (1992) *Simplicity and Complexity in Games of the Intellect*, Cambridge, MA: Harvard University Press.

[113] See, eg, Michael Strevens (2003) *Bigger than Chaos: Understanding Complexity Through Probability*, Cambridge, MA: Harvard University Press.

[114] See Philip Pond (2020) *Complexity, Digital Media and Post Truth Politics: A Theory Of Interactive Systems*, Cham: Palgrave Macmillan.

[115] See, eg, Ronald J Allen (2011) 'Rationality and the Taming of Complexity' *Alabama Law Review* 62: 1047–71.

[116] See, eg, Justus Buchler (1966) *Metaphysics of Natural Complexes*, New York: Columbia University Press.

Index

Lightning Source UK Ltd.
Milton Keynes UK
UKHW010035231122
412689UK00004B/50